Studies in the English Renaissance

John T. Shawcross, General Editor

Changing the Subject

*Mary Wroth and Figurations of Gender
in Early Modern England*

Naomi J. Miller

THE UNIVERSITY PRESS OF KENTUCKY

Scholarly publisher for the Commonwealth,
serving Bellarmine College, Berea College, Centre
College of Kentucky, Eastern Kentucky University,
The Filson Club, Georgetown College, Kentucky
Historical Society, Kentucky State University,
Morehead State University, Murray State University,
Northern Kentucky University, Transylvania University,
University of Kentucky, University of Louisville,
and Western Kentucky University.

Editorial and Sales Offices: The University Press of Kentucky
663 South Limestone Street, Lexington, Kentucky 40508-4008

Library of Congress Cataloging-in-Publication Data

Miller, Naomi J., 1960-
    Changing the subject : Mary Wroth and figurations of gender in
early modern England / Naomi J. Miller.
        p.   cm. — (Studies in the English Renaissance)
    Includes bibliographical references and index.
    ISBN 0-8131-1964-2 (alk. paper)
    1. Wroth, Mary, Lady, ca. 1586–ca. 1640.   2. Women and literature
—England—History—17th century.   3. Authorship—Sex differences.
4. Sex role in literature.   5. Renaissance—England.   I. Title.
II. Series.
PR2399.W7Z76   1996
828'.309—dc20   95-26151

To my four children
Fiona, Isaiah, Damaris, and Elias
whose presence in my life puts everything in place

Contents

Acknowledgments

Many institutions and individuals have supported me during the writing of this book, leaving me with many debts of gratitude. I was assisted in my research by an American Council of Learned Societies Grant-in-Aid, a National Endowment for the Humanities Travel to Collections Grant, a Newberry Library Fellowship, a University of Arizona Small Grants Award, a University of Arizona Women's Studies Advisory Council Summer Faculty Stipend, and, in the earliest stages of my work, a Whiting Fellowship in the Humanities. I am particularly grateful to the Viscount de L'Isle for permission to quote from the De L'Isle manuscript collection of Sidney family letters housed at the Kent County Archives Office in Maidstone, England, where I spent two summers, and to the Newberry Library for permission to quote from the manuscript continuation of Wroth's *Urania*.

Preliminary versions of my work on Wroth appeared in the volume of essays that I co-edited with Gary Waller, entitled *Reading Mary Wroth: Representing Alternatives in Early Modern England* (Univ. of Tennessee Press, 1991), as well as in *Renaissance Englishwomen in Print: Counterbalancing the Canon*, edited by Anne Haselkorn and Betty Travitsky (Univ. of Mass. Press, 1990), in *Studies in English Literature* 29 (1989), and in various conference papers, although all of that material has been substantially altered in the present book.

My work on Mary Wroth began at Harvard, under the guidance of Barbara Lewalski, who encouraged me to travel to the various archives that provided the primary materials for my research, to give my first conference paper on Wroth, and to move far beyond the confines of my early attention to Wroth in graduate school, in order to write this book. I have appreciated her incisive comments throughout the many stages of my work. The New England Seminar on Women in the Renaissance and the Reformation, and the new Society for the Study of Early Modern Women, have brought me into contact with many scholars whose writings and advice I have valued over the years, including Pamela Benson, Susan Frye, Elizabeth Hageman, Ann Rosalind Jones, Anne Lake Prescott, Carolyn Ruth Swift, Betty Travitsky, and Susanne Woods. Special thanks go to Mihoko Suzuki, with whom I have shared not only the MLA Committee on the Status of Women in the Profession, but also many conversations on the status of women in Renaissance studies.

From the very earliest stages of my work until the present moment, I have been fortunate to have received generous counsel from other Wroth scholars at every step of my path. Margaret Hannay and Josephine Roberts have aided and encouraged me, most particularly through our regular meetings at conferences, for many years. Gary Waller proved to be a wonderful correspondent, as well as an enthusiastic co-editor, during our work in gathering together the collection of essays on Wroth, which also had the beneficial result of bringing me into contact with still other Wroth scholars, such as Nona Fienberg and Mary Ellen Lamb, whose work has helped to foster my own.

My greatest debt of gratitude for the present shape of the book rests with Elaine Beilin and Heather Dubrow, whose incisive, challenging, and affirming comments on the manuscript enabled me to sharpen and refine my argument in instances too numerous to detail here, and in many cases to articulate ideas that had been overly embedded in the prose of my drafts. In an even more elementary sense, these two scholars have guided and inspired me to find my own voice as a scholar since my earliest days in the profession, and continue to assist others with the greatest generosity. I would also like to thank John Shawcross, whose Renaissance series is a valuable resource in the field.

During my years at the University of Arizona, I have benefited from the presence of many exceptional friends and colleagues: in the Renaissance, Meg Lota Brown, Fred Kiefer, Peter Medine, and John Ulreich; in Women's Studies, Susan Aiken, Karen Anderson, Laura Berry, Myra Dinnerstein, Lynn Fleischman, Kari McBride, Beth Mitchnek, Judy Temple, Susan White, and Lynda Zwinger; and in general, Martha Gilliland, Mimi Gray, and Annette Kolodny. With Daniel Cooper Alarcón I have shared not only office space, but also many timely conversations which have eased the trials of junior faculty life. And I continue to learn from my students, both past and present, including Ann Brigham, Chalon Emmons, Huong Huynh, Alexander Macleod, Tyler Smith, and Eric Switzer.

In writing my sixth chapter, on bonds between women, I have often been reminded of my gratitude for the trenchant advice and unstinting support of my friends around the country, with whom I have shared everything from the challenges of graduate school and assistant professorships to the production of books and children. I continue to rely upon Emily C. Bartels, Meg Lota Brown, Anne Davies, Carol Ann Johnston, Laura Lunger Knoppers, and Naomi Yavneh, for shared speech and much more. Maureen Kelly has been a constant source of sustaining humor and affection. And always, I am renewed by the wit, wisdom, exemplary common sense, and caring of Mary Thomas Crane.

Over the years, I have learned a great deal from the quite different models of engagement with higher education provided by my mother, Nobuko Ishii, and my father, David K. Eiteman. My sister, Marcia Ishii-Eiteman, is the best there is. In Tucson, I have particularly appreciated the presence of extended family: Marion Miller, Irwin Weinberg, and Rosi Weinberg. Deeper gratitude than I can express goes to June Brechbiel and Sharon Peters, for so wonderfully looking after and caring for my children while I worked on this project.

Finally, I thank my husband, Hugh Miller, for making everything possible through the past seventeen years of marriage. I have dedicated this book to my four children, Fiona, Isaiah, Damaris, and Elias, who were born and have grown during the years in which I was writing this book, and who share the reading of books with me every day.

1

Figurations of Gender

The subject of the present book is not singular, but multiple: figurations of gender in early modern England, as viewed in relation to the works of a particular, indeed quite singular, writer: Lady Mary Wroth (c. 1587-1653). I have chosen the term "figuration," which is defined in the OED as both "the action or process of giving shape or determination to a certain form" and "the resulting form or shape," in order to consider at once the ongoing construction of the gendered subject in early modern England and specific representations of female subjectivity that both resulted from and continued to revise that process of construction. While many recent critical studies of gender and culture in early modern England have confined themselves to canonical male authors such as Shakespeare and Milton, I have chosen to study the gendering of discourse in female-authored texts as well, and to concentrate on Mary Wroth, whose oeuvre offers an alternative lens through which to view gender relations in the early modern period.[1]

Mary Wroth wrote the first sonnet sequence in English by a woman, *Pamphilia to Amphilanthus* (1621), one of the first plays by a woman, *Love's Victory* (printed for the first time in 1988), and the first published work of fiction by an Englishwoman, *The Countess of Mountgomeries Urania* (1621; first modern edition published in 1995).[2] Wroth is noteworthy not simply for her gender as a woman writer in a period dominated by male voices, but for the range of her authorship as well: whereas other English women writers at that time are known for single texts or for their work in single genres, the volume and diversity of Wroth's texts amply attest to her multifaceted attention to figurations of gender. At the same time, the fact that Wroth was forced by members of King James's court to withdraw *Urania* only six months after its publication and to leave the court herself in disgrace—in part precisely because her choice of a secular romance narrative was deemed inappropriate for a woman—underscores the gendered perspective of outsider and "other" which invests her authorial voice with its particular angle on her culture.

Previous critics have treated Wroth primarily in relation to her male literary predecessors, most notably in the Sidney family, without much attention to other contemporary voices. Although the understandable emphasis

1

upon Wroth's relation to her Sidney family heritage has produced several illuminating readings, the simultaneous relevance of her culture's multiple discourses on gender has not been explored in sufficient detail. As Valerie Wayne has pointed out, approaching the past through dominant discourses heightens the risk of appropriation of women's voices, and prevents our being able to distinguish among available ideologies.[3] Thus while my own discussion of Wroth includes considerable attention to the significance of her family connections, I endeavor to uncover alternative connections and disjunctions as well. Instead of treating Wroth's texts solely as literary works, I undertake to explore Wroth's engagement with a variety of cultural discourses regarding gender. I examine Wroth's discursive relation to contemporary literary and cultural texts as well as her rewriting of the gendered constructions of influential predecessors, both within and outside her family, in order to probe not simply "the subject" of gender in her works, but the changing subject of gendered representations in the early modern period. At the same time, by looking at multiple discursive contexts, I hope to recall attention to Wroth as a subject in her own right, rather than treating her, as several other critics have done, primarily as already written by the dominant voices of her male predecessors. Thus I read Wroth in relation to a broad range of early modern English and continental authors, both male and female, from Philip Sidney, Spenser, Shakespeare, and Honoré d'Urfé to Mary Sidney, Aemilia Lanyer, Elizabeth Cary, and Marguerite de Navarre. Furthermore, my study treats the interactive dynamic linking Wroth's texts not only with literary works, but also with female-authored diaries, letters, and mothers' advice books, as well as with monarchs' speeches, handbooks for women, polemical pamphlets, and political correspondence. Only by scrutinizing a range of cultural discourses in light of figurations of gender can we examine the ideological underpinnings of that culture's constructions of subjectivity.

Given women's widespread subjection to patriarchal and often misogynist systems of social and sexual order in early modern England, one might ask when and even whether it is possible to discuss women both as culturally constituted subjects and as agents of change. Although the varied prohibitions on early modern women's speech have been well documented, particularly in studies of male-authored texts, less has been written about the sometimes bold, sometimes subtle discursive strategies appropriated or devised by women writers themselves in their efforts to achieve agency in the face of the social forces impelling their subordination. While it would be misleading to celebrate these sometimes vexed or fragmented efforts as examples of women's triumphant mastery of their culture's discourses, nevertheless it is important to analyze both the achievements and the limitations that characterized early modern women's attempts to write voices of their own, as well as the historical and social conditions that variously hindered or enabled the emergence of those voices. In my study of Mary Wroth's texts in relation to figurations of gender in early modern England, I attend not only to historical evidence of the oppression of women and the silencing of feminine speech, but also to the multiple ways in which women writers ended silences and escaped constraints, and even occasionally worked to "fashion femininity" in emancipatory terms.[4]

When literary critics of gender and culture in early modern England appropriate a canonical figure such as Shakespeare as a focal point for discussion, they frequently interpose references to other (usually less canonical) writers or cultural texts with the expressed intention of provoking thought rather than providing extensive coverage of all the texts touched upon. In choosing the works of Mary Wroth as my own focal point, I would like to make clear that I am not concerned to "do justice" to each author I mention, but rather to locate my reading of Wroth's texts among a variety of cultural as well as theoretical discourses. Given the tension between the space constraints of my study and the sheer amount of surface involved, I will not provide a comprehensive survey of figurations of gender in the period (conceptually as well as practically unattainable in any case), so much as offer a selective scrutiny, in which in-depth soundings of Wroth engage with select moments from other texts.[5] Accordingly, instead of endeavoring to discuss an entire text in a single chapter, I have chosen to extend my analysis of many texts across several chapters, in order to re-view those texts from different angles as the book proceeds. I have selected particular texts and moments of representation within texts not because they are the most representative, either of "the author's" position or of figurations of gender in "the Renaissance"—as if either could be located in completely fixed terms—but rather because of their particularity of intersection with each other in shaping the ongoing construction of gendered subjectivity in early modern England.

Many scholars have called attention to the social and rhetorical obstacles confronting Renaissance women who attempted to write within genres structured by male categories and dominated by masculine discourse. Faced with these obstacles some writers, such as the authors of the feminist pamphlets of the period, adopt a defensive stance in seeking to refute the stereotypes presented by misogynistic treatises.[6] Mary Wroth, however, chooses not to portray women only reactively, in relation to patriarchal norms, but rather to explore, in her fictions, the possibilities encoded within a culture defined *by* women's voices as well. For example, Wroth reconfigures the "heroine/confidante" pattern governing the presentation of female homosocial bonds in both native and continental literary antecedents, to establish more equality of voice and role in her representations of ties between women. Here her emphasis on mutuality rather than hierarchy in female friendship intersects with the writings of other Jacobean noblewomen: surviving letters and diaries written by women of the period attest, as I will show, to close and complex personal friendships among women of the courtly class to which Wroth belonged.

On one level, Wroth changes the subject of Renaissance representations of desire through her treatment of women's approaches to questions of identity and sexual difference, emphasizing homosocial bonds between women at once in relation to and in contradistinction from the heterosexual bondage of passion often imposed upon women by husbands and lovers, fathers and brothers. On another level, by contrast to male-authored depictions of woman-as-object, Wroth changes "the subject" by representing women as at once subject to patriarchal authority and yet working to claim positions as speaking subjects with independent existences as well. When Wroth's texts are viewed in relation to both female- and male-authored figurations of gender, her participation in what Catherine Belsey sees as the "instability" evident in the utterances attributed to women because they seemingly "speak with equal conviction from incompatible subject-positions" can be understood not as confusion or inconsistency, but as an ongoing attempt to represent female subjectivity in multiple terms.[7]

I read Wroth's constructions of female subjectivity in light of Luce Irigaray's celebration of woman as the speaking subject of difference, rather than simply the opposition or mirror-image of man.[8] Where previous critics of Wroth have tended to position her repeatedly in terms of her mirror-image opposition to a handful of male familial and literary predecessors, I would argue that Wroth's figurations of gender are not simply oppositional, but in many ways "other" in emphasis. The limitations associated with the valorization of "difference" arise in part from critical tendencies to substitute "opposition" for "difference," or "sexuality" for "subjectivity," missing the range of discursive positions from which "difference" can be constituted. By exploring the mutually constitutive potential linking Wroth's texts with a variety of marginal as well as dominant discourses, I endeavor to address the discursive interdependence of early modern figurations of gender. Along those lines, I am concerned to investigate the simultaneous complexity and instability of relations between speech and subjectivity, agency and voice.

Mary Wroth represents women-as-subjects not according to a single model of feminine identity, which would indicate simply reverse stereotyping in response to dominant contemporary definitions of womanhood, but rather through multiple examples of identity formation. Wroth pays special attention to the impact of female homosocial bonds, focusing upon affiliation, however ambivalent, as a governing characteristic in the development of women's subjectivity. Where many of Wroth's male literary predecessors construct their fictions of desire upon extremes of romantic conflict, placing unremitting emphasis upon struggles between the sexes, Wroth highlights complex connections among women that predate, coexist with, and outlast the continually changing examples of conflict between the sexes. At notable moments, Wroth's works re-present the potential resilience of female discourse in a world where fluctuations in romantic fortune may be determined by male lovers, but possibilities for subjectivity are forged in the bonds between women.

Furthermore, Wroth's bold juxtapositions of discursively empowered female characters with equally compelling examples of silently victimized or passively obedient women open a new space in the midst of the dominant ideologies of her culture for constructing female subjectivity in unexpectedly multiple terms. Instead of reading Wroth's texts simply as valorizations of mirror-image gender differentiation, where female constancy is opposed to male inconstancy, feminine victimization to masculine agency (and a marginalized Sidney family woman to a canonized Sidney family man), I am interested in examining the potential challenge to gendered norms posed by the multiplicity of speaking positions for women in her texts.

Must female chastity necessarily be read as social subordination, for example, because it is prescribed as such by the conduct manuals of the period? Must familial obedience necessarily be seen to engender silence, or marital constancy to erase the possibility for female agency, along the lines of the overdetermined positions accorded a Cordelia or a Desdemona in the popular drama? I would like to suggest that, viewed afresh, the texts of Wroth and other female authors can be seen to offer alternatives not simply of degree but more substantially of direction to the gendering of agency and subjectivity in early modern English discourses. In Wroth's texts in particular, chastity offers some women opportunities for social freedom even as it imposes patriarchal constraints upon others. Likewise, while some of Wroth's mothers accede to the voice of fatherly authority in the family, others speak out. And while some of Wroth's female characters relinquish their agency under the bonds of matrimony, others locate in the constancy of female friendship an opportunity to assert parameters of subjectivity beyond the control of inconstant husbands or lovers.

I find that Wroth's insistent inscription of female subjectivity in multiple rather than simply dualistic or oppositional terms represents not simply a record of the social diversity of women's voices, or variety for variety's sake, then, but more daringly a complex attempt at rewriting those cultural discourses that presume to contain women's potential for agency in a handful of prescribed pairings of voice and role. To look beyond the ideology of victimization which has shaped many critical readings of Renaissance women's lives and works is not to evade the truth of social circumstances, but rather to recognize the possible existence of another truth to tell. Between subordination and

mastery lies a spectrum of discursive positions—my aim in this study is to
examine the spectrum of Wroth's constructions in relation to the fluctuating
figurations of gender in her culture. Indeed, the intersections between Wroth's
texts and those of her cultural contemporaries disclose the presence of tensions
between representations of potential victimization and potential empowerment across a range of early modern figurations of gendered subjectivity.

In his introduction to a recent collection of essays in materialist criticism entitled *Subject to History*, David Simpson urges the importance of moving
the ongoing debate about agency and subjectivity beyond the polarities of
either "total self-empowerment" or "total determination," to engage increasingly with "the difficult and perhaps indecisive registers of the middle range."
Simpson's thoughtful call for recognition of the extent to which "subjects
may be sometimes passive, sometimes active, and sometimes both at once in
relation to different subcultural positions held simultaneously" offers the possibility for identifying not so much a choice as a concatenation of representations of agency and subjectivity within single texts as well as across cultural
periods.[9] Indeed, critics as various as Carol Thomas Neely, Barbara Lewalski,
and Heather Dubrow have been working to suggest alternatives to the one-
sided model of discourse as implied disempowerment which has dominated
much new historicist treatment of early modern texts, with its emphasis on
omnipotent determination in the construction of subjectivity. Neely maintains, for example, that she does not think that "character need be subsumed
entirely under 'textual strategies', that 'desire' or 'sexuality' can be satisfactorily
explained as simply an example of class conflict, or that individual subjectivity
is absolutely controlled by the dominant ideology."[10] Lewalski states that she
has more interest in "attending carefully to what [Jacobean] women manage
to express than in reading through them (again) the all-too-true story of what
the culture managed to repress," adding that "their literary gestures of resistance matter."[11] Similarly, in her recent study of Petrarchism, Dubrow interro-
gates assumptions about subjectivity and patriarchy that have been cited to
deny the possibility of female agency, stating that her goal is "not to deny repression, but rather to build a model that does full justice to its complexities,
including those that open the door to some measure of resistance."[12] In my
own study of Wroth and figurations of gender in early modern England, I endeavor to expand some of the commonly observed boundaries between seemingly disparate sets of critical territories, with the aim of "changing the
subject" of early modern studies sufficiently to attend to the gendering of
those cultural as well as theoretical discourses that employ, in Simpson's
words, "the difficult and perhaps indecisive registers of the middle range."
     The historical parameters of my study have been sharpened invaluably
by the impressive work of an array of social historians who have expanded the

consideration of early modern figurations of gender beyond the previously accepted boundaries defined by Lawrence Stone's influential 1977 study, *The Family, Sex, and Marriage in England, 1500-1800*.[13] The writings of Keith Wrightson, Linda Pollock, Ralph Houlbrooke, Alan Macfarlane, and J.A. Sharpe, for example, illuminate many aspects of familial relations in early modern England, even as the studies of David Underdown, J.P. Sommerville, and Linda Peck address more overtly political intersections of courtly and popular culture.[14] More concentrated attention to the implications of gender, particularly for Renaissance women, can be found in the incisive studies of Susan Amussen and Margaret King, as well as in the early essay collections of Berenice Carroll and of Renate Bridenthal and Claudia Koonz, and the more recent collections of Mary Prior, Barbara Hanawalt, and Valerie Fildes.[15] My own indebtedness to these historical studies will be immediately apparent in the body of my discussion, where I draw upon the work of Wrightson, Underdown, Amussen, King, Ezell, Wiesner, and Crawford, among others, in working to define the tensions that distinguished social conditions for women in early modern England. Rather than positioning a "historical" chapter at the beginning of a primarily literary study, however, I have chosen instead to explore nonliterary as well as literary discourses in historical terms throughout each chapter.

Over the past decade, an exciting explosion of scholarship has also occurred in the recovery and analysis of writings by Renaissance women. Much of the literary critical work on English Renaissance women thus far has been historical and formalist in orientation, and has broken significant new ground primarily in uncovering the existence and asserting the importance of many previously unrecognized and noncanonical authors.[16] Only now that the existence of women writers has been acknowledged have critics such as Elaine Beilin, Elaine Hobby, Ann Rosalind Jones, Marilyn Williamson, Tina Krontiris, and Barbara Lewalski been able to move forward and begin to build, to pay more sustained attention to these women writers as individuals rather than simply "exceptions," and to explore some of their varied and multiple relations to early modern English culture.[17]

At the same time, as Margaret Ezell has pointed out in her 1993 analysis of the challenges of writing women's literary history from a feminist perspective, "to a striking degree women writing before 1700 are still not part of the 'tradition' as it is currently formulated." Ezell remarks further that although increasing numbers of excellent studies of individual figures have been appearing, "the theoretical model of women's literary history and the construction of women's literary studies as a field rest upon the assumption that women before 1700 either were effectively silenced or constituted in an evolutionary model of 'female literature' an early 'imitative' phase, contained and co-opted in patriarchal discourse."[18] In the case of Wroth, assumptions of "imitative" or "co-opted" discourse certainly can be seen to have shaped some of the critical treatment of her texts. My own study of Wroth's relation to figurations of gender in early modern England examines the extent to which Wroth's texts work to interrogate rather than simply to mirror the canon, thus exposing some of the fissures of gender ideology within the discourses of her culture.

I would supplement Ezell's analysis of women's literary history with the observation that a type of "Noah's ark" perspective can be identified in the frequent positioning of women authors in direct relation to already canonical or culturally powerful male figures. The resultant juxtapositions seemingly legitimate the attention to the female half of a given "pair," as an otherwise "minor" woman is linked with an acceptably recognizable patriarch. This "couples" approach has been particularly evident in the cases of Mary Sidney, the countess of Pembroke and sister to Sir Philip Sidney, and Lady Mary Wroth, niece to the same Sir Philip Sidney. The patriarchal pedigrees of both women have provided them with ready-made legitimation on the margins of the canon through their connections to the powerful male figures of the Sidney and Herbert/Pembroke families.[19]

Since the details of Mary Wroth's life have been amply rehearsed in other studies and will be addressed in subsequent chapters of my own study, I will provide here only a brief biographical sketch.[20] Mary Wroth was born in 1587, the first child of Robert Sidney (later Viscount de L'Isle and earl of Leicester) and his wife, Barbara Gamage, and niece to both Sir Philip Sidney and Mary Sidney, the countess of Pembroke. Wroth spent her childhood at Penshurst, the Sidney family estate, and came to court in the late years of Queen Elizabeth's reign. Following her marriage to Sir Robert Wroth in 1605, Wroth maintained an active presence in court circles. She gave birth to a son, James, one month before her husband's death in 1614. When her son died two years later, the estate reverted to her husband's uncle, leaving Mary Wroth to face her husband's debts. Subsequently, she engaged in an affair with her cousin, William Herbert, third earl of Pembroke, bearing two illegitimate children, William and Catherine, and maintaining ties with her circle of friends despite her reduced standing at court. The first portion of *Urania* was likely composed during these years, and was published in 1621 with her lyric sequence, *Pamphilia to Amphilanthus*. Her play, *Love's Victory*, and the second portion of *Urania* were probably written in the early 1620s. Wroth raised her children with support from both the Sidney and Pembroke families, and lived until 1653.

Much of the previous critical attention to Mary Wroth has focused upon the significance of her family ties. In his 1988 edition of *Love's Victory*, for example, Michael Brennan declares in the introduction that "to do her full justice, we should attempt to view Lady Mary not as an individual literary figure but rather as an important member of a talented network of writers drawn from the families of the Sidneys and the Herberts." With a sharper critical focus, Margaret Hannay positions the countess of Pembroke in relevant relation to her brother in her 1990 study entitled *Philip's Phoenix: Mary Sidney, Countess of Pembroke*. Mary Ellen Lamb's excellent 1990 analysis of the "Sidney family women" is likewise entitled *Gender and Authorship in the Sidney Circle*, and argues that "for his sister, daughter, niece, and an anonymous poet in his family or circle, Sir Philip Sidney's name provided a competing discourse enabling authorship," adding: "They were not only women, they were Sidneys." In her 1990 essay on Wroth's *Urania* poems, Maureen Quilligan observes that "Wroth's membership in the Sidney family goes a long way toward explaining how she could overcome the massive social injunctions against female authority that functioned throughout the Renaissance to silence female would-be writers," concluding that "the shared family gives [Mary Wroth and Philip Sidney] an experience as similar as we are likely to get for two writers of the period." Yet again, Lewalski comments about Wroth that "she claimed her status as author from her Sidney family heritage." And most recently, Gary Waller positions Wroth primarily in relation to her cousin, William Herbert, as well as to her father and her uncle, in his 1993 study entitled *The Sidney Family Romance*.[21] While these studies offer many thoughtful and illuminating readings of Wroth's texts that encompass other influences than those in the immediate Sidney family, their collective emphasis upon Wroth's familial connections has not addressed some of the provocative intersections between her texts and the other discourses of her culture. Furthermore, for all the range of theoretical approaches represented by these different critics, from formalist to psychoanalytic, they nevertheless focus with remarkable consistency on the literary texts and biographical details of the Sidney family members concerned, leaving relatively untouched the equally complex relations between Wroth's texts and nonliterary, nonfamilial, and female-authored figurations of gender in early modern England.

Despite the evident attractions of bringing critical attention to bear on an uncanonical woman writer by relating her to a canonical male author—not least of which is a built-in audience already familiar with the canonical male author—it is important to recognize that the minor woman in such bipolar studies ceases to be the subject, and in losing the status of a subject in her own right, becomes, most often, merely a foil for the male figure after all. In examining early modern women writers who have been positioned on the margins of the canon, moreover, we need to recognize that margins are also boundaries, which include as well as exclude: what circumscribes also *defines* what is at the center. Put another way, Gayatri Spivak suggests that "the margin" can be thought of not simply as opposed to the center, but as "an accomplice of the center," so that historically the margins become "the place for the argument, the place for the critical moment."[22] In the texts of some early modern women, the feminized margins of discursive authority become the place for argument after all, enabling women's voices to resonate across the social constraints intended to produce their silence. And in those cases where margins are recognized to be permeable, competing cultural discourses on gender can be regarded as mutually transformative.

Critical studies of canonical texts and dominant institutions tend to ignore what Teresa de Lauretis has described as the "space-off" of marginal discourses, a term drawn from film theory for "the space not visible in the frame but inferable from what the frame makes visible." Yet as de Lauretis points out, the "space-off" or "elsewhere" of these discourses exists both concurrently and in contradiction with the apparently hegemonic discourses, and the movement between them produces a tension of multiplicity.[23] In fact, although some evolution-based narratives of women's literary history have tended to segregate the writings of early modern women from canonical male-authored texts by grouping their letters, diaries, and unpublished manuscripts together under the label "private," Ezell has convincingly demonstrated the "public," circulatory nature of many of those writings, concluding that they often form part of a "dialogue" with other, printed texts rather than standing as discrete documents.[24] Only when the connections between literary and nonliterary discourses, canonical and noncanonical voices, male- and female-authored texts, the center and "elsewhere," are examined can "the subject" of women not only be defined, but changed, and the cultural complexities of gendered subjectivity be explored.

Although in recent decades, as noted above, critics have treated Wroth primarily in relation to male literary figures and trends, the response of some of King James's courtiers to the publication of *Urania* in 1621 suggests the presence of conflicting notions of what was acceptably literary and what nonliterary, what was appropriate for a woman to write, and what right a voice from "elsewhere" had to depict, let alone attack, the "center." Letters that document the court furor indicate that Wroth's gender, her choice of genres, and her social position outside the inner circle of power whose vagaries she was exposing rendered her authorship unacceptable. In fact, although the topical allusions to various court scandals which intermittently mark Wroth's narrative clearly antagonized some of the most powerful males in King James's court, thus jeopardizing her subsequent standing in courtly circles, it is quite likely that her marginalized political position had already shaped her writing voice, rather than vice versa.[25]

The objections of King James's male courtiers to the book's satirical references to their private lives forced Wroth to withdraw *Urania* from sale only six months after its publication.[26] Her primary attacker, Edward, Lord Denny, charged that Wroth had slandered himself and his family in using his personal affairs as the basis for her story of Seralius and his father-in-law. In lashing back, Denny specifically chose to make Wroth's gender an issue, lambasting her not only for her topical allusions to his life, but just as scathingly for her effrontery as a woman in presuming to write secular fiction and poetry, by contrast to the apparently pious femininity associated with her aunt's translations of religious poetry. Addressing Wroth in a poem as a "Hermophradite in show, in deed a monster," Denny advised her to "leave idle books alone / For wiser and worthyer women have writte none."[27] The resulting suppression of Wroth's text had long-range consequences: twenty-eight copies of the published *Urania* and only one copy of her unpublished continuation of the romance survive today, while the first complete edition of her romance did not appear until 1995. Certainly, this publication history attests to the cost of "changing the subject" in early modern England.

Moreover, while past discussions of the court scandal associated with the publication of *Urania* have treated "the court" as if it were a single entity, it is important to take into account the troubled gender relations underlying the power struggles between the court of King James, which suppressed the published (and "public") text, and the court of Queen Anne, whose ladies had been known to defy the king's wishes with the queen's support on other occasions. Indeed, as Linda Peck argues in her introduction to a collection of essays on the "mental world of the Jacobean court," the multifaceted court of the king, the queen, and Prince Henry spoke with a "polyphony of cultural voices." Expounding upon that characterization, Malcolm Smuts and Leeds Barroll have explored the conflicts within court society, which at once affected and reflected not only literary trends, but quite specifically the shifting positions of women in early modern England.[28] The complex cultural base for the court attack suggests why it is important to position Wroth in relation to the varied discourses on gender in her society, rather than confining the context of her works to her immediate literary and familial predecessors. Although several critics have shared the assumption that family connections give Mary Wroth and Philip Sidney an experience as similar as we are likely to get for two writers of the period, I would argue that the fact of their sexual difference renders any overreliance on similarities—familial, literary, and otherwise—problematic. By reading Wroth in relation to her culture as well as her family, I aim to scrutinize her authorial stance while uncovering some of the usually sublimated tensions associated with the gendering of subjectivity in early modern England.

In the three centuries following the attempted erasure of Wroth's texts from the public record, critical silence ensued. In the first half of the twentieth century, Wroth earned only brief and usually dismissive mention in studies of the English novel by J.J. Jusserand and Ernest A. Baker, and in surveys of women writers by Frederic Rowton and Bridget MacCarthy.[29] The first modern edition of *Pamphilia to Amphilanthus*, edited by Gary Waller, appeared in 1977, followed by Josephine Roberts's edition of the complete poems in 1983, and Michael Brennan's edition of Wroth's play in 1988. The 1980s witnessed the appearance of numerous articles on Wroth, while the 1990s have marked the publication of the first collection of essays devoted to Wroth; the book-length studies of Mary Ellen Lamb and Gary Waller, which devote significant attention to Wroth's works; and, finally, the first modern edition of *Urania* in 1995.[30]

Yet for all the burgeoning of critical interest in Wroth, several limitations can still be noted. Beyond the tendency to pair Wroth with dominant male familial and literary predecessors is the common treatment of her literary works as discrete texts, separable for purposes of critical discussion into individual chapters or portions of chapters, rather than capable of being read in relation to each other as well as to a range of contemporary discourses that form larger patterns of gender figuration in the culture. The most potentially disturbing tendency, however, is one that sporadically but repeatedly surfaces in a variety of critical responses to Wroth as well as to other Renaissance women, and that can be termed "victim feminism." Although critics such as Theodora Jankowski maintain that "to say that those women were 'chattels' is not to be complicit in making them so, but is an attempt to reclaim them as constructed/victimized/marginalized/objectified by the patriarchal society that *made* them chattels," Ezell points out that studies that focus on the "means of repression" rather than on the "modes of production" result too often in readings of early modern female coterie or manuscript writers as "docile victim[s] of a patriarchal literary system."[31] Even among critics apparently sympathetic to Wroth's accomplishments can be discerned an impulse to read Wroth consistently as a "victim" of her culture, which has far-reaching implications for our apprehension of Wroth as a "subject."

Although feminist insofar as it is concerned with a woman writer's relation to her patriarchal culture, this approach can result in a dramatic foreclosure of the possibilities for identifying subjecthood in female-authored texts. Carolyn Ruth Swift articulates one manifestation of this position in asserting that "Wroth reveals the loss of identity that women experience in a society that victimizes them."[32] A more sophisticated version of this approach emerges in Waller's analysis of Renaissance women's writing, which suggests that "we must look particularly at the gaps, silences, and margins of the subject . . . not so much on what women's writings 'say' so much as what they did or could not say, and why."[33] Certainly it is true that feminist critics must often start with an assessment of the "gaps and silences" in their subjects' texts, and yet, as Jane Marcus points out, "we val-

orize the victim at our own peril," because elevating sexual victimization
"robs women of a sense of agency in history."[34] The "feminist aesthetics of
power" which Marcus suggests as an alternative can be glimpsed in Patricia
Yaeger's study of "emancipatory strategies in women's writing," which
argues that we need to "pay less attention to women's silences and more attention to the ways women address men's silences."[35] And, I would add, we
need to analyze the ways women have entered into dialogues with other
women's texts as well, and have expanded the discursive potential within
their own texts in order to engage the multiple figurations of gender in their
culture. Along similar lines, Karen Newman has recently argued that we
have exhausted the usefulness of the "traffic in women" paradigm, because
"reading woman repeatedly as the object of male exchange constructs a
victim's discourse that risks reinscribing the very sexual politics it ostensibly
seeks to expose and change."[36] My own analysis of the relation between
Wroth's texts and the gendered discourses of early modern English culture
considers how she works to "change the subject," most particularly in inscribing women's voices not only as gaps and silences but also as discursively empowered, if embattled, and in constructing women's subjectivity
not as singular but as multiple.[37]

I have structured my discussion according to the cultural constructions
of femininity associated with different roles for women in the early modern
period, as inscribed, idealized, and interrogated by Wroth's texts in relation
to a range of social and literary discourses which, taken together, compose a
"multilogue" regarding figurations of gender.[38] Thus my second chapter,
"Dark Lady: This Self Which Is Not One," considers women's roles in sexual
and domestic relation to men, as lover and beloved as well as wife and
widow. My third chapter, "Matriarch's Daughter: Ties That Bind," explores
mothers' and daughters' relations within patriarchal family structures. My
fourth chapter, "Sovereign Subject: The Politics of Gender," addresses
women's positions within English court society, from monarchs to socially
marginalized "subjects". My fifth chapter, "Engendering Discourse: In a
Different Voice," scrutinizes the subjective authority of women as readers
and writers. My sixth and final chapter, "Between Women: Becoming
Visible," focuses upon bonds between women both as grounds for and challenges to female subjectivity. In exploring the dynamic relation between
Mary Wroth and her culture, I am concerned to present not a litany of influences, reifying my subject with reference to already canonical writers, but
rather a scrutiny of difference, considering the implications of gender in
constructions of subjectivity during the early modern period. My aim is to
explore a range of the sometimes ambiguous or seemingly contradictory textual discourses that attended Mary Wroth's efforts to claim a voice not just as
a second-generation Sidney and a "second sex" author in a misogynist court

culture, but as a seventeenth-century woman writer with a diverse cultural heritage and legacy.

I should note that while my particular critical approach has been shaped in significant ways by current trends in Renaissance criticism, most particularly by the perspectives of new historicist and materialist feminist critics with their insistence upon the importance of material culture, I draw as well upon alternative feminist approaches not as commonly found in studies of early modern England, including the varied discourses of French and American psychoanalytic feminists. The multiple lines of divergence between new historicism and feminist criticism find some resolution in the materialist feminist approaches practiced by critics from Valerie Wayne to Peter Stallybrass, Jean Howard to Catherine Belsey, as well as by other critics whose work does not as clearly fit under the materialist label—from Margaret Ferguson and Ann Rosalind Jones to Carol Thomas Neely, Karen Newman, and Mary Beth Rose—who can yet be considered "feminist historicists."[39] Nevertheless, other feminist perspectives more common to criticism of the modern than the early modern period can aid in the identification of additional areas of concern to Renaissance gender studies. I can best situate my own feminist historicist approach to figurations of gender in the early modern period by surveying briefly some of the most significant distinctions between these critical perspectives, which have helped to clarify the evolving parameters of my own critical "difference" as a feminist.

As it is by now common to observe, Renaissance studies have benefitted immeasurably from the wide-ranging attention of new historicist and cultural materialist critics, from Stephen Greenblatt and Louis Montrose to Jonathan Dollimore and Alan Sinfield, to the network of material practices which surrounds every text. Yet, as Neely has pointed out, the effect of many of these critical approaches has been paradoxically to further oppress women, repress sexuality, and subordinate gender issues.[40] Feminist criticism(s) at large, on the other hand, extend the boundaries of the new historicist truism that interpretation is crucially bound up with power, in pointing to gender as a significant determinant of any interaction between text and reader. As Margaret Homans remarks, to study gender difference from a woman's perspective is to begin to redress the appropriation of women's lives by androcentric critics of culture.[41] Some of the specific challenges that feminism poses to new historicism and cultural materialism along these lines can be located in feminist constructions of the subject as gendered, by psychoanalytic feminists as divergent as Nancy Chodorow and Luce Irigaray, Julia Kristeva and Hélène Cixous.[42]

While only a handful of Renaissance critics have included any references to the French feminists in the course of their discussions, Margaret Ezell stands out among scholars of Renaissance women's writings in stating

explicitly that her intent is to draw upon "the practices of two schools of critical methodology sometimes presented as being unsympathetic or insensitive
to feminist investigations of the past . . . French feminist literary theory and
new historicism." Ezell asserts that her goal in effecting this juxtaposition is
not to "suggest that the ultimate goal of feminist literary history is to recover
l'écriture féminine," but rather to "use the provocative insights into the nature
of 'the feminine' and on the act of interpretive reading provided by these ahistorical, psycholinguistic feminisms to produce sparks off the seemingly iron
facade of Anglo-American feminist literary history." In related terms, Eve
Sedgwick has urged the value of recruiting "the representational finesse of de-
constructive [French] feminism in the service of a more historically discrimi-
nate mode of analysis."[43]
     More typical, however, of critics who claim a strongly new historicist
orientation is the wholesale dismissal of "essentialist or psychoanalytic" feminist criticism found in Jankowski's study of women and power in early modern
drama. Jankowski sets out to oppose her "historicist-feminist" approach to what
she terms "the basically essentialist nature of the psychoanalytic feminist critical project," maintaining the necessity of "eliminating essentialist/psychoana-
lytic methodologies" in order to achieve her own brand of "historicist feminist
criticism." Although I agree with Jankowski about the need for a criticism that
is "flexible and open to the consideration of those historical texts which record
the nature of gender identity and gender definition in the early modern
period," I would argue that such a criticism can benefit from openness to
psychoanalytic feminist approaches as well. If the theories of psychoanalytic
feminists are brought to bear upon the findings of social historians rather than
"eliminated" from consideration, the result may be a criticism which, in the
words of Ezell, "has something of value to say to us about recognizing and ap-
preciating difference, not just in our time or in a transhistorical, timeless state,
but also in the historical past." Ezell's advocacy of "feminist historicism" is
thus more nearly allied to my own interests in conjoining new historicist and
materialist feminist approaches with the insights of French feminist theory
than is Jankowski's resolutely antipsychoanalytic "historicist feminism."[44]
     In fact, the frequent objection that French feminists are attempting to
define an "essential" natural or innate femininity needs to be balanced against
the recognition that the thrust of French feminist projects frequently involves
a contestation of patriarchal constructions at the level of cultural representation itself. Maggie Berg provides a particularly illuminating analysis of
Irigaray, for instance, which submits that "she posits a feminine essence not
in order to trap women in deterministic definitions but to enable them to
escape cultural definitions defined by men." Along these lines, Irigaray,
Cixous, and Kristeva can be seen to view the unconscious not as the cause
but rather as the consequence of women's social experience.[45] Likewise,

Diana Fuss points out that "essence" in Irigaray's writings need not be viewed
as the unitary, monolithic, in short "essentialist" category that anti-essentialists
so often presume it to be, suggesting instead that "to the extent that Irigaray
opens the question of essence and woman's access to it, essentialism represents not a trap she falls into but rather a key strategy she puts into play, not a
dangerous oversight but rather a lever of displacement."[46] Irigaray's insistence
upon the discursive nature of the conditions that determine women's sexuality, or Kristeva's attention to the multiplicity of female expressions and preoccupations, then, can be regarded not as limiting women's identities to their
bodies, but rather as opening the possibility that exploring the historical conditions under which women's sexuality is lived must entail exploring the language through which female subjectivity is expressed as well.

Interestingly, even while American and French feminists level and
counter charges of "essentialism" against each other, they constantly risk
being lumped together under an essentialist label by other critics.[47] "Non-
essentialism" has become a supposed virtue which many otherwise competing
schools of critical theory claim for themselves. Feminists, however, have
begun to scrutinize the definition, use, and implications of the apparently de-
rogatory label "essentialism" more carefully. Instead of accepting the apparent
choice posed by nonfeminists between an "essentialist feminine subject" and
a "genderless subject produced by discourse," feminists are insisting upon the
need to examine constructions of women's subjectivity both within language
and at specific historical moments, to refuse the separation of the empirical
from the symbolic, of the material from the discursive, of sex from gender.[48]
Thus de Lauretis reclaims the use of the term "essential" by asserting that
"feminist theory is all about an essential difference, an irreducible difference,
though not a difference between woman and man, nor a difference inherent
in 'woman's nature' (in woman as nature), but a difference in the feminist
conception of woman, women, and the world."[49] The importance of "difference" to feminist theory, moreover, encompasses not just an oppositional construction of male-female difference, but a relational construction of the
differences among and within women as well. "The subject" for feminist
theory, then, becomes not singular but multiple: to adapt Irigaray's phrase, this
subject which is not one. Historically specific as well as linguistically discrete
constructions of female subjectivity can be conjoined to "change the subject"
from an "essentialist" set of oppositional polarities to an interactive dynamic of
differences, which can be scrutinized not solely as culturally (pre)determined
artifacts, but also as active agents in shaping cultural figurations of gender.

Even as materialist feminist critics provide a necessary corrective to the
depoliticizing tendencies of some new historicist approaches, particularly in
relation to women, their analyses of the material conditions of life in the past
can usefully be expanded in response to the approaches of both French and

American psychoanalytic feminists without abandoning considerations of the historicity of culture. While materialist feminists emphasize their concern with "the social and the economic, as opposed to the purely psychological, and with historical difference, as opposed to the universal and essential categories of 'woman' or 'patriarchy'," even these apparent oppositions must be worked through as feminist attention to the early modern period continues to evolve.[50] In discussing the cross-pull of different imperatives associated with recent feminist theories of agency, Nancy Fraser observes that "*either* we limn the structural constraints of gender so well that we deny women any agency *or* we portray women's agency so glowingly that the power of subordination evaporates," concluding that "either way, what we often seem to lack is a coherent, integrated, balanced conception of agency, a conception that can accommodate both the power of social constraints and the capacity to act situatedly against them."[51] While to recognize this lack is not easily to redress it, in my present study of Wroth and figurations of gender in early modern England I endeavor consciously to chart a course between denial and celebration of agency and subjectivity in feminist historicist terms. My concern is thus with the psychological as well as the social, and with the historicity of figurations of gender in both early modern discourses and contemporary feminist criticism.

I realize that to some of my potential readers, not only is Wroth not Shakespeare, she is "not-Shakespeare," a marginal woman writer, whose sporadic appearances on academic syllabi, or in recent critical articles or larger studies of Renaissance women writers, often attest to precisely that: her identity as "not-Shakespeare," as an absence rather than a presence in the canon, a name to be invoked in a politically correct display of knowledge rather than a writer to be read. Yet as Teresa Brennan has pointed out, what is at stake for feminist critics is the definition of woman as "other-than a non-man."[52] In order to be able truly to rewrite the canon, it is important to be able to read women writers as presences, not just absences, to read texts, not just contexts. And instead of using male authors as touchstones to validate critical attention to women writers, it is more illuminating to interrogate the multiple conjunctions and disjunctions that emerge when "dominant" and "marginal" texts are juxtaposed. In my present study, I offer a feminist reading of figurations of gender in early modern England through the lens of the works of Mary Wroth, whose writings changed the subject of my own.

2

Dark Lady

This Self Which Is Not One

In *This Sex Which Is Not One*, Luce Irigaray observes that female sexuality has always been conceptualized on the basis of masculine parameters, and she proposes a redefinition of woman as *"neither one nor two."* In Irigaray's terms, woman is "indefinitely other in herself."[1] Irigaray's focus upon the multiple discursive potential of female sexuality has important implications for any examination of "difference" in male- and female-authored constructions of subjectivity. Early modern women writers in England were faced on all sides with masculine parameters, with definitions of female sexuality and subjectivity as "other" in mirror-image relation to masculine standards and assumptions, within male-authored texts ranging from handbooks for women to Petrarchan sonnet sequences. Yet their own discourses, in letters and diaries, poems and plays, expose the difficulties of attempting to voice divided selves and represent the potential power of female subjectivity in multiple terms. Instead of accepting masculine definitions of woman simply as other in relation to man — however divided those definitions of man might be — some early modern women authors were able to explore versions of the "otherness in themselves" (to borrow Irigaray's language), through their discursive engagement with gender relations in their culture.

In this chapter, I am particularly concerned to examine representations of women's roles in sexual and domestic relation to men, as lover and beloved, wife and widow. Whereas women can be mothers and daughters, rulers, writers, and friends in relation to other women as well as to men, as will be discussed in the succeeding chapters, conventional Renaissance conceptions of the beloved, wife, and widow underscore women's accepted (and typically subordinate) relations to the "other" sex.[2] The underlying connections between the roles can be glimpsed in their paradoxically oppositional interdependence. Thus Petrarchan constructions of the female beloved as a potentially unattainable object of desire, seemingly controlled by the male gaze, represent the flip side of the conduct manuals' concern with wives whose refusal to accept subordination as domestic chattels might suggest the presence of disquietingly ungovernable sexual passions of their own. Likewise, the social constraints publicly proclaimed appropriate for widows reveal a large measure of the cultural anxiety generated by the prospect of widows' freedom from husbandly authority.

Furthermore, the conventional gendering of responsibilities can be disrupted, reversed, and further transfigured by women endeavoring to rewrite their positions as objects of male authority and desire in order to claim some degree of agency as speaking subjects. Thus a female sonneteer might adopt the voice of lover rather than simply beloved, for example, while a widow might dare to assume the discourse of authority previously preempted by her husband. Wroth's texts, significantly, represent female characters in multiple combinations of roles as lover and mother, wife and widow, ruler and writer, whose voices bespeak both confidence and discouragement, and whose experiences, far from projecting an idealized roster of feminine triumphs, instead span a gamut of relationships from abandonment to independence which can be seen to reflect the complex and often conflicting constructions of gender in early modern England.

While Irigaray tends to counterpoise the feminist potential of "the future" against a patriarchally determined "present," which seemingly subsumes all past constructions of female sexuality, her insights can illuminate the gendered dynamic informing past social orders as well. Irigaray asserts that "in our social order, women are 'products' used and exchanged by men" with the status of "merchandise" or "commodities." Irigaray maintains, further, that "the use, consumption, and circulation of their sexualized bodies underwrite the organization and the reproduction of the social order, in which they have never taken part as 'subjects'," and questions "what modification would this process, this society, undergo, if women, who have been only objects of consumption or exchange, necessarily aphasic, were to become 'speaking subjects'."[3] Although Irigaray predicates her question on the assumption that women have not yet had an opportunity to become "speaking subjects," Margaret Ezell has challenged the notion that l'écriture féminine exists only in the future of women's writings, suggesting instead that "perhaps we have simply been looking for it in the wrong places in the past, or our construction of a historical narrative has hidden it in sight."[4] In scrutinizing the multiple constructions of subjectivity that emerge in early modern figurations of gender, I refer to some of Irigaray's insights in identifying moments, however vexed, in which women struggle to become "speaking subjects" in the face of the patriarchal sexual politics of their culture.

Notions of "difference" inevitably structure both male-authored representations of subjectivity in which woman stands for "other," for the object of a masculine subject, and the constructions of each female author/other who seeks to define an/other subject for herself. On the one hand, sexual identity seems to go hand in hand with sexual difference, yet when differences in subjectivity as well as sexuality are interrogated, an implicit gap between identity and difference can be recognized. When the cultural norms for identity are based on identification with a group, class, or category, then identity based on difference—that is, a woman's identity as "other"—results, in practical terms, in a "self which is not one." Thus when women attempt to construct identities for themselves, to speak with voices of their own, they must begin from the multiplicity of their "otherness," not simply as in difference from men but as in "otherness in themselves."

Julia Kristeva perceptively calls for a "demassification of the problematic of *difference*" in defining sexual identity, in order to analyze "the potentialities of *victim/executioner* which characterize each identity, each subject, each sex."[5] The identification of such potentialities allows for a consideration of women's voices in terms other than those solely of a victim's discourse. As noted in chapter 1, although some critics might maintain that identifying women as victimized by the patriarchal society that objectified them is only a reflection of historical fact, nevertheless, as Jane Marcus points out, to "valorize the victim" is to risk erasing the simultaneous evidence for some degree of women's agency in history.[6] Among the limitations of an ideology of female victimization, then, is the failure sufficiently to address—in historicized as well as theoretical terms—the potentialities of "victim/executioner" which Kristeva has suggested may characterize each sex as well as each subject. Furthermore, when the two-dimensional construction of sexual identity as a male/female opposition is replaced with a three-dimensional model which takes account of differences within as well as between genders, then Eve Sedgwick's choice of the schema of "the triangle" as a register "for making graphically intelligible the play of desire and identification by which individuals negotiate with their societies for empowerment" can be extended from examples of male homosocial desire to heterosocial figurations of gender.[7]

While it has become fairly conventional, if still useful, to observe that "the male subject's (hetero)sexuality depends upon the repression and control of the female Other,"[8] the female subject's sexuality cannot be defined in similarly hierarchical terms without resorting to a victim's discourse once again. On the other hand, the concept of "male subjectivity" becomes, as Marjorie Garber has observed, a "theoretical back formation from 'female subjectivity,' where the latter evolved as a politically necessary critique of the universal subject, 'man'."[9] How, then, can issues of male and female subjectivity and sexuality be balanced in a consideration of early modern figurations of gender when the comparative terms of such a bilateral discussion are inherently unequal? I find the concept of the triangle useful here as well, particularly in considering how the feminist subject, to use Rosi Braidotti's words, "fastens on to the presence of the other woman, of *the other as woman*," and even posits "the recognition of the otherness of the other woman" as the first step toward redefining women's identities.[10] Although in some circumstances this notion of "the other woman" might reinscribe a victim's discourse, still in many cases the recognition of otherness in homosocial terms can prove to undermine binary constructions of female subjectivity as the inverse of a masculine model. Rather than deriving models of female subjectivity solely from the "otherness" of sexual difference, then, we can explore the "otherness" of sexual identity for different women, both written by and writing against the gendered preoccupations of their culture.

In my own study, instead of drawing misleading (because apparently symmetrical) parallels between male and female subjectivities, I have chosen to focus upon the disjunctions that mark early modern constructions of female subjectivity, in order to uncover some of the ideological underpinnings of that culture's figurations of gender. My decision to juxtapose contemporary feminist theories with early modern discourses reflects my agreement with Nancy Fraser's articulation of the need to recognize "complex, shifting, discursively constructed social identities" as an alternative to "reified, essentialist conceptions of gender identity, on the one hand, and to simple negations and dispersals of identity on the other."[11] By exploring discursive constructions of gender relations in the early modern period, it is possible to historicize contemporary feminist accounts of women's agency and subjectivity.

In his analysis of domestic relations in English society, Keith Wrightson presents evidence that a fair degree of unsupervised contact was permitted between young people of both sexes in the early modern period, while Ralph Houlbrooke, Alan Macfarlane, and J.A. Sharpe, among others, have extended Wrightson's analysis of marital bonds in early modern England.[12] In Mary Wroth's case, numerous letters attest to her interaction with a peer group that included her cousin William Herbert as well as several close female friends. Interestingly, Wroth had two illegitimate children by that same cousin during her widowhood, at a time in the early seventeenth century when Wrightson has noted the emergence of a temporary peak in the illegitimacy ratio in England.[13] To a certain degree, Wroth's relation to her first cousin can be viewed in light of Houlbrooke's analysis of the exceptionally high endogamous tendencies among the nobility and gentry in southern and midland England, which resulted in the emergence of terms such as "Kentish cousin" to allude to the wide knowledge of kindred common in that county (which included the Sidney family estate of Penshurst), or Macfarlane's discussion of the extent to which first cousin marriage was legal if often unapproved.[14] The presence of not only one, but two offspring resulting from Wroth's extramarital relations with William Herbert, however, violated social norms in a highly visible manner, regardless of how accepted more discreet sexual relations between first cousins might have been. Wroth's willingness to transgress the social constraints considered appropriate to her sex extended from sexual to verbal license in her roles as mother and author, in a period when both modes of conduct on the part of women were liable to invite social ostracization and punishment.[15]

Examining moral, religious, and dramatic texts, Mary Beth Rose argues that there is a shift in sixteenth- and early seventeenth-century England from the dualistic conception of women as either transcendently idealized or physically degraded to the Protestant celebration of marriage as the predominant, authoritative sexual discourse.[16] In both cases, however, women are represented as objects to be valued or devalued by male-authored discourse. Early modern conduct books voice consistent concern with the chastity and decorum not only of unmarried women and of wives, but of widows as well, demonstrating the masculine parameters of culturally approved forms of desire, based upon the relationship between a desired (female) object and a desiring (male) subject.[17] The other side of (male) desire is understood to be (female) chastity, which simultaneously elicits and validates the prescribed direction of that desire. This subject/object dichotomy is perpetuated in the rhetoric of marriage treatises which maintain that husbands are to control wives in practice, no matter how affective their relationship in theory.[18]

At the same time, Heather Dubrow calls attention to a variety of inconsistencies in the conduct books on marriage which suggest that attitudes toward marriage in both Tudor and Stuart England were characterized by contradictions, ambivalences, and flux. The very intensity and frequency of pronouncements on the wife's inferiority and necessary subordination to her husband may well have been reactive, Dubrow suggests, encoding a defensive response to types of power achieved by women in the culture.[19] Still, the evident cultural preoccupations with regulating women's behavior within (and through) the marriage bond indicate the prevalence of ideological objectifications of women.

Furthermore, a double standard of sexual conduct operated beyond the scope of the marriage manuals, according to which women, whether married or unmarried, were expected to contain their sexual appetites, while men could and did participate both in conjugal relationships for the purpose of procreating male heirs and in extramarital relationships for love, companionship, and sexual pleasure, although such behavior was condemned in a number of the manuals. Susan Amussen has ably documented the extent to which the consequences of illicit sexuality, the type of attention paid to them, and the ways they were punished, differed for women and men. Indeed, Amussen's analysis of defamation cases suggests that "honesty" had one meaning for women and another for men, with women's honesty subject to determination and judgment on the basis of their sexual behavior, so that "reputation was a gendered concept in early modern England."[20] Thus a male courtier such as William Herbert, for example, suffered few consequences for his sexual relationships with various women, while the social ostracization endured by his female cousin and lover, Mary Wroth, for the two illegitimate children she bore William Herbert during her years of widowhood has been well documented.[21] Social historians have outlined many ways in which widows enjoyed power in certain areas that married and never-married women did not, ranging from estate management and promotion of their children's interests to litigation and performance of public duties. Nevertheless, sexual or verbal license on the part of widows entailed the risk of social or legal punishment potentially all the more severe for the perceived threat posed by a widow's anomalous position in Jacobean culture as a woman freed from the practical constraints of patriarchal authority.[22]

The sexual double standard did not go unremarked upon in Renaissance defenses of women, particularly when women's voices were raised in counter-attack to misogynist pamphlets. One of the earliest and boldest defenses written under the name of a woman, Jane Anger's *Protection for Women* (1589), warns that "at the end of men's fair promises there is a Labyrinth," and asserts directly that "we are contrary to men because they are contrary to that which is good."[23] This kind of dichotomous rhetoric becomes at moments more clearly triangulated in the major pamphlet war that erupted in 1615 with the publication of Joseph Swetnam's *The Arraignment of Lewd, idle, froward, and unconstant women,* and the responses of Rachel Speght, Esther Sowernam, and Constantia Munda. Swetnam accuses women of duplicity in conventionally abusive terms, labeling them "earthly serpents" and asserting that "a woman which is fair in show is foul in condition . . . the fairest woman hath some filthiness in her," while Sowernam turns Swetnam's invective back upon himself in admonishing him "to forbear to charge women with faults which come from the contagion of Masculine serpents."[24] Both sides appropriate the image of the serpent, the original "other" in the garden of Eden, in order to conflate the opposite sex with the perpetrator of "the Fall." At the same time, Swetnam's mode of attack focuses upon the otherness of women's sexual difference, which can be defined only according to the circular argument that "women are women."[25] His subsequent warning that a woman is like "a pumice stone, for which way soever you turn a pumice stone, it is full of holes," represents women as unfaithful in sexually suggestive language even while constructing femininity in terms of absence and lack.[26]

Cultural anxieties linking sexual difference with sexual identity can be identified in foreshortened form in the 1620 pamphlet debate over masculine attire for women. *Hic Mulier; or, The Man-Woman* attacks the "Female-Masculine" of "these new Hermaphrodites," betraying fears that the autonomy of male subjectivity can be threatened by women *not* visibly detectable as "other."[27] In fact, as Linda Woodbridge has pointed out, the image of the bare-breasted woman with a sword associated with the controversy is not that of a woman pretending to be a man but indeed that of a hermaphrodite.[28] The not-so-subtle connections between the controversy over cross-dressed females and the transgressive act of female authorship can be glimpsed in the label of "Hermophradite" affixed to Mary Wroth by Edward Denny, the male courtier who was antagonized by her authorship.[29] Interestingly, the initially feminist response of *Haec Vir; or, the Womanish Man*, asserting women's right to freedom from the social bondage of "custom," modulates by the close of the pamphlet into a call for men to reassert their masculine subjectivity by reaffirming their sexual difference from women: "be men in shape, men in show, men in words, men in actions, men in counsel, men in example." Banishing the threateningly ambivalent image of the hermaphrodite, *Haec Vir* promises the restoration of women's ornamental, subordinate, sexual identities in relation to men: "Then will we love you and serve you; then will we hear and obey you; then will we like rich Jewels hang at your ears to take our Instructions."[30]

While the ideological fault lines of sexual difference run through the conduct books, marriage treatises, and polemical pamphlets of the period, for the most part perpetuating rather than challenging dichotomous figurations of gender, an examination of personal letters and diaries provides a rather different perspective on early modern constructions of gendered subjectivity. Women's roles as wives and widows still emerge in relief against a backdrop of patriarchal authority, but frequently in reaction to the absence rather than the immediate presence of men. In her study of gender, family, and social order, Amussen has explored the ways in which simple subordination of women to their husbands is an inadequate description of spousal relations in early modern England, given the gap between the ideology of the household manuals, most of which were written by Puritan clergymen for whom the family was a spiritual institution, and the actuality of households in which the wife was responsible for the day-to-day education and supervision of both children and servants.[31] Educated women of the aristocratic class, whose correspondence and diaries have survived, often managed entire country estates in the absence of their husbands on court business in London or abroad, or maintained those same households as widows.[32] Assuming practical responsibilities only intermittently supported by their culture's manuals and treatises, some of these women produced their own cultural texts, or their voices were written into the letters and diaries of others, documenting their struggles to define selves both "other" than their husbands and even, occasionally, "other in themselves."[33]

Although Lady Mary Wroth's mother, Lady Barbara Sidney, was not one of those women whose own written words have survived in the form of a diary or many letters, the correspondence between her husband, Robert Sidney, and his steward, Rowland Whyte, represents various aspects of her situation during her husband's frequent absences abroad. While Mary Wroth's relationship with her mother will be addressed more fully in the next chapter, the existing documentation of her mother's relationship with her father, as detailed in the Sidney family correspondence, sheds light upon the "woman's part" in an upper-class marriage in early modern England. Whyte writes Robert Sidney in 1595 to inform him of the birth of his fourth son (and future heir), Robert, adding: "my Lady herself all day yesterday tooke your Lords absence as a great part of her affliction and burst out into these words, that now she had most cause for your presence and comforte, yt was not gods will for her to have yt."[34] Subsequent letters from Whyte convey Barbara Sidney's unhappiness at enduring her husband's continued absence, and her plans to join him in Flushing with the children.[35] At the same time, Whyte documents her exemplary care for the Sidney estate at Penshurst.[36] Robert himself writes frequent letters to his wife, assuring her of his affection and instructing her of his wishes regarding the estate in matters ranging from the hiring of servants to the maintenance of the landscape.[37] Wielding both authority and responsibility, even if not at her choice, Barbara Sidney found herself mediating between the roles of obedient wife and estate manager, nurturing mother and governing parent.

The costs and consequences of male absence in marriage emerge more clearly from the woman's point of view in the next generation, within the correspondence of Mary Wroth's sister-in-law, Dorothy, countess of Leicester, with her husband, Robert Sidney, second earl of Leicester (the same Robert whose birth Whyte announced in the 1595 letter cited above). Dorothy Sidney's letters to her husband are filled with expressions of affection and references to the sadness and "dis[com]forts that your absence doth bring."[38] Embracing the role of loving wife, she nevertheless finds language to convey her position which quite vividly attests to her self-confidence as a speaking subject. In one case, she passes judgment on her husband's brother-in-law with a stinging wit which cuts directly through the stylized courtly civilities defining accepted interchange between the sexes in early modern England: "this night your newe brother in law is come to visitt me wich is a verie extravagant civilitie for I never saw the mans face in my life, and I have not hard on[e] word from your sister since her marieg wich makes me wonder the more at this caviliers complement, what shee finds in him I do not know but if he be not a verie ase I am deseaved."[39] No "cavalier's compliment" can prevent the countess of Leicester from naming this courtier for the "ass" she finds him to be. Such boldly explicit language suggests that wifely affection not only may not have restrained women from voicing their judgments with authority, but may even have empowered their discourse within marriage, a possibility not often considered in literary historical discussions of spousal relations in early modern England.

A further extension of this freedom of speech emerges in the countess of Leicester's addition of "passion" to the conventional virtues prescribed for wives in the marriage treatises. As early as 1588, the term "passion" was associated not only with commanding or vehement emotions in general, but more particularly with amorous feelings, and even, by the decade in which this letter was composed, with explicitly sexual desire.[40] The countess assures her husband that she is "*bodie and soule* yours with all the constansie *pasion* and fedilitie that ever was found in any creature," and in a subsequent letter apparently responds to the expressions of sexual desire in one of her husband's letters to her:

> I will not defer my takeing notise of sume paseges in your last wich I read with a litle shame but no dislieke for nothing can be unwellcome to me that brings with it any show of your affection, neather need I many per-swaisions to give you in my thoughts what I beleeve you desier . . . and you wronge me if you thinke me defective in any thing that belongs to a most sincer *pationate* L[ady], for if thear be on[e] in the world that can love above all others I am deceaved if I am not shee.[41] [Emphasis mine.]

Furthermore, she reminds her husband on several occasions of her responsible management of his "businesses" both in the estate and at court, and justifies the frank speech which on one occasion has offended him by reminding him that honest discourse should be grounded in friendship rather than subordina-tion: "Though you are pleased to give me much of your affection and to desier mien, yeet will you not alow me the libertie of a frend which I am sure maie be prejudiciall to you, but if you will have me to saie nothing but what I am sure agrees with your humor I can conforme my selfe to it and had I not an ex-traordinarie *pastion* for you I should have brought my selfe to that comple-sance longe since."[42] (Emphasis mine.) Professing passion rather than chastity, substituting vividly written speech for silence, the countess transfigures rather than rejects the cultural ideal of wifely obedience from a model of subordina-tion to one of freely offered opinions, equally shared sexual desire, and even a claim—howsoever honored in the breach rather than the observance—for the "libertie" of friendship.

The letters of Wroth's sister-in-law bear witness to the validity of Amussen's observation, upon examining the records of defamation suits in the ecclesiastical courts, that many women did not emphasize obedience to hus-bands either in their own reputations or in their evaluations of each other. In-stead, Amussen has found extensive evidence that women were most concerned with their reputations for chastity and fidelity rather than obedi-ence.[43] The countess of Leicester's role as wife may thus be regarded as en-compassing seemingly conventional cultural terms, with a not-so-subtle assertive addition ("constansie *pasion* and fedilitie"), even as her letters docu-ment the presence of an articulate female voice in marriage, subtly but surely rewriting some of her culture's ideological figurations of gender and providing, in the process, what Amussen has termed "a covert critique of relations within the family."[44] Quite evidently not all early modern women's voices need be forged by outright oppression, not all female subjects need enter discourse through the conscious experience of victimization.

In other cases, however, opposition can prove empowering. Some early modern women diarists left behind quite detailed written records of their experiences which attest, more specifically than the letters discussed above, to the struggles involved in defining women's "selves" in a patriarchal culture. While diarists such as Lady Margaret Hoby (who entered the Sidney family circle through marriage) confined their entries primarily to daily business rather than personal reflections, others, such as Lady Anne Clifford (linked both to Margaret Hoby and subsequently to Mary Wroth through marriage and kinship ties), asserted their identities in writing as speaking subjects.[45] Anne Clifford married her husband Richard Sackville, earl of Dorset, in 1608, three years after her contemporary, Robert Sidney's daughter Mary (born three years before Anne), married her husband Sir Robert Wroth. Both women were active in the court of James I and Queen Anne, participating in several court masques, including a joint appearance in The Masque of Beautie in 1609. Both gave birth to their first children in 1614. As mentioned above, in the early years of her widowhood Mary Wroth also bore two children to her cousin, William Herbert, third earl of Pembroke; six years after Anne Clifford's first husband died, she married Philip Herbert, fourth earl of Pembroke and William Herbert's brother. Throughout their adult lives, Anne Clifford and Mary Wroth maintained a friendship with one another which is documented in the pages of Clifford's diary. Even as Mary Wroth seems by all accounts to have experienced a troubled relationship with her husband Robert, so Anne Clifford and her husband Richard were perpetually in disagreement, in Clifford's case over the issue of her continuing battle to gain her inheritance of land from her uncle. In many ways, then, the marriages of both women attest to the accuracy of Amussen's observation that marital breakdown was a constant reminder of the failure of life to conform to the prescribed "gender order." Along these lines, Barbara Lewalski explores the extent to which the figure of Clifford provides an instance of sustained public opposition to patriarchal authority.[46]

Anne Clifford describes in her diary how her husband directed her to accept the judges' determination of a monetary award in exchange for the land, and how, when she repeatedly refused, he attempted to punish her with his absence in London:

> All this time my Lord was in London where he had all and infinite great resort coming to him. He went much abroad to Cocking, to Bowling Alleys, to Plays and Horse Races, and commended by all the world. I stayed in the country having many times a sorrowful and heavy heart, and

being condemned by most folks because I would not consent to the agree-
ments, so as I may truly say, I am like an owl in the desert" [May 1616].[47]

In subsequent accounts of her relationship with her husband, Anne Clifford
documents the physical consequences of their sporadic arguments ("This
night my Lord should have lain with me but he and I fell out about matters"
[April 1617]), and her continued resistance to his wishes concerning her land
("After supper my Lord and I had a great falling out, he saying that, if ever my
land came to me I should assure it as he would have me" [December 1619]).[48]
Refusing to submit to her husband's will and to the pressure of (male) public
opinion, Clifford had the support of her mother and her female friends, as will
be discussed in subsequent chapters, while at the same time she articulated
her experience of isolation in the pages of her diary. Clifford's appropriation of
the image of "an owl in the desert," recalling Psalm 102, functions to convey
an early modern woman's recognition of the "otherness in herself" when she
sets that self against the dictates of the husband who presumes to rule her. De-
fying her culture's construction of the gendered subordination proper to a wife
and then a widow, Anne Clifford fought publicly throughout her life for her
legal right to claim an inheritance of land, even while maintaining the autonomy of her private voice in her diary.

     Like her contemporary Anne Clifford, Lady Mary Wroth turned to
writing as an expression of autonomy during a difficult marriage and widowhood, in her case producing a sonnet sequence, a play, and a prose romance
which represent women's struggles to become speaking subjects. Soon after
her wedding, a letter from her father to her mother recounted a visit from
Robert Wroth to complain about Mary Wroth's "carriage towards him," concluding dryly: "It were very soon for any unkindnesses to begin."[49] Ben Jonson,
who dedicated The Alchemist to Mary Wroth and addressed several poems to
her, reported to Drummond of Hawthornden that "my Lady Wroth is un-
worthily married to a jealous husband."[50] Her trials as a wife only increased as
a widow when her husband died in 1614, one month after the birth of her son
James, leaving her a legacy of £1,000 and an estate £23,000 in debt. Again like
Anne Clifford, Mary Wroth engaged in ongoing legal disputes to preserve her
land and her financial standing, in one letter asking her father to protect the
wardship of her son James from the "medling" of her husband's brothers, who
were attempting to claim "the lease of the land till hee come of yeeres."[51] Less
than two years later, her young son died, and Wroth's brothers-in-law possessed the land she had been attempting to preserve.

     While the social options available to widows, whom Houlbrooke has
identified as occupying a large proportion of the adult population at any given
time in the period, varied according to financial rank and class, many women,
like Mary Wroth, found themselves potentially vulnerable to reductions of

their status through conditions such as widowhood.[52] At the same time, the fact that widowhood could often prove empowering, discursively if not financially, is borne out by court records of women of different classes daring to speak up in efforts to preserve their positions, as widows, in the social hierarchy.[53] Much of Wroth's written work was quite probably produced during the difficult years of her early widowhood, when she was forging roles for herself as a lover, a mother, and a writer.

Before turning to her texts, it is important to situate Mary Wroth's exploration of the multiple discursive potential of female subjectivity in relation to the abundant literary as well as nonliterary figurations of women's sexual "identity" and "difference" in her society. The Petrarchan objectification of the beloved which recurs in many Renaissance sonnet sequences, for example, frequently figures forth a type of "dark lady," however fair in appearance. A distant and unattainable object of desire—beautiful and virtuous on the one hand but proud and cruel on the other—the female beloved is often characterized by a quality of elusiveness that serves both to perpetuate male desire and to allow masculine constructions of her identity that are not limited by any professed subjectivity on her part. While the recipient of voluble praise from the sonneteer, the sonnet lady often remains voiceless herself within the poems, her description serving more to indicate the exclusive nature of the sonneteer's passion and ingenuity in love than to reveal her own character.

Nancy Vickers's well-known explication of Petrarch's use of the blazon indicates how the fragmentation of Laura into different body parts encourages a distorted view of the woman as an assortment of scattered particulars to be assembled by the male sonneteer's governing eye.[54] As Louis Montrose has subsequently pointed out, "the Petrarchan persona is a distinctly masculine subject explicitly fashioned in relation to a feminine other . . . the Petrarchan lover worships a deity of his own making and under his own control; he masters his mistress by inscribing her within his text, where she is repeatedly put together and taken apart."[55] Central to the representation of "woman viewed" is the issue of sexual difference—Vickers suggests that the encounter between Petrarch's Actaeon and Diana, both hunters, is "a confrontation with difference where similarity might have been desired or even expected," and leads to the man's desire to descriptively dismember the threat posed by this glimpse of female sexuality as "other" than the male norm.[56] Once again, female subjectivity is erased by masculine inscriptions (Ovid's, Petrarch's, Actaeon's) of the "difference" of female sexuality. Such literary inscriptions of the sexual difference of the beloved are not far removed, in cultural terms, from the anxieties and prohibitions regarding women's behavior inscribed in the conduct manuals and sermons on marriage, linking the "otherness" of the apparently unattainable beloved and the seemingly attained wife after all.

Potentially even more disturbing to the male Renaissance sonneteer as well as the conduct manual author is not difference alone, but rather the possibility that the objectified sonnet mistress or wife may herself seek to become a speaking subject. Newman has noted how the fragmentation of the female body into parts in both wedding sermons and love poetry focuses not only on the genitals but also on the mouth as source of speech.[57] Where the Protestant preacher Henry Smith associates chastity with silence in a good wife ("As the open vessels were counted uncleane; so account that the open mouth hath much uncleannes"), both Philip Sidney and his brother Robert produced lyric sequences in which the lady, albeit briefly, is given a voice.[58] In the Eighth Song of *Astrophil and Stella* and the Sixth Song of Robert Sidney's untitled sequence, the lady speaks her love within a third-person narrative frame that places both lover and beloved at one remove from the first-person frame of the larger sequence. The lady's voice in each case heralds or reflects a further separation from the lover, leaving the sonneteer's song "broken."[59] Yet despite the apparent potential for autonomous speech written into the female beloved's voice, the latter portions of both sequences are devoted to reducing the woman to silence once more, as in the wedding sermons, in order to perpetuate the music of the lover's complaint.[60] By contrast, Mary Wroth transforms the role of the lady in her own sequence from a breaker into a maker of songs. In *Pamphilia to Amphilanthus*, the woman appears not as an object of adoration but as a lover, not as a muse but as a poet. When the "sonnet mistress" becomes the sonneteer, the conventional rhetoric of the lyrics has the potential to serve unexpectedly as a feminine discourse of sexual difference. At crucial moments, Wroth's lyrics work even more particularly to encode not simply an oppositional or "mirror-image" discourse in relation to Petrarchan conventions, but a woman poet's voicing of the "otherness in herself."

As Dubrow convincingly argues in her analysis of the counterdiscourses of Petrarchism, just as being silent is not the same as being silenced, so "speech is not necessarily an unqualified source or sign of power." Dubrow goes on to caution that "the voice of the Petrarchan mistress should not invariably be crammed into the category of disempowered silence," citing instances in which some Petrarchan mistresses achieve agency even in silence, while some Petrarchan poets manifest prolific speech without agency.[61] Dubrow's useful reminder of the complexities and ambiguities in the linkage between speech and agency illuminates the potential significance of Wroth's lyric sequence, not as an unqualified representation of successful female agency merely because the woman has a voice, but rather as an evolving articulation of competing cultural conceptions of voice and otherness.

Most often, of course, Renaissance sonneteers dwell upon the potential duplicity of the woman neither as voice nor as "other in herself," but as other than the professedly constant male lover. In the twenty-third sonnet of the *Amoretti*, for example, Spenser counterpoises Penelope's deception of her suitors through the covert unweaving of her "web" with his beloved's destruction (with "one word") of his own "whole years work" of discourse.[62] Spenser's recasting of the tale so that the male poet alone has the power to weave language into artistic creation, his beloved retaining only the power of speech to "undo," exposes the male sonneteer's fear of female speech as competitive with and destructive of his own. The doubled "self" of the sonnet mistress emerges in conventionally negative terms with Spenser's descriptions of her as "fayre . . . but cruell and unkind, . . . proud and pittilesse, . . . hard and obstinate" (*Amoretti* #56), followed by the warning that such a "proud fayre" can only mistakenly be "assured of her selfe" (*Amoretti* #58). In other words, this (female) self which is not one cannot claim its own subjectivity, because there is no basis other than self-deceit upon which to found any such claim.

In many of the other sonnet sequences of the period, authored by such poets as Samuel Daniel (*Delia* [1592]), Michael Drayton (*Idea* [1594]), Bartholomew Griffin (*Fidessa* [1596]), and Richard Lynche (*Diella* [1596]), the problematics of female sexual identity are repeatedly inscribed in terms of duplicity, duality, and "difference." Often the duality consists of an opposition between insistently blazoned physical beauty and consistently demonized behavior (considered only in relation to the male speaker's desires), so that Daniel complains: "Faire is my Love, and cruell as she's faire," while Drayton observes: "An evill spirit your beautie haunts Me still," naming his beloved "sweet Angell Devill" in consequence.[63] In a classic scattering of body parts, Griffin details the beauty of his mistress's hair, eyes, cheeks, lips, hands, breasts, and feet, concluding: "But ah the worst and last is yet behind, / For of a Gryphon she doth beare the mind," while Lynche caps a similar blazon with the warning that "yet a Tygresse hart dwells in this mold."[64] According to such figurations, the woman is merely a "mold" of physical beauty, possessed by an "otherness" so alien to the male speaker that only beast metaphors will serve to objectify her presence. The figure of a "gryphon"—itself a type of "blazon," with the head and wings of an eagle and the body and hindquarters of a lion—conveys particularly well the mingled fascination and repulsion engendered by the spectacle of female sexuality as a fabulously monstrous power inhabiting a deceptively familiar, because apparently human, body. Obsessed by sexual difference, these sonneteers project their fear of "otherness" outward upon the voiceless objects of their desire.

Although Shakespeare alters the polarized figurations of gender that obtain in other Renaissance sequences by "triangulating" the dynamics of desire—to cite Eve Sedgwick's illuminating formulation—the presence of the young man does not engender a new treatment of sexual identity and difference, other than to underscore the dominant subjectivity of the poet-speaker.

Just as in other sequences, Shakespeare's "Dark Lady" is convicted, by implication, of "false women's fashion," and of "fairing the foul with art's false
borrow'd face."[65] The poet counters the deceptiveness of the Dark Lady's discourse, identified in "her false-speaking tongue," with his own ability to "lie
with her" likewise (Sonnet #138), producing a conflation of verbal and sexual
intercourse which reduces the woman, once again, from a potentially speaking subject to a sexualized physical object. While the young man is represented early in the sequence in notably singular, if physicalized, terms—as when
"another self" for the young man can be imagined to occur only through pro-
creation rather than duplicity (Sonnet #10), and ultimately even that self is
collapsed into the singular subjectivity of the speaker's "own self" (Sonnet
#39)—the Dark Lady's duality is repeatedly reinscribed in the latter portion of
the sequence, emphasizing the speaker's fear that "thy sweet virtue answer not
thy show" (Sonnet #93).

Joel Fineman has suggested that the Shakespearean subject or "I" finds
its voice when the homosexual imagery of praise is displaced by the rhetoric of
heterosexual desire, and when the conflict between "true vision" and "false
language" transforms "a poetry based on visual likeness . . . to a poetry based
on verbal difference," indicating "a progress, in other words, from man to
woman."[66] From the "visual likeness" of male sexual identity to the "verbal difference" of female sexual identity, the masculine parameters of Shakespeare's
treatment of "woman as other" leave no room for an/other self in the sequence than the (male) poet's "I." Even the young man, another male, remains confined to the status of object, as the sequence resolutely refuses any
representation of multiple subjectivity, gendered male or otherwise.

Sedgwick goes further than Fineman in exploring the implications of
"gender assignment" in Shakespeare's "sexual triangle," maintaining that "the
woman finds grouped with her femaleness an overwhelmingly, eschatalogi-
cally negative moral valuation, . . . suggesting that she is the container and
others are the thing contained." In related terms, I would argue that the dynamics of triangularized passion, which emphasize loving only where, and because, others love, work to the negative valuation of the lady as an object of
both male figures' desires, when the speaker complains to the young man that
"thou dost love her because thou know'st I love her" (Sonnet #42), and accuses the lady in turn of taking "me from myself" and engrossing "my next
self" as well (Sonnet #133). Possessing no value or "self" of her own, then, the
lady operates as both impetus and obstacle to the bonds between men, themselves conflicted in their mutual attraction. Sedgwick concludes that despite
the potentially balanced juxtaposition of young man and Dark Lady as dual
objects of the poet's desire, beneath the rhetorical representation of counterparts and complementarity "one gender is treated as a marginalized subset
rather than as an equal alternative to the other."[67]

The gendered dynamic governing such container/contained metaphors can be identified not only in Shakespeare's sonnet sequence, but in subsequent lyric figurations of gender in early modern England as well. The pervasiveness of these metaphors throughout the period can be glimpsed as late as 1648, with Robert Herrick's "Julia poems" in *Hesperides*, one of which concludes:

> Then Julia let me wooe thee,
> Thus, thus to come unto me:
> And when I shall meet
> Thy silv'ry feet,
> My soul I'le poure into thee.[68]

Once again, the masculine "soul" is poured into a female container, reifying the act of sexual intercourse in "metaphysical" terms. More nearly contemporary with Wroth is Ben Jonson, whose *Works* (1616), containing both his *Epigrams* and *The Forest*, yields evidence of some relation between his poems and those of his acquaintance, Mary Wroth.[69] As Ezell has documented, women writers' manuscript circles included men as well as other women, professional writers and critics as well as brothers and in-laws, fathers and cousins.[70] Indeed, not only does Jonson dedicate his *Epigrams* to William Herbert, Mary Wroth's cousin, and place his long poem celebrating the Sidney family estate, "To Penshurst," near the beginning of *The Forest*, but he includes two poems to Mary Wroth herself. Yet another poem, in *The Underwood*, asserts that since "exscribing" Wroth's sonnets, Jonson has become "a better lover, and much better poet,"[71] suggesting (flattery apart) some mutual exchange of their poems over time.

At the same time, closer examination of the images in the two epigrams reveals the pervasive duality in Jonson's poetic construction of a female object of praise. *Epigram* #103, for example, calls attention to Wroth's family identity as "a Sidney, though unnamed," initiating the long critical tradition, discussed in the first chapter, of reading Mary Wroth primarily in relation to her prominent family. As Kathleen McLuskie has observed, Jonson's poems make explicit the inclusion of "certain categories of women in the approved world of men," particularly those whose social status was assured by their male relatives.[72] Jonson's "naming" Wroth as a Sidney thus substitutes familial identity for individual subjectivity.

In *Epigram* #105, Jonson declares to Wroth that if all past nymphs, muses, and graces had been lost, "who could not but create them all from you?" These multiple roles, however, are types rather than "selves," and furthermore are clearly intended to be male-authored rather than self-fashioned on Wroth's part, as revealed in the pronoun use of such lines as: "He that but saw you wear the wheaten hat / Would call you more than Ceres, if not that." Jonson concludes that Wroth is "nature's index," the ultimate compliment

from a male poet who claims the Adamic prerogative of naming the partici-
pants in that index, whether with the names of "Ceres" or "a Sidney." Of
course the concepts of "index" and "subject" are mutually exclusive, in that
Jonson's use of "nature's index" serves as a kind of exploded blazon, with a
single female object of praise standing in for multiple noteworthy women,
without any claim to a "self of her own." Jonson's hierarchical figuration of
gender can be glimpsed further in poems such as *Forest* #7, entitled "Song
That Women Are but Men's Shadows," and *Underwood* #20, which accuses
women of being "outward, fresh from spots, / But their whole inside full of
ends and knots." Although the poems of Jonson and his peers in many cases
can be seen implicitly to reify female power in the very act of denying it, still
the underlying impetus of their poetry supports the deconstruction of women
as speaking subjects. Once again, to use Sedgwick's words, one gender is
treated as a marginalized subset rather than as an equal alternative to the
other, and once again femaleness is associated with a negative moral valuation, as a container with conflicting "inside" and "outward" appearance.

   Maureen Quilligan has argued persuasively for the likelihood that, as in
the case of Wroth and Jonson, Wroth and John Donne could easily have
known of each other's work.[73] By contrast to Jonson and the sonneteers,
Donne's poetic rhetoric initially seems remarkably egalitarian with regard to
relations between the sexes. Rather than always representing women as duplicitous and doubled, "other" to the men who desire them, Donne in notable
instances celebrates unions between the sexes in which two selves apparently
become one: "If our two loves be one, or, thou and I / Love so alike, that none
doe slacken, none can die."[74] Yet in the opening conditional, "if," as well as in
the subtle falling off from the initial "one" to the less rhetorically confident
"alike," can be detected an implicit concern with sexual difference after all.
The activity of naming surfaces in "The Canonization" in another attempt to
represent sexual union:

> Call us what you will, wee are made by such love;
>   Call her one, mee another flye,
> We'are Tapers too, and at our owne cost die,
>   And wee in us find the'Eagle and the Dove.
>   The phoenix riddle hath more wit
>   By us, we two being one, are it.
> So to one neutrall thing both sexes fit,
>   Wee dye and rise the same, and prove
>   Mysterious by this love.

The resort to metaphorical triangulation in order to make "both sexes fit" one
"neutrall thing" results in a mystery, a claim for love itself as "other" in uniting
two individuals within a single identity beyond sexual difference. Donne in

fact repeatedly relies upon such metaphorical triangulation in order to represent multiple versions of such a union, from the two bloods mingled in the
flea ("The Flea") to the two feet of twin compasses ("A Valediction: forbidding
mourning") to the two souls "interinanimate[d]" by love into a single "abler
soul" ("The Extasie"). For Donne, successful union seems in these cases to require an obliteration of sexual difference, along with a concomitant substitu-
tion of "love" itself for subjectivity.

At the same time, the unequal mobility of the twin feet of the compasses
hints at a hierarchical figuration of gender, made explicit in the conclusion to
"Aire and Angels":

> Then as an Angell, face, and wings
> Of aire, not pure as it, yet pure doth weare,
> So thy love may be my loves spheare;
> Just such disparitie
> As is twixt Aire and Angells puritie,
> 'Twixt womens love, and mens will ever bee.

This construction of love does not so much contradict the celebrated unions
beyond sexual difference in the other poems as it exposes a more basic concern
with the gendering of sexual passion itself, rather than simply the gendering of
individuals. Why, after all, does the poet need to resort to such a multiplicity of
metaphors to convey union if not for the classic reason that if he does not con-
vince his mistress of the purity of his (male) love, the desired union cannot in
fact take place? In "Aire and Angels," the dimensions of the poet's task become
apparent: "mens" love "will ever bee" purer than "womens love," and thus
at best women's love can only serve as the "spheare" or container of men's passion, which must constantly attempt to surmount, erase, or subliminate,
through language, the troubling "otherness" of the lady. Objectified into
molds, hollowed out into containers, the female beloveds of male poets in early
modern England are expected (or at least urged) to wait for male-authored discourse to construct them into fitting receptacles for male desire.

How might this gendered dynamic be altered when women poets claim
the position of speaking subjects? Mary Wroth was by no means the first early
modern woman to gender the lyric "I" female, and thus her poems can be
read not simply in opposition to her male predecessors and contemporaries,
but in relation to continental and English women poets as well. By the sixteenth century, Europe already had an established tradition of secular writing
by women, including the poetry of the French women troubadours of the
twelfth and thirteenth centuries, Christine de Pizan's defense of women in
The Book of the City of Ladies (1405), Marguerite de Navarre's *Heptaméron*
(1558/59), and the love lyrics of Pernette du Guillet (*Les Rhymes*, 1545),
Louise Labé (*Sonnets*, 1555), and Veronica Franco (*Terze rime*, 1575).

Recent critics of the women troubadours, or *trobairitz*, who have attempted to identify qualities that distinguish the women's poems from those of the male troubadours who preceded them, call attention to a consistent thread of suffering running through the poems, a greater tendency to address the lover directly, and a frequency of reference to a past state that no longer obtains.[75] The early and often subtle revisions of a male-dominated tradition of love poetry which can be glimpsed in the lyrics of the women troubadours become more explicit three centuries later in the love poems of Guillet, Labé, and Franco. Ann Rosalind Jones has provided several illuminating analyses of these poets, stressing their attempts to bring new emphases and fundamental questioning to their chosen poetic modes. With regard specifically to the Petrarchan mode, Jones concludes that a European woman poet such as Labé "reverses" the relationship of distant, silent lady and longing, speaking lover, of observed and observer, on which Petrarchan poetry depends.[76] I find that Wroth, by contrast, "changes the subject" through a more complex and at the same time more ambivalent approach to male-authored figurations of gender than simple reversal, writing in response to a wider range of cultural discourses than masculine love poetry alone.

The less evidently assured "reversals" of convention found in English Renaissance women poets have led critics such as Gary Waller to hypothesize that these poets were provided only with "gaps, silences, and the role of the other, within male discourse." Reading them solely against the standards of their male literary predecessors, Waller finds that "no less than Astrophel's Stella or Drayton's Idea, they are fixed as 'images,' objects of gaze and analysis, within languages they did not invent and do not control."[77] Yet to start from the assumption of their passivity, objectification, and lack of control is to reinscribe them yet again according to the male-authored figurations of gender which their voices attempt to engage and revise. The evidence of frank speech in letters and diaries by women such as the countess of Leicester and Anne Clifford suggests that we must not too hastily read victimization and silence into the literary texts of their peer, Mary Wroth, without looking at the same time for evidence of speaking subjects in her hundreds of pages of poetry and prose, and investigating the ways in which she entered into dialogues with female-authored as well as male-authored discourses on gender.

Often, indeed, poets such as Wroth, Aemilia Lanyer, and even Elizabeth I voice the ambivalence and alienation of writing against cultural discourses that have constructed women's selves as dual, duplicitous, and ever other. At the same time, they themselves work to represent conventional metaphors in unconventional contexts or voices, and struggle to change the subject of the metaphors by claiming subjectivity for themselves. Even such an apparently conventional Petrarchan poem as Queen Elizabeth's "On Monsieur's Departure," with its alternating metaphorical extremes, opens out at the end of the first stanza with the poet's ambiguous figuration of her "self": "I am and not, I freeze and yet am burned, / Since from myself another self I turned."[78] For a woman, and a queen, to declare "I am and not" reads differently than does the same complaint from the pen of a male Petrarchan lover, as women constantly faced the erasure of their potential subjectivity within cultural constructions of gender, and as the queen in particular, with her "two bodies," grounded her princely authority in her doubled identity as monarch and woman—"this self which is not one."[79] In light of this doubled identity, Elizabeth's observation that "from myself another self I turned" may perhaps refer not only to "Monsieur," but also to her own alternating celebration and suppression of her femininity, in self-fashioning such roles as mother to her people and prince to her kingdom.

In *Salve Deus Rex Judaeorum*, Aemilia Lanyer reconfigures the mirroring potential of verse, traditionally claimed by male Renaissance poets to depict women as objects in mirrored opposition to their own subjectivity, in the service of constructing femininity in female-authored terms. Thus she urges Queen Anne, in the first dedicatory poem, to "Looke in this Mirrour of a worthy Mind, / Where some of your faire Virtues will appeare," and further urges "all vertuous Ladies in generall" to "let this faire Queene not unattended bee, / When in my Glasse she daines her selfe to see."[80] The "mirror" of Lanyer's verse can reflect the potential multiplicity of female subjectivity, when women "read" each other rather than suffering themselves to be written and read by men. Along related lines, Lanyer represents Lucy, countess of Bedford, not as a passive receptacle for masculine desire, but rather as an active agent of that passion for Christ over man which originates within "the closet of your lovely breast . . . where your selfe doth rest" ("To the Ladie Lucie, Countesse of Bedford," 2, 4).

Lanyer further recontextualizes the conventional Petrarchan blazon for her praise of Christ as "more true a Lover" than any man (*SDRJ*, 672), conjoining Petrarchism with the Biblical imagery of the Song of Songs in an address to the countess of Cumberland:

> His lips like skarlet threeds, yet much more sweet
> Than is the sweetest hony dropping dew,
> Or hony combes, where all the Bees doe meete;
> Yea, he is constant, and his words are true,
> His cheekes are beds of spices, flowers sweet;
>   His lips like Lillies, dropping downe pure mirrhe,
>   Whose love, before all worlds we doe preferre.   [*SDRJ*, 1314-20]

By choosing the same technique of praise used by male poets to construct their mistresses, Lanyer turns the blazon convention inside out, empowering women (in this case herself and the countess of Cumberland) as active contemplators rather than passive objects of contemplation.[81] Kari McBride points out that by assigning to Christ the traits and characteristics of both lovers of the Canticles, Lanyer merges male and female, implicitly calling into question the way Petrarchan conventions of love poetry appropriated the descriptive materials of the Old Testament poems.[82] Unlike the figure of the Petrarchan mistress, Christ is also present to his admirers rather than absent, and thus the poet's expression of loving praise can be predicated on achieved rather than forever deferred union, between two subjects (bride and groom) rather than subject and object.

On the one hand, Lanyer's sexualization of Christ as bridegroom can be compared to Donne's rhetoric in the *Holy Sonnets*, yet Donne could never this comfortably conjoin the erotic and the spiritual—his address to Christ as bridegroom focuses upon the troublingly sexualized role of Christ's spouse, "Who is most true and pleasing to Thee then / When she is embraced and open to most men" (*Holy Sonnet* #18). For a woman poet, the spousal relation to Christ is naturally gendered female, and thus Lanyer can speak with a woman's authority in identifying Christ as the only "constant" and "true" lover and beloved in one, "whose love, before all worlds we doe preferre." Furthermore, Lanyer reconfigures the container/contained metaphor in feminine terms, describing the countess of Cumberland not as a hollowed-out receptacle for masculine desire, but rather as a vessel for her own love for God: "You loving God, live in your selfe confined / From unpure Love . . . Your perfit sight could never be so blind / To entertaine the old or yong desires / Of idle Lovers" (*SDRJ*, 1547-51). Finally it is as women that she and the countess of Cumberland ("we") choose to "preferre" Christ, and thus it is as a woman poet that Lanyer is able to adapt Petrarchan discourse to a feminine mode of praise.[83]

Near the end of *Pamphilia to Amphilanthus*, Mary Wroth's poet-speaker contrasts the "true forme of love" in her thoughts with those "ancient fictions" that conjure shapes from the stars.[84] Even as she makes deliberate reference to the "olde fictions" of Arcadia in her prose romance, *Urania*, in order both to relate and differentiate her narrative from that of Philip Sidney, so she changes the subject of "star-struck" Petrarchan sequences, from *Astrophil and Stella* on, in rewriting male-authored "fictions" to body forth the "true forme" of a woman's desire. In light of her sister-in-law's bold assertion of "pasion" for Wroth's brother, and Lanyer's feminine revision of the Petrarchan blazon, discussed above, Wroth's own representations of sexual identity and difference in love become more understandable than when viewed as an isolated woman's implausible attempt to counter dominant male-authored discourses. Both as a woman and a woman poet, Wroth could fashion her voice in relation to the voices of other women as well as men, writing in response to multiple cultural figurations of gender.

A number of critics have focused on identifying the seeming limitations associated with women's voices in Wroth's lyric sequence as well as her prose romance.[85] Although it is possible to identify examples of victimization in the texts, an interpretive focus on masculine domination and feminine pain and passivity results in readings that tend to obscure or even erase the presence of alternative constructions of female subjectivity in Wroth's works. Both Beilin and Lamb, however, go beyond narratives of victimization in examining constructions of female heroism in Wroth's works. Beilin links Wroth's authorial approach with that of Aemilia Lanyer, in arguing that Wroth uses Pamphilia to create "another variation on a familiar figure, the true Christian woman," able to serve as a female hero who challenges "the normal masculine standards of heroism."[86] Lamb draws distinctions between different types of female heroism in her highly perceptive analysis of the writings of the Sidney family women, suggesting for example that while Wroth's aunt, the countess of Pembroke, provided positive female models by depicting heroic women in her translations of Petrarch and Garnier, her characters serve as "models of negation" because of their definition according to male perspectives. Lamb further argues that the "heroics of constancy" which pervades Wroth's texts testifies to the sublimated presence of "anger as a central motive for authorship."[87]

More recently, Dubrow's reading of Wroth's "conflicting and conflicted approach to autonomy in general" in *Pamphilia to Amphilanthus* makes a convincing case for the need to take stock of "the surrender of power which co-exists so uneasily with Wroth's assertion of it."[88] Given the evident circulation of competing cultural discourses on gender in both literary and nonliterary, male- and female-authored texts in the period, it is important to scrutinize *Pamphilia to Amphilanthus* not only for signs of dominant masculinist ideologies, but also for alternative signs of emergent female subjectivity. Thus in the discussion that follows, I examine Wroth's juxtaposition of dominant and subversive ideologies of gendered subjectivity in relation to the discourses of her culture.

I find that in *Pamphilia to Amphilanthus* Wroth counterpoises speech and silence, absence and presence, in such a way as to decenter the authority of the male beloved, so that it is the woman, as speaking subject, who commands if not the entirety, then at least the balance, of the discourse.[89] By contrast to the male love poets discussed above, Wroth gives the speaker's voice in her lyric sequence to the woman, thus silencing the man and simultaneously undermining the stricture of female silence so emphasized in Renaissance directives for women. Pamphilia's insistence upon her constancy can be read in relation to Susan Amussen's observation that early modern women's defenses of their reputations centered upon their chastity, with little concern for silence or obedience.[90] The discourses on constancy attributed to early modern women thus differed from those attributed to early modern men, in that constancy in the former case could be associated with, rather than divorced from,

female speech and even agency. Wroth's treatment of constancy may be regarded in historicist terms, then, less as a self-destructive idealization of a
dominant masculinist ideology, or even as a sublimated representation of religious faith or repressed anger, than as a manifestation of women's potential
to transform strictures upon their actions into enabling grounds for discourse.
Such discourse can contest patriarchal constructions of women's "essence" on
the level of cultural representation itself. As in the defamation suits surveyed
by Amussen, what is at stake in Wroth's texts is not simply female behavior,
but female speech. Where a focus upon identification of gaps and silences in
a woman writer's texts presumes a model of effective speech based on masculine discourse, a consideration of a range of female-authored discourses allows
for less potentially reductive critical readings in gendered terms.

By contrast to many male love poets who periodically blame their personal trials upon the harshness of their ladies, Wroth's speaker moves beyond
blame or self-pity to celebrate the "true forme of love" apart from the caprice
of her male beloved—even, for example, as Wroth's sister-in-law, the countess
of Leicester, asserts her "pasion" apart from her husband's refusal to allow her
"the libertie of a frend." In structuring her sequence around a woman's voice,
Wroth does more than simply reverse the conventional relationship of male
lover and female beloved in the manner, for example, of Louise Labé. Instead,
Pamphilia speaks not solely as a lover focused upon the beloved but as a
woman cognizant of the shared female experience of suffering for love. In her
voicing of the inclusive rather than exclusive nature of her passion, Pamphilia
refuses to speak from the margins of discourse as an isolated woman in love.
Writing at once within and against the gendered figurations of her patriarchal
culture, Wroth uses not the egocentrism of masculine rhetoric but Pamphilia's feminine awareness of mutuality to empower her lyric voice.

Pamphilia to Amphilanthus opens with a dream vision in the first sonnet
which establishes the female speaker's initial loss of identity, when "sleepe
deaths Image did my senceses hiere / From knowledg of my self" (P1). Venus
and Cupid succeed in "martiring" the dreamer's heart so that Pamphilia awak-
ens as a "lover," a newly acquired role which initiates her discourse. Because
the male beloved is absent except for the presence of his name in the title,
Wroth from the first places the emphasis directly upon the speaking voice of
the female lover.[91] The evolving dynamic among the central characters soon
differentiates Wroth's perspective from that of her male literary predecessors,
allying her more clearly with a female poet such as Lanyer, who also worked to
transfigure Petrarchan traditions. In Wroth's sequence in particular, the
speaker's relation to Cupid shifts when the sonneteer is a woman. For example, whereas Philip Sidney presents the figure of Cupid as both ally and
rival to Astrophil in the pursuit of the female beloved (AS #11), Wroth's
Cupid becomes the female poet's suitor. Thus Pamphilia finds herself in the

position of denying Cupid's suit while affirming her constancy toward her male beloved (P8).[92]

Wroth further delineates the altered relation of her female speaker to Cupid in order to revise the conventionally masculine metaphor of battle. The male sonneteers regularly represent the lover's predicament in martial terms, outlining the speaker's attempts on the one hand to conquer the beloved's heart (Philip Sidney, AS #61, #69; Robert Sidney, #7; Spenser, Amoretti #14), or on the other hand to resist captivity himself, when faced with his beloved's arsenal of beauty (Philip Sidney, AS #53; Robert Sidney, #15, #18, #33; William Percy, Coelia #1). Ben Jonson even links Cupid's arms specifically with Wroth in one of his sonnets addressed to her, identifying "in your verse all Cupid's armory, / His flames, his shafts, his quiver, and his bow, / His very eyes are yours to overthrow" (Underwood #28). Wroth, however, shifts the focus of the strife, so that her speaker's conflict is with Cupid rather than with her beloved: "Am I thus conquer'd? have I lost the powers / That to withstand, which joy's to ruin mee? / Must I bee still while itt my strength devowres / And captive leads mee prisoner, bound, unfree?" (P16). Here are encoded the potential victimization and loss of liberty that have focused previous critical attention—from scholars otherwise as various as Swift and Beilin, Waller and Lamb—upon Wroth. At the same time, Wroth's verse inscribes speech rather than silence, and Pamphilia's question can be read as posing a contestation of agency rather than a loss of identity, suggesting a starting point for resistance rather than a concluding point for denied anger.

While the male love poets emphasize the strength of their efforts to preserve their autonomy, surrendering only when "no power is left to strive" (Robert Sidney, #18), Wroth's female speaker demonstrates her passion without the masculine emphasis on aggression. All the "powre" and aggressive strife are left to Cupid, while the lady admonishes him that "'tis cowardise, to strive wher none resist" (P8). Asserting that "I ame thy subject, conquer'd, bound to stand" (P8), Pamphilia paradoxically claims a voice from the very position of subjection.[93] Furthermore, by displacing the focus of the conflict onto Cupid, the female lover maintains the prerogative of choosing her beloved willingly. By acknowledging rather than resisting her passion, she is enabled to reject the authority of Cupid's "boyship" once she has directed her love toward Amphilanthus (P8). Both as a lover and as a poet, Wroth's speaker prefers to take the initiative in offering her affections through song directly to her beloved rather than prolonging a martial engagement with Cupid.

Jeff Masten argues perceptively that the "nascent" subjectivity in Pamphilia to Amphilanthus is both "private and privative," alluding to the sonnet in which Pamphilia declares herself "possesst" by "the hellish speritt absence" (P52).[94] The language of "possession" certainly seems to indicate a representation of a "self which is not one," a subject striving to claim a voice not overdetermined by her beloved's absence. At the same time, the speaker's ability to look forward to a future when "I ame my self, and blest" (P52), suggests an underlying determination to maintain her position, however privative, until her willed constancy triumphs over the inconstancy of her beloved. Thus although the speaker's female subjectivity may be shaped in part by male absence—as was that of Wroth's mother and sister-in-law—it is increasingly defined by her speaking voice, and possesses the power to endure and outlast that "hellish speritt" by its discursive presence in the sonnets themselves.

In the crown, or *corona*, of fourteen sonnets at the heart of the sequence, Wroth further explores the problematics of female subjectivity. One of the first instances of the *corona* in English occurs in Philip Sidney's *Old Arcadia*, in the form of ten linked dizains (*Old Arcadia* #72), while Robert Sidney includes an incomplete crown of sonnets in his sequence. By choosing the same form for inclusion in her sequence, Wroth doesn't hesitate to engage head-on with these literally patriarchal precedents, while at the same time fashioning her own crown as a testament to the emerging power of the voice of the lady. Indeed, the pervasive image of a "strang labourinth" (P77), in which the speaker must find "the thread of love"—the opening and governing image of Wroth's *corona*—can be read in direct relation both to Robert Sidney's description in his sequence of "the saving thread" which "the maze unwound" (Pastoral #9), and to the background myth of Theseus and Ariadne as well. In Robert Sidney's sequence, the "saving thread" turns out to be the lady's faults, which can bring the lover to his senses so that he can change his mind and relinquish love, described as a "maze" along the lines of the labyrinth housing the Minotaur, from which Theseus escaped with Ariadne's help. According to one version of the myth, Ariadne—whom Nancy Miller has argued persuasively is "troped as masculinity's feminine other"—provided Theseus with the thread, only to be abandoned by him and left alone on the island of Naxos to commit suicide in despair.[95] Embedded in Robert Sidney's use of the thread-and-maze image, therefore, is a trope of masculine abandonment of the feminine other, justified as masculine escape from feminine wiles, with the understated possibility that female sexuality is perceived as the monstrous power lurking at the center of the maze of male desire.

By contrast to this oppositional constitution of the sonnet mistress as "other" in every sense, Wroth reclaims the image of a "labourinth," along the lines of Jane Anger's reference to the "Labyrinth" of male promises, to explore the possibility of a female subjectivity that can not only endure the male lover's abandonment, but even prevail.[96] The "thread" in Wroth's sequence is not, in simple reversal of Robert Sidney's sequence, a list of male faults, but rather a "thread of love" (P77), which emerges through the power of female discourse to unwind a maze of male inconstancy. As the final line of each sonnet in the *corona* is repeated in the first line of the successive sonnet, Pamphilia's voice itself becomes her thread of love expressed, revealing her chosen path through the labyrinthine turns of her male beloved's fluctuating behavior, and allowing Wroth to enter into a "dialogue" with her father's and uncle's texts. In her study of the "idea of the labyrinth," Penelope Doob has indicated that mazes are both single—to the "maze treader," whose vision is severely restricted—and double—to the "maze viewer," who sees the pattern whole, as simultaneously incorporating both order and disorder, clarity and confusion, unity and multiplicity.[97] Read as a trope not simply for masculine abandonment, but for emergent female subjectivity as well, Wroth's "strang labourinth" becomes at once a trial for the woman lover suffering her beloved's absence, and a testament to the woman poet's ability to view the pattern whole, inclusive of that future time when "I ame my self, and blest."

Early in the *corona*, Wroth highlights the issue of constancy from a female point of view. In the third sonnet, the speaker describes the testing ground of true love: "Heere are affections, tri'de by loves just might / As gold by fire, and black deserned by white, / Error by truthe, and darknes knowne by light, / Wher faith is vallwed for love to requite" (P79). In the trial of affections, faith is valued and true love proves "constant as fate" (P79). The series of similes, from "gold by fire" to "darknes knowne by light," outlines a knowledge based on contrarieties, an identity for the lover based on "difference." When Wroth's diction is viewed as offering a dialogue with the discourse of her male predecessors, however, it becomes apparent that her concern is less with the oppositional relation between the genders than with the different figurations of women's subjectivity constructed by male- as opposed to female-authored discourse. For eight lines of her monorhymed sonnet, Wroth chooses two of the same ending words—"might" and "light"—as Philip Sidney uses for his monorhymed sonnet in the *Old Arcadia*. Sidney's sonnet, significantly, is attributed to Gynecia, who is tormented by her selfish desire to betray her marriage for adulterous love of Pyrocles. In that sonnet, Gynecia invites "clowdie feares" to close her sight (*Old Arcadia* #72), while in Wroth's sonnet, Pamphilia declares that "noe clowde can apeere" to dim the light of true love (P79). The deliberately allusive echoes of the earlier sonnet serve to emphasize the contrast between Sidney's inconstant Gynecia and Wroth's constant Pamphilia, revealing not a gap or a silence erasing female agency but rather an active re-vision of the female subjectivity of the lover.

The third sonnet of Wroth's crown also alludes to the third sonnet of Robert Sidney's crown, in which the speaker professes his faith to his beloved, yet admits that he has loved others before her. In excusing his behavior, he argues that "Love gave me not to them, he did but lend" (Robert Sidney, #13), and offers a justification in the following sonnet: "Ah let not me for changing blame endure, / Who only changed, by change to find the best:" (Robert Sidney, #14). Wroth demonstrates her awareness of that particular justification of change in her own depiction of the relationship between lover and beloved, yet in her case she attributes that position to Amphilanthus. When Pamphilia remarks upon her beloved's inconstancy in *Urania*, he replies that "none can bee accused . . . for their change, if it bee but till they know the best, therefore little fault hath yet been in me: but now I know the best, change shall no more know me."[98] Pamphilia's response is simply that "every change brings this thought." Within the *corona*, Wroth emphasizes not a man's egocentric quest for "the best" object of desire as a justification for change, but rather a woman's assertion of love beyond male inconstancy as a justification for female subjectivity. In place of patriarchal Renaissance conceptions of constancy as rare in women and optional for men, Wroth represents constancy—along the lines of the women defending their reputations in defamation suits—as one potentially empowering parameter of female sexual identity.

Later in the *corona*, Wroth inscribes the possibility of mutual love between the sexes in terms that suggest a response to her contemporary, John Donne. Wroth claims for love the power "to joine two harts as in one frame to move; / Two bodies, butt one soule to rule the minde," adding that love "doth inrich the witts, and make you see / That in yourself, which you knew nott before" (P82). Instead of resorting to a third "other" (whether phoenix, compass, or flea) to define union in terms of obliterated sexual difference, Wroth allows for the "otherness in themselves" of both lovers. Still possessed of "two bodies," the lovers enrich rather than erase each other's subjectivity, each learning to see "that in yourself, which you knew nott before." In Wroth's figuration of gender, love is not a substitute for subjectivity, but rather an opportunity for sexual connection which can include difference on both sides, for a union between two equal subjects rather than "container and contained." Even as contemporary theorists such as Irigaray look to future women writers for inscriptions of the multiple "otherness" of female subjectivity, Mary Wroth can be seen to be carving out a discursive space among early modern English figurations of gender within which she can associate the "otherness" of women, previously constructed as objects of desire, with both sexes configured anew as agents of passion. The masculine parameters of her culture's dominant discourses can be viewed as providing not so much the boundaries, then, as the starting point for Wroth's representation of the "otherness" of her own voice as a female poet.

Like Wroth's poems, her play concentrates on the gendered relations between lover and beloved within courtship, while her prose romance spans women's roles from courtship through marriage and widowhood. Even as the male-authored drama and prose fiction of the period, as well as contemporary continental romances in circulation in early modern England, established patterns of gender relation that alternately suppress or demonize female sexuality, some women authors refused to reduce women's roles, and voices, to the handful of recognizable stereotypes embedded in the texts of their male predecessors and contemporaries. A comparative evaluation of the fictions of female as well as male authors in the early modern period begins to suggest the divergent parameters of gender-fashioning which confronted Mary Wroth. Consequently, Wroth's own characterizations in her play and prose romance may be seen to reveal patterns of gender relation which at once refract and multiply the positions accorded women in the popular texts of her culture.

Continental romances such as Jorge de Montemayor's *Diana* and Honoré d'Urfé's *Astrée* were arguably almost as well-known and popular in early modern England as some of the prose romances by English authors such as Thomas Lodge and Robert Greene. Montemayor's *Diana* would certainly have been accessible to Mary Wroth in Bartholomew Yong's 1598 English translation, while she could have read the early volumes of d'Urfé's *Astrée* either in English translation or directly in French, in the early 1600s.[99] By the same token, she would quite likely have been familiar with the even earlier depictions of the gendered play of desire in the female-authored continental romance of Marguerite de Navarre, which appeared in the mid-sixteenth century and was first translated into English during Elizabeth's reign.[100]

Although the female characters in many of the tales in Marguerite de Navarre's *Heptaméron* seem initially to be objectified in the manner of male-authored texts from Boccaccio's *Decameron* to d'Urfé's *Astrée*, the female victims of the many rape attempts which mark the text frequently emerge as bold, virtuous, or intelligent, while the stance of the male aggressors can be viewed as concomitantly problematic. And in representations of the marriage bond, as P.A. Chilton has remarked, alongside those tales urging the wife's moral influence as a remedy for male inconstancy can be found a small number of stories "claiming something approaching a symmetry of sexual rights in marriage."[101] Furthermore, the connecting commentary between the tales provides quite varied perspectives on the relations between the sexes, particularly as the male and female narrators frequently present conflicting interpretations on gendered grounds, adumbrating the discursive strategies of Wroth's texts.[102]

Early in the *Heptaméron*, for example, one male character named Dagoucin gives voice to a desire to obliterate feminine difference in love, effectively erasing any possibility of female subjectivity: "No man can know . . . where his other half is to be found, this other half with whom he may find a union so equal that between the parts there is no difference . . . For if she whom you love is your true likeness, if she is of the same will, then it will be your own self that you love" (113). Similar expressions of egocentric passion are embedded in many male-authored English sonnet sequences. In Marguerite's *Heptaméron*, however, such a view is immediately challenged, on the one hand by some of the other male characters, who argue with his terms, and on the other hand by the vocal assertions of a number of female characters throughout the narrative, who present their own quite different views on love and desire. Repeated attempts on the part of the male storytellers to objectify women are met by counterassertions of agency and subjectivity on the part of the female storytellers, leading to heated debates which effectively serve to problematize the gendering of authority and desire.

One of the male narrators, Saffredent, actually admits that men "devise the most angelic appearance we can, to cover up the devil inside, and thus disguised, we receive a few good favours before we're found out" (165), confessing to a duplicity more conventionally attributed in male-authored romances to women than to men. Furthermore, one of the female narrators, Longarine, uses her tale to demonstrate that "there are women who are just as courageous, just as intelligent and just as shrewd as men" (188). Nevertheless, when the most respected female narrator, Oisille, attempts to outline differences among women, Saffredent refuses to allow her argument, instead urging the objectification of all women in terms of their sexualized bodies: "All the same, . . . you *are* all women. You can cover yourselves up becomingly with all the finery you like, but the fact remains that anyone who looks carefully underneath all those skirts will find that you *are* all women!" (202).

No single gendered perspective, male or female, dominates the course of Marguerite's narrative, as the characters not only argue with members of the opposite sex, but differ with others of the same sex as well. Although the characters variously assert that "more men are deceived by women than women by men" (Dagoucin: 460), or that "women love more deeply than men" (Nomerfide: 533), Oisille's observation that "one should not judge anyone but oneself" (490) speaks to the heart of the interpretive commentary in the *Heptaméron*, in which both men and women are represented as having the capability for judgment as well as speech. When one of the male characters, Geburon, admits that after listening to all the tales and commentary thus far, he is "amazed by the varied nature of women's love" (373), his admission suggests the capacity of the narrative itself to represent female subjectivity and desire in more expansive terms than typically found in male-authored romances. The multiple perspectives of the narrators in Marguerite de Navarre's *Heptaméron* open the text to equally multiple interpretations, allowing cultural figurations of gender to be queried rather than reified, and granting the discursive potential of the female narrators as speaking subjects.

Whether focusing upon the power of constancy or of inconstancy in love, critics of male-authored continental romances such as *Diana* and *Astrée* have not tended to remark upon the pervasive connections within these texts between representations of sexual desire and sexual identity.[103] Yet both Montemayor and d'Urfé center the dynamics of desire upon the title female characters, whose rejections of their faithful male lovers initiate the plots. Not only Montemayor and d'Urfé, but Sidney, Lodge, and Greene as well construct their fictions upon extremes of romantic conflict, placing unremitting emphasis upon struggle and tension between the sexes that is resolved by the union or reunion of male and female characters in pairs, the traditional unit of the romance. The continental female beloveds represented by Diana and Astrée are additionally plagued by jealousy and caprice which contrast sharply with the patient fidelity of the male lovers represented by Syrenus and Celadon. Furthermore, throughout *Diana* and *Astrée* the female characters, for all their manipulative schemes, are subject to domination and control by the male characters. Diana is punished for her inconstancy by marriage to a jealous husband, Delius, and suffers jealousy herself at the happiness of her former lovers. Astrée grieves throughout most of the work for the loss of her lover which she herself has precipitated, but is virtually possessed by that lover at the same time, when Celadon returns in the guise of the druidess Alexis to enjoy many lingering and explicitly described views of Astrée's unsuspecting and frequently naked female body—at one point desiring, "Argos-like, that he had a body all of eyes."[104] In both these texts, the female characters are objectified by the male gaze, reduced by masculine discourse to a conflation of their sexualized bodies and their inconstant behavior, which establishes at once their sexual difference and their negatively gendered identity as false women.

Interestingly, the male-authored image of female sexuality as a dangerous labyrinth surfaces yet again, in d'Urfé's construction of feminine discourse in a letter from Astrée to Celadon: "I am full of suspitions, extreamly Jealous; I am exceeding hard to be won; and very easily lost; quickly offended, but abominably hard to be pleased: my will must be destiny it selfe; my opinions must passe for reasons, my commands must be inviolable Lawes. Shepheard, be wise, and keep out of this dangerous Labyrinth."[105] This could be the portrait of a fickle female mistress by any male sonneteer, as discussed above, with the difference that in d'Urfé's text the woman actually does have a voice, but a voice already written—or, to use Elizabeth Harvey's term, "ventriloquized"—by male-authored configurations of female sexual identity.[106] In a further twist on the notion of sexual difference, both d'Urfé and Philip Sidney place central male protagonists in female disguise, and then provide examples of apparently shared female discourse between Astrée and "Alexis," and Philoclea and "Zelmane," which are actually controlled by the men masquerading as women.

Constance Jordan suggests that Pyrocles/Zelmane signals "the oxymoronic union of self and other which Sidney will demonstrate to be the basis, first, of the stability of the couple, and thus the family; and second, of the state."[107] The stability of this "oxymoronic union" is not surprisingly based on a gendering of "self" as male and "other" as female, so that it is ultimately against the "otherness" of female masquerade that Pyrocles/Zelmane must work to reclaim the full extent of "his" subjectivity, without Sidney ever needing to grant comparable subjectivity to Philoclea, the female object of Pyrocles's desire. At the same time, as both Lamb and Margaret Sullivan have pointed out, Pyrocles's discomfort with his female garb indicates the persistent associations of weakness and vulnerability with female passion.[108] It is worth noting that the two female characters who do assume male disguise and fight—Parthenia and the "original" Zelmane—so far from assuming full subjectivity, instead do not survive. Within Sidney's text, apparently only a male can successfully transform the "otherness" of a gendered disguise into personal empowerment.

Spenser's Britomart seems to be another case altogether, in that she successfully assumes not only a masculine disguise, but an apparently masculine agency as well, which allows her to defeat any number of male challengers on physical as well as moral grounds. Nevertheless, it is important to keep in mind that Britomart finds her identity as a lover by gazing into her father's mirror, which significantly reflects back to her not her own image, but rather the image of Arthegall.[109] In Irigarean terms, then, Britomart first learns to define herself not as a speaking subject of difference, but rather as "other" in relation to a masculine subject. Furthermore, the image of Arthegall initially proves disabling rather than empowering to Britomart's potential agency as a woman, causing her to be stricken with traditionally feminine tears and weakness until she is informed by Merlin of her appointed feminine destiny as Arthegall's future spouse. In the meantime, Britomart's reflexive identity as a lover requires that she sublimate her own femininity through the adoption of a masculine disguise until she can enter the gendered completion offered by union with Arthegall.[110]

A number of critics have explored the extent to which Shakespeare's comic heroines seem able to use male disguise as a catalyst that allows them to transcend the social limitations of their gender.[111] Assuming new roles through cross-gender disguise, protagonists such as Rosalind and Viola acquire at the same time new voices which allow them to cloak feminine desire with masculine discourse. On the other hand, as Jonathan Goldberg points out, in a play "it is not necessarily a sign of power to have a voice, not necessarily a sign of subjection to lose it."[112] Although Shakespeare's heroines may temporarily acquire "male" voices, the comic denouements of the plays in question require their return to the subjection expected of wives, underscoring the illusory nature of their discursive authority as "male" subjects. At the same time, the drama does open seemingly new options for women's speech by contrast to the verse and prose romances, and thus merits further investigation as an index of those cultural figurations of gender which contextualize Wroth's inscription of women's voices. Moreover, Wroth's own interest in dramatic productions while active in the Jacobean court is evidenced by her participation in performances of Jonson's *The Masque of Blackness* (1605) and *The Masque of Beauty* (1608), as well as by her attendance at numerous other masques. Indeed, Wroth may well have witnessed court performances of such plays as *Othello* in 1604 and *The Winter's Tale* in 1611.[113]

"It is not the fashion to see the lady the epilogue," comments Rosalind at the end of *As You Like It*, proceeding to deliver the epilogue apparently as "she" likes it nonetheless, before concluding with an acknowledgment that she is no lady after all, but a boy playing a woman's part. In becoming Ganymede, Rosalind (like Pyrocles/Zelmane) apparently escapes the confines of a single position, a single voice, a single gender. But whereas Pyrocles resolutely represents his masculinity as strength to Musidorus throughout the course of his disguise, Rosalind consistently admits the limitations of her feminine identity to Celia, particularly with regard to her inability to control her own speech: "Do you not know I am a woman? when I think, I must speak" (*AYLI* III.ii.249-50). At the same time, Rosalind's avowal might also be read, at least in part, as contesting cultural mandates regarding women's silence. Even as female-authored texts begin to define multivocal approaches to gender relations in the early modern period, so some male-authored texts contain notable examples of women's voices.

By contrast to the female-authored texts, however, which often open out in multivocal terms as they progress, the emphasis in many male-authored texts, including *As You Like It*, returns women to silence. Thus Rosalind's frank address in the epilogue turns out to undermine the apparent power of feminine discourse when the actor calls attention to the male identity which empowers his speech. Stephen Greenblatt suggests that the cross-dressing of Rosalind, Portia, and Viola in fact underscores Renaissance conceptions of the emergence of male identity, so that "Shakespearean women are in this sense the representation of Shakespearean men, the projected mirror images of masculine self-differentiation."[114] Once again reduced to mirror images, these "heroines" are unable finally to claim voices of their own, and must repeatedly speak with the voices of men or be silent.

Elizabeth Cary's *The Tragedy of Mariam, the Fair Queen of Jewry* (1613), on the other hand, tackles the very same issues of feminine speech and identity that repeatedly surface in the male-authored social comedies of early modern England, yet with the difference that women are not represented simply as "other" than men, and as such useful for focusing conceptions of masculine identity, but rather emerge as deeply divided within and among themselves. Lady Elizabeth Tanfield Cary, viscountess Falkland, was born two years before Lady Mary Wroth, another daughter and heiress of an upper-class

Renaissance family. Married to Henry Cary, later first viscount Falkland, three years before Mary Wroth married Robert Wroth, Cary found herself trapped, even as were her female contemporaries Wroth and Anne Clifford, in an unhappy union. In 1625, after twenty-three years of marriage, Cary publicly professed Catholicism and suffered the social consequences of disinheritance from her family, separation from her husband and children, and subsequent penury.

Several critics have scrutinized the stifling effects of patriarchal authority within marriage upon Cary's female characters, and have remarked upon the manifold connections between Cary's depiction of domestic and political tyranny in Mariam's marriage to Herod and her own experience of married privation.[115] With regard more specifically to Cary's relation to the representation of tyranny in her primary source, Josephus's *Antiquities of the Jews*, I find that Cary deconstructs Josephus's determinedly patriarchal "frame," not by eliding the significance of Herod's masculine tyranny, but rather by consistently directing her audience's attention outside the scope of that frame, to the "space-off" (to use de Lauretis's terms) associated with women's speech.[116] Without clearly independent voices to distinguish them from each other, the women in Josephus's narrative serve more to illustrate the extent of Herod's ruling supremacy than to define speaking positions for themselves. While the speeches of Cary's female characters cannot dislocate the centrality of the male patriarch, they nevertheless serve to redraw the boundaries of domestic authority that frame the patriarch's power.

Cary opens her play with Mariam's acknowledgment of the dangers of female discourse: "How oft have I with public voice run on?" (I.i.1), revealing a concern underscored by other characters' observations that "unbridled speech is Mariam's worst disgrace" (III.iii.183).[117] In the face of expected social subordination, Mariam learns to claim a space as a speaking subject not by assuming male disguise, as do Shakespeare's heroines, but rather by relying upon her "self-experience" (I.i.9). At the same time, her experience of a "self which is not one" emerges in the polarization of her discourse when she addresses herself alternately as "you" as well as "I." Believing Herod to be dead, and thus assuming that the power of Herod's "tongue" to enforce a state of married subjection far removed from her earlier "virgin freedome" is finished, Mariam finds nevertheless that her widowed state at the beginning of the play only subjects her voice to further scrutiny from society (I.i.39, 72).

It soon becomes apparent that not only "public" but also private speech can sully a woman's reputation, when Constabarus rebukes Salome, a flamboyantly assertive female figure in many ways opposed to the modest Mariam, in terms that emphasize spousal responsibility: "how much you wrong your name, / Your race, your country, and your husband most! / A stranger's private conference is shame," adding: "A virtuous woman crowns her husband's head"

(I.vi.375-77, 396). This is language that could be lifted directly from the marriage treatises, and yet Salome herself deconstructs patriarchal directives, querying "why should such privilege to man be given? / Or given to them, why barr'd from women then?" (I.iv.305-6). As David Underdown has indicated in his analysis of the period's preoccupation with scolding women and unruly wives, the figures of women who defied the authority of their husbands threatened the entire patriarchal order.[118] Salome's brazen defiance of her husband leads him to question the very standards of sexual difference upon which gendered behavior is supposed to rest: "Are Hebrew women now transformed to men? . . . Suffer this, and then / Let all the world be topsy-turvèd quite" (I.vi.420, 422-24). Subsequently, Constabarus resorts to the most polarized language of the Petrarchan sonneteers on the duality and deception of women:

> You creatures made to be the human curse,
> You tigers, lionesses, hungry bears,
> Tear-massacring hyenas: nay, far worse,
> For they for prey do shed their feigned tears.
> But you will weep, (you creatures cross to good)
> For your unquenched thirst of human blood. . . .
> You are to nothing constant but to ill,
> You are with nought but wickedness indued:
> Your loves are set on nothing but your will,
> And thus my censure I of you conclude.
> You are the least of goods, the worst of evils,
> Your best are worse than men: your worst than devils. [IV.vi.315-20, 345-50]

But where the male sonneteers examined above couch their representations of women as wild beasts and devils in the language of courtship and desire, Cary places these descriptions, in heightened form, in the mouth of a "wronged" husband, revealing the potentially enormous hate and fear of female sexual difference which can erupt when a woman violates the male-authored norms of her culture.

Mariam herself refuses to adopt the role and language of a traditional Petrarchan mistress, scorning to lead Herod "captive with a gentle word, . . . Or other speech than meaning to afford" (III.iii.164-65). Yet for all her efforts to speak only what she means, she cannot escape her husband's construction of her as unfaithful simply because she has a voice "other" than his. Not surprisingly, Herod's accusations of infidelity on Mariam's part employ language as polarized as that used by Constabarus against the unfaithful Salome:

> Now do I know thy falsehood, painted devil
> Thou white enchantress . . .
> A beauteous body hides a loathsome soul . . .

... Hell itself lies hid
Beneath thy heavenly show.   [IV.iv.175-76, 178, 203-4]

Whether chaste or promiscuous, honest or deceptive, women in Cary's play, as
in her society, are subjected to the dichotomization of a masculine rhetoric
which links autonomous speech with feminine deceit. Significantly, the one
female character who does not speak in conflict with the others is also the epitome of feminine silence and subjection to male authority: namely, Graphina,
who does not appear in the *Antiquities*. Graphina actually can be seen to function as a striking foil for the other female characters, pointing up their emergent
assertions of agency and subjectivity, not only despite but through their conflict
with one another, as well as their varying degrees of resistance to patriarchal authority, by contrast to her own passivity and self-doubt. Cary's representation of
the strengths as well as the limitations of feminine discourse accordingly encompasses a wider range of women's voices than typically allowed for in either
the male-authored treatises or literary narratives of the period.

While the varied voices of Cary's female characters are framed by the experience of male tyranny, Wroth extends the opportunity for her female characters to find voices of their own with reference to a wider range of gender
relations than appear in Cary's play. When viewed in relation to the texts of
Elizabeth Cary and Marguerite de Navarre, Anne Clifford and the countess of
Leicester, Jane Anger and Esther Sowernam, as well as Shakespeare and
Sidney, Montemayor and d'Urfé, the marriage treatises and the polemical
pamphlets, Wroth's texts reveal evidence of the competing discourses of femininity that marked her culture, even as they "change the subject" by further
representing the possibility that difference can not only constrain but also empower women's voices in domestic relation to men.

   Mary Wroth's play, *Love's Victory*, has received significantly less attention than her lyric sequence and her prose romance, at least in part because
until the first complete edition of the play appeared in 1988, it could only be
read in an incomplete manuscript at the Huntington Library, while the sole
complete manuscript resided in a private collection.[119] The four pairs of lovers
in the play, interacting with three other rival lovers, confront the discursive
problematics of courtship and desire between the sexes which *Pamphilia to
Amphilanthus* explores exclusively from the woman's perspective, and which
Urania expands into the realms of marriage, parenthood, and widowhood.
Looming over the central courtship relation in the play is the prospect of
forced marriage—between Musella and her dead father's choice, Rustic,
rather than her beloved Philisses—which drives the young lovers toward a
Romeo-and-Juliet–like climax in which permanent disaster is averted only
through the presence of mind of Silvesta, one of Musella's female friends.

Behind the play's Petrarchan vocalizations of desire loom the hierarchical pronouncements of early modern marriage treatises, in which acceptable parameters of female sexuality were defined by the father's choice and the husband's will.

Wroth's response to these cultural constraints on women emerges not only in her representations of fiercely independent female lovers, such as Pamphilia and Musella, who claim the right to choose their male beloveds willingly, but also in her attention to a character such as Silvesta, who, once having suffered the bondage of desire, now locates her freedom in her chastity:

> Now love's as farr from mee as never knowne,
> Then bacely tyde, now freely ame mine owne.
> Slavery, and bondage with mourning care
> Were then my living, sighs, and tears my fare,
> Butt all thes gone, now live I joyfully,
> Free, and untouch'd of thought butt chastity. [I.157-62]

Although Silvesta is not unique among romance protagonists in professing freedom from desire after suffering a rejection in love, her difference emerges in her steadfast assertion of a new subjectivity for herself, which cannot be shaken even by the presence of a faithful male suitor, the Forester. In examining cultural responses to virgin women in early modern England, Jankowski points out that in a society that denied women autonomy, "the discourse of virginity carried encoded within it the notion of an anomalous female nature that was threatening to established Christian notions of woman's submissiveness and subordination."[120] While conventional romance protagonists who repudiate love usually live to eat their words, either suffering all the greater a fall for their professed independence from desire, or finding themselves social outcasts in a couples' culture, Wroth presents a female character strong enough to remain single to the very end of the play, and yet so central to the social world of the lovers that she alone brings about a positive resolution to the conflicting dynamics of desire which threaten to destroy that world.

Musella, on the other hand, initially experiences a dislocation of identity through desire, proclaiming an absent presence for herself: "for oft'nest when I'me heere / I ame as if I were an other wher" (I.289-90). She comments upon her subjection/subjectivity ("Sorry I ame I should your subject bee" [I.334]) when forced to accept the unwelcome advances of Rustic, proffered in the form of a parodic Petrarchan blazon ("Thy Eyes, doe play / Like Goats with hay" [I.340-41]). Wroth allots more classic Petrarchan discourse to Lissius, who casts women in conventionally dichotomous beast images before he himself falls prey to desire: "For wee showld women love butt as owr sheep / Who beeing kind and gentle gives us ease, / But cross, or straying, stuborne, and unmeeke, / Shun'd as the wulf, which most owr flocks disease" (II.67-70).

To use Irigaray's terms, both Rustic and Lissius attempt to conceptualize female sexuality on the basis of masculine parameters, suppressing the possibility of female subjectivity in their metaphoric representations of women's "otherness." Where conventional male Petrarchan sonneteers admit no challenges to their objectification of women in similar language, by not allowing female speech to disrupt their discourse, Wroth follows Lissius's observation with an immediate challenge from Musella, who is able to take issue with the masculine parameters of such discourse through her own subjection to desire.

When the pairs of lovers finally achieve union at the end of *Love's Victory*, Wroth moves beyond the Petrarchan insistence on sexual difference, as well as the Donnean obliteration of the signs of that difference, in language that recalls the possibility of mutual love between the sexes inscribed in *Pamphilia to Amphilanthus*. Lissius's declaration that "tow bodys wee ar, yett have butt one hart, / Then rather joine then lett such deere love part" (V.529-30) echoes Pamphilia's claim that love has the power "to joine two harts as in one frame to move; / Two bodies, butt one soule to rule the minde" (P82). Once again, still possessed of "tow bodys," the lovers enrich rather than erase, engage rather than escape, each other's subjectivity, each learning to see "that in yourself, which you knew nott before" (P82). Although the issue of female subjectivity is complicated in the play by a variety of voices of both genders not present in the lyric sequence, Wroth nevertheless undertakes in both texts an exploration of courtship as an opportunity for sexual connection between the sexes which can include difference on both sides.

In her prose romance, Wroth vastly expands her treatment of female subjectivity beyond the initial confines of the lover/beloved relationship which provide the focal point for figurations of gender in *Pamphilia to Amphilanthus* and *Love's Victory*. Not only does Wroth prepare a much broader canvas of characters and action for *Urania* than for her play and lyric sequence, but she treats the gendered dynamics of sexual relations across a significantly expanded time frame, which distinguishes her romance not only from her other texts but also from the romances of her male predecessors, whether in prose, verse, or drama. Unlike the primarily youthful protagonists created by Sidney and Spenser, Montemayor and d'Urfé, for example, Wroth's characters grow from youth to maturity, with three generations represented, enabling a consideration of the continuity of relationships over time. Wroth thus explores the issue of constancy and inconstancy in love, so central to the romance tradition, in a temporal framework which extends beyond the immediate formation and dissolution of bonds among the protagonists.

Wroth further alters generic conventions in order to re-present the problematics of female subjectivity through the voice of a woman, a speaking subject of difference. Whereas *Diana* and *Astrée* open with the laments of faithful male lovers rejected by the title female characters, and the *New Arcadia* commences with the mourning of Strephon and Claius over the departure of their beloved Urania, Wroth's narrative opens with Urania herself mourning not for love of a man, as does Britomart after confronting the image of Arthegall in the mirror, but rather over the question of her identity *as a woman*. Unlike Sidney's Urania, Wroth's protagonist is no absent ideal, but a very present female. Having just discovered that the shepherds who raised her are not her real parents, and that her origins are unknown, Urania cries out to herself: "Of any miserie that can befall woman, is not this the most and greatest which thou art falne into? Can there be any neare the unhappinesse of being ignorant, and that in the highest kind, not being certaine of mine owne estate or birth?" (1). The plight of Urania, and of another of Wroth's "lost shepherdesses," Veralinda, can be linked more directly to Shakespeare's Perdita than to the lamenting male shepherds of the prose romance tradition, yet Wroth heightens the tension of unknown identity beyond the example of *The Winter's Tale* by insisting upon the relevance of gender. For a woman to lack knowledge of her family origins in a patriarchal society is to lack a social identity. Given that kinship reckoning in early modern England was "ego-focused," with an individual identifying kindred on the basis of their relationship to the self, Wroth's dramatic opening exposes both the difficulty and the enabling potential of Urania's emerging attempt to construct her own subjectivity.[121] Without the patriarchal parameters of "estate or birth" to define identity, Urania must come to terms with the "otherness in herself" in locating a position both from which to speak and from which to identify her kindred.

Having assumed the security of her identity through "the love of those [she] tooke for parents," Urania grieves to learn "the contrary, and by that knowledge not to know my selfe" (1). Her complaint on the one hand addresses her lack of "identity" in the sense of "essential sameness or oneness" with others—in this case her parents—while at the same time providing a starting point for the construction of an individual subjectivity through her interaction with others separate from herself, and her concomitant recognition of the otherness in her "selfe" which is no longer one. Swift concludes from Urania's plight that "Wroth reveals the loss of identity that women experience in a society that victimizes them," while Waller suggests with a somewhat different emphasis that *Urania* "dramatizes the difficulties and the contradictions involved in constructing viable subject positions for women outside the dominant masculinist ethos."[122] At the same time, it is necessary to attend to alternative patterns not simply of loss or suppression but also of recognition and reclamation of female identity in Wroth's texts. Urania's awareness of her loss indeed initiates her emerging articulation of her subjectivity through a process of social interaction rather than cultural victimization. By positioning Urania's lament at the beginning of her narrative, Wroth establishes both the power of gender to shape discourse and the importance of self-awareness as a starting point for female constructions of identity. It is precisely outside the dominant masculine ethos that Wroth situates Urania's attempt to construct a position as a speaking subject, in order to dramatize both the challenges and the possibilities that attend such construction.

In expressing her suffering at the opening of the narrative, Urania composes a poem to her "Eccho," whom she finds "answere gives like friend of mine owne choice," and "onely she doth my companion prove" (2). By identifying the friend of her "owne choice" in the echo of her own voice, Urania is taking the first step toward embracing that otherness in herself which, in Irigarean terms, must provide the basis for her emergent subjectivity. The absent and often dark lady of the Petrarchan sonneteers becomes, in Urania's revision of Petrarchism, an absent presence, an elusive yet supportive echo of her own female discourse.[123] Most significantly, Urania addresses her poem not to a male lover, but to a female "friend" who is at once herself and not herself, thus erasing the masculine parameters of Petrarchan representations of desire. "Neither one nor two," to use Irigaray's phrase, Urania defines herself as a speaking subject by composing a poem in which the woman is not an object of male desire, and female subjectivity begins to emerge in multiple terms.

When Urania subsequently does fall in love for the first time, she constructs her suffering subjectivity not in relation to her male beloved, Parselius, but in relation to "miserie" itself as a female companion (21), along the lines of Pamphilia's address in the lyric sequence to "Night" as a female friend in time of grief. Urania's initial loss of a socially determined identity thus leads her to discover feminine parameters of self-fashioning. Furthermore, instead of accepting the role of "other" to Parselius's "self," she overturns the Petrarchan dynamics of desire, regarding Parselius as "her other selfe" (33). Having already confronted the otherness in herself when faced with the obliteration of her assumed social identity, Urania is enabled to view the male as "other" to *her* "selfe" rather than vice versa.

Wroth emphasizes the enabling effect of Urania's self-fashioning when the lovers are caught in a storm near the coast of Cyprus, and Urania adopts a protective role with Parselius: "she did feare, but seeing his, she dissembled hers, in care of not further harming him" (37). Far from being a relatively helpless female in the mold of the heroines of Montemayor or d'Urfé or even Sidney, whose female characters rely upon the bravery of males to protect them, no matter how great their personal courage, Urania shields her male beloved from the knowledge of her fear precisely because, having embraced him as "her other selfe," she is able to identify his fear in her own. And where the bravery of Spenser's Britomart is associated with her masculine garb as warrior, and is in any case not privileged in comparison to that of Arthegall, Wroth's Urania needs no cross-gender disguise to articulate her courage or protect her male beloved, given the emphasis of the narrative here on emotional and psychological rather than simply physical threat and strength. It is not Urania's absence of fear but rather her presence of mind which underlies her subjectivity. As the narrative progresses, she becomes a model of agency for both sexes, so that her younger brother, Leonius, is criticized for his state of mind under an enchantment by comparison to his sister: "Can Uranias Brother, Uranias picture, Uranias self in the masculine bee thus babied, thus besotted, thus fooled?" (II: fol. 59). While Britomart appears as a feminine version of the male warrior whom she glimpsed in the mirror, the male knight Leonius is represented as a masculine version of Urania's "self."

Far more frequently than Urania or some of her other peers, Pamphilia must endure the isolation of several "enchantments" in the process of defining her subjectivity within the courtship relation. These enchantments culminate in the "hell of deceit" episodes near the end of the published *Urania*, where Pamphilia and Amphilanthus are separated and encounter Spenserian visions of the other being tortured for love. Searching for her lover in the forest where they have lost each other, Pamphilia comes upon a "Crowne of mighty stones" and pulls open a door in the greatest stone to discover a *tableau vivant* "as in the hell of deceit," in which Amphilanthus stands bound before one of Pamphilia's rivals for his love, Musalina, who is preparing to raze the name of Pamphilia from his exposed heart (493). Amphilanthus meanwhile encounters a similarly illusory vision in the forest, revealing Pamphilia lying dead with her breast cut open and his name engraved in burning flames upon her heart (554). In both instances, when the lovers attempt to break into the *tableaux* they are cast out, and awaken from trances to find the vision vanished and the entrance closed.

This double enchantment recalls the *tableau* in Book III of *The Faerie Queene* where Britomart observes Busyrane torturing Amoret by carving characters in "living blood" upon her exposed heart. However, in Spenser's text the male en/acts the enchantment while the women suffer or watch, whereas in Wroth's text, both male and female lovers are subject to enchantment and potential objectification through separation, and must determine their own courses of action in response.[124] At the same time, the "hell of deceit" enchantment in Wroth's text underscores some of the particular challenges to subjectivity facing the woman in love, when Pamphilia must view Amphilanthus in the company of an/other woman—who subsequently manages to win his attention away from Pamphilia for a time—while Amphilanthus views Pamphilia's (dead) body purely as an object which, however troubling, does nothing to threaten the chivalrous position of lover according to which he defines his masculine subjectivity. Indeed, Amphilanthus is soon distracted from the scene of Pamphilia's torture by a vision of two other women (one of whom is Musalina) requiring rescue from peril.

When Pamphilia and Amphilanthus are finally reunited near the end of the published *Urania,* Wroth indicates Pamphilia's still divided subjectivity at this point in the courtship relation, characterizing Pamphilia's soul as "without her selfe, because in an other body returned" (557). Although Wroth's language here recalls her representation of the courtship relation as "two bodies, but one soule" in *Pamphilia to Amphilanthus* (P82) and *Love's Victory* (V.529-30), her prose romance focuses less on the idealized potential of such a union than on the actual fault lines of sexual difference which may separate the "two bodies," dividing the woman's soul in particular from "her selfe." The divided self of the culturally objectified dark lady thus informs Pamphilia's experience of desire within much of the published text, underlying not only her frequent separations from her absent lover, but also her isolation from her potential female friends, without whom she is unable to define a stable discursive context for her constancy.

Although Wroth's representation of Pamphilia's constancy in the published *Urania* might seem to support the general conclusion of some of the critics cited above, that constancy for women may be regarded as "a defensive posture at best, an assigned and unavoidable role within an aggressively patriarchal situation at worst,"[125] that conclusion appears less absolute when some of Wroth's alternative constructions of constancy in the figures of other female characters such as Urania are examined, and even more so when Pamphilia's own evolving discourse on constancy in the unpublished manuscript continuation of Wroth's text is taken more fully into account. In addition, while the critical estimation of female constancy as necessarily a defensive and overdetermined stance owes much to twentieth-century psychoanalytic observations which have informed my own as well as other critics' readings of early modern texts, I find that it is important to take into consideration as well the potential for agency embedded in some of the other female-authored constructions of constancy in early modern England discussed above.

Like both Cary and Lanyer, despite their differing subjects, for example, Wroth in fact takes pains to distinguish between the emergent subjectivity of different women lovers by representing alternative female responses to desire in the courtship relation. In some senses, Urania and Pamphilia serve as polarized representations of female desire throughout much of the published text. Just as Urania regards her first lover, Parselius, as "her other selfe" (33), so Pamphilia refers to Amphilanthus as "her other selfe" (492), but with the difference that Urania perceives her lover's "otherness" while they are still together, in the context of coming to terms with the "otherness in herself," while Pamphilia is divided by Amphilanthus's absence into a "self which is not one." Urania, furthermore, learns to recognize not simply erotic desire, but also friendship as a basis for enduring relations between the sexes. After she is deserted by Parselius when he becomes enamored with another woman, Urania is freed from the bonds of her initial passion through the aid of a wise woman, Melissea, and grows to love Steriamus instead. She comes to recognize that her love for Steriamus is actually based upon their longstanding friendship, which dates from the beginning of the narrative, observing that she may "in a kind" present him with her first affection after all, "for I liked you before I loved the other" (220). Instead of configuring a triangulation of desire along the lines of Shakespeare's sonnets, then, where the voiceless dark lady serves as a doubled object of desire in the competition for affection which defines the homoerotic attraction between the men, Wroth represents a woman's ability not only to recognize the significance of mutual friendship as a preexisting condition for love, but also to give voice to her choice.

In the manuscript continuation of *Urania*, the tensions of courtship between Pamphilia and Amphilanthus modulate into the further complications of a secret marriage, as Wroth exposes both the insecurity underlying the male lover's repeated tendency to objectify the woman, and the ingenuity empowering the female lover's discursive revision of subjection to desire. Anxiety about female sexual betrayal on the male lover's part pervades most male-authored configurations of the dynamics of desire in sonnet sequences, plays, and romances, as well as marriage treatises and polemical pamphlets, as discussed above. The importance of visual corroboration of jealous suspicions, so evident in *Othello*, for example, can be linked to the masculine construction of feminine sexual identity in terms of sexual difference. Thus in Marguerite de Navarre's *Heptaméron*, it is a male character who insists upon visual corroboration of the "difference" of feminine identity: "anyone who looks carefully underneath all those skirts will find that you *are* all women!" (202). Katherine Maus's argument that "the jealous male represents the spectator at his most agonizingly involved and his most scandalously marginalized" can be applied to Amphilanthus's position in Wroth's romance, when he notices the king of Tartaria gazing upon Pamphilia's beauty and retires abruptly in a sulk.[126] In linking Amphilanthus's jealous outburst to a question of visual interpretation, Wroth's romance responds to seventeenth-century commonplaces concerning the danger of wandering eyes. Along related lines, Nancy Miller has convincingly explored the extent to which a woman's awareness of male scrutiny becomes an integral part of feminine identity, "of woman's sense of herself as sighted and sited in a dialectics of power."[127] Significantly, where popular manuals of female conduct stress the necessity for the female to restrain the compass of her gaze, Wroth re-presents the issue as a male problem.

Amphilanthus justifies his behavior in highly objectified terms of consumption and desire, explaining that "he grudged any eyes should feed on that rich fruict of her beauty butt his owne, and onely his" (I: fol. 14). Amphilanthus's lament here recalls the desire of d'Urfé's male protagonist for a "body all of eyes," the better to observe/consume his beloved. Pamphilia's response—

that "eyes are wanderers, and fasting will seeke to feed on any food . . . and soe itt may bee some may endlesly enough looke on mee" (I: fol. 14)—seems apparently not to repudiate her lover's Petrarchan objectification of her beauty, allowing him to conceptualize her sexuality according to conventionally masculine parameters of consumption. Elsewhere in the scene, however, Wroth's representation of their relative positions reveals an increasingly confident assertion of subjectivity on Pamphilia's part which Amphilanthus is not yet able to grasp. Explicitly revising Shakespeare's presentation of male jealousy in *Othello*, Wroth represents the woman's part not as a passive object but as an active participant with an emerging voice of her own.

When Pamphilia finds Amphilanthus after his disappearance, for example, flung upon her bed in the throes of his jealousy, she inquires "what is the cause" for this behavior, when she herself has given him "noe cause" to grieve, eliciting in response only Amphilanthus's query: "Is itt soe my onely soule" (I: fol. 14). This exchange can be compared, in both language and content, to the scene in which Othello, consumed by jealousy, comes upon Desdemona in her bed, exclaiming: "It is the cause, it is the cause, my soul. / Let me not name it to you, you chaste stars. / It is the cause" (*Othello* V.ii.1-3). Reversing this pivotal Shakespearean depiction of jealousy, Wroth situates the male lover in the supine position upon the bed, and represents the effectiveness of female discourse in breaking down the masculine barrier of jealousy through direct communication.

Amphilanthus excuses his jealousy by explaining "thatt while we are butt lovers I am suspitious, love never having the true heigth of zeale in love till the knott never to bee untide bee tied, therfor knitt that, and noe more shall you see mee suspect" (I: fol. 14v). Instead of arguing with his construction of the situation, Pamphilia replies: "butt for the knott you demaund, I ame reddy to ty that with all sincerity, affection, and obedience requisitt for my part to performe" (I: fol. 14v). By appropriating for herself a conventional feminine position of obedience, Pamphilia preempts and thus disarms the disciplinary strategies enacted by the jealous male lover. At the same time, her acknowledgment of the nature of this "part" as a "performance" suggests her capacity to distinguish between the constancy that she chooses to maintain her subjectivity and the obedience that she enacts to calm Amphilanthus's jealousy. Even as the countess of Leicester makes a case for the "libertie" of friendship, conjoined with obedience in marriage, in defusing her husband's defensive reaction to the frank speech of her letters, so Pamphilia successfully deflates her lover's defensive posture without compromising either her constancy or her self-confidence. Encoded within her apparent submission, then, is a resistance to masculine assumptions of authority which links her to Cary's *Mariam*. The difference between the two can be discerned in Pamphilia's ability not only to endure but to prevail, particularly through her speech in the manuscript continuation of *Urania*. Mariam's voice, by contrast, is ultimately constrained by the historical details of Cary's source, so that Mariam—like Desdemona—is finally and permanently silenced by her husband.

Pamphilia and Amphilanthus subsequently engage in a secret wedding ceremony before several witnesses, including Urania, which is performed "nott as an absolute mariage though as perfect as that, beeing onely an outtward Serimony of the church, this as absolute beefore God and as fast a tiing, for such a contract can nott bee broken by any cause whatsoever (I: fol. 14v). As Roberts has illustrated, this type of *de praesenti* marriage contract was indeed considered as binding as a church wedding in early modern England.[128] The not uncommon occurrence of such contracts can be gathered both from the fact that Mary Wroth's brother, Robert Sidney, was secretly married to Lady Dorothy Percy in 1616, and from a reference in a letter from Dorothy to Robert, twenty years later, concerning a secret marriage between two lovers "with out the knowleg or consent of thear parents".[129] In covert terms, then, Pamphilia and Amphilanthus experience the transition from courtship to marriage that marks the maturation process of all the major protagonists in the romance. Unlike the other characters, however, their marriage remains secret, and is later violated by Amphilanthus's public wedding to the queen of Candia when he mistakenly believes Pamphilia to be unfaithful. As a result, Pamphilia subsequently agrees to a public marriage with Rodomandro, the king of Tartaria, although the original contract between herself and Amphilanthus is recalled by scattered references throughout the narrative, such as Urania's description of Pamphilia as Amphilanthus's "truest wife" (II: fol. 51). Faced with a social identity which is overdetermined not merely in familial terms, as will be discussed in the next chapter, but even in spousal terms, Pamphilia begins to forge new parameters for a subjectivity that is not singular, bound by social definitions of female sexuality and domesticity, but rather multiple, encompassing both public roles and private self.

While the courtship and marriage relation provides one context for emergent female subjectivity, Wroth moves beyond the dark lady trope to indicate how Pamphilia's ability to come to terms with the tensions between her roles and her self, her social identity and her personal subjectivity, is predicated upon her growing ability to fashion a voice for her desire. By defining her constancy in relation to her love, rather than in defensive response to a jealous lover, Pamphilia, as a speaking subject, decenters the repeated absences of that lover through an increasingly empowering revision of her own subjection to love. Where Anne Clifford preserves her subjectivity in the face of the punitive absences of her husband by maintaining the privately resolute discourse of her diary entries, Pamphilia safeguards the continuity of her discourse from the instability of changeable male response by resolving to maintain her constancy, whether in the presence or absence of Amphilanthus. At the same time, significantly, Wroth provides more than one articulation of women's relation to love, counterpointing Pamphilia's dedication to constancy with Urania's emphasis on female agency. Thus Urania actually criticizes Pamphilia's "bondage" to love, asserting that women must not let "want of courage and judgement make us [love's] slaves," and advising Pamphilia that even the virtue of constancy is not absolute, but rather culturally constructed with "limits to hold it in" (399-400). In Wroth's narrative, the presence of two women produces two voices, not a single "female" perspective on love.

Furthermore, Wroth does not restrict her representation of emergent female subjectivity in *Urania* to her female protagonists' struggles with heterosexual desire, but rather takes care to include figures of female chastity as well, along the lines of Silvesta in *Love's Victory*. One such figure, who changes her name from Allarina to Silviana (a name which itself echoes the name of Silvesta) when she takes a vow of chastity, celebrates her freedom from "love to which [she] late was slave" (187). As in the case of Silvesta, Silviana's liberty extends to her release from the divided self of the conventional Petrarchan dark lady: "Then finding this true vertue in my selfe, and my poore selfe returned to me againe, I did embrace it in the same true sort that love held me, and so we did agree. I love my selfe, my selfe now loveth me" (187). When she embraces her self, when she utters the love of a self freed from the parameters of masculine conceptualizations of female sexuality, when, in brief, her lips speak together, Silviana gives voice to an empowering discourse of women's potential for agency. Addressed specifically to Pamphilia, Silviana's speech thus charts the emergence of female subjectivity in obliquely "Irigarean" terms, which Pamphilia herself comes to appreciate further through just such dialogue with female friends over the course of the narrative.

It is in the voice of one woman speaking to another, after all, that Irigaray observes: "If we keep on speaking sameness, if we speak to each other as men have been doing for centuries, as we have been taught to speak, we'll miss each other, fail ourselves," adding: "How can I say it? That we are women from the start. That we don't have to be turned into women by them, labeled by them, made holy and profaned by them. . . . If we don't invent a language, if we don't find our body's language, it will have too few gestures to accompany our story."[130] While I would not go so far as to argue that *Urania* inscribes the language of women's bodies directly along the lines "embodied" and embedded in Irigaray's text, nonetheless I would suggest that the refusal to accept masculine discursive parameters which marks the interchange between the most vocal of Wroth's female characters indicates the presence of an insistent undercurrent of "speaking difference" in this early modern woman writer's texts.

Throughout Wroth's lyric sequence, play, and prose romance, women appear as speaking subjects with an emerging capacity, if not always sufficient assurance, to fashion selves through discourse. Transfiguring the fragmented

objectification of female sexuality which characterizes the culturally determined role of dark lady in the male-authored conduct manuals and marriage
treatises, sonnet sequences and romances of the period, Wroth represents a variety of female characters whose voices come to define feminine parameters
for a figuration of subjectivity that is "neither one nor two," neither singular
nor dual, but multiple. Wroth's consistent foregrounding of female discourse
to distinguish the dynamics of heterosexual desire within the courtship relation underscores the extent to which her female protagonists are able to voice
their passion as emergent speaking subjects, whose female predecessors include Jane Anger and Esther Sowernam, Anne Clifford and the countess of
Leicester, Marguerite de Navarre's Oisille and Elizabeth Cary's Mariam.

Whereas male-authored inscriptions of the oppositional difference of
female sexuality in early modern England tend to erase any potential figuration of women's subjectivity "other" than as an echo, shadow, or mirror-image
reversal of masculine sexual identity, some of Wroth's female characters learn
to find words for the "difference within," for that "otherness in themselves"
which shapes their experience of courtship and heterosexual desire. Even as
Clifford chooses the image of an "owl in the desert" to represent her gendered
experience of isolation and alienation in a patriarchal society, while conveying
at the same time the potential power of a bird of prey at home in the night, so
Wroth's texts combine women's experiences of abandonment and independence, self-doubt and self-assertion, in formulating feminine parameters of
sexual identity and difference. Yet the roles of lover, wife, and widow, bound as
they are to the "other" sex, provide only the starting point for Wroth's figurations of emergent female subjectivity. As the succeeding chapters will indicate, women's identities as mothers and daughters, rulers and subjects, readers
and writers, and sisters and friends, afforded early modern women authors in
general, and Wroth in particular, multiple positions from which to interrogate
dominant cultural constructions of gender difference.

3

Matriarch's Daughter

Ties That Bind

Why does the verb "to father" signify "to beget," while the verb "to mother" represents not only the act of giving birth, but also an ongoing responsibility to nurture? Why does "patrimony" signify "inheritance from one's father," reifying the patriarchal line, while "matrimony" represents "the rite or state of marriage," in which a bride is given from father to husband? Behind the definitions of the *Oxford English Dictionary* lie multiple cultural figurations of gender which at once reflect and shape the political and familial structures of Western societies. The texts of Mary Wroth offer several alternative constructions of maternity which reconfigure some of the literally "patriarchal" strategies of her male predecessors, while bearing witness to the complex range of familial bonds represented by her female contemporaries.

Even as some early modern women authors claimed maternal authority as the justification for their transgressive voices, or located within mother-daughter bonds a space for women's speech, so Wroth works to define some feminine parameters for discourse and subjectivity along maternal lines. The nascent traces of maternal discourse in Wroth's lyric sequence are expanded into an explicit narrative of maternity in her play, and find extended expression in the multiple maternal bonds, both literal and figurative, that inform her prose romance. The discourses of maternity across Wroth's texts provide occasions for intersections of female authority and subjectivity which subvert the overdetermined domestic positions accorded women in many male-authored texts, and offer instead glimpses of mothers with the status of speaking subjects. While by no means all of the maternal figures represented by Wroth can be labeled "good mothers," nevertheless the maternity of several of Wroth's major female protagonists extends significantly beyond the duties of sexual reproduction, to enable both communication and differentiation among successive generations of women.

A number of feminists have exposed the tendency of traditional psychoanalytic criticism to construct the mother always as "other" to the infant subject, typically gendered male, without allowing the mother herself the status of a speaking subject or "author."[1] At the same time, even feminist psychoanalysts who privilege the role of the mother tend to focus on the effects of maternal authority more consistently than on the implications of maternal subjectivity. The "daughtercentricity" of a number of feminist psychoanalytic discourses, which attend more to conditions of "being mothered" than to experiences of mothering, is only just beginning to be scrutinized.[2] Furthermore, as long as psychoanalysis fails to examine the ideological underpinnings of specific cultural constructions of maternity, the challenges confronting both maternal and filial discourse are sublimated in more general discussions of maternal functions.

Whether looking to the *OED* or to the theories of psychoanalysts such as Jacques Lacan, one finds that gendered discourse produces gendered definitions, so that "paternity" in Lacan's framework, for example, depends on signification, while "maternity," represented as a prediscursive state, apparently does not.[3] The concepts of "maternal discourse" and "maternal subjectivity" are implicitly erased, then, by Lacan's oppositional construction of the mother's role in relation to masculine parameters of speech and subjectivity. The French feminists, meanwhile, work to engage Lacan directly in psychoanalytic terms. While Julia Kristeva's attention to the mother's body emphasizes the importance of maternal presence to the development of a subject-in-process, Luce Irigaray and Hélène Cixous work to define a female poetics that addresses the language of both mother and daughter as speaking subjects.[4] Furthermore, despite the distinctions necessitated by her object-relations approach, Nancy Chodorow shares with Irigaray and Cixous a concern with "the mother as subject," and a commitment to exploring the "intersubjectivity" arising from "the *mutual* recognition of the other and the self" (emphasis mine) which underlies, among other issues, the mother/daughter dynamic.[5]

In increasing numbers, feminist critics of a variety of disciplines are calling for an acknowledgment of the often socially effaced link between daughter and mother, and working to uncover a female heritage and genealogy to counter the common universalizing of male subjectivity. Indeed, when the social specificity of women's identities is attended to, the theories of Chodorow and the French feminists may be drawn upon to illuminate possibilities for differentiation *among* women in nonphallocentric terms. If mother and daughter, for example, are accorded the status of speaking subjects by each other, rather than serving as the silent "other" for male subjects, then familial bonds between women can measure not only similarity, but also difference. Where the Law of the Father designates maternity as a prediscursive state, the mother/daughter relation can emerge as a new paradigm with its own discursive parameters, in which connection with the "other" woman opens up possibilities for a "woman-identified" construction of the subject, or a female "intersubjectivity."

Although women writers have often been read as daughters in relation to actual or literary "fathers" (as is the case for Mary Wroth in relation to

Philip and Robert Sidney), when the women authors are mothers as well as mothers' daughters themselves, their written relation to their own female fore-bears, contemporaries, and successors acquires new resonances of authority and subjectivity. The figure of the mother then can no longer be relegated to the (silenced) position of the "other," the passive mirror in which the child searches for (his) reflection, the prediscursive body written by the language (and governed by the Law) of the Father. Specifically, when both mother and daughter speak with the voice of the "author," the "otherness" of female sub-jectivity can be defined not simply against men, but among women.

The proliferation of studies by social historians on the composition of the family in early modern England, which range from attention to parenting and kinship relations, through consideration of the conditions of childhood, to more recent analyses of gender(ed) relations within the family, has shaped current critical perceptions of Renaissance mothers and mothering roles in strikingly different ways. Lawrence Stone's focus upon the increased power of the husband and father over the wife and children, making him a "legalized petty tyrant within the home," in conjunction with, among other factors, "the lack of a unique mother figure in the first two years of life," leads him to the conclusion that family relations, particularly between upper-class parents and children, were characterized by "at best a calculating indifference and at worst a mixture of suspicion and hostility, tyranny and submission, alienation and rage."[6] By contrast, Ralph Houlbrooke's survey of early modern diaries, auto-biographies, and letters, which relates preponderantly to the most highly liter-ate social groups (such as that represented by the Sidney family), presents evidence of strong bonds of both paternal and maternal affection, with mater-nal influence playing an important part in the early upbringing of both boys and girls. Furthermore, given the continuity of child care and household management issues, as well as the frequency of lying-in visitations for child-birth, Houlbrooke substantiates the cultural regard for the bond between mother and daughter as "the strongest and most enduring of those between members of the nuclear family."[7] In a direct refutation of Stone's emphasis on the brutality of family relations, J.A. Sharpe similarly makes the point that writers on familial matters throughout the period regarded the tie between parent and child, particularly with respect to maternal love, as "one of the closest of human bonds."[8]

Just as more recent social historians of the family have worked to revise the frame of reference created by Stone, so scholars such as Leah Marcus and Linda Pollock, who have focused their attention upon the conditions of child-hood in sixteenth- and seventeenth-century England, have exposed the limi-tations of Philippe Aries's influential argument in *Centuries of Childhood* that childhood as a state did not exist, and that children were harshly disciplined.

Marcus calls attention to the importance of examining the handling of child subjects in imaginative literature in relation to more widely articulated social attitudes and actual social behavior, while Pollock focuses upon diaries, auto-biographies, and newspaper reports of court cases concerning child abuse, in order to refute both Aries's and Stone's emphases on the harshness of parental discipline with evidence that brutality was the exception rather than the rule, and that the parent-child relationship was "very much a dyadic one," with the wishes of children being "both respected and accommodated.[9]

Despite their otherwise divergent perspectives, a number of the studies mentioned above share with Keith Wrightson's influential survey of English social relations a tendency to use male-authored texts as the basis for generali-zations about "parents," with little discussion of mothers as distinct from fa-thers (apart from scattered references to maternal affection), and with little differentiation between the relations of male and female children to same-sex and opposite-sex parents.[10] The recent studies of Susan Amussen and Margaret King, and the essay collections of Mary Prior and Valerie Fildes, however, have uncovered and analyzed a wealth of historical material on the significance of gender relations in the early modern family, which has bearing upon any con-sideration of maternal authority and subjectivity in early modern England.

In examining manuals for householders and the wills of women as well as men, Amussen points out first that relationships within the household were reciprocal, and second that household relationships were all different. The multiplicity of models indicates at once that there could be no single concep-tion of authority, and that women might and indeed did conceive their posi-tions within the family hierarchy and economy in divergent terms. Thus women with land, for example, disposed of their property in their wills quite differently than did men: 13.7 percent of the men who left land left it to one daughter, while 34.6 of the women did; of those with more than one child mentioned in their wills, 6.7 percent of the men but 30 percent of the women left it to one daughter, while 41.8 percent of the men and only 25 percent of the women left it to one son. Not only did women give more authority and power in the form of land to their daughters than did their husbands, but they were also far more likely to choose daughters, or indeed other women, as exec-utors of their wills than were men. Amussen concludes from her review of these statistics that "the behavior of women in writing their wills opens a small crack in the patriarchal facade of early modern England," exposing the inade-quacy of relying wholly upon prescriptive statements from sources such as the household manuals as guides to social "reality," because women's lives were lived "in tension with prescription."[11]

While Stone had pointed to the widespread usage of wet-nurses among upper-class families as evidence of the tenuousness of the maternal bond, Dorothy McLaren's much more extensive survey of nursing practices suggests that upper-class mothers selected wet-nurses very carefully, with great concern for the well-being of their infants.[12] King reviews further evidence indicating that aristocratic mothers' involvement in their children's well-being often continued well into adolescence and even adulthood, leading her to conclude that "motherhood was clearly a deep commitment for certain privileged women of the Renaissance, as it was the central task, for many years of their lives, for nearly all of them."[13] Similarly, Patricia Crawford probes the complex relation between the potentially oppressive patriarchal "ideology of the good mother" and women's actual experiences of maternity in early modern England, which offered them opportunities in practice to establish potentially empowering positions for themselves as subjects.[14]

When a literary critic such as Jonathan Goldberg argues that "the family functioned in the Renaissance to reproduce society," maintaining in explanation that "the body is inscribed in a social system," his apparent reliance on the historical terms of the analogy between the family and the state, from Aristotle to the Renaissance, obscures the co-existence of alternative constructions of the family in early modern England, which functioned less to "reproduce society" than to deconstruct some of the patriarchal parameters of familial authority.[15] As Amussen has pointed out, "ambiguous relations within the family undermined the analogy between the family and the state," which must be recognized at best to be only "an analogy, not an equation."[16] Abstracted references to "the" family as a unitary presence, then, or even more troublingly to "the" body in purportedly nongendered terms, fail to address questions concerning the gendering of social definitions of "family" and "body" as well as "state" which have been raised by some of the recent social historians cited above. Goldberg's silence regarding the relevance of sexual relations in both familial and state "systems" thus implicitly reifies the "fatherly authority" he purports to scrutinize, erasing the significance of female subjectivity within "the politics" of the family.

Furthermore, Goldberg's emphasis on the supremacy of fatherly authority can be contrasted with Margaret Ezell's analysis of the politics of the family in terms of the role of "the patriarch's wife." Ezell distinguishes between theory and practice, maintaining that the patriarch's wife in fact could wield considerable power on a private level, however subjugated in public pronouncements. Ezell points out that the repressive consequences of patriarchalism for women are manifested more in the literature of the period than in letters, diaries, and statistical reconstructions of domestic patterns.[17] Similarly, Heather Dubrow's extensive analysis of early modern marriage manuals suggests that, despite their advocacy of patriarchal authority, the marriage manuals repeatedly acknowledge the wife's power within the family as well, occasionally even according her the status of a "governor" of the family, albeit a subsidiary one.[18] When one looks beyond male-authored representations of the patriarch's wife alone to the familial discourses binding mother and daughter, the dominant lines of domestic patriarchalism can be opened to further reinterpretation across a range of cultural texts. Subverting the prevalent rhetoric supporting fatherly authority, the constructions of maternity that mark both male- and female-authored texts indicate not only the presence of deep-seated ambivalence regarding the implications of maternal power, but also the emergence of strategies of female self-assertion both within and outside the family.

In early modern England, tensions between tropes of sexual reproduction and discursive production mark the texts of female authors in particular, revealing the strains as well as the challenges facing women who attempted to establish positions for themselves as speaking subjects within the familial structures of the culture.[19] Whereas many early modern treatises on the nature of women were written by men and addressed to men in their roles as father and husbands, the feminist pamphlets in defense of women, as well as the popular mothers' advice books, provided a counter-discourse which often attempted to reclaim publicly the mother's importance in the patriarchal structures of family and society. Jane Anger's "Protection for Women" asserts in 1589, for example, that women are "more excellent than men" because "our bodies are fruitful, whereby the world encreaseth."[20] Even Joseph Swetnam's misogynist 1615 pamphlet, "The Arraignment of Lewd, idle, froward, and unconstant women," concedes that women's suffering in childbearing far surpasses any physical discomfort experienced by men: "Amongst all the creatures that God hath created, there is none more subject to misery than a woman, especially those that are fruitful to bear children, but they have scarce a month's rest in a whole year, but are continually overcome with pain, sorrow, and fear . . . There is no disease that a man endureth that is one half so grievous or painful as childbearing is to a woman.[21]

At the same time, Swetnam takes care to distance himself from his mother's body, asserting that "I am weaned from my mother's teat and therefore nevermore to be fed with her pap" (191). In her counterattack, Constantia Munda seizes upon Swetnam's reference to his mother in order to frame the terms of the debate over women in relation to a mother's authority over any man, who literally owes his life to her body: "If she had crammed gravel down thy throat when she gave thee suck or exposed thee to the mercy of the wild beasts in the wilderness when she fed thee with her pap, thou couldst not have shown thyself more ungrateful than thou hast in belching out thy nefarious contempt of thy mother's sex."[22] "Thy mother's sex" can be said to define the very existence of the male sex, indicating why male-authored treatises spend so much ink enforcing perceived boundaries between the sexes, lest men's identities be swallowed up by the mothers from whose bodies they issued forth. Indeed, in the *Hic Mulier/Haec-Vir* controversy, the threat of women's potential "masculinity"—"for since the days of Adam women were

never so Masculine: Masculine in their genders and whole generations, from
the Mother to the youngest daughter" — is couched in terms that reveal the
fear that the mother/daughter relation in particular can somehow encompass
a masculinity that excludes respective fathers and sons.[23]

By representing the female body as a mother's body, both attackers and
defenders of the female sex sometimes collapse the significance of the mother's
position within the family into a consideration of her physical responsibilities.[24] Because upper-class mothers tended to use wet-nurses, who were usually
lower-class women with children of their own, a class-bound reproductive pattern emerged in the period, consisting of perpetually pregnant wealthy
mothers and perpetually nursing poor mothers.[25] The use of "the mother's
body" thus varied according to class lines. Less variable was the result of the
tendency in the pamphlet wars of 1615-1620 to represent the mother as the
sum of her bodily functions, so that whether bearing children or nursing them,
mothers were treated more often as voiceless objects of discussion than as
speaking subjects in their own right. Only a rare aristocratic woman such as the
countess of Lincoln was able to "write her body" in Cixousian terms, using
metaphoric mother's milk as her ink, as indicated by her publication in 1622 of
a treatise which advised women to suckle and was dedicated to her daughter-
in-law, who was breastfeeding.[26]

In addition to the formal treatises and the attacks and defenses of
women, pamphlets that eulogized or condemned individual women construct
maternity in deliberately overdrawn terms, revealing the gendered domestic
politics which masked structures of household authority in early modern
England. In the case of Elizabeth Crashaw, death in childbirth provided the
impetus for a 1620 pamphlet eulogy entitled *The Honor of Virtue*, which
terms her a "Phoenix" for giving up her own life to bear a child, and praises
"her singular motherly affection to the child of her predecessor" (that child
growing up to be the poet Richard Crashaw).[27] On the other hand, a condem-
natory pamphlet entitled *A pitiless Mother* (1616) attacks Margaret Vincent—
who murdered two of her children apparently in the belief that she could
save their souls, since she was being forced by her husband to raise them
as Protestants despite her own conversion to Catholicism — as "Tigerous"
and "wolfish" for her "unnaturall" violation of the dictates of maternity. The
ideology of the mother's body provides grounds in this case for the condemnation of a woman "who by nature should have cherished them with her own
body, as the Pelican that pecks her own breast to feed her young ones with
her blood," and instead behaves more monstrously than "the Viper, the en-
venomed Serpent, the Snake, or any Beast whatsoever," in taking her
children's blood, "nay, her own dear blood bred in her own body, cherished in
her own womb." The pamphleteer accordingly labels Vincent a "Creature not
deserving Mother's name," and represents her subsequently failed suicide at-

tempt not as an effort to join her dead children, but rather as further evidence of her damnation.[28]

Embedded in the narration of the pamphlet on Vincent is the implication that this tragedy resulted from a woman's misguided attempt to direct her husband, opposing an incipient and subversive maternal authority to his rightful fatherly authority. Thus the pamphlet documents Vincent's repeated "persuasive arguments to win her husband to the same opinion" after her conversion to Catholicism, resulting in his "many times snubbing her with some few unkind speeches which bred in her heart a purpose of more extremity."[29] Vincent's maternity becomes the battleground upon which is enacted a competition for authority within the household, when she determines upon her duty to liberate her children, through the extreme measure of death, from the false spiritual rule of her husband. Confronted with the dead bodies of his children, Vincent's husband reproaches her with reference to their frequent arguments regarding "this damned Opinion" of Catholicism, underscoring the discursive fissures between them. In replying that "this had never been done if thou hadst been ruled and by me converted," Vincent asserts her position as a speaking subject in the face of her husband's authority one final time, before her conveyance to prison and a sentence of death.[30] The unsettling figure of Margaret Vincent bears witness to the fact that maternal care, at once contested and contestatory, potentially monstrous and self-sacrificial, could extend to issues not simply of physical reproduction, but of domestic authority as well.

To return to Goldberg's terminology, if the family functions to "reproduce" society, the question of "whose body" is responsible for that reproduction has implications for any determinations of authority. In the case of the eulogy, the mother's body is praised as a rightful sacrifice for the life of her child, which brings honor to her husband's name and thus "reproduces," in familial terms, the social stature of the patriarch. In the case of the condemnation, a woman's attempt to reclaim her children's souls by sacrificing their bodies, which are at once her body as well ("her own dear blood bred in her own body"), is represented in ideological terms not simply as a crime of murder, but more significantly as a mother's repudiation of patriarchal authority. Despite the prevalence of prescriptive representations of fatherly authority, then, the fact that the family in practice was often associated with the mother's body can be said to render problematic, at the very least, any direct familial "reproduction" of the social patriarchy.

When mothers begin to claim speaking positions for themselves not simply as reproductive bodies, but as authors, issues of authority and authorship collide. Although the countess of Lincoln located her authorship quite literally in the "issue" of the mother's body (both child and milk), other women found voices originating with the mother's authority within the family as a social system. Addressing their books of advice to their offspring, these mothers claimed the rightful maternal privilege of authority over children. Furthermore, those women writing about their roles as mothers, such as Dorothy Leigh in *The Mother's Blessing* (1616), or Elizabeth Joceline in *The mothers legacie to her unborn child* (1624), stressed the dignity and strength which they brought to that role rather than simply which they garnered from it. Elizabeth Joceline actually wrote in anticipation of the birth of her first child, assuming the voice of a mother while pregnant in order to convey her "desire" for maternity to her as yet unborn daughter.[31] Nine days after the birth of the baby, Joceline died, leaving behind her maternal instructions regarding the religious upbringing of her daughter.

Dorothy Leigh, on the other hand, composed a book of advice for her three sons while still living, explaining in her dedicatory preface that she could conceive of no better way of directing her children than "to write them the right way."[32] While acknowledging that writing is considered "a thing so unusual" among women, Leigh locates the origins of her authorship in her "motherly affection," and asserts the authority of her words over her sons, daring to assume, in Joan Larsen Klein's words, a position analogous to the role of minister, that is, "a spiritual leader of men."[33] Furthermore, Leigh links her status as a speaking subject with her written authorship, claiming that "my mind will continue long after me in writing."[34] At several moments in her text, Leigh even associates the power of her written words with the text of the Bible, which her sons may learn to read "in their own mother tongue," under the direction of her "many words," so that they may gather food for the soul "out of the word as the children of Israel gathered manna in the wilderness."[35] While Leigh takes care never to substitute the authority of her text for that of the Bible, the conflation of her maternal words with the "mother tongue" of the Bible suggests her power as a mother to provide verbal and spiritual nourishment for her children.

Although Leigh addresses her book to her sons, Klein argues that the very fact that she caused her book to be published reveals a conscious intention to reach a wider audience which was clearly intended to be women, particularly given that she addresses women directly (speaking throughout the book of "we women"), and counsels her sons concerning matters that involve women and children.[36] Leigh's construction of the marriage relationship stresses the woman's position as equal to the man, for "if she be thy wife, she is always too good to be thy servant and worthy to be thy fellow." Furthermore, she presumes upon her authority as a mother in assuring her sons that "if you get wives that be godly and you love them, you shall not need to forsake me," whereas "if you have wives that you love not, I am sure I will forsake you."[37] Leigh thus uses her maternal authority to safeguard the marital positions not of her sons but rather of her future daughters-in-law, suggesting her solidarity with her potential audience of other women.

The popularity of the mothers' advice books indicates that the issues they addressed were of concern to a significant portion of the populace. Leigh's *The Mothers Blessing*, for example, went through sixteen editions between 1616 and 1640, leading Mary Beth Rose to conclude that "the mothers' self-representations were neither obscure nor eccentric, but rather available, accessible, and well received by a relatively sizeable audience."[38] At the same time, Rose calls attention to the emergence of an increasingly problematic status for motherhood in early modern England, particularly with regard to issues of parental power and authority. Thus in the male-authored tracts, the maternal authority associated with the responsibilities of educating children and arranging marriages is frequently erased or undermined by conflating "mothers" and "parents," or by foregrounding fathers in their place. Rose points out, moreover, that in the dramatic discourses of the period the best mother is frequently an absent or dead mother.[39]

In the mothers' treatises, by contrast, maternal authorship is represented as a transgressive activity justified by sacrificial love for the children. Writing metaphorically from "beyond the grave," and thus beyond the scope of traditional cultural constraints, these mothers presume to assert their authority through a legacy not of money or of land, but of words. Rose argues that the revolutionary implications and "logical incoherence" of these female-authored treatises—based upon the mothers' discursive strategy of "self-cancellation" through death followed by their "self-presentation" as authoritative agents—indicate why their representations of motherhood could not be reproduced or appropriated by a public, popular discourse like Shakespeare's drama, despite the fact that they were moderately well known and well received.[40] For a writer such as Mary Wroth, however, the fact of shared gender renders the discourse of the mothers' advice books accessible on an entirely different level than would have been the case for her male literary peers. Indeed, Wroth's representations of motherhood can be found both to appropriate and to transform the familial dynamics, from self-cancellation to self-presentation, encoded within the social treatises of "other" author-mothers.

Coexisting with the mothers' advice books, the diaries and letters of literate women record private experiences of maternity in both physical and social terms, encoding some of the discursive instability associated with women's roles as both authoritative mothers and subservient wives. In her analysis of many such private records, Crawford finds that women at the upper social levels devoted an immense amount of time and energy to their mothering, while drawing upon female networks of support and advice from their own mothers and their friends.[41] The public (and published) discourse of the mothers' advice books thus finds a private parallel in the intimate discourse shared among women within their households and recorded in their diaries and letters. Aristocratic women such as Lady Anne Clifford, the countess of Pembroke, and Lady Barbara Sidney adopted varying strategies suitable to the social role of matriarch, detailed in their private papers, which indicate their attempts in practice to exercise agency, particularly with regard to their children, in the face of the "fatherly authority" claimed by their husbands.

In her recent study of hospitality in early modern England, Felicity Heal maintains that women who used the household as a locus of social action were enabled to demonstrate a certain measure of authority and self-definition within the domestic sphere. Similarly, Newman observes that women of different classes, although always ideologically subject, had authority over men in the persons of servants and children, the less wealthy or wellborn.[42] At the same time, household manuals such as John Dod and Robert Cleaver's popular A Godlie Forme of Householde Government (1598) attempted to create separate spheres of responsibility for husband and wife within the family, locating the wife's authority paradoxically in her visible submission to her husband.[43] In examining the contradictory definitions of power relations in the family, Belsey suggests that the woman's position as both authoritative mistress and subjected wife is consequently "unfixed." Where the terms "husband", "father," and "master" designate at once positions of authority and different sets of subordinates, the equivalent terms for women—"wife," "mother," and "mistress"—prove mutually incompatible. Belsey concludes that mothers, in particular, unsettle male-authored discourse "to the point where the price of coherence is their repeated elimination."[44] Female-authored texts, on the other hand, can be seen to restore some measure of authority to maternal discourse even as they explore the limitations and ambiguities attendant upon women's efforts to claim speaking positions in resistance to a familial ideology predicated upon their silence.

Women's diaries, as might be expected, were much more apt than contemporary men's diaries to center around the household, occasionally exploring the boundaries of domestic authority in the process.[45] For a woman such as Lady Anne Clifford, whose social sphere encompassed courtly as well as domestic circles, the diary provided a private space within which to query cultural norms even as she reflected upon the domestic dynamics of her household. Clifford lived to see the birth of seventeen grandchildren and nineteen great-grandchildren, in the process laying claim to a role, as matriarch, far more enabling as well as challenging than the initial role of wife detailed in her description of her first marriage. At the same time, Clifford's narration of her close relation to her own mother illuminates her identity as a daughter, and suggests that her assumption of matriarchal authority may have been empowered as much by daughterly loyalty as by her own maternal responsibilities.

In the first portion of her diary, which covers events in the year of 1603, Clifford recounts the power struggles between her mother and her father which occurred when she was thirteen years old. Writing as a daughter, she consistently emphasizes the perspective of her mother over that of her father. In one passage, Clifford observes that her mother was "not held as mistress of the house, by reason of the difference between my Lord and her, which was grown to a great height," while in another passage she describes her own relation to her father's authority: "Sometimes my Mother and he did meet, when their countenance did show the dislike they had one of the other, yet he would speak to me in a slight fashion and give me his blessing."[46] The "difference" between her mother and father emerges for the young Anne as a difference not only of point of view, but also of power. The lessons learned from that difference can be gathered in the latter portion of the diary from Clifford's implicit reliance upon her mother during her own power struggles with *her* "Lord" and husband over the business of the disputed land, as when she writes in April of 1616 that "for some 2 nights my Mother and I lay together and had much talk about this business."[47] Along these lines, Lewalski observes that Clifford's self-definition and sense of empowerment even while engaged in marital conflict can be traced to her close identification with her mother, who served as primary strategist and comrade in arms for her daughter.[48]

Exercising his fatherly authority in an attempt to force his wife to submit to him, Clifford's husband uses her daughter Margaret ("the Child" — named for Anne's mother) as a counter to be moved against his wife, even as Clifford's father had attempted during her own childhood to slight his wife by acknowledging directly only his daughter. Thus on 3 May 1616, Clifford notes in her diary that she received "a letter from my Lord by which I might see it was his pleasure that the Child should go the next day to London, which at the first was somewhat grievous to me, but when I considered that it would both make my Lord more angry with me and be worse for the Child, I resolved to let her go," and on 9 May she details a further "letter from my Lord to let me know his determination was, the Child should go live at Horsely, and not come hither any more so as this was a very grievous and sorrowful day to me." Little more than a week after the loss of her daughter through Margaret's departure for Horsely as ordered, Clifford receives "the heavy news of my Mother's death which I held as the greatest and most lamentable cross that could have befallen me."[49] Bereft of both mother and, for a time, daughter, Anne Clifford continues to give voice to her identity as a daughter and a mother in her diary, expressing her unwavering determination to fight for her daughter's interests even as her own mother had taken her part.

One year after her mother's death, in June 1617, Clifford describes herself as "still working and being extremely melancholy and sad to see things go so ill with me and fearing my Lord would give all his land away from the

Child." Even as Clifford's father had given land already entailed upon her to his brother, precipitating her interminable struggle with her uncle over that land in her adulthood, so Clifford received news in July 1617 that her husband "was setting his land upon his Brother."[50] Hedged about by a patriarchal system designed to protect the dominant interests of men, Clifford continued to fight in her own case for the authority to possess her land, until with the deaths of her uncle in 1641 and his son in 1643 without male issue, the property for which she had fought for thirty-eight years finally reverted to her. Mary Wroth was not as fortunate, living to witness as a widow first the attempt of her husband's brothers to claim the wardship of her son, James, in order to take over Robert Wroth's land, and subsequently, with the death of her son, their successful possession of that land. Clearly mothers and daughters in early modern England confronted complex obstacles when they endeavored to pursue their own interests in opposition to the domestic authority of their male relatives. At the same time, texts such as those discussed above survive to document the existence of some women who moved beyond sexual reproduction to discursive production in an effort to establish positions as speaking subjects within the familial structures of their culture.

In Wroth's case, multiple configurations of the father-daughter bond can be identified within the Sidney family correspondence, exposing competing constructions of family relations. The letters that Robert Sidney received from his steward, Rowland Whyte, during his frequent absences abroad throughout Mary's childhood, and the letters he wrote to his wife, Barbara, throughout their married life together, document in explicit terms his relation to his firstborn daughter, while implicitly conveying the existence of a distinctly separate mother-daughter bond. Robert regularly inquired after the young Mary's well-being in letters to her mother, instructing Barbara, for example, to "make much of little mall."[51] At the same time, Robert encourages his wife to consider visiting him abroad without the older children, commenting that "they are not so yong now, but that they may wel bee from their Mother"—released, in other words, from the bonds of maternal authority, viewed as excessive in the eyes of the father. Along these lines, Robert asserts in the same letter that "I know your delight in them makes yow not care what is best for them," adding: "I know also, that a better and more carefull mother there is not, then you are; and indeed I doe not feare anything so much as your to much fondnes."[52] Robert's admonition thus praises his wife's maternal care on the one hand, while questioning from a masculine perspective, on the other hand, the judgment of maternal affection upon which an author/mother such as Dorothy Leigh bases the authority of her voice.

During the same time period, Whyte remarks upon Mary's desire for more direct contact with her father: "I wold to god your Lordship wold bestow a lettre upon mistress Mary, yt wold greatly encourage her to doe well, for since you sayd you wold wryte, she by her speaches shewes a longing for yt."[53] For his part, Robert's concerns in letters to his wife, even in that very month when Mary longs to hear from him, rest much more directly with the upbringing of his oldest son than with his firstborn daughter. Reminding Barbara of the "difference" between paternal and maternal spheres of authority, Robert writes: "For the girls I cannot mislike the care yow take of them: but for the boies yew must resolue to let me haue my wil. For I know better what belongs to a man then yow do. Indeed I wil haue him ly from his maide for it is time, and now no more to bee in the nurcery among women."[54] Robert's assertion of *his* "wil" can refer at once to his fatherly authority and to his firstborn son, William Sidney, whom he desires to be released from the traces of his mother's governance and "to much fondnes." In deciding to relegate him to the care of a male "schulmaster," Robert maintains that his son "lieth stil with his mayds and doth not learn anything," and advises Barbara to "have the boy delivered to his charge onely, and not to have him when hee is to teach him to bee troubled with the wemen."[55] Fatherly authority in Robert Sidney's letters, then, works in opposition to rather than conjunction with the domestic authority of "the wemen" where sons are concerned.

Just the previous month, Robert had congratulated Barbara on her "happy deliuery" of another child, concluding that he was waiting to hear "what *your* little girls name is" (emphasis mine).[56] Daughters, in Robert Sidney's view, may belong for a while to their mother, but "the boies" must come under the father's charge. Indeed, even in Mary's adulthood, Robert often communicated with his daughter through her mother, conveying to Barbara his arrangements for Mary's engagement and marriage to Robert Wroth, and subsequently voicing concerns about the apparently difficult relationship between his daughter and son-in-law.[57] As Belsey points out in her analysis of the discursive instability of wives and mothers within the family hierarchy, shifting from subordination to authority and back, the coherence defined by "masculine terms" of subjectivity is threatened each time "feminine terms" are placed alongside them.[58] Robert Sidney's expressed preference for his son not to be "troubled with the wemen" thus suggests an underlying unease with the potential power of female domestic authority over emergent masculine subjectivity.

Growing up "in the nurcery among women," subject to "the Law of the Father" while being marginalized in his discourse, Mary Wroth learned to speak with her father in "his" language, even while beginning to grant women voices of their own in her poetry, drama and fiction. In one of the few surviving letters in Mary Wroth's own hand, she writes in 1614 to urge her father to protect the interests of her son from her brothers-in-law, as mentioned above, by assuming the wardship of James himself. Wroth reminds Robert Sidney that "itt is now your part to bee his Father being left both wayes in blood, and charge unto you." Signing herself "My Lordships most obedient daughter," Mary Wroth attempts to carry out her maternal responsibility to her child by calling upon the paternal authority of her father.[59]

Interestingly, Wroth writes her mother's voice into the conclusion of her letter to her father, explicitly mentioning that her mother has "comanded" her to "deliuer thus much" in her place. In fact, the family dynamic which emerges in much of the Sidney correspondence for this period reflects a frequently absent father, abroad or at court, with a firm and constant mother holding both family and household together in her husband's absence. The ending of Wroth's letter, in which she sends her mother's love, makes clear that she is writing to her father while at her mother's side at Penshurst, the Sidney family home, which, while in every social and legal sense her father's house, functioned throughout Wroth's life as her mother's domain and her own place of refuge.

Recent critical analyses of Wroth's family history have tended to emphasize the socially visible role of the father. Waller, for example, finds that Wroth was "dominated by men, or more accurately by her internalization of the socially constructed power of men," concluding that her life "shows a consistent struggle to come to terms with her idealization of the distant father." Basing his reading on the Freudian construct of the idealized father's power in "the patriarchal family romance," Waller emphasizes in Wroth's writing "signs of what might be described as neurotic displacement, vulnerability to depression, and helpless passivity before the father figure," despite his much briefer acknowledgment that the very act of writing "seems to have opened up both material and psychological agency that confounds the masochistic stereotypes by which she was otherwise interpellated."[60] While Waller's focus on vulnerability and passivity in Wroth's writings produces a perceptive analysis of her position in the "family romance," I am concerned to pursue the evidence of emerging signs of agency which is less fully scrutinized in Waller's study.

Certainly it is possible to locate Wroth's simultaneous resistance and subjection to her father and her uncle, her husband and her lover, within her textual configurations of male characters. Yet in examining the range of Wroth's representations of familial dynamics, I find that it is important to consider as well the less discussed importance of her mother, whose bond with her daughter surfaces repeatedly in a range of Sidney family letters. From her childhood, when her nine-months-pregnant mother refused to be separated from the eight-year-old Mary, who had the measles, to her adulthood, when she retired to her mother's company at Penshurst to recover from a miscarriage, Mary Wroth was able to count on the loving presence of her mother in times of trouble.[61] Furthermore, her mother's authority "in the nursery among women" translated, for Wroth, into educational and social instruction as well as emotional support, very likely informing Wroth's own representations of the mother-daughter bond in her texts.

Wroth's aunt and godmother, Mary Sidney, the countess of Pembroke, must be recognized as a further model of female authority, who was at once an "other" author-mother. Margaret Hannay has explored, in illuminating detail, indications of the bond between Wroth and her aunt, which originated with Mary's frequent visits to her godmother at Wilton or Baynards Castle, and continued into adulthood with the countess's assistance in the preparations for Mary's wedding to Robert Wroth.[62] In a letter to Barbara Sidney during Mary's childhood, the countess of Pembroke sends "my blessing to my pretey Daughter," who was also her namesake.[63] Raised "among women" such as her mother, who governed Penshurst in her father's absence, and her aunt, who not only turned Wilton into a gathering place for writers, but also wrote poetry and plays of her own, Mary Wroth was able to fashion her own role as author and mother in more complex terms than a reading of her texts primarily in relation to the "dominant" father figures in her life might seem to suggest. Wroth's texts thus must be viewed not only in relation to the "patriarchal" discourses of her father and her uncle, but also in relation to her significant matrilineal heritage.

While the male-authored social treatises examined above frequently construct mothers in terms of their bodily functions, male-authored literary texts in early modern England often tend to erase or even deconstruct the "mother's part." In the case of the lyric, physical aspects of maternity are typically either sublimated or appropriated in order to reproduce masculine desire, while women's speech is represented, if at all, more often as destructive than (re)productive. One blatant example of masculine appropriation can be found in the opening sonnet of the most famous of Wroth's "dominant" father figures, Philip Sidney, whose poet-speaker proclaims himself "great with child to speake" (AS #1). By conflating masculine and feminine fertility in a single image of discursive childbirth, Astrophil projects his desire in language at the same moment that he attempts to override any exclusively female claim to reproductive authority. At the same time, the emphasis upon the troubling lack of control in labor—"helplesse in my throwes" (AS #1)—points to an underlying ambivalence associated with the male speaker's appropriation of a feminized speaking position.

When Astrophil subsequently observes: "I cannot chuse but write my mind, / And cannot chuse but put out what I write, / While those poore babes their death in birth do find" (AS #50), his seemingly frustrated labor results paradoxically in a phallic delivery, as the initial "fulnesse" of his thoughts, which "swell and struggle forth" until Stella is "exprest," bodies forth the poem's completion apparently successfully after all. Stella herself, as the simultaneous recipient and product of Astrophil's discourse—"these lines . . . bare sweet Stella's name" (AS #50)—is effectively divorced from any consistently discursive role of her own. And yet the brief appearance of Stella's voice in the Eighth Song, which leaves Astrophil's song "broken," exposes fissures in the sonneteer's own discourse. The tensions that mark the male sonneteer's use of metaphors of female fertility in Astrophil and Stella thus indicate at once the potential power of maternity and the male speaker's need to contain or transform that potential in masculine terms.

Even as female-authored tracts such as the mothers' advice books work to inscribe maternal authority within a social framework, some early modern women poets sought to justify their transgressive voices with reference to an authority gendered female. Aemilia Lanyer, for example, situates her volume of religious poems, Salve Deus Rex Judaeorum, within a framework of matriarchal authority, opening with a dedicatory poem to the "Renowned Empresse, and great Britaines Queene, / Most gratious Mother of succeeding Kings," and concluding with a country-house poem, "The Description of Cooke-ham," which celebrates the feminine power encoded in the mother-daughter bond between the countess of Cumberland and Lady Anne Clifford. In light of this matriarchal emphasis, it becomes possible to view the volume not simply as a "Book of Good Women" in the tradition of Christine de Pizan, but even more particularly as a lyric commemoration of "good mothers and daughters."[64]

The opening poem's praise of queen Anne as once and future queen-mother modulates by the poem's conclusion into a celebration of Nature, "that goodly Creature, Mother of perfection" ("To the Queenes most Excellent Majestie," 152). The next dedicatory poem, to Princess Elizabeth, looks backward to the "Phoenix of her age," Queen Elizabeth herself, also described in resolutely matriarchal terms as "that deare Mother of our Common-weale" ("To the Lady Elizabeths Grace," 4, 7). Subsequent dedications, such as those addressed to "the Ladie Susan, Countesse Dowager of Kent, and daughter to the Duchesse of Suffolke," to "the Ladie Katherine, Countesse of Suffolke" and mother to "noble daughters," and to "the Ladie Anne, Countesse of Dorcet" and daughter to the countess of Cumberland (the principal patron of the volume), repeatedly construct the mother-daughter bond as a prime source not only of female security, but also of women's subjectivity.

In the dedicatory poem to Anne Clifford, for example, Lanyer disparages men who have proven unworthy of their responsibilities as "Gods Stewards," and in their stead praises Anne "as Gods Steward . . . In whom the seeds of virtue have bin sowne, / By your most worthy mother" ("To the Ladie Anne," 55, 57-59). Lanyer's emphasis on maternal rather than paternal lineage extends from the "seeds of virtue" to the more explicit education provided by the mother, who has "so well instructed" her daughter that no further "art" is necessary to complete her education ("To the Ladie Anne," 93-94). Lanyer's construction of the mother's part, then, can be linked to the proclamations of Dorothy Leigh in her "mother's advice book," which locate both wisdom and authority in maternal affection, by contrast to Robert Sidney's dismissal of "to much fondnes" on the part of the mother of his own children.

Following upon the dedicatory poems, Lanyer's prose epistle "To the Vertuous Reader" anticipates Constantia Munda's attack on Joseph Swetnam for denigrating his "mother's sex," when she berates "evill disposed men, who forgetting they were borne of women, nourished of women, and that if it were not by the meanes of women, they would be quite extinguished out of the world, and a finall ende of them all, doe like Vipers deface the wombes wherein they were bred" ("Vertuous Reader," 19-23). Instead of reducing women to the sum of their domestic responsibilities, however, Lanyer underscores the spiritual as well as physical significance of the mother's role by reminding her readers that "our Lord and Saviour Jesus Christ" was "begotten of a woman, borne of a woman, nourished of a woman, obedient to a woman" ("Vertuous Reader," 40, 43-45). In emphasizing the necessity of a woman's presence for Christ's conception, Lanyer links the divine power of God with the female authority of maternity. Lanyer stresses Christ's origins not as the "son of man" so much as the son of God and a woman, while men are portrayed in the body of her poem as sinners and crucifiers of Christ. Furthermore, the fact that Christ was not simply "borne of a woman," but also "obedient to a woman"—accepting not simply the divine authority of God but also, in human terms, the maternal authority of Mary—expands the significance of women's capacity for maternity from purely physical to spiritual terms.

Lanyer's long poem on Christ's Passion extends her focus on maternal authority with a detailed defense of "our Mother Eve," whom Lanyer represents as accepting the fruit from the serpent "for knowledge sake," while Adam was merely beguiled by its "faire" appearance (SDRJ, 763, 797-98). Again expanding her consideration of female authority beyond merely physical limits, Lanyer asserts that men, despite their boasting, owe not only their bodily lives ("You came not in the world without our paine") but also their very knowledge to the first mother: "Yet Men will boast of Knowledge, which [Adam] tooke / From Eves faire hand, as from a learned Booke" (SDRJ, 827, 807-8). Subsequently, Lanyer moves from Eve, the mother of all mankind, to Mary, "deere Mother of our Lord," whose maternity elevates her to the position of "most beauteous Queene of Woman-kind" (SDRJ, 1031, 1039). Writing in Protestant terms, Lanyer finds a way to appropriate the Virgin Mary as a model, not as Catholic intercessor but as exemplary mother. Her emphasis, indeed, rests with Christ's identity as the son of Mary and the son of God, in that order, as when she recounts Gabriel's message that "this blessed Infant borne of thee, / Thy Sonne, The onely Sonne of God should be" (*SDRJ*, 1071-2). While Dorothy Leigh asserts that "man can claim no part in" Mary's redemption of all women from the shame of the fall, Aemilia Lanyer goes even further in maintaining both the originary innocence of Eve and the power of Mary's position not only as unsubordinate to any man but as bearing the authority of a mother over Christ as well.[65] Maternal subjectivity within the poem on Christ's Passion thus manifests itself both within Eve as seeker and source of knowledge and within Mary as queen-mother of "Heavens bright King" (*SDRJ*, 1088).

In the final poem in the volume, "The Description of Cooke-ham," Lanyer represents a female Eden in which the mother-daughter bond between the countess of Cumberland and Anne Clifford simultaneously embraces Lanyer and empowers her to assert her own subjectivity in discursive terms.[66] Unmarked by the presence of men, Cookham emerges at once as a locus of female authority and a vision of female community, which I will discuss more extensively in the following chapters. Lanyer celebrates the countess's powers of both governance and learning, addressing her as "(great Lady) Mistris of that Place," and praising her use of the estate as a site for the transmission of knowledge from mother to daughter, "where many a learned Booke was read and skand" ("Cooke-ham," 11, 161). By contrast to Eve's expulsion from Eden after her initial pursuit of knowledge, the already learned countess of Cumberland departs Cookham of her own accord to accept other social responsibilities as a figure of female authority. Even as the poet is left to lament the loss of female companionship, she transforms that separation into grounds for establishing a voice of her own, thus articulating her discursive connection with the maternal inspiration of the countess. Taken as a whole, Lanyer's volume of poems shares with the female-authored social tracts a concern with attending to the mother's role, while developing the grounds for discourse outlined by the mother's advice books, in which maternal authority is represented as an important context for female subjectivity.

Mary Wroth's poems offer at once several alternative and sometimes competing configurations of maternity which extend the discursive constructions of the early modern women writers discussed above, illuminating gender differences in procreative terms. At the same time, Wroth's explicit reconfigurations of lyric forms and strategies common to the sequences of Philip and Robert Sidney in particular indicate the parameters of her ongoing attempt to deconstruct the boundaries of her "paternal" inheritance in order to fashion a voice of her own. Wroth's attention to maternity extends from the opening sonnet of *Pamphilia to Amphilanthus*, where Venus's maternal authority results in the speaker's subjection to love as Cupid shoots Pamphilia upon his mother's order, to many other sonnets in which she transforms the Petrarchan conceit of Night, referred to as "unjust night" by Robert Sidney's speaker (Sonnet #6), into a comforting maternal presence.[67] Wroth thus writes mothers as social entities into a lyric form previously dominated by a masculine obsession with women as bodily parts to be "emblazoned."

At the same time, Wroth rewrites specific elements of her father's lyric sequence in terms that explore the significance of her relation, as a patriarch's daughter, to her father's house. One of Robert Sidney's sonnets, which begins by comparing the speaker to an alchemist, develops into a study of the speaker's metaphorically endless travels:

> The endless alchemist, with blinded will,
> That feeds his thoughts with hopes, his hopes on shows,
> And more his work proves vain more eager grows
> While dreams of gold his head with shadows fill,
> Feels not more sure the scourge of flatt'ring skill,
> When in false trust of wealth true need he knows,
> Than I, on whom a storm of losses blows
> And tides of errors run: yet sail on still
> While my corrupted sense doth think it sees
> The long sought land of rest, and while to bliss
> I think there is a way, though yet I miss.
> Thus shunning to have lost, I still do leese,
> And hope and want: and strive and fail: and prove
> Nor end with joys, nor end from cares in love.   [Sonnet #17]

In her own Sonnet #10, Wroth develops the "traveler" comparison at more length, while directly echoing the syntax of her father's sonnet:

> The weary traveller who tired sought
>   In places distant farr, yett found noe end
>   Of paine, or labour, nor his state to mend,
> Att last with joy is to his home back brought;
> Finds nott more ease, though hee with joy bee fraught;
>   When past is feare, content like soules assend;
>   Then I, on whom new pleasures doe dessend
>   Which now as high as first borne bliss is wrought;
> Hee tired with his paines, I, with my mind;
>   Hee all content receaves by ease of limms;
>   I, greatest hapines that I doe find
>   Beeleefe for fayth, while hope in pleasure swimms;
> Truth saith t'was wrong conseite bred my despite
> Which once acknowledg'd, brings my harts delight.   [P11]

On the most obvious level of comparison, the first, fifth, seventh, and eleventh lines of the sonnets express dichotomously opposed states of mind: "The endless alchemist, . . . Feels not more sure the scourge . . . Than I, . . . I think there is a way, though yet I miss" versus "The weary traveller . . . Finds nott more ease, . . . Then I, . . . I greatest hapines that I doe find / Beeleefe for fayth." Yet in another sense, Wroth's sonnet provides not so much a reversal of her father's sonnet as a reconfiguration of its terms. She appropriates her father's metaphor of a weary traveler—a comparison, it might be noted, which fits his many trips abroad—and brings that traveler home: "Att last with joy is to his home back brought." Where Robert Sidney's speaker has lost his way, Wroth's speaker finds "beeleefe for fayth." The traveler's return home becomes Wroth's starting point, an opportunity to reshape her father's metaphor so as to emphasize not literal journey or physical absence, but frame of mind.

While Wroth returns the traveler to his house in order to claim that house as a metaphoric point of reference in Sonnet #10, she elsewhere rewrites the dynamics of familial authority within the home. In the father's house are many dwelling places. During much of Wroth's childhood, as evidenced in the family letters discussed above, it was not her frequently absent father but rather her mother and herself who inhabited that house. Where Robert Sidney's speaker journeys perpetually, Mary Wroth's speaker apparently dwells. Welcoming the maternal presence of "Night" in the face of male absence (P43), Wroth's female speaker finds comfort, if not "in the nurcery," then certainly "among women." In effect, Wroth writes her mother into her father's house, where she has been, for Wroth, all along.

Wroth's attention to the maternal body itself diverges sharply from the approach adopted by her other paternal forebear, Philip Sidney, who appropriates pregnancy as a metaphor for his male speaker's discursive fertility. As Susan Friedman has remarked, women writers' uses of the childbirth metaphor, unlike phallogocentric male uses of the same metaphor, frequently result in subversive inscriptions of female (pro)creativity which rely upon the marks of gender difference.[68] In Wroth's sequence pregnancy leads to miscarriage, within a lyric inscription of the body's betrayal of its own fertility which comes to represent the female speaker's recognition of the precarious relation between desire and language:

> Faulce hope which feeds butt to destroy, and spill
>   What itt first breeds; unaturall to the birth
>   Of thine owne wombe; conceaving butt to kill,
>   And plenty gives to make the greater dearth . . .
> For hope deluding brings us to the pride
> Of our desires the farder downe to slide.   [P40]

Writing not as a man borrowing a convenient metaphor from the body of the opposite sex, but rather as a woman who has herself suffered the physical and emotional loss of miscarriage, Wroth represents the cost of self-deception in distinctly female terms. "Faulce hope" in an unfaithful lover results in a miscarriage of desire, and a concomitant challenge to the (re)productive authority of the female poet. Even as the countess of Pembroke intensifies the imagery of miscarriage in her metaphrase of Psalm 58, by describing the "formlesse eyes" of "the Embrio, whose vitall band / Breakes er it holdes," so her niece and poetic successor, Mary Wroth, lays claim to the authority of maternal discourse with her own lyric inscription of miscarriage.[69] Certainly the (pro)creativity in Wroth's sequence exhibits more commonality with the pattern of gestational losses recorded in other early modern women's diaries and correspondence than with Astrophil's phallic fertility.[70]

As Wroth's sequence progresses, metaphors of pregnancy and childbirth resurface in a pointed attack upon the falsehood of male sonneteers, who disguise their lust with the name of love in order to "begett / This childe for love, who ought like monster borne / Bee from the court of Love, and reason torne" (P85). In Wroth's dramatic reconfiguration of the obstetrical terms of Philip Sidney's opening sonnet, then, Astrophil's claim to be "great with child to speake" (AS #1) only underscores the monstrosity of "lust . . . faulcely nam'd" as love (P85), resulting not in true (re)productive fertility, but rather in "faulce hope which feeds butt to destroy . . . conceaving butt to kill" (P40). Far from being the product of her male lover's discourse like Stella, Pamphilia undermines the "faire showes" (P40) of lustful male lovers by exposing the false premises of their discursive fertility. In place of the miscarriage of desire resulting from the deceptive practices of such male lovers, Pamphilia celebrates the "light of true love," which "brings fruite which none repent" and offers a "wombe for joyes increase" (P78). Focusing upon the womb, Wroth produces her own subversive inscription of female (pro)creativity, which relies upon the marks of gender difference to assert the capacity of women, both as lovers and as poets, to give birth to their own language of desire.

Throughout her lyric sequence, Wroth expands on the notion of "fruite" in terms that link the "wombe for joyes increase" with nature as a maternal force, even as Lanyer describes Nature as "that goodly Creature, Mother of perfection" in the first dedicatory poem to *Salve Deus Rex Judaeorum* ("To the Queenes most Excellent Majestie," 152). Whereas male poets such as Jonson and Robert Sidney offer detailed descriptions of the natural landscape under the rubrics of fatherly authority or masculine desire, both Lanyer and Wroth relate their images of nature to women's experiences. In "To Penshurst," for example, Ben Jonson finds in the lush abundance of nature on Robert Sidney's estate evidence of the moral fruitfulness of his patriarchal household, where the lady is "noble, fruitful, chaste withal," the children may be called "his own" by the "great lord," and the lord himself has not merely built, but "dwells" (90-91, 102). Robert Sidney uses the same gardens and orchards of Penshurst as metaphors to express his speaker's suffering desire. In one sonnet, Robert Sidney's speaker compares himself with "forsaken woods, trees with sharp storms oppressed, / Whose leaves once hid the sun, now strew the ground," and with "gardens, which once in thousand colours dressed / Showed nature's pride, now in dead sticks abound" (Sonnet #31), while in a later song he depicts his heart as a deserted garden where "nettles of grief" and "briars of care" have replaced the "flowers of hope" (Song #22). Whether claiming the fruitfulness of the orchards as a triumph of fatherly authority, or linking the "weeds" in the garden to the suffering of the male lover, both Jonson and Robert Sidney thus represent the landscape of Penshurst in distinctly masculine terms.

In "Cooke-ham," on the other hand, Lanyer inscribes a mutuality of relation between the natural landscape (already gendered female by her previous celebration of nature's maternal perfection) and its female inhabitants, who give as much pleasure to the estate as it gives to them. The ladies' departure brings wintry desolation to the landscape, which actively mourns rather than merely passively reflects their absence. Wroth also configures the garden as a site of female loss, invoking the maternal presence of Night in the opening of one of her sonnets, and proceeding to relate her own experience of absence to the physical lament of the landscape over summer's departure:

The very trees with hanging heads condole
Sweet sommers parting, and of leaves distrest
In dying coulers make a grief-full role;
Soe much (alas) to sorrow are they prest.
Thus of dead leaves her farewell carpett's made:
Theyr fall, theyr branches,all theyr mournings prove;
With leavles, naked bodies, whose huese vade
From hopefull greene, to wither in theyr love,
If trees, and leaves for absence, mourners bee
Noe mervaile that I grieve, who like want see. [P22]

Subject to the absence of her male beloved, Wroth's speaker sees her own loss encoded in the trees' loss of leaves, the devastation wrought upon the garden by winter.

At the same time, by developing her representation of the garden in terms of seasonal change, Wroth expands the metaphor to explore the possibility of rebirth. By contrast to her father, whose speaker self-pityingly complains that his garden of love is "to desert grown" (Song #22), Wroth reconfigures the garden metaphor near the end of her sequence by transforming the fading and fallen leaves of Sonnet #19 (P22) into fading and fallen blossoms:

[O noe lett love his glory have and might]
Bee given to him who triumphs in his right
Nor vading bee, butt like those blossooms fayre
Which fall for good, and lose theyr coulers bright
Yett dy nott, butt with fruite theyr loss repaire. [P88]

Just as spring follows upon winter, linking the fallen leaves of Sonnet #19 with these fallen blossoms, this sonnet looks forward to the fruit which results from that loss and indeed repairs it. Consistently juxtaposing "fruite" and "birth," Wroth finds that male lust results in "a timeles, and unseasonable birth," producing "fruit of a sowre, and unwholsome ground" (P86, P87), which contrasts with the "wombe for joyes increase" associated with the faithful female lover (P78). In Wroth's treatment of the garden, then, male absence ceases to be a dead end or "desert" for the female lover, serving rather as a potential prelude to discursive creation. Wroth's speaker uses her male lover's absence to empower her own lyric voice rather than complaining of victimization. Over the course of the sequence, so pervasively shaped by the absence of the beloved, Wroth moves ultimately to decenter that loss by celebrating the "fruite" of her female speaker's discourse, in a womb of her own. Even as women authors of the treatises and the mothers' advice books work to highlight maternal authority as a basis for their transgressive act of writing, or women diarists such as Anne Clifford find room for voices of their own in the domestic accounts of their journals, or women poets such as Aemilia Lanyer locate a productive context for female discourse within the mother-daughter bond, so Mary Wroth writes not simply as her father's daughter, but as a mother and mother's daughter herself. The female speaker in *Pamphilia to Amphilanthus* thus gives voice not only to heterosexual passion, but to a nascent maternal subjectivity as well, which appears in increasingly developed terms in Wroth's other texts.

In moving from Wroth's poems to her play and prose romance, it is useful to examine representations of maternity in other early modern plays and romances, in addition to the cultural texts discussed above. Although mother-figures, when they appear, tend to enact more significant roles in these dramatic and fictive genres than in male-authored lyric poetry, nonetheless, as Mary Beth Rose has pointed out, the best mother often seems to be an absent or dead mother. Rose attributes this pattern to the fact that mothers are construed largely in terms of a private world of individual desire, in which an overindulgence of maternal love—characterized as "to much fondnes" in the letters of Robert Sidney discussed above—poses a potential threat to fatherly authority.[71] Lest excess maternal "fondnes" undermine the familial balance of power, paternal restraint often operates as a powerful force within both social and literary texts. Wroth's constructions of maternity, then, respond both to the explicit erasures and sublimated anxieties which inform male-authored representations of the mother's part, and to alternative (re)presentations of maternity which surface in female-authored texts as well.

Wroth's uncle, Philip Sidney, in fact introduces the central female characters in his *Old Arcadia* in the context of their social containment by the male head of the family, when Gynecia appears with her daughters in the protective custody ordered by Basilius. Almost immediately, the issue of "to much fondnes" arises in inverted terms which undercut the reliability of maternal authority, when Gynecia sets herself against her own daughter, vowing that she will not allow Philoclea to supplant her in "Cleophila's" affections: "the life I have given thee, ungrateful Philoclea, I will sooner with these hands bereave thee of than my birth shall glory she hath bereaved me of my desires" (*OA*, 92). Gynecia's bondage to passion transforms the familial bond between mother and daughter into an occasion for conflict rather than nurturance. Soon, Gynecia comes to perceive the domestic hierarchy itself in inverted terms: "The growing of her daughter seemed the decay of herself. The blessings of a mother turned to the curses of a competitor" (*OA*, 122). Unable to govern her desire for Cleophila/Pyrocles, Gynecia cannot maintain her maternal authority over her daughters. The conflict between maternal and erotic functions in the figure of Gynecia can be said to result, in Irigarean terms, in the repeated objectification of the woman.[72] When Gynecia comes to trial at the conclusion of the *Old Arcadia*, she further defines herself as the inversion of each of her social and familial roles, culminating in the role of mother: "I am the subject that have killed my prince. I am the wife that have murdered my husband. I am a degenerate woman, an undoer of this country, a shame of my children" (*OA*, 382). No longer even able to claim the title of "mother," Gynecia names herself "shame" instead, and submits to the objectifying discipline of Euarchus's patriarchal authority, from which she is released only by the resurrection of the original patriarch, Basilius. Although Gynecia has not killed her children, her rejection of her husband's rightful authority over her and consequent mistreatment of her daughters positions her, at least temporarily, at the margins of society like Margaret Vincent, that "Creature not deserving Mother's name."[73]

Sidney expands upon his representation of maternity as a threat to patriarchal authority with the figure of Cecropia in the *New Arcadia*, whose "to much fondnes" for her son, Amphialus, works directly to undermine Basilius's governorship of the community. Only Gynecia, in fact, is able to recognize Cecropia's hand in the intrusion of a lion and a bear into the pastorals (*NA*, 125), and her maternal warning to Pamela and Philoclea prepares them for their later persecution by their aunt. Cecropia's maternity, even more than Gynecia's, works malignantly in inverse proportion to the heroism of her offspring. Thus Amphialus is described as "being (like a rose out of a brier) an excellent sonne of an evill mother" (*NA*, 363). In Sidney's configuration of gender, male heroism can evidently flourish despite a man's origin in the mother's body. At the same time, the objectification of the woman's body in his text is underscored by a piece of advice fashioned to represent the mother's perspective, when Cecropia encourages her son to renew his suit to Philoclea by urging him to "know thy selfe a man, and shew thy selfe a man: and (beleeve me upon my word) a woman is a woman" (*NA*, 453). Of course, in the case of Amphialus's rival, Zelmane, a "woman" is not a woman when she is a man, and thus Cecropia's pronouncements on gender difference prove not only misguided, but useless. Mothers such as Gynecia and Cecropia serve in both versions of the *Arcadia* less to signify maternal power than to reify, through their very failings, the forces of fatherly authority that they unsuccessfully attempt to displace.

In Book III of Spenser's *Faerie Queene*, the female warrior figure of Britomart is represented as necessarily separated from the forces of maternal nurturance, taken from "nourses tender pap" to be "trained up in warlike stowre" (III.ii.6). Significantly, she is stricken with love for Arthegall in "her fathers closet" while gazing into Merlin's magic mirror, upon seeing not her own face but rather a male image reflected back at her—a conflation of masculine forces which effectively overwhelm her emergent femininity (III.ii.22). The mother-figure in this narrative is Britomart's nurse, Glauce, who calls Britomart at once her "deare daughter" and her "dearest dread" (III.ii.39), suggesting her fears at being unable to protect her charge from the world outside "the nurcery." Indeed, when Britomart falls ill with desire, Glauce's maternal remedies prove impotent, producing instead a "miscarriage" of aid which underscores her feminine ignorance (III.ii.51-52). Only when Glauce brings Britomart to Merlin, yielding her ineffective position as female nurse to the fatherly authority of the male magician who immediately sees through her "womanish guyle," is Britomart healed, by the power of masculine learning rather than feminine superstition (III.iii.17-19). Once again, as in Sidney's *Arcadia*, the failures of a mother-figure reify the forces of fatherly authority. In Wroth's *Urania*, by contrast to Spenser's *Faerie Queene* in particular, the female magic of the wise woman, Melissea, is not displaced by any greater masculine authority, and stems from a combination of learning and insight rather than "guyle" or superstition.

In other popular male-authored romances of the period, from Montemayor's *Diana* and d'Urfé's *Astrée* to Lodge's *Rosalynde* and Greene's *Pandosto*, mothers tend either to be absent or subsumed under the more general appellation of "parents," who are most notable for attempting to block the romantic pairings of the younger generation. As critics from Rose to Montrose have noted, Shakespeare's romantic comedies provide particularly striking examples of the erasure of the mother from the domestic hierarchies of the family. Focusing upon *A Midsummer Night's Dream*, for example, Montrose points out that the mother's part is wholly excluded from Shakespeare's account of the making of Hermia and Helena as their fathers' daughters. Furthermore, when Titania attempts to claim the role of foster mother to her friend's son, displacing the relationship between wife and husband with a maternal bond between women, Theseus successfully disrupts that bond with the insertion of his fatherly authority. Montrose concludes that the play's "overcompensation" for the "natural fact" of maternity suggests how "patriarchal norms are compensatory for the vulnerability of men to the powers of women."[74] Nevertheless, however threatened patriarchal norms may seem, the play manages to contain the potential powers of maternity within the bounds outlined by paternal discourse.

While some of Shakespeare's late romances seem to confront maternity more directly than his romantic comedies, at least to the extent of providing mother-figures or even mothers who claim authority over daughters in the early portions of the plots, those mothers are characteristically shunted aside as the plot evolves — by dying, retiring to the confines of a nunnery, or even becoming a "statue" — in order to allow the fathers opportunities for unmediated confrontations with their daughters. The potential authority of the absent mothers is thus deflected upon their daughters, whose physical resemblance to their mothers only underscores their lack of concomitant standing in the domestic hierarchy, allowing them ultimately to comfort their fathers without challenging the parameters of paternal authority.

Cymbeline, named for the king, father, and head of the domestic hierarchy, seems, for example, initially to erase mothers only to reinscribe the subversive power of their absence. While Cymbeline's queen serves as an evil stepmother-figure to Imogen and Posthumus, who have both lost their own mothers, the very concept of "mother" becomes a kind of touchstone which serves to reveal the emotional and psychological states of the lead characters throughout the play. Imogen's initial gift of her mother's diamond to Posthumus as a pledge of faithful, chaste love prepares the ground for Posthumus's diatribe against the female sex, and most particularly against women as mothers, when he believes Imogen to be false:

> Is there no way for men to be, but women
> Must be half-workers? We are all bastards,
> And that most venerable man which I
> Did call my father, was I know not where
> When I was stamp'd. Some coiner with his tools
> Made me a counterfeit; yet my mother seem'd
> The Dian of that time. So doth my wife
> The nonpareil of this.   [II.v.1-8]

Conjoining his mother and his wife, Posthumus attacks "the woman's part" within himself and within all men, who cannot escape the curse of being born of woman. Imogen, on the other hand, even while adopting a "man's part" in her disguise, reclaims the role of "mother" as a regenerative force, asserting that "hardness ever / Of hardiness is mother" (III.vi.21-22). With the death of the evil queen at the end of the play and the restoration of the king's sons, however, the patriarchy undergoes a regenerative transformation in which Cymbeline can claim to be "a mother to the birth of three," thus effectively reinforcing his position as head of state and family by appropriating any remaining power of "the mother's part" for the father.[75] Whether despised or praised, then, the woman's part in *Cymbeline* is finally defined not only by men, but through men as well, so that the presence or absence of real mothers bears an increasingly redundant relation to the play's discourses of maternity.

The Winter's Tale, on the other hand, opens not with a wicked stepmother but with a queen and mother whose visibly pregnant state signifies maternity incarnate. Leontes's recurring anxiety that his son, Mamillius— whose very name connotes life-sustaining mother's milk—is more linked to his mother than to the world of male bonding represented by his father, has its counterpart in Robert Sidney's concern that his son be removed from his mother's immediate sphere of authority "in the nurcery among women." Threatened by the blatant sexuality embodied (literally) by Hermione's pregnancy, Leontes in effect finds her guilty of "to much fondnes," with the result that his anxieties about his son are displaced onto Polixenes as an alternative object of his wife's affections. In retaliation, Leontes strikes directly at Hermione's identity as a mother by commanding that her children be taken from her. The play's attention to maternity resurfaces at the conclusion, where it is first and foremost as a mother that Hermione is released from her statuesque immobility, confiding to her daughter that she "preserv'd" herself explicitly "to see the issue" of the oracle's promise that her child was alive. This restoration of the mother-daughter bond comes literally second, however, to Leontes's own reunion with his daughter, and the play closes with Leontes silencing the most vocal mother-figure in his court ("O, peace, Paulina!") and getting the last word. In the end, to borrow Jonathan Goldberg's words from another context, fatherly authority reigns supreme.[76]

In Elizabeth Cary's *Mariam*, on the other hand—published two years after the first performance of *The Winter's Tale*—mothers are neither absent nor dead. On the contrary, most of the female protagonists, with the notable exception of Salome, are mothers whose relation to their children directly shapes their interaction with each other, and whose voices challenge fatherly authority from a range of positions.[77] Both Cary and Mary Wroth were mothers who chose what Susan Suleiman has termed "the indirections of fiction" as a place for maternal discourse, by contrast to the more explicitly factual rhetoric of the mothers' advice books and diaries.[78] In Cary's case, her public profession of Catholicism in 1625 (after twenty-three years of marriage) resulted in her disinheritance by her father and her separation from her husband and children, shedding some retrospective light upon the strong mothers in her play. Furthermore, the fact that six of Cary's eight surviving children chose vocations in the Catholic church, and that one of her daughters found a voice of her own to write her mother's biography, suggests some measure of the enduring resistance to patriarchal authority embedded in Cary's words. Interestingly, *The Lady Falkland: Her Life*, authored by Cary's daughter, testifies to Cary's often trying relationships with her own mother and mother-in-law, as well as to Cary's enduring bonds with her children.[79]

Cary develops Alexandra and Doris as mothers in much greater detail than does her source, Josephus, and foregrounds Mariam's maternity in relation to both those figures.[80] Furthermore, instead of constructing mothers along the exaggeratedly one-sided lines of pamphlet eulogies or condemnations such as *The Honor of Virtue* or *A pitiless Mother*, Cary represents mothers as speaking subjects whose discourse serves to reveal both their strengths and shortcomings. While Belsey's reading of *Mariam* focuses upon "a wife's right to speak, to subjectivity, to a position from which to protest," treating the implications of Mariam's position as both wife and subject, her more general analysis of the "discursive instability" of women as both authoritative mothers and subservient wives, mentioned earlier, is directly relevant to any consideration of Cary's representations not only of wives but of mothers in the play as well.[81] I find that the mother-figures in *Mariam*, from Alexandra to Doris to Mariam herself, in fact are enabled by their maternity to define positions, however admittedly discontinuous, from which to speak and protest apart from their apparent subordination as wives and as women subject to the patriarchal tyranny of Herod. Indeed, the discursive potential of Cary's maternal characters offers striking parallels to the developed representations of mothers in Wroth's play and prose romance.

Cary's play presents the double-edged potential of maternal discourse quite vividly in the example of Mariam's mother, Alexandra.[82] Following the initial news of Herod's death, Alexandra urges Mariam to cast off Herod's patriarchal authority, declaring: "My curse pursue his breathless trunk and spirit" (I.ii.83). Although Alexandra is hardly the idealized mother-figure of the pamphlet eulogies, neither can she be termed a "pitiless Mother," or simply a meddler who, as in Josephus's *Antiquities*, treats her children primarily as weapons in a power-struggle with Herod. Indeed, it is with the united voice of a mother and a daughter that Alexandra curses Herod for the deaths of Mariam's brother, Aristobolus, and grandfather, Hircanus. Furthermore, Alexandra's speech underscores how her ambitions for her own daughter, whom she believes could have outmatched Cleopatra in becoming the bride of Antony and "empress of aspiring Rome" (I.ii.199), were foiled by Herod's aggressively preemptive wedding to Mariam. In railing against Herod's powers, Alexandra laments the possession of her daughter—whom she calls "my

Mariam" (I.ii.79, 180)—by Herod, in effect registering the loss of both her children to Herod, the one through marriage as surely as the other through death. While Belsey suggests that the drama of the period typically represents mothers, if at all, as negotiators between fathers and children,[83] in *Mariam* patriarchal authority has the potential to obstruct the mothering process itself, particularly in removing children from the scope of maternal authority, as in the case of Alexandra.

Identifying her daughter with herself in familial terms, Alexandra observes to Mariam that "this his hate to thee may justly prove, / That sure he hates Hircanus' family" (I.ii.125-26). Significantly, it is in the discursive liberty afforded by Herod's presumed death that Alexandra voices her estimation of Herod's capacity to wish "that Mariam might be slain" (I.ii.130), unexpectedly adumbrating the outcome of the play. In the meantime, Mariam's only defense of Herod to her mother emphasizes his decision to take her children for his heirs, rather than those of Doris, his former wife. Mariam's speech suggests that some measure of her loyalty can be explained by Herod's decision to privilege her maternity not simply over that of Doris—"nor did I glory in her overthrow"—but over his own paternal investment in his firstborn son as well:

> He not a whit his first-born son esteem'd,
> Because as well as his he was not mine:
> My children only for his own he deem'd,
> These boys that did descend from royal line.
> These did he style his heirs to David's throne;
> My Alexander if he live, shall sit
> In the majestic seat of Solomon,
> To will it so, did Herod think it fit.   [I.ii.134-42]

Rather than attributing her tears at Herod's death to her wifely duty, then, Mariam emphasizes the fruition of her maternal hope and pride through Herod's "will." Mariam's use of the possessive pronoun in referring to her son as "my Alexander" serves as a further echo of her own mother Alexandra's investment in "my Mariam."

Although relegated in Josephus's text to the marginal position of a castoff former wife who has no voice, Doris proves to be a very present mother in Cary's reconstruction of ties that bind. Doris returns to Jerusalem with her own son, Antipater, in *The Tragedy of Mariam*, and attempts to repossess for her son the honor which she herself has been denied as a wife. In claiming a speaking position for herself as a mother, Doris even professes herself willing to disregard Herod's cruelty to her within marriage should he agree to advance the fortunes of her son: "Let him but prove as natural to thee, / As cruel to thy miserable mother: / His cruelty shall not upbraided be / But in thy fortunes. I his faults will smother" (II.iii.267-70). The verbal conjunction of "mother"

and "smother" here suggests what might be termed, in Belsey's words, "a discontinuity of being," in that Doris is willing to "smother" her potential subjectivity as an abused wife in return for recognition of the fruits of her maternity.
The speaking positions of wife and mother can be seen to be radically discontinuous in the examples of both Doris and Mariam, when maternal ambition
subsumes the effects of wifely subordination to tyranny.

Near the end of the play, when Doris confronts Mariam before her execution, Cary represents their interaction as a standoff not simply between
two competing wives, but more compellingly between two rival mothers.
Given both mothers' preoccupation with their sons, Doris's complaint that
Mariam "robb'd from me the glory of my life" (IV.viii.586) may as likely refer
to the fate of her son as herself. In revenge, Doris extends her curse, as one
mother upon another, from Mariam to her children. When Mariam seeks to
protect her children ("Curse not mine infants" [IV.viii.606]), Doris responds
by redoubling her curses ("plague the mother much: the children worse"
[IV.viii.616]) and declaring to Mariam: "I do hope this boy of mine / Shall one
day come to be the death of thine" (IV.viii.623-24). Even in rivalry, Mariam
and Doris are concerned less with the man to whom they both have been
married than with their children, whose fates will reflect posthumously upon
their own.

Alexandra, by contrast, is represented as repudiating her daughter as
Mariam approaches her execution. Whereas Alexandra's earlier discourse of rebellion surfaced in the face of Herod's presumed absence through death, his
presence apparently transforms her into a type of pitiless mother, who "did
loudly rail" upon her daughter "as if nature she did quite forget" (V.i.35-36). Yet
just as the behavior of the "pitiless Mother" excoriated in the pamphlet can be
read as a response to patriarchal tyranny, so Alexandra's "unnatural" repudiation of Mariam can be viewed as a public attempt to placate the tyrant who has
executed one of her children and is about to execute the other. Revealingly,
Alexandra's observation that Mariam had already "liv'd too long" (V.i.42)
echoes her earlier prediction that Herod would be the death of her daughter.
Predictably, Herod's response to Alexandra denigrates the very maternal identity that his authority has functioned to disassemble: "Base pickthank devil!
Shame, 'twas all her glory, / That she to noble Mariam was the mother: / But
never shall it live in any story— / Her name, except to infamy, I'll smother"
(V.i.45-48). Once again, the conjunction of "mother" and "smother" exposes a
discontinuity of being, but in this case the smothering of the maternal bond
can be regarded as a social manifestation of the effects of patriarchal discourse
as much as a failure of "nature."

Mariam's final utterance in Cary's play proclaims the potential of male
tyranny to silence female speech—Herod's "sentence" causes her literally to
"loose [her] breath" (V.i.73)—even while her prediction that Herod will

repent her death in three days proves able to shape not only Herod's repentance but even his choice of an inscription for his future gravestone: *"Here Herod lies, that hath his Mariam slain"* (V.i.258). Known ultimately in relation to "his" Mariam, Herod's final words are contained by her own. The varied voices of the play's mothers, however, cannot be confined so neatly within a single epitaph, forming instead a discursive collage of maternity which encompasses conflict and rivalry as well as nurturance and affection. Maternal authority in *Mariam* admittedly is short-lived and has a price, but significantly it finds expression in more than one voice, defining a range of speaking positions for the simultaneous subjection and subjectivity of women.

The competing maternal voices in Elizabeth Cary's play, as well as the assertive proclamations of the mothers' advice books, expose a far more variable range of representations against which to read Mary Wroth's narratives of maternity than do the examples of mothers constructed by Wroth's literary "fathers" alone. In particular, the emphasis placed in female-authored texts upon the power of mothers' voices, rather than simply their bodies, to sustain or to subvert their offsprings' positions as speaking subjects, as well as the glimpses of mothers with self-proclaimed speaking positions of their own, suggest the extent to which Wroth's multiple constructions of maternity extend an ongoing engagement with issues of maternal authority and subjectivity in her culture.

Wroth's play, *Love's Victory*, contains two mother-figures whose voices suggest in preliminary form the co-existing maternal discourses of empowerment and ambivalence which surface in *Urania*. The play opens with the voice of the mother implicated in its title: Venus, Goddess of Love. Even as *Pamphilia to Amphilanthus* commences with Venus instructing her "deare sonne" to "martir" the heart of the speaker (P1), so the first scene of *Love's Victory* sets forth Venus's desire to bring lovers into subjection to her power through the wiles of her son, Cupid. This first mother-figure in the play exercises her considerable maternal authority in order to assure the recognition of that authority among the play's lovers, who are cast in a child-like relation to her. Furthermore, Venus's maternal relation not simply of "fondnes" for, but more strikingly of authority over, Cupid in particular is underscored in their conversations, with Cupid repeatedly inquiring: "Like you this, mother?," and Venus replying: "Son, I like this well" (I.427).

Although Venus appears through much of the play to be concerned with causing the lovers to suffer, by its conclusion she reveals a nurturing side to her authority as well, declaring: "Lovers bee nott amas'd, this is my deed, / Who could nott suffer your deere harts to bleed" (V.487-88). As a mother who is *not* also a wife, Venus proves less subject to the discursive instability which marks the conjunction of those roles in Cary's play. Instead, her maternal

authority can appear threatening as well as liberating, constraining as well as
nurturing, without becoming "discontinuous." By contrast to male-authored
depictions of Venus which emphasize the physicality of her sensual female
body (as, for example, in Shakespeare's popular *Venus and Adonis*), Wroth's
Venus is more notable for the scope of her maternal authority than for any
descriptions of naked blazoned body parts.[84] The very range of her powers
indeed serves to effect an expansion in traditionally conceived notions of the
discursive capability of maternal figures.

The other maternal figure in the play is the widowed mother of Musella, the central female protagonist, whose relation to her mother initially recalls the conflicts between lovers and overbearing parents in the romances of
Montemayor and d'Urfé, Sidney and Shakespeare. Although in generic terms
Wroth's play bears some resemblances to the pastoral tragicomedies of Tasso,
Guarini, Daniel, and Fletcher,[85] Wroth's attention to the role of the mother
distinguishes her play from theirs. Rather than generalizing the conflict to one
of parents versus children, as in the domestic treatises of the period, Wroth focuses specifically upon the mother-daughter bond, in a family in which the
father is dead and there is no son. That domestic configuration in itself diverges from those in most male-authored constructions of the familial hierarchy, such as the narratives of Sidney, Spenser, and Shakespeare discussed
above. The mother-daughter bond represented in Wroth's play is threatened,
however, by fatherly authority from beyond the grave, when Musella's mother
betroths her daughter to Rustic, according to her husband's instructions but
against Musella's will. When Musella's friend, Simeana, urges her to express
her hate for Rustic to her mother, Musella replies: "Alas, I'have urg'd her, till
that she with teares / Did vowe, and grieve she could nott mend my state /
Agreed on by my father's will which bears / Sway in her brest, and duty in
mee" (V.11-14). Musella's mother is no insensitive tyrant, but rather a woman
bound by the strictures of a marriage not completely unlike that of Mary
Wroth's own mother, Barbara, whose husband could write her that "for the
boies yew must resolue to let me haue my wil." The difference is that in Mary
Wroth's family, the "father's will" pertained more directly to "the boies" than
"the girls," and Barbara Sidney maintained her ties with her daughters
whether her husband was present or absent. Mary Wroth herself, however,
was well acquainted, both through her own experience of widowhood and that
of friends such as Anne Clifford, with the privations that the deceased
"father's will" could impose upon the children, quite beyond the powers of
the widowed mother to redress. The simultaneous suffering of mother and
daughter within her play, then, exposes the inequities of a patriarchal system
in which, on a social level distinct from the mythic maternal authority of
Venus, a daughter might not be able to receive "mother's advice" after all.

In Musella's case, her inability to "governe butt my mother's will" intersects with her own willed choice to accept Rustic's offer of marriage against
her better judgment (V.53, 69-72), so that only her friend Silvesta can help her
to escape the betrothal by providing Musella and Philisses with a potion which
seemingly causes their deaths. When Silvesta attributes Musella's fate to "her
mother growne her foe, and death her freind" (V.335), Musella's mother responds by accepting all the blame, and hoping that "death alone, my freind, /
Shall mee release" (V.399-400). As the will of the father, compounded by the
lying speeches of the villain Arcas, extends beyond death to constrain the lives
of mother and daughter, both look to death itself to serve as the friend which
each can no longer be to the other.

In the event, once the lovers are revived from their apparent deaths,
mother and daughter find not only their bond restored, but also their shared
discourse renewed. While Musella's mother had disavowed the ability to express her "true grief . . . by words" (V.354), registering instead the pain that
Arcas's false speech about her daughter had inflicted upon her (V.389-94), her
daughter's "rebirth" allows her to speak directly to Musella:

> Joy now as great as was my former woe,
> Shutts up my speach from speaking what I owe
> To all butt mine; for mine I joye you are
> And love, and blis maintaine you from all care.
> Pardon my fault, injoye, and blessed bee,
> And children, and theyr children's children see.   [V.497-502]

Even as Hermione, restored to Perdita, speaks only to her daughter—"Tell
me, mine own, / Where has thou been preserv'd?" (WT, V.iii.123-24)—so
Musella's mother addresses only her beloved daughter: "for mine I joye you
are / And love." Yet while Shakespeare cuts off Hermione's speech to her
daughter and does not include that daughter's reply, concluding instead with
the pronouncements of the king and father, Wroth puts into words the fruition of a mother's blessing in motherhood itself: "And children, and theyr
children's children see."

Significantly, Musella's reply to her mother is a concomitant request for
forgiveness and expression of affection: "Pardon mee first who have your
sorrow wrought, / Then take owr thanks whose good your care hath brought"
(V.503-4). The significance of the mutual affirmation between mother and
daughter in this scene can be read suggestively in relation to Cixous's assertion
that "there always remains in woman that force which produces / is produced
by the other," as well as in relation to the mutual support between mothers and
daughters recorded in numerous journals and letters of the period, including
those of Wroth's family examined above.[86] Wroth represents the potential for

extended maternal authority when even Philisses addresses Musella's mother as "Mother, for soe your gyfte makes mee you call" (V.507), in thanking her for her blessing. Rather than reproducing the paternal appropriation or erasure of the mother's part which marks the behavior of father-figures from Sidney's Basilius to Shakespeare's Cymbeline, Wroth locates a sufficiency of parental authority in a female figure. Initially disparaged by the other characters, Musella's mother finally receives honor from all for her enduring love for her daughter.

At the same time, Silvesta reminds the lovers that Venus "the prayse must have whose love to you / Made her desend on earth and your cares view" (V.513-14). As the ultimate maternal authority figure in the play, Venus pronounces sentence upon the villain, Arcas, and accepts the acclaim for "Love's Victory." Freed of the constraints of dead fathers and male villains, the characters finally celebrate the love of mothers. "Love's Victory," then, signifies not only the happy couplings of the male and female characters, but the finally enduring authority of the loving mothers as well. Admittedly, the mothers in *Love's Victory* share with the mothers in *Mariam* the capacity to inflict suffering as well as to extend protection to those in their charge. But unlike the mother-figures in Sidney's *Arcadia* or Shakespeare's *Cymbeline* and *The Winter's Tale*, who tend to resemble the idealized or demonized mothers of the pamphlet eulogies and condemnations, the mother-figures constructed by Cary and Wroth speak with complex voices whose range deconstructs the exaggerated boundaries of male-authored stereotypes and offers instead glimpses of mothers with the status of speaking subjects.

In Wroth's *Urania*, the attention to maternity as a potential intersection of female authority and subjectivity that informs *Pamphilia to Amphilanthus*, and is developed more fully in *Love's Victory*, can be identified as an important issue from the start. Urania's opening lament over her lack of knowledge of her family origins signals, as discussed earlier, both the difficulty and the potential empowerment which can attend a woman's attempt to fashion a position from which to speak, outside the patriarchal parameters of "estate or birth."[87] After initially mourning the absence of parents whose identities could stabilize her own, Urania particularizes her lament to the absence of the female parent, in comparing herself to her lambs: "Miserable Urania, worse art thou now then these thy Lambs; for they know their dams, while thou liue unknowne of any" (1). Subsequently, when she comes upon a lamb wandering lost, she returns to the subject of her own desire for a mother:

> Poor Lambe, said she, what moane thou mak'st for losse of thy deare dam? what torments do I then suffer, which never knew my mother? thy misse is great, yet thou a beast may'st be brought up, and soone contented

hauing food; but what food can bee giuen me, who feede on nothing but Despaire, can that sustaine me? No, want of knowledge starves me, while other things are plentifull. [16]

Like the authors of the mothers' advice books, Wroth privileges maternal nurturance over physical nourishment in giving voice to Urania's longing for her mother. Urania's recognition of the importance of mothering to the development of "knowledge" of oneself shapes her subsequent mothering of her own children, as well as her ability to help other female characters to define feminine parameters of self-fashioning throughout the narrative.

Pamphilia, on the other hand, inhabits an overdetermined familial identity, not only as a royal patriarch's daughter, but also as the King of Pamphilia's "Neece, who by his gift was to enjoy that kingdome after his decease, and therefore bore that name likewise given by him" (82). Far from experiencing Urania's problem of not knowing her parents, Pamphilia finds herself flanked by a strong father and a strong uncle—family bonds not unlike those of Mary Wroth—while being courted by the most heroic of princes. Wroth further acknowledges her own familial heritage by forming Pamphilia's name from a combination of syllables which echoes the names of Pamela and Philoclea. Small wonder, then, that Wroth represents Pamphilia's concern with asserting and preserving authority as an author, as well as autonomy as a lover and ruler.

Throughout *Urania*, Wroth juxtaposes figurations of gender with family bonds, exposing the problematic gendering of authority and subjectivity within familial structures. One male character takes care to distinguish between the sexes, for example, in commenting upon the admirable self-control of a lady following the death of her beloved: "O women how excellent are you, when you take the right way? else, I must confesse, you are the children of men, and like them fault-full" (36). This judgment of course depends upon a male conception of "the right way" in the first place, and assumes a masculine capability to evaluate the faults of women as fathered by men.[88] On the other hand, when another male character inveighs against women's lightness and jealousy, having lost the favor of his own beloved, it is Urania's future husband, Steriamus, who reminds him that "your mother was a woman, and you must be favour'd by an other, to be blessed with brave posterity" (159). Such a reminder balances the earlier perspective of women as "the children of men" with a recognition of the engendering role of women as mothers. Furthermore, Wroth's distinction between the reproductive agency of mothers and the limitations associated with "the children of men" underscores her own discursive capacity to move beyond the characterizations of her male predecessors in the romance tradition, transforming those "children of men" through her representation of relationships not only between the sexes, but also within the family structure itself.

Steriamus's acknowledgment of maternal power additionally recalls
Pyrocles's exploration of his male identity in the *Arcadia*: "if I be anything, . . .
I was to come to it born of a woman and nursed of a woman" (OA, 21). Yet
Pyrocles relegates that dependence to his origins while maintaining the autonomy of his present state, assuring Musidorus that in spite of his Amazon attire
"there is nothing I desire more than fully to prove myself a man in this enterprise" (OA, 22-23). By contrast Steriamus, whose subsequent marriage to
Urania represents one of the most stable unions in the romance, underscores
the terms of male dependence upon women as mothers not only as a past connection, but also as a present and future one: "you must be favour'd by an
other, to be blessed with brave posterity." In effect, Wroth shifts the focus
from the mother's body as a fortuitous conjunction of womb and breasts to the
mother's role as author of posterity. While the importance of women's childbearing capability is acknowledged by numerous male-authored domestic
treatises, Wroth's emphasis not merely on the physical procreative potential of
women, but on their maternal authority as well, links her narrative to the texts
of female polemicists such as Jane Anger and Constantia Munda and author-
mothers such as Dorothy Leigh and Elizabeth Joceline.

The parental relation to children is not always a benign one in *Urania*,
particularly when fathers and daughters are involved. In many cases, the
father's will enforces upon the daughter an unwelcome betrothal which results
in the daughter's experience of a divided subjectivity, a "self which is not one,"
as discussed in the previous chapter. One female character named Bellamira,
for example, observes regarding the cost of obeying her father's choice of
husband, "Thus more then equally did I devide my selfe" (334). Another
female character, Limena, finds that her accession to "her fathers will" produces self-loathing, "for consenting in shew to that which was most contrarie to
it selfe" (5). In an echo of the relation between Musella and her mother in
Love's Victory, Limena's mother comes upon evidence that suggests that her
daughter is dead, and is "readie to die with her, as if shee had brought her forth
to bee still as her life, that though two, yet like those eyes, that one being struck
in a certaine part of it, the other unhurt doth lose likewise the sight: so she
having lost her, lost likewise all comfort with her" (14). Wroth's repeated treatment of actual or potential mother-daughter bereavement forms a revealing
counterpoint to Adrienne Rich's observation that "the loss of the daughter to
the mother, the mother to the daughter, is the essential female tragedy."[89] The
mother/daughter paradigm in the case of Limena seems to operate along the
lines explored by Irigaray and Cixous, in which possibilities for female subjectivity depend upon connection with the "other" woman. In fact, it is Urania the
motherless who is responsible ultimately for restoring Limena to her mother,
when she urges Limena's lover, Perissus, to keep searching for her rather than
succumbing to the passivity of despair.

Other examples of oppressive "fatherly authoritie" (207) surface throughout the romance, as when one father binds his daughter to his will by choosing
to "shut her up in a Towre, wherein he then kept (in her) his choisest Treasure,
till this day of her Marriage" (36). Even when the father is absent or dead, the
father's house can function as a site of imprisonment. In one series of episodes,
the queen Meriana is taken captive by an unsuccessful suitor and displayed on
the top of the palace with her head cut off and placed on a pillar. When her
lover, Rosindy, breaks into the palace to recover her dead body, he hears her
voice, and discovers her to be walled up but still alive. It turns out that
Meriana's captor had appropriated for his own use a "counterfeting device"
which he found in the palace, described as a pillar big enough to stand up in,
but appearing made to hold a head upon, and created "by her father, a man ex-
cellently graced in all arts, and especially in prospectives" (133). The device of
showing an apparently decapitated female head serves as a deliberate twist on
the Sidnean episode in which Cecropia makes a false display of Philoclea's
head in a bloody basin before Pyrocles, in revenge for Philoclea's refusal to love
Cecropia's son, Amphialus (NA, 563). Wroth transforms Sidney's possessive
mother-figure into a possessive male lover who is using a device designed by
the heroine's father, thus rewriting the threat of excessive maternal "fondnes"
to convey instead the oppressive effects of masculine lust conjoined with paternal devices of containment.

In writing against the effects of fatherly authority, Wroth encodes within
her text direct references to the influential father-figures in her own life. After
Urania's first lover, Parselius, abandons her to marry Dalinea, he sees a vision
of Urania in a dream, and explains to his wife that he must temporarily leave
her because "hee saw all Arcadia on fire, the earth flaming, and in the mid'st
his father burning, who with lamentable cryes demanded helpe of him" (125).
As Jeff Masten has pointed out, Wroth here stages the burning of "Arcadia"—
not simply the country but Philip Sidney's text as well—within a context that
exposes male inconstancy, while consigning a "father" to the same flames.
Masten further suggests that Parselius's subsequent reference to his wife with
the phrase "shee, deare shee," borrowed from the opening sonnet of *Astrophil
and Stella*, constructs male-authored sonnet discourse as "inauthentic, feigned
invention with particular and devastating effects for the constant women who
are its objects."[90] Certainly the exposure of Parselius at this point conveys the
inadequacy of fatherly authority to cover for male inconstancy.

Subsequently, however, when Urania is happily matched with Steriamus and Parselius proves faithful to his wife, Wroth seems less concerned to
focus upon male inconstancy or even, in oppositional terms, upon her uncle's
and father's texts, than to stake out a new center of discursive authority within
her own text, based upon specifically female as well as familial bonds.[91] In the
manuscript continuation of *Urania*, when Parselius arrives in the course of his

travels at Tempe, he compares the landscape favorably with literary descriptions of Arcadia: "[Poets] in their olde fictions doe most strangely rave on the desarts, and rarenesses of the pleasant Arcadia, butt to mee this seemes as pleasing, rare, and farr more delightfull because more richly stored with Varieties" (II: fol. 3v). No longer preoccupied with "burning" her uncle's text, Wroth can assert the "Varieties" of her own text to be "farr more delightfull" than "olde fictions" of Arcadia.

Before considering the familial bonds linking the major female protagonists in Wroth's narrative, I would like to examine several subplots involving familial bonds which problematize maternal authority and subjectivity, and which can serve as reference points for an examination of the configurations of maternity in the main plot. These subplots attest in even more extreme terms than those represented by Cary to the discursive instability and discontinuity which attended women's attempts to mediate among competing discourses of domestic authority in early modern English society. In Wroth's depiction of one domestic quarrel, for example, "the father tooke part with the Son in law, the Mother with the Daughter; to that extremity this flew, as no fire flamed or sparkled higher" (438-39). The "burning" here divides the family not along generational lines, but rather along gender lines, with the mother taking her daughter's part in an effort to preserve her daughter's "spirit, that disdaind to be curbd." In an act of discursive violation with sexual connotations, the daughter's husband breaks open his wife's "Cabinets" in a futile attempt to find evidence of infidelity in her letters (439). But when the father takes up a dagger to "kill his daughter, and so cut off the blame, or spot, this her offence might lay upon his noble bloud," the husband intervenes unexpectedly as "the shield of her defence," evidently preferring to reserve exclusive penetration rights for himself (439). The narrative concludes with mention of the fruit of that penetration in the form of two children, with the wife's death following immediately thereafter. In the absence of the wife, accompanied by the silent disappearance from the text of her mother, the children are raised by the husband and his father-in-law, whose combined "fatherly authority" appears to have succeeded in curbing the "spirit" of the women in this instance after all.

An even more troubling representation of the potential conflict between maternal and erotic bonds surfaces in a story of two lovers who seek the support of a woman who is at once "Mother to the youth, and Governesse to the Princesse" (443). When they hail her as "a mother, and a friend to love," her repetition of their phrase in her response at once inverts and sexualizes the conventional discourse of maternity: "A friend to love, cryd the old woman, and a mother? 'Tis true I am both, and they have brought my miserie" (445). In admitting to a sexuality that has resulted in a violation of social norms, this mother constructs herself in a rhetoric as monstrous as that to be found in the most misogynist of the male-authored polemical tracts:

> I blush in foule guiltinesse, I mourne in the knowledge of my sinne, I am more faulty then ever woman was, and a meere staine to my sexe: you cannot, my dearest heart, enjoy this Lady, nor you (sweet Lady) have your love: I am the Monster that keepes the gates against you, and the Serpent that deserves death from you for double injury. . . . I am the ground brought forth this poyson; wonder not, but shun me as the Pestilence. I am not to bee neerer suffer'd then the Plague; for such I am to you, to you (deare two) the life of my poore life: the reson of all this was love, and your love by this sinfull love is cross'd; you are, poore soules, deceiv'd and couzened; turne your affections now to chaste and just desires, for you are (ah that I must say so) Brother and Sister, children to one man.   [446]

The mother here assumes all the guilt, both for the act of "sinfull love" which led to the birth of a child out of wedlock, and for the narrowly averted incest between her children. In naming herself monster, serpent, pestilence, and plague, she defines herself not in terms of her passion for a man, but rather in terms of her failure as a mother who has brought injury to her children. Thus her declaration that she is "more faulty then ever woman was" reflects her perception of the destructive effects of her sexuality upon her maternity.

Viewed in light of Irigaray's observation that when women allow themselves to be subjected to a hierarchical choice between erotic and maternal functions they accede both to the objectification imposed by a desiring male subject and to a masculine ideology of reproduction,[92] this mother in Wroth's narrative can be seen to bear witness to the destructive potential of such an ideology of reproduction for maternal subjectivity. Significantly, while the mother's death immediately after her confession and burial by her son is shortly followed by the deaths of both lovers, consumed by grief, the father in question maintains his position of honor as a prince, and sees to a stately burial for his children without being touched by any blame. Wroth's own experience of social ostracization associated at least in part with the illegitimate children she bore her cousin, by contrast to William Herbert's secure position at court, provides a historical frame of reference for her inscription of the vexed relation between maternity and sexuality, which can be conjoined with Irigaray's psychoanalytic frame.

In counterbalance to the many subplots in which tyrannical fathers subject their daughters to unhappy betrothals, and mothers accede to patriarchal objectification or oppression, Wroth represents the familial bonds among the major female protagonists in unusually supportive terms, including a number of strong maternal figures as well as several illegitimate children who are accepted by their extended families rather than associated with maternal shame or failure.[93] One of the strongest bonds which emerges over the course of the narrative is that between Pamphilia and her widowed aunt, the queen of Naples, who is at once "her most honord friend" (314) and the "matchlesse" mother of Amphilanthus (316). Margaret Hannay has convincingly noted the likenesses between the fictional queen of Naples and the actual countess of Pembroke—Mary Wroth's aunt and the mother of her sometime lover, William Herbert—which include the description of the queen of Naples as "rare in Poetry" (415-16).[94] Wroth emphasizes not simply the affection between the two women, but even more importantly their shared freedom of speech: "No time was lost betweene them, for each minute was fild with store of wit, which passed betweene them, as grounds are with shadowes where people walke: and the longer they discoursed still grew as much more excellent, as they, to nightward seeme longer" (316). The strength of this surrogate mother-daughter bond resides in their discourse, which reflects their positions as speaking subjects even as shadows upon the ground reflect the positions of their bodies. This emphasis upon the empowering potential of feminine discourse distinguishes the maternal bonds in the main plot from those in the subplots discussed above, where mothers are silenced or "smothered" by a masculine ideology of reproduction. Wroth expands upon Pamphilia's closeness to both her mother and her aunt in the course of the narration of Pamphilia's wedding to Rodomandro, king of Tartaria. Even as Pamphilia's mother takes her aside for a supportive conversation during the days preceding the wedding (II: fol. 19), so the queen of Naples assists Pamphilia during the wedding ceremony itself (II: fol. 22v), in an echo of the assistance provided Mary Wroth by her own mother and aunt in preparation for her wedding to Robert Wroth. Furthermore, when the queen of Naples becomes aware of the prior bond between her niece and her son, she takes the opportunity to let the two remain in contact after Pamphilia's wedding, and remains close to Pamphilia herself (II: fol.23v). As Barbara Lewalski has pointed out, Wroth's representation of intergenerational bonds fostered particularly by the sympathy and agency of women extends into the next generation when Pamphilia takes over the maternal role of her aunt in offering aid and counsel to her own niece and nephew.[95]

The queen of Naples, of course, turns out to be not only the mother of Amphilanthus, but the long-lost mother of Urania as well, and her bond with her own daughter proves as significantly enduring, once recognized, as that with her niece. In the manuscript continuation of the romance, Wroth describes the union of Urania and Steriamus, where "blessed with many children they thought fitt to looke to the breeding of them, and soe resolved to send their eldest daughter to her grandmother the brave and discreet queen of

Naples" (I: fol. 8). The mother-daughter connection, which was broken when Urania was not raised by her mother, can now be restored by her decision to allow her mother to "looke to the breeding" of her own daughter. Over time, the queen of Naples receives several other grandchildren and great- nieces and nephews into her charge, becoming the central matriarchal figure in the romance.

Even as Pollock's review of early modern diaries, memoirs, autobiogra- phies, and letters suggests that most parents were acutely aware of and con- cerned for their children, so Houlbrooke's analysis of familial structures mentions that children of upper-class parents were often sent to live with their grandparents when quite small.[96] The children in Wroth's narrative are simi- larly sent away for care, but significantly entrusted not to "grandparents" or "kindred" in general, but rather to the explicitly female authority of the queen of Naples, whose maternity is not subsumed or erased by any parallel figure of fatherly authority. In Wroth's own culture, Crawford documents the extent to which "women enjoyed sharing in the care of their grandchildren, and wrote with pleasure of their grandchildren's activities," and observes that "it was in old age, especially as grandmothers, that wealthier women enjoyed most social respect."[97] By contrast to the familial dynamics encoded in many of the domes- tic treatises, which surface in *Love's Victory* or in some of the *Urania* subplots, moreover, the queen of Naples's authority over her children and grand- children is not compromised by any relics of her late husband's will.

At the same time, the vulnerability of this idealized domestic hierarchy to social disruption becomes evident when several of the royal children are captured en route to the court of the queen of Naples.[98] Over the course of the manuscript continuation of the narrative, although many male knights at- tempt to rescue the children, culminating at long last in the predictable suc- cess of Amphilanthus (II: fol. 65v), the children are protected and preserved in the meantime by yet another figure of female power, the wise Melissea. Lewalski suggests that Melissea's much-enhanced role in the second part of the manuscript "substitutes in the supernatural realm for the powerful female protectors children are seen to need in the dangerous passage to adulthood but may no longer readily find," concluding that Melissea "presents a fantasy of female agency exercising beneficial control."[99] I would add that the "bene- ficial control" attributed to both the unmarried Melissea and the widowed queen of Naples may be seen to represent the potential for a female agency specifically unfettered by the oppressive patriarchal authority which blocks the speech and actions of some of the "victimized" mothers and daughters in the subplots, as well as the female figures in a text such as Cary's *Mariam*.

Even as Urania and Pamphilia are able to look to Melissea and the queen of Naples in fashioning empowering positions for themselves as women, so their own positions, as mentioned earlier, provide models of authority for the next generation. The centrality of Urania's role in particular, not only as the title character of the romance, but also as a maternal model of authority and subjectivity, becomes evident when her children as well as her nieces and nephews reflect upon her position in determining their own. Writing against yet another strong paternal figure, Wroth borrows the names of characters from *The Winter's Tale*, with slight alterations, only to radically revise the operative familial dynamics of Shakespeare's plot. The betrothal of the "shepherdess" daughter of the ruler Leonius and the young prince Floristello thus recalls the betrothal of the "shepherdess" daughter of Shakespeare's Leontes and the young prince Florizel. In Wroth's romance, however, it is the present friendship of the young lovers' mothers which contextualizes their bond, by contrast to the past rivalry of the lovers' fathers which contextualizes the bond in *The Winter's Tale*. Wroth's "lost shepherdess," Lindavera, is the daughter not only of Leonius but more significantly of Veralinda, whose name as well as identity complement those of her daughter, while the prince Floristello is the son of Urania. The friendship between these two female protagonists influences their children, as well as other characters, far more directly than do the roles played by their husbands.

Floristello, for example, reflects upon the pastoral appearance of his beloved in relation to the example of his mother, observing: "yett why may she oh why may shee nott bee other, her spiritt is as high as an Emperess; was nott my mother a sheapherdes, yes, and the fairest, loveliest Urania" (I: fol. 32). With further reference to his mother, Floristello resolves to love this seeming shepherdess apart from her potential to "bee other" than she appears, even as Urania was first loved for her worth rather than for her class or family position. At the same time, Lindavera justifies her right to give voice to her love for Floristello, despite her humble appearance, by considering that "Urania, the beautie and wonder of the world for worthe, was butt a shepherdese as I ame in showe when Steriamus first loved her, when Parselius first loved her . . . I may bee as great as shee" (I: fol. 37). Veralinda's daughter proceeds to live up to her mother's assertion that a woman can "bee the Emperess of the world, comaunding the Empire of [her] own minde" (I: fol. 40v), by her confident discourse with Urania's son.

Where Shakespeare's plays, as discussed earlier, often address conflict with fathers in the absence of mothers, Wroth refigures that familial dynamic in her own work to emphasize connections both with and of mothers. This is not to say that the bonds between mothers and daughters in Wroth's narrative remain free of tension, as the problematizing of maternal authority in many of the subplots indicates. Rather, the variety of dysfunctional families depicted in the subplots exposes the potentially disabling effects of patriarchal authority upon women in the domestic hierarchy, even as do Cary's representations of competing maternal figures. At the same time, Wroth moves beyond the reactive boundaries of Cary's text, in which women are defined primarily by their relations to men, in order to forge a framework of female-authored discourse more akin to the subtly polemical stance of the mothers' advice books, in which women are enabled to claim voices of authority over the next generation. Even as Rose characterizes the discursive strategy of the mothers' advice books as extending from "self-cancellation" through death to "self-presentation" as authoritative agents, so Wroth juxtaposes maternal self-cancellation in her subplots with a striking measure of self-presentation among her major female protagonists. In restoring to mothers not only a discourse of their own, but also a significant influence upon the emergent subjectivity of their offspring, Wroth's narrative can productively be viewed, then, both in contrast to the "paternal" models offered by a plethora of male-authored texts, and in direct relation to the texts of other "author-mothers," from Elizabeth Cary to Dorothy Leigh.

Margaret Homans has questioned if and when it is possible to stop excluding and killing the mother for the sake of representation's projects, and whether "the mother and the linguistic practices she and her daughters share, tainted as they are by the patriarchal culture with which they are intertwined and by which they come into being, [can] be recuperated for gynocentric, perhaps even for feminist projects."[100] With more specific reference to the cultural discourses of early modern England, Mary Beth Rose has suggested that "once construed in the 'public' rhetoric of authority, as well as in the 'private' vocabulary of nurture and desire, motherhood presents a test case for female power."[101] The many instances of mother-daughter bonds evidenced in female-authored texts in early modern England, ranging from the unpublished diaries and correspondence of aristocratic women to the published mothers' advice books, from Lanyer's poetry and Cary's play to the biography of Cary by her daughter, produce, collectively, a multitude of discourses on maternity. As a test case for female power, motherhood cannot maintain easy victory in such texts, but mothers and daughters can and do begin to claim voices of their own.

The nascent maternal subjectivity that underlies *Pamphilia to Amphilanthus* and emerges into the open in *Love's Victory* proves central to the shared linguistic practices of mothers and daughters, aunts and nieces, in *Urania*. Published the year that Wroth's mother died, and alluding on its title page to Wroth's bond with her author-aunt, the countess of Pembroke, Wroth's *Urania* offers many compelling examples not simply of paternal tyranny but also of maternal power. By juxtaposing oppressive instances of fatherly authority with the frequently liberating effects of maternal presence, in figures ranging from the queen of Naples to Urania herself, Mary Wroth re-presents the absent, dead, malevolent, or merely incompetent mothers who haunt the texts of her paternal forebears as speaking subjects in their own right, whose maternal authority is able to empower shared female discourse. In some instances of maternal discourse, Wroth moves beyond the purview of her female contemporaries as well, in conjoining a private rhetoric of authority within the family with a public vocabulary of nurture and desire within the state. As ruling mothers, then, Wroth's major female protagonists inhabit a state of maternity which, far from being restricted to sexual reproduction, works to authorize the emergent subjectivity of each successive generation. At the same time, as the next chapter will indicate, the gendering of authority within the family can operate to shift the balance of sexual power within the state as well.

4

Sovereign Subject

The Politics of Gender

The ambivalence about female independence which marks the debate over women's roles during the reign of King James suggests the presence of deep-seated anxieties regarding women's cultural authority, which can be traced, at least in part, to the double-edged politics of gender in the Jacobean court. Against James's proclamations of the theoretical bases for his masculine authority must be balanced the challenges to that authority in practice on the part of women, from Queen Anne to Lady Anne Clifford, and from Esther Sowernam to "Hic Mulier." Although instructed to remain chaste, silent, and above all obedient, Jacobean women can be found who ignore at least the latter two injunctions in the attempt to voice not their subjection, but rather their gendered subjectivity. Furthermore, those women whose writings threatened the normative social order of female subordination could refer at least implicitly back to the gynecocratic rhetoric of Queen Elizabeth, which performed the successful balancing act of combining the discourses of both subject and monarch, woman and ruler. James's reliance upon the singular discourses of patriarch and king produced, by contrast, a vacuum of power constantly in danger of collapsing in upon itself in the face of the disregard of assertive female subjects.

The problematically doubled positions of Elizabeth I and Anne of Denmark as both queens and women served to a certain extent to enable the emergent voices of some of their female subjects, even as the queens' exceptional standing in their societies underscored the discursive limitations remaining for those who could not speak as both subject and sovereign. For Mary Wroth and peers such as Anne Clifford, for example, the court society surrounding James I and Anne of Denmark provided an arena for political action which was admittedly shaped by a backlash against women in the wake of Elizabeth's powerful reign, but which nevertheless offered an opportunity to engage in the social plays for power that defined the politics of gender in upper-class circles. Writing under a misogynist king who proclaimed the absolute authority of the monarch while himself remaining under the shadow of the powerful gynecocracy of his predecessor, and writing as well in response to the alternative configurations of courtly power associated with Anne of

Denmark's circle of female confidantes, women such as Anne Clifford and
Aemilia Lanyer, Elizabeth Cary and Mary Wroth used their own strategic discourses of sovereignty to assert their positions as speaking subjects despite, or
in some cases because of, their political marginalization.

In her works, Mary Wroth responds to the examples of the two female
sovereigns, under whom she was born and in whose court she participated,
and to the constructions of sovereignty in the works of other female authors, as
well as to the representations of female rule by male authors ranging from
King James and Philip Sidney to Spenser and Shakespeare. Wroth works not
to split the figure of the female sovereign into exemplary or monstrous types,
as did some of her male contemporaries, so much as to multiply the possibilities for sovereignty within women's discourse. At the same time, extending the
configurations of female sovereignty provided by women authors such as Cary
and Lanyer, Wroth critiques the gendered play of power in courtly circles
through her own representations of the discursive relations between gynecocracy and gynecology, sovereignty and sexuality, authority and subjectivity.

Luce Irigaray contends that "every operation on and in philosophical
language, by virtue of the very nature of that discourse—which is essentially
political—possesses implications that, no matter how mediate they may be, are
nonetheless politically determined." Consequently, Irigaray poses the question
of whether or not a "woman's politics" is possible within "an order prescribed
by the masculine." Only when a "woman's politics" works not simply to re-
distribute the power, but rather to challenge the forms and nature of political
life, the contemporary play of powers and power relations, Irigaray maintains,
can it begin to modify women's status within the culture. Irigaray's juxtaposition of "the power of discourse" and "the subordination of the feminine"
suggests further that only when a "woman's politics" succeeds in deconstructing the apparent "sexual indifference" of a culture's discourses to reveal the
deeply gendered bias ingrained within that culture's structures of power can
the "specificity" of feminine discourses begin to be heard.[1] Although Irigaray
focuses upon the language of twentieth-century psychoanalysis, her question
about the possible existence, let alone survival, of a "woman's politics" might
also be posed with regard to the cultural discourses of early modern England.
When the apparent "sexual indifference" of the most public of such discourses
is examined in relation to the gendered structures of power within which those
discourses are voiced, a pervasive sexual bias is revealed.

In early modern England, the possibility of a "woman's politics" must be considered first in relation to the female monarch who presided over her culture's
structures of power for over four decades, which included the first seventeen
years of Mary Wroth's life. Certainly the politics of gender in both the Elizabethan and Jacobean periods was deeply shaped by the presence and legacy

not simply of a woman on the throne, but of a woman ruler who was able to command her male subjects through adept use of her society's discourses of sexual difference in the face of resistance and even opposition. Indeed, in the very year of Queen Elizabeth's accession, John Knox published his treatise condemning gynecocracy, *The First Blast of the Trumpet Against the Monstrous Regiment of Women* (1558), in which he asserts that female rule is contrary to Nature, an insult to God, and finally "the subversion of good Order."[2] Elizabeth's presence on the throne consequently signified to Knox and his supporters the ultimate violation of what Irigaray has termed "an order prescribed by the masculine." At the same time, John Knox's "blast" found a response in two unpublished manuscripts by Henry Howard, earl of North-ampton—one entitled "The Dutifull Defense of the Lawful Regiment of Women"—which not only supported the legitimacy of women rulers, but fur-ther argued that "women weare endowed with reason which is the rule of gov-ernment as wel as men, that they had equal dominion over creatures, that possession was given to both."[3] An important question to consider in relation to a political climate thus riven with controversy is whether the implications of Elizabeth's sovereignty for her female subjects were limited to a simple re-distribution of power, or posed a more deep-seated challenge to the contem-porary play of powers and power relations.

A number of critical essays on Elizabeth over the past decade have dis-cussed the effects of her rule upon the male courtiers who surrounded her and, in many cases, authored representations of her figure as queen.[4] Although crit-ics such as Allison Heisch have treated the queen as an "honorary male" whose speeches only underscore her extraordinary position, more recent studies probe the gendered implications of Elizabeth's strategies of power.[5] Both Leah Marcus and Theodora Jankowski, for example, read the self-presentation of Elizabeth's speeches in relation to Renaissance dramatic re-presentations of the queen, while Mary Thomas Crane and Susan Frye attend to the tensions informing Elizabeth's relation to a wide range of "subjects," both within and outside the immediate circles of the court.[6] Focusing more specifically upon Elizabeth's significance for sixteenth- and seventeenth-century women au-thors, Lisa Gim examines texts about Elizabeth I by Anne Bradstreet, Bathsua Makin, and Marie Catherine d'Aulnoy. Gim argues that, unlike contemporary male authors of royal panegyrics, these women authors stress specifically trans-gressive behavior, and concludes that Elizabeth provided women with a recog-nizable representation of gender transgression in her discursive power as a writer, speaker, and poet, as well as in her political agency.[7] My own analysis of Wroth's discursive relation to the figures not only of Elizabeth I, but also of James I, and James's wife, Anne of Denmark, attends to the gendered politics of "sovereign subjects" in early modern England, in order to examine both the constraining and the enabling effects of these royal models upon Wroth's extensive representations of female sovereignty in both political and personal terms.

From the first, with her speech to Parliament in the year of her accession concerning the issue of marriage, Elizabeth I played on the politics of gender in claiming authority for her discourse. Declaring that she had made her own "choice of a husband, the kingdom of England," Elizabeth reminded the members of Parliament that every one of them "and every Englishman besides, are my children."[8] Even as the prescribed subordination of wives to husbands was transformed by this "wife's" proclamation of her choice as her own, so the authority of maternity allowed this virgin "mother" to remind her "children" that her word, in effect, was law. Almost ten years later, still addressing the issue of marriage and succession, Elizabeth asserted the possibility of female autonomy, both in connection with and distinction from gynecocracy: "I am your anointed Queen. I will never be by violence constrained to do anything. I thank God I am endued with such qualities that if I were turned out of the realm in my petticoat I were able to live in any place in Christendom."[9] Whether in crown or petticoat, whether anointed queen or exposed woman, whether defined by gynecocracy or gynecology, Elizabeth maintained her sovereignty as a speaking subject, who would "never be by violence constrained to do anything." While simply making that claim did not release Elizabeth from the gendered constraints of her culture, her juxtaposition of the "sexually indifferent" language of political autonomy with the implicitly sexualized discourse of a woman clothed only in a petticoat served to re-gender the politics of discourse from a woman's point of view.

Throughout her reign, the queen reminded her subjects not only that the gendered frailty of her body coexisted with the enduring authority of a monarch—"I know I have the body but of a weak and feeble woman, but I have the heart and stomach of a king, and of a king of England too"—but also that she could speak the language of both subject and sovereign: "I have known what it is to be a subject, and I now know what it is to be a sovereign."[10] Instead of wholly relinquishing the private for the public sphere, replacing subjection with sovereignty, Elizabeth learned as a female monarch to move in both worlds, to speak in both languages. Furthermore, although her position as sovereign subject remained unique to her person, her discourse provided subsequent women authors with a model of the balancing act required of a woman of power speaking within "an order prescribed by the masculine."[11] If the play of powers and power relations in Elizabeth's court responded more to a "monarch's politics" than to a "woman's politics," nevertheless the success of her gynecocracy shaped the possibilities not just for Renaissance dramatists, but for women speakers who were not rulers in early modern England as well. For Anne Clifford and Aemilia Lanyer, Elizabeth Cary and Mary Wroth, the discursive self-fashioning of Queen Elizabeth served to a limited but nevertheless significant extent to authorize their own voices both implicitly and explicitly even after her reign was over. Despite the social gap that accompanied their subjection to her sovereignty, women authors could define themselves not simply as subjected bodies but also as speaking subjects in relation to Elizabeth's feminization of the monarch's position.

The speeches of King James, on the other hand, attempted to dismantle the gendered implications of his female predecessor's power by focusing attention less on the singular woman who ruled before him than on women in general as sexual bodies needing to be ruled. James was concerned to emphasize not successes of gynecocracy, in other words, but rather weaknesses of gynecology. Even in his writings during Elizabeth's reign, James characterized the drawbacks of female rule in sexualized rather than politicized terms, describing the legacy of the king his grandfather as a "double curse . . . to the land," because his heir was a "Woman of sexe, and a new borne babe of age."[12] Subsequently in the same piece of writing, *Basilikon Doron*, James revealed his tendency to estimate women's capabilities as a function of their bodies, in advising his son to "choose your Wife as I advised you to choose your servants . . . For if a man wil be careful to breed horses and dogs of good kinds, how much more careful should he be, for the breede of his owne loines?"[13] Servants, horses, dogs, and women could all be put to bodily use from James's point of view, with little regard for the spiritual "helpmeet" view of wedlock propounded in contemporary marriage treatises.

In *The Trew Law of Free Monarchies* (1598), James expounded upon the "reciprock and mutuall duetie" between a king and his subjects in politically gendered terms, warning, for example, against the "Sirene songs" of rebellion.[14] Far from being "sexually indifferent," then, James's discourse was explicitly misogynous. His repeated insistence upon his role as "father" of his subjects can be read, at least in part, as a reactionary response to Elizabeth's assertion of maternal authority over her own subjects ever since her accession to the throne of England forty years earlier. Although James initially applied the label of "mother" to the "commonwealth," he proceeded to compare a commonwealth in a state of rebellion to "an undaunted young horse that hath casten his rider," effecting a transposition of maternity and horses which once again cast women, even when used as metaphors, at the bottom of the political hierarchy.[15]

At the time of his own accession to the throne of England, James reversed Elizabeth's matrimonial metaphor to assert: "I am the Husband, and all the whole Isle is my lawfull Wife."[16] One effect of James's rhetoric here is to feminize the kingdom itself, problematically supplanting and regendering the Petrarchan discourse of his predecessor's court, so that his male courtiers bear an unsettlingly feminine relation to his authority which seems to require the legitimation implicit in James's use of the term "lawfull." At other moments, however, James's language serves paradoxically to feminize his own position. Stephen Orgel has suggested, for example, that in James's refiguration of the monarch's position "mothers became unnecessary," because the father-king could supply all the "nourish-milk."[17] Yet in attempting to control women by "incorporating" them, James allowed the politics of gender to undermine the fatherly authority of his discourse. In effect, James metaphorically re-gendered his kingly body in order to supply an implicit gynecological lack, while actually only underscoring his distance from his predecessor's successful gynecocracy. Given that Elizabeth, as Marcus points out, was becoming a powerful political symbol in Jacobean London, James's rhetoric of fatherly authority can be viewed as disclosing the implicit instability of the domestic hierarchy it was concerned to invoke.[18]

In focusing upon James I as "the articulate and visible center of society," the supreme figure of authority for his culture, Goldberg discusses how James's attacks on women exhibit "strategies of discursive power . . . that *ensure* the monarch's freedom and truth" (italics mine). Although Goldberg himself acknowledges in his general discussion of family portraiture that "behind patriarchal and filial assertions loom vast maternal powers," he nevertheless concludes that both in the example of James and in "the politics of family life" in general, "fatherly authority reigns supreme."[19] In any example of attempted appropriation, however, there is the danger that the consumer may find himself consumed. Indeed, when James's "strategies of discursive power" are examined in relation to those of Elizabeth, his attacks on women seem able less to "ensure" his position than to expose his own anxiety about his lack of female powers, while his "second body" begins to appear less like that of God's lieutenant than like a hermaphroditic shadow of the powerful figure of the queen.

In her historical analysis of the use of familial metaphors in early modern discussions of political and social order, Amussen notes that the multiplicity of available models resists the imposition of any single conception of authority. If the family was a little commonwealth, Amussen points out, the governor of the larger one might be viewed from differing perspectives as father, husband, or master, with relative rather than absolute authority in each sphere.[20] One effect of James's representation of the "maternal" aspects of his fatherly authority thus is to call up the specter of the "vast maternal powers" of his predecessor which he was so concerned to resist. Scrutinized from this angle, the defensive rhetoric of James's speeches gives some indication that the royal patriarch was engaged in a discursive struggle against the absorbing force of Elizabeth's gynecocratic creativity.

For all the attention that literary critics have paid to the figures of Queen Elizabeth and King James, there has been less discussion of the court of Queen Anne, which provided an alternative model of female authority during James's own reign. The court controversy engendered by the writings of Mary Wroth, which previously has been discussed primarily with reference to a court viewed as singular and self-contained, thus must be examined in relation to a much wider range of cultural trends both within and outside the competing "courts" of the period.

Leeds Barroll makes a convincing case for the importance of the court of Anne of Denmark, "the first Stuart queen," in providing political opportunities for advancement to a number of ambitious and talented women. Barroll's examination of the "vastly underestimated new court of the Queen Consort" in the early years of James's reign draws attention to her establishment of a formal structure for a concentrated network of patronage in the arts, which counterbalanced James's own literary influence. Lucy, countess of Bedford, was one of the most powerful noblewomen in what Barroll terms the "Essex group" (named for courtiers associated with the late earl), which played a central role in arts patronage in Queen Anne's court.[21] Other members of the group included Robert Sidney, Mary Wroth's father, who became the queen's Lord High Chamberlain; William Herbert, earl of Pembroke, Mary Wroth's lover, who became the king's Lord Chamberlain and Master of Revels; Susan de Vere, one of Mary Wroth's closest friends and the dedicatee of *Urania*, who married William Herbert's younger brother Philip, and was a great favorite of Queen Anne; the countess of Rutland, Mary Wroth's cousin and Philip Sidney's daughter; Barbara Sidney, Mary Wroth's mother and a good friend of the well-placed countess of Bedford; and, not least, Mary Wroth herself, whose close connections with court circles thus extended, through friends and family, beyond the hostile reaction provoked in King James's court by the publication of *Urania* in 1621.

The oppositional tensions marking the relations between Queen Anne's court and the court of King James receive particular attention in Barbara Lewalski's analysis of the ways in which the masques and entertainments that the queen produced or sponsored affirmed the worth of women. Lewalski argues that Queen Anne's choice of favorites and close friends was grounded as much in oppositional politics as personal attraction, and concludes that Queen Anne's court was perceived as a "separate female community," marginalized yet powerful.[22] The writings of some of the women in these competing courtly circles indeed testify both to the social constraints and the discursive challenges associated with women's voices in upper-class circles. In some instances, the politics of gender served to deconstruct the established parameters of courtly power relations along lines of sexual difference.

When Lady Anne Clifford, for example, records in her diary her impressions of the accession of King James and the funeral of Queen Elizabeth, the latter significantly takes precedence over the former. After devoting a couple of sentences to the "peaceable coming-in of the King," Clifford turns to the

funeral ceremonies for the queen. She describes in some detail the participation of her mother and aunt in these ceremonies, which included sitting
up at night beside the queen's corpse at Whitehall, and attending the funeral
procession to Westminster. For her own part, Clifford observes that she was
not allowed to participate "because I was not high enough, which did much
trouble me then, but yet I stood in the church at Westminster to see the so-
lemnities performed."[23] At the age of thirteen, Clifford mourns the passing of
the queen and takes note of the attendance of the prominent women of the
realm upon that passage.

Fourteen years later, Clifford records her own interaction with Queen
Anne as well as King James over the business of her disputed family lands.
As J.P. Sommerville has noted in his study of politics and ideology in early
modern England, property held a central position in the debate on "the liberties of the subject" under James. At issue in Clifford's case, furthermore, were
the "liberties" of the female subject, so that the face-off between "absolute
royal power" and "absolute property," to use Sommerville's terms, was a gendered conflict in the political arena.[24] When Anne Clifford and her husband
had an audience with the king on 18 January 1617, James requested that they
"put the whole matter wholly into his hands." Although her husband consented, Clifford herself refused to yield any ground, literally, to the king: "I
beseech'd His Majesty to pardon me for that I would never part from Westmoreland while I lived upon any condition whatsoever. Sometimes he used
fair means and persuasions and sometimes foul means but I was resolved
before so as nothing would move me."[25]

Unawed by James's attempted display of fatherly authority, Clifford proceeded "to the Queen's side," where the advice that she received exposes the
operation of an active politics of gender within the court. Clifford's account of
the queen's "warning not to trust my matters absolutely to the king lest he
should deceive me"[26] suggests that James's "strategies of discursive power" over
women were not as effective after all as he might have wished, to the extent
that Queen Anne apparently felt free to undermine his authority by taking
"the woman's part" at court. At another audience two days later, Clifford continued to defy the king's discursive authority, observing: "The King asked us all
if we would submit to his judgment in this case. My Uncle Cumberland, my
Coz. Clifford, and my Lord answered they would, but I would never agree to it
without Westmoreland at which the King grew in a great chaff."[27] If James's
vaunted authority could be reduced by one woman to "a great chaff," the likelihood that similar episodes occurred, even if recounted only in the pages of
private diaries or between women, must not be discounted in attending to the
gendered politics of discourse within the culture.

As a close friend of Anne Clifford as well as a frequent participant in
court activities, Mary Wroth would likely have been privy to such episodes

among her acquaintances, in addition to her own dealings with the king and queen. Her husband, Robert Wroth, was knighted by James I in 1603, the year before they were married, and subsequently hosted the king's hunting expeditions quite frequently at Loughton Hall. James even appointed Robert Wroth as a riding forester, with the responsibility of leading the king's expeditions in search of game in the royal forest of Essex.[28] Like Anne Clifford, then, Mary Wroth was faced with an apparently difficult marriage to a favorite male courtier of the king. Also like Anne Clifford, Wroth turned to Queen Anne in seeking support for early petitions on the behalf of both herself and her husband that required the king's approval, before the publication of *Urania* during her widowhood resulted in James unequivocally taking the part of his male courtiers in expressing displeasure at Wroth's presumption as an author.[29] Even James's "kindness" to women of Wroth's circle can be seen to have been equivocal at best and objectifying in any event, as in the case of Wroth's sister-in-law, Dorothy, countess of Leicester, who wrote of her embarrassment to her husband after visiting the court: "In his Majestie I found an inclination to show me sume kindnes, but he could not finde the waie; at last he told me that he perseaved I was to kind to my husband, when he was with me, wich kept me leane, for he thought me much fatter then I use to be, this short speeche was worse to me then an absolute silence, for I blushed and was so extreamlie out of countance that all the companie laughed at me."[30]

Wroth's own position in Queen Anne's court ultimately proved unstable as well. After the death of her husband in 1614 and her son in 1616, Wroth was left in perilous financial circumstances, and lost her position in Queen Anne's intimate circle of ladies. Wroth's standing at court was further jeopardized by the successive births of her two illegitimate children by William Herbert, third earl of Pembroke, whose reputation for sexual dalliance was already well known.[31] With the death of Queen Anne in 1619, followed by the scandal associated with the publication of the first part of *Urania* in 1621, Wroth's public exclusion from court circles was assured, although she continued to maintain close ties with female friends such as Susan Herbert and Anne Clifford. Wroth's experience of the politics of gender within court circles can be seen to have shaped the representations of women as rulers and subjects in her works as surely as Clifford's encounters with James and Anne shaped the assertive entries in her diary.

The female authors of the polemical tracts demonstrate a related awareness of the relevance of examples of gynecocracy to the politics of gender in their society. Esther Sowernam, for example, refers to the example of Elizabeth, in suggesting that the queen's combination of gynecocracy and femininity produced not simply an exceptional woman, but a model for the masculine sex as well: "Elizabeth our late sovereign, not only the glory of our Sex, but a pattern for the best men to imitate."[32] Constantia Munda also celebrates "the forces of Gynaecia," calling men's attention less to women as models than to women as mothers, whose maternal authority implicitly authorizes masculine discourse itself.[33]

Whereas Sowernam and Munda foreground femininity in defending women, the Hic Mulier figure is attacked by the male author of the tract by that name for being too "masculine." King James himself had ordered his clergy to "inveigh vehemently in their sermons against the insolence of our women" dressed like men.[34] The *Hic Mulier* pamphleteer argues that since cross-dressing obscures the sexually unique features of women's bodies to such an extent that women can "*be* manlike not only from the head to the waist, but to the very foot and in every condition" (italics mine), this apparent "sexual indifference" poses a threat to the masculine structures of power in the culture.[35] In defense of Hic Mulier, the female author of *Haec-Vir* chooses to use the language not of gynecology but of sovereignty: "I was created free, born free, and live free; what lets me then so to spin out my time that I may die free?" "Hic Mulier" articulates a position for herself as a sovereign subject in thus asserting her ability to perform "all the rights and offices due to my Creation."[36] Even as Elizabeth proclaimed her autonomy as a speaking subject who "will never be by violence constrained to do anything," whether in crown or petticoat, so "Hic Mulier" defies the constraints of male (and kingly) authority in defending her right to cast aside her own petticoat should she so choose.

The connections between political and literary discourses in the courts of both Elizabeth and James produced gendered representations of authority and subjection which elide some of the boundaries between actual and fictive monarchs and subjects. In poetry, male-authored sonnet sequences have been treated as models for the power structure of the Elizabethan court in particular, representing acts of political courtship within a patronage system dependent on the queen or other female patrons.[37] Analysis of the politics of gender in these accounts tends both to originate and terminate with the voices of frustrated male courtiers, whose discourse is seen in large measure as a play for power and authority over an either actively or passively resistant female. The positions of male poets within the Jacobean court, by contrast, have been viewed almost entirely in relation to James alone, resulting in discussions of homosocial bonding and, more often, competition, under the rubric of patriarchal authority. Thus Jonathan Goldberg suggests that Jonson's poems, particularly "To Penshurst," admit the king into the text in order to present "an image of absolute totality, an inclusive fantasy of containment," so that ultimately "the poet's speech constitutes the truth of society" and his words "maintain the state." Marking the play for power among men in the absence of women as speaking subjects—an absence underscored by the emphatically reproductive fertility with which Jonson delimits Barbara Sidney's role in this poem addressed to her husband—fatherly authority once more reigns supreme, with "the truth" of society located in the "representative" voices and figures of Robert Sidney, Ben Jonson, and James I.[38]

When the poet is a woman, however, the play for patronage and the politics of gender acquire quite different resonances, underscoring the importance of viewing Mary Wroth's constructions of sovereignty in relation to the discourses of other women as well as men. Aemilia Lanyer, for example, actively solicits the patronage of a number of women in her *Salve Deus Rex Judaeorum*, from Queen Anne to Lady Anne Clifford. Furthermore, as discussed in the previous chapter, whereas the patronesses of male poets are cast predominantly as objects of heterosexual desire, Lanyer's patronesses emerge as maternal and filial subjects whose bonds with each other provide the basis for the poet's celebration of a "community of good women." Appropriately, then, Lanyer chooses to open *Salve Deus* with a dedicatory poem not to the king, but rather to "the Queenes most Excellent Majestie." Although unable to preside over a present gynecocracy, Queen Anne has, according to the terms of Lanyer's dedication, a gendered basis for her sovereignty over future generations of monarchs, of whom she is the "most gratious Mother." Lanyer specifically refers to the queen's sex in explaining the basis for the central portion of her poem:

> Behold, great Queene, faire Eves Apologie,
> Which I have writ in honour of your sexe,
> And doe referre unto your Majestie,
> To judge if it agree not with the Text:
>   And if it doe, why are poore Women blam'd,
>   Or by more faultie Men so much defam'd?
> ["To the Queenes most Excellent Majestie," 73-78]

Considering that the most prominent of the men responsible for defaming women in early modern England was James I himself, Lanyer's bold appeal to the queen's judgment fashions a direct line of communication between women which excludes the king, even as Anne Clifford's receipt of the queen's advice in the matter of her disputed lands strengthens her decision to disregard the king's authority. Furthermore, Lanyer represents her text as a mirror that reflects not just the authority but also the comfort and inspiration apparently provided her by the example of female sovereignty, when she identifies Queen Anne and Princess Elizabeth as the "glittring Suns" which grace her "Glasse" and reflect comfort to her "spirits" (97, 98, 101).

Just as Clifford records her mourning at the passing of Queen Elizabeth, so Lanyer observes that she herself lives "clos'd up in Sorrowes Cell, / Since great Elizaes favour blest my youth" (109-10). Even the favor of the present queen cannot erase the memory of the most powerful female of the age, described by Lanyer in the next dedicatory poem as "deare Mother of our Common-weale" ("To the Lady Elizabeths Grace," 7). The figure of Elizabeth I, at once subject and sovereign, becomes a mother-figure for all the commonwealth, and a model of female autonomy whose example Lanyer uses strategically to empower her own discourse on women. The representative conjunction of Queen Elizabeth, Queen Anne, and Princess Elizabeth thus forms a generationally spaced triumvirate of powerful royal women, notably unmarked by any references either to King James or to Prince Henry, whose death occurred in 1612, one year after the official publication of *Salve Deus Rex Judaeorum*.

In the actual verses of "Eves Apologie," as in her dedication to Queen Anne, Lanyer again refers to the judgment of the male ruler's wife over that of his own—in terms that anticipate Wroth's representations of ruling women in her play and prose romance—in appealing to Pontius Pilate to "heare the words of thy most worthy wife, / Who sends to thee, to beg her Saviours life" (*SDRJ*, 751-52). Lanyer argues that Eve's fault in "giving to Adam what shee held most deare" pales in light of Pilate's decision to condemn Christ to death, observing that "her sinne was small, to what you doe commit" (*SDRJ*, 764, 818). Consequently, Lanyer makes a striking case for equality between the sexes:

> Then let us have our Libertie againe,
> And challendge to your selves no Sov'raigntie;
> You came not in the world without our paine,
> Make that a barre against your crueltie;
> Your fault being greater, why should you disdaine
> Our beeing your equals, free from tyranny?
>   If one weake woman simply did offend,
>   This sinne of yours, hath no excuse, nor end.
> To which (poore soules) we never gave consent,
> Witnesse thy wife (O Pilate) speakes for all;   [*SDRJ*, 825-34]

In Lanyer's gendered reconfiguration of the politics of the crucifixion, Pilate's wife becomes a spokesperson for the innocence of all women, while the figure of Pilate, who chooses to disregard his wife's advice and betray the Savior, embodies the guilt of all men. Given this construction of gender relations, Lanyer points out that men have no basis for their claims of "Sov'raigntie" over women. Instead, Lanyer uses the language of sovereignty to argue for women's equality. Female sovereignty remains to be realized, later in the poem, in the figure of Mary, "deere Mother of our Lord" and "most beauteous Queene of Woman-kind," whose virginity guarantees that she is "from all men free"

(*SDRJ*, 1031, 1039, 1078). The eternal queen of womankind and the past queen of the commonwealth thus share through their virginity a common "Libertie" from male tyranny.

Subsequently, Lanyer celebrates sovereign agency in a list of famous women, from Deborah and Judith to the queen of Sheba, "whose glorious actions did appear so bright, / That powrefull men by them were overthrowne" (*SDRJ*, 1466-67). In a line that reflects the bent of the entire poem, Lanyer calls attention to the divine justice of "making the powrefull judged of the weake" (1536), suggesting that it is indeed by the judgment of worthy women, however marginalized within a patriarchal society, that "powrefull men" can be "overthrowne." Sovereignty and subjection thus can coexist within a female-authored representational frame. Lanyer's account of the queen of Sheba's meeting with Solomon, however, concedes no ground to superior fatherly authority, but rather maintains that "here Majestie with Majestie did meete, / Wisdome to Wisdome yeelded true content / One Beauty did another Beauty greet" (1585-87). By insisting that the countess of Cumberland "remaine[s] as Queene" (1557) in the midst of this catalogue of exceptional women, Lanyer authorizes her own position as speaking subject of this "Queene," whose sovereignty is underscored by her position as "Mistris" of the self-sufficient female community represented in "The Description of Cooke-ham."

Mary Wroth's poems engage the language of sovereignty not, as with Lanyer, in religious terms, but rather in relation to the play for power encoded in male-authored discourses of Petrarchism. At the same time, Lanyer's insistence upon the potential coexistence of subjection and sovereignty in examples not simply of exceptional women, but indeed of all women desiring "Libertie" from male "tyranny," aligns her strategic stance as a female author representing the politics of gender with that of Wroth. The discursive struggles to affirm the possibility of female agency and autonomy which mark *Pamphilia to Amphilanthus* have led Gary Waller to conclude that Wroth's sequence expresses "a masochism born of frustrated wishes to emulate the apparent freedom of men."[39] Viewing the poems as an exercise in failed Petrarchism, however, obscures the possibility that a female speaker may adopt another response to male authority than that of emulation. Ann Rosalind Jones argues, for example, that Wroth's poems were strategic attempts to put an end to her exclusion from James's court, and to resist her own disappearance into the categories of failed courtier and silenced woman.[40] Although Jones's argument is based on the assumption that Wroth's poems were written in response to her diminished standing in courtly circles after the death of her husband in 1614, their composition preceded (and perhaps contributed to) her more public ostracization after the publication of *Urania*, with the poems attached, in 1621.

As Catherine Gallagher has remarked, women's exclusion from political sub-jecthood can foster not merely efforts to achieve inclusion so much as re-visions of subjectivity in feminine terms.[41] When Wroth's sequence is viewed not as a masochistic emulation of male privilege nor as a reactionary attempt to regain favor at a male-dominated court, but rather as a revisionary assertion of emergent female subjectivity in a Petrarchan frame, then the apparently conflicting discourses of sovereignty and subjection within the sequence can be seen to reveal some of the conditions experienced by women as subjects in early modern England.

Both discourses come into play early in the sequence, in poems such as the sonnet acknowledging the speaker's conquest by Cupid: "Beehold I yeeld: lett forces bee dismist; / I ame thy subject, conquer'd, bound to stand" (P8). As discussed in chapter 2, Wroth's speaker here carves a speaking position from the very condition of subjection. Yet far from stopping at this acknowl-edgment of subjection, the speaker proceeds to proclaim her sovereignty over Cupid after all: "Yett this Sir God, your boyship I dispise; / Your charmes I obay, butt love nott want of eyes" (P8). Although constrained by the power of love, Pamphilia nevertheless refuses to demonstrate respect for Cupid's au-thority, even as Clifford left the king "in a chaff" at her similar disregard for his authority. While conventional discourses of Petrarchism place the male speaker in embattled conflict at once with Cupid and his beloved, the female speaker in Wroth's sequence maintains her autonomy even in subjection by distinguishing between Cupid and the object of her desire.

Furthermore, just as Clifford's departure from the king to repair to Queen Anne's side resulted in the strengthening of her inclination to disre-gard James's authority once possessing the support of the queen, so Pamphilia turns from addressing Cupid to addressing Night, whose maternal signifi-cance has already been discussed, and whom Jones has suggested may be a figure for Queen Anne herself.[42] Pamphilia is attracted to the feminine authority of Night on the basis of her "sad attire," which refuses to raise "some mens phant'sies higher" (P17), and thus remains free of what Lanyer termed the "tyranny" of male "Sov'raigntie." Female lovers can claim some degree of sovereignty even in subjection, then, by embracing sober attire, and refusing to make a play for power in the Petrarchan terms that define women as the sum of their blazoned attractions to "mens phant'sies."

The relevance of courtly power relations surfaces in Pamphilia's rejec-tion of the "pleasing pastimes" of hunting, "hauking," discourse, and music, which produce a false "daylike night" at court, thus robbing her of her compan-ion, Night (P26). In a subsequent sonnet, Pamphilia questions "What pleasure can a bannish'd creature have / In all the pastimes that invented arr," conclud-ing: "Noe, / I ame bannish'd, and no good shall find / Butt all my fortunes must with mischief bind / Who butt for miserie did gaine a birth" (P44). The ambiguous phrasing of the final line allows for at least two readings: one, that the speaker has gained a birth for misery alone, and alternatively, that the speaker could still gain a birth except for the blocking power of misery. The image of "gaining a birth" recalls the earlier sonnet on miscarriage, in which "faulce hope" proves "unatural to the birth" of its "owne wombe, conceaving butt to kill" (P40). Whereas the miscarriage sonnet inscribes the female speaker's recognition of the precarious subjectivity of the desiring woman, the "bannish'd creature" sonnet allows for the possibility that banishment—in other words, exclusion from political subjecthood—can lead, despite or even through misery, to the birth of a new position for a woman as a speaking subject. As Pamphilia observes in the following sonnet, "Who's us'd to sorrow, griefe will nott destroy" (P45). Instead, her discourse acquires authority from her suffering.

Masten maintains that Wroth uses Sonnets P26 and P44 to displace "public, male exhibition" with a discourse seeking to record a "private authenticity of feeling." On the other hand, as Jones points out, the political vocabulary of some of the poems works to stage the speaker's self-sufficiency as a public spectacle.[43] Occasionally, Pamphilia even voices the "private authenticity" of her suffering desire through the "public, male exhibition" associated with the position of the sovereign ruler. In the text of *Urania*, for example, Pamphilia reads aloud a sonnet written by another woman, in whose voice she identifies her own plight: "Had I not happy beene, I had not knowne / So great a losse, a King depos'd, feeles most / The torment of a Throne-like-want, when lost, / And up must looke to what late was his owne" (U33). The sonnet concludes with the question, "My Paradice of joy gone, doe I live?", to which Pamphilia replies: "Yes I doe live . . . but to what end?" (409). In identifying with a deposed king, Queen Pamphilia juxtaposes her political sovereignty with her subjection to passion, reimagining her personal loss in political terms. At the same time, her acceptance of the validity of another woman's discourse to convey the "private authenticity" of her own feelings distinguishes her subjectivity from the egocentric individuality of male Petrarchan sonneteers, each of whom insists upon the unique intensity of his particular condition. Finally, Pamphilia's affirmation that even in loss she still does "live" recalls the tone of Queen Elizabeth's assertion that even if she "were turned out of the realm in [her] petticoat," she would be able "to live in any place in Christendom."

"Bannish'd" by choice from courtly pastimes, identifying with the condition of a ruler turned out of the realm, Pamphilia nevertheless affirms that her suffering has not erased her subjectivity, but rather has multiplied her possibilities for expression. Pamphilia moves between the discourses of subjected lover and autonomous sovereign, adopting both public and private registers of diction, even as Queen Elizabeth combined the discourses of both subject and monarch, woman and ruler, in asserting her own self-sufficiency. The parallels between Pamphilia and Elizabeth I, which appear in even greater detail in the prose text of *Urania*, serve to contextualize the paradoxical presence of a dual language of sovereignty and subjection in the poems.

Critiquing the gendered plays for power enacted in contemporary court circles and in popular male-authored literary texts, Wroth explores configurations of female sovereignty in her play and prose romance in terms that intersect with the representations of sovereign women in the texts of Lanyer and Cary, Anne Clifford and Queen Elizabeth herself. The vocal female characters in *Love's Victory* and *Urania* on the one hand provide a potential re-vision of the enforced silence and passivity of the Jacobean female masquers, of whom Wroth was one, while on the other hand serve to re-gender the language of sovereignty appropriated for masculine use by such writers as Sidney, Spenser, and Shakespeare.

   Philip Sidney's first literary work, *The Lady of May*, in fact marks his debut as a courtier with a tribute to the monarchical ideal embodied by Queen Elizabeth.[44] The question posed to the queen by the May Lady and her mother is based on a condition of female subjection, however, rather than sovereignty. The May Lady's mother explains to the queen that while "other women think they may be unhappily cumbered with one master husband; my poor daughter is oppressed with two," and requests, along with her daughter, that the queen choose which suitor is more fitting.[45] The bulk of the ensuing performance before the queen is occupied not by dialogue among mother, daughter, and queen, but rather by the lyric competition between the suitors Espilus and Therion, echoed by the arguments of Dorcas and Rixus. In the end, the queen chooses Espilus to be the "master husband" of the May Lady, her royal presence thus serving, within the terms of Sidney's entertainment, to validate patriarchal authority after all.

   By contrast to *The Lady of May*, *The Countess of Pembroke's Arcadia* has been praised by Constance Jordan for containing a "powerful exposition of the notion of androgyny as the foundation for a defense of woman and more especially of women's rule," and for providing an "extended feminist critique of various aspects of patriarchy." Jordan's analysis is based upon the premise that Sidney's text is "feminist" to the extent that it gives "a positive value to the feminine aspect of male behavior in private life."[46] On the other hand, Sidney's text can be regarded as less than feminist to the extent that it is arguably overdetermined by fatherly authority, with the presence of not one but two male monarchs, Basilius and Euarchus, whose sovereignty ultimately prevails not simply over the errant but recognizably heroic princes, but less favorably over the feminine crimes and misdemeanors of the weak Gynecia and wicked Cecropia.

The revised *Arcadia*, which is Jordan's concern, differs significantly from the *Old Arcadia* in the addition of the figure of Cecropia, whose specifically female lust for Basilius's monarchical power threatens his kingdom more deeply than his own irresponsibility. Betraying her proper gendered role as submissive subject and patriarch's sister, Cecropia plots to supplant her brother and king, Basilius, with her son, Amphialus. Sidney underscores the contrast between "evill mother" and "excellent sonne" when the narrator maintains that Amphialus "was utterly ignorant of all his mothers wicked devises; to which he would never have consented" (NA, 363). In the revised text, furthermore, it is Cecropia who is responsible for releasing the lion and bear at the time of the pastorals, "knowing that they would seeke their food there, and devoure what they founde" (NA, 365). The intrusion of the beasts into the circumscribed pastoral meadow not only elicits the heroic response of the male princes within the meadow, but also reveals the malignant intentions of a female would-be ruler outside those bounds. Admittedly Sidney provides some examples of admirable women with the figures of Pamela and Philoclea, yet however socially acceptable their rejection, in different forms, of the flawed maternal authority of Gynecia and Cecropia, the princesses must learn to submit to the discipline of fatherly authority before they can assume their appropriate positions within society.

While the dominant politics of discourse in the canonical texts of Spenser and Shakespeare have received a wealth of critical attention, the relevance of female sovereignty to subjectivity has been less discussed.[47] In the case of *The Faerie Queene*, studies by Susanne Woods and Pamela Benson have begun to explore the gendered implications of Spenser's constructions of "female regiment."[48] Common to the readings of both Benson and Woods is a focus upon Spenser's privileging of traditionally "feminine" attributes, from beauty to chastity, in representing successful female regiment. Interestingly, the feminine attributes of Spenser's women rulers can be linked to masculine objectifications of women across a range of texts in early modern England.

Moreover, I find that Spenser's representations of female sovereignty, whether positive, as in the case of Britomart, or negative, as in the case of Radigund, are not only connected to feminized attributes of chastity or ungoverned sexuality, virtue or vice, but are also separated from considerations of discursive subjectivity. Britomart's early trial of strength in the Castle Joyeous, for example, results in her transformation from an object of desire in the eyes of a sexually "sovereign" woman, Malecasta, to an object of aggression to be penetrated by the "gaze" and weapon of a male knight, Gardante, before she vanquishes her attackers with the aid of Redcrosse Knight, without ever claiming a voice as a speaking subject. Subsequently, in the House of Busyrane, the weapon of a male aggressor again draws Britomart's blood when she attempts to wrest Busyrane's knife from his hand. Poised upon the brink of silent vengeance, Britomart is stopped by Amoret, who requires the male speaking voice of the magician to release her from the spell. When Amoret prostrates herself to the ground before the seemingly male presence of Britomart in gratitude for being restored to a "perfect hole" (FQ, III.xii.39), the juxtaposition of the two figures underscores Britomart's use of her sovereign strength in masculine terms to restore another woman to her expected position as perfect container, or "hole," for the (legitimate) desire of her male lover.

The much later conflict between Britomart and Radigund is staged not only in silence, with Britomart refusing to engage with her opponent's "conditions" in speech, but in overtly bestialized terms which recall the reductive language of the male sonneteers, discussed in chapter 2:

> Ne either sought the others strokes to shun,
> But through great fury both their skill forgot,
> And practicke use in armes: ne spared not
> Their dainty parts, which nature had created
> So faire and tender, without staine or spot,
> For other uses, then they them translated;
> Which they now hackt and hewd, as if such use they hated,
> As when a Tygre and a Lionesse
> Are met at spoyling of some hungry pray,
> Both challenge it with equall greedinesse: [FQ, V.vii.29-30]

Whether cast as honorable or usurping, both female warriors here are represented as women who are violating their femininity in the exercise of their sovereign strength, translating "their dainty parts" into "other uses" than nature had intended, and appearing in consequence possessed of "equall greedinesse" and bestial violence. Significantly, Britomart's victory over Radigund results in her exercise of her sovereignty "as Princess" to restore the patriarchal order, as she "the liberty of women did repeale, / Which they had long usurpt; and them restoring / To mens subjection, did true Justice deale" (FQ, V.vii.42). Female sovereignty viewed in these terms serves to reproduce rather than deconstruct the subjection of women in the society at large. In the narratives of Mary Wroth's play and prose romance, by contrast, women rulers are represented not only or even primarily in relation to male subjects, for whom their strength can appear to be a violation of their femininity, but in relation to a range of assertive female subjects as well. The idealization and/or demonization of female regiment in The Faerie Queene thus gives way in Urania to a complex figuration of the relation between female sovereignty and subjectivity, at once potentially more empowering and less absolute, more ambivalent and less reductive than those found in many male-authored texts.[49]

Certainly the figure of the virgin queen, so crucial to Spenser's epic, appears in noticeably refracted form during the Jacobean age, transmuted from seemingly glorious sovereign to an ambiguous symbol of female rule which still overshadows the court of Elizabeth's male successor. The splitting of female sovereignty into acceptable and unacceptable alternatives can be viewed, for example, in Jonson's Jacobean masques. Given that Wroth herself, as noted earlier, participated in performances of *The Masque of Blackness* (1605) and *The Masque of Beauty* (1608), while her friends such as Anne Clifford and Susan Herbert, the countess of Montgomery, performed in other masques such as *The Masque of Queens* (1609), Jonson's representations of female sovereignty reflect a politics of gender in the Jacobean court with which Wroth would have been intimately familiar. From absolutist containment to gendered subversion, the masques encode a range of interpretive possibilities.[50]

In *The Masque of Queens*, for example, an antimasque of witches and hags precedes the celebration of worthy historical queens, pitting demonized female figures, "fraught with spite," against twelve aristocratic ladies.[51] The witches, "all differently attired," represent in Jonson's own words "a spectacle of strangeness producing multiplicity of gesture" (321). Even among themselves, then, without reference to the queens whose subsequent appearance dispels them, the witches can be seen to embody both multiplicity and difference associated with femininity. The spectacle of Jonson's witches relies upon "difference" in oppositionally gendered terms as well, with boys playing the speaking witches' parts while noblewomen played the silent queens, subjected to a discourse not their own. Given that witches historically were associated with scolds and domineering wives, all of whom were viewed as rebelling against their places in the social and gender hierarchies, the suspect and disorderly speech of Jonson's witches serves to privilege the socially silent/silenced state of the courtly women taking the queens' parts.[52] At the same time, it is important to remember that even the apparently constraining parameters of masque production could not eliminate the assertive court voices of women such as Anne Clifford, whose overtly rebellious speech had the power, discussed above, to put the king "in a chaff."

Some readings of the masques suggest that Jonson celebrates a sovereign world of masculine self-sufficiency in which the authority of poet and king are one. In *The Masque of Queens* in particular, Suzanne Gossett argues that Jonson takes pains to suppress any indications that the queens were historically or traditionally powerful, dangerous, or even masculine by idealizing them in passive terms, while stripping the actual queen of political significance by depicting her in the dependent position of a consort-queen.[53] Stephen Orgel goes further to suggest that Jonson uses the Perseus myth in *Queens* in order to convey the power of male heroism to "overcome the Medusa," or to appropriate the feminine rhetorical power embodied by the Gorgon's head, and consequently emphasizes the "fantasy of masculine self-sufficiency which underlies Jacobean conceptions of literary and political authority."[54]

As Lewalski has pointed out, however, Jonson himself credited Queen Anne with the governing concepts for several of the masques, including the idea of black-faced Africans in *The Masque of Blacknesse* and the idea for the antimasque of witches in *Queens*. By representing herself and her ladies as black African beauties, then, the queen can be seen to be associating them with the feared and desired "others" imagined by contemporary explorers, and linked with female danger and power. In *Queens*, moreover, Lewalski argues that the queens appropriate rather than destroy the power of the witches, and themselves represent figures of violence with the historical power to overturn gender norms. The attempted containment of the power of these militant queens by identifying James as the epitome of all merit thus cannot succeed, because the trajectory of power in the masque finds completion in the female referent of Queen Anne rather than King James.[55] As in James's own reference to the "nourish-milk" of his fatherly role, attempted supplantation need not necessarily be read as resulting in successful containment, but rather may be viewed as exposing gendered fissures of authority which reveal the patriarch's dependence upon the enabling powers associated with the seemingly marginalized "other."

Certainly *Queens* and several of Jonson's other masques both opened discursive possibilities for subversion of governing conceptions of gender and authority, and directly involved a number of the prominent women of the court, including Mary Wroth and her peers, in productions that enact some of the tensions informing the competing courts of the king and the queen. Those tensions extend from the dichotomizing of female figures as either monstrous or virtuous to the silencing of actual women's voices in production, as only the boys playing the hags and witches were allowed to speak. In plays authored by women at the same time, however, such as Cary's *The Tragedy of Mariam* and Wroth's *Love's Victory*, women's voices bespeak their own discursive possibilities for subversion, representing spectacles of production of subjectivity in the face of attempted containment by fatherly authority.

Shortly before the publication of Wroth's works, the appearance of Cary's *Mariam* offered an ideologically ambivalent statement regarding the implications of a "public voice" (I.i.1) for women, which anticipates some of the political tensions associated with public female discourse in both *Love's Victory* and *Urania*. The same conditions of patriarchal tyranny that empower some of the women's voices in Cary's and Wroth's texts work to hinder the speech of others, unsettling the gendered dichotomizing of mastery and subjection, speech and silence, which marks conduct manuals of the period. Focusing upon Cary's protagonist, Belsey observes that Mariam herself is a subject who speaks from a definite position, even when this is one of inner conflict.[56] Lewalski suggests, from another angle, that the figure of Mariam allows Cary to explore the possibility and power of nonviolent or passive resistance, associated with claiming the right to speech, for "queen-wives" subjected at once to domestic and state tyranny.[57] Given the examples of Cary's resistance to the tyranny of her own husband, discussed in chapter 2, as well as Queen Anne's resistance to the domestic and state authority of James I, discussed above, Cary's competing representations of women's voices serve at once to reflect and rework the particular historical and social conditions that shaped the experience of a range of women, from subject to sovereign, in early modern England.

In the case of Mariam, her sovereignty as "the monarch of Judea's Queen" (I.i.58) arises not from her marriage to Herod, but rather from her position as the granddaughter of Hircanus, the rightful king. It is thus *her* hereditary sovereignty that has brought Herod *his* title, rather than vice versa. And yet, Mariam herself recognizes that her "public voice" can jeopardize her sovereignty, and that her chastity alone cannot preserve her "breath," or speech, from censure (IV.viii.526). In an extended reflection on Herod's choice of herself over the famous Queen Cleopatra, Mariam observes that even though the renowned power of Cleopatra's "face" was despised by Herod in favor of her own, her own neglect of "humility," as evidenced in her bold speech, was enough to bring about her sentence of death at Herod's command (IV.viii.543-70). As Sohemus remarks about the queen, "unbridled speech is Mariam's worst disgrace, / And will endanger her without desert" (III.iii.183-84). The "bridling" of female speech associated with Mariam's proper position in society establishes limits to female subjectivity as well as sovereignty throughout the play.

Conflicts of subjectivity and subjection extend beyond the parameters of Mariam's perspective alone to shape the simultaneous emergence and suppression of more wide-ranging possibilities for female discursive sovereignty. For example, the power of maternal discourse in *Mariam*, as noted in the previous chapter, emerges only to be deconstructed when mothers attempt to claim public rather than private voices for their concerns. Thus although Alexandra can speak frankly in urging her daughter Mariam to cast off Herod's patriarchal authority after the initial report of his death, her private cursing of Herod modulates into a public cursing of her own daughter when she is confronted with the tyranny of the living Herod's sovereignty. Each of the mothers in the play, whether Alexandra, Doris, or Mariam herself, in fact can be seen at moments to subordinate her femininity to the power of the tyrant's discourse, whether in apparent denial of the power of maternal bonding, as in the case of Alexandra, or in the service of maternal responsibility over an emergent desire for wifely resistance, as when both Mariam and Doris gloss over Herod's faults in light of their hopes that he will treat their offspring well.

At the opposite end of the spectrum from the mothers in the play is the figure of Salome, whose promiscuous sexuality is inextricably associated with her outspoken voice. When Salome attempts to assert her autonomy as a woman, declaring "I'll be the custom-breaker: and begin / To show my Sex the way to freedom's door" (I.iv.309-10), she receives scorn rather than sovereignty as her portion in society, not only from her castoff husband, Constabarus, but from the patriarch who has solicited her advice as well. Thus Herod repays Salome with curses for the very voice that he called upon her to use: "Accursèd Salome, hadst thou been still, / My Mariam had been breathing by my side" (V.i.157-58). As one of the few women who is *not* a mother, Salome attempts to use female sexuality rather than maternity to establish a public speaking position for herself, and is dismissed as verbally untrustworthy in consequence.

Furthermore, for all the opposition between the sexually promiscuous figure of Salome and the chaste figure of Mariam, the two women share a common problem of finding themselves unable to voice their subjectivity in public terms without opprobrium. The power of discourse in the patriarchal society of Cary's play, to refer once more to Irigaray's terms, is predicated on the subordination of the feminine voice, whether sexually aggressive or restrained. In assessing the political significance of Cary's play, Ferguson maintains that Mariam's anxiety over her "culpable public speech" reflects Cary's own concern with the problem of "the woman author's *signature*" in her culture.[58] Cary's play thus conveys the extent to which women authors faced a discursive politics of gender in Jacobean England that worked preemptively to prohibit, or reactively to silence, women's speech if not publicly authorized by the male sovereign.

From the authority figures of Venus and Musella's mother to the assured female voices of Silvesta and Musella herself, the female characters in Wroth's *Love's Victory* endeavor, more concertedly than in Cary's play, to appropriate the language of sovereignty to express their fears and desires. At the same time, Wroth explores the limits of female sovereignty in the face of fatherly authority, in situations where an individual woman's voice is not sufficient to overturn the Law of the (dead) Father. Ultimately, it is the collective power of women's voices, much like the enabling discourse between women in Lanyer's "To Cooke-ham," that facilitates the distinct if arduous emergence in Wroth's play of an order prescribed by the feminine, with "love's victory" conceived in terms of the sovereign matriarchal powers of Venus and, at long last, of Musella's mother as well.

At the beginning of the play, Venus's opening words express her concern with maintaining her sovereignty: "Cupid, me thinks wee have too long bin still / And that thes people growe to scorne our will" (I.1-2). Noting some resemblances between *Love's Victory* and Sidney's *The Lady of May*, Margaret

McLaren observes that Wroth's choice of Venus as an analogue of female power in her play may be read as a "delicate compliment" to the presiding part played by Queen Elizabeth in Sidney's work.[59] Although it is certainly true that the action of both plays is subject to the influence of female authority, in Sidney's play the queen can only sit and observe and pass judgment upon the worth of the "master husbands," while in Wroth's play the goddess takes an active part in the affairs of the lovers, even as Queen Anne, in Wroth's own experience, was likely to engage in domestic politics involving the ladies in her court. Furthermore, the male voices which dominate the body of Sidney's play give way in *Love's Victory* to a multiplicity of female voices which take repeated precedence at crucial moments in the plot over the discourse of men. Thus Venus gives Cupid the orders, Silvesta instructs the Forester to keep his distance from her, and Musella tells off Lissius when he compares women to sheep.

Unlike the May Lady, then, Wroth's female characters are looking neither to be chosen by a "master husband" nor to have such a master chosen for them. Instead, they attempt to assert their own sovereign right to choose, whether between suitors, as with Musella and Simeana, or between marriage and chastity, as with Silvesta. In the latter case, Wroth makes it clear that Silvesta's choice of chastity arises not from her subjection to social pressures, but rather from her desire for "freedom." Where Cary's Salome sought to proclaim her liberty through sexual promiscuity, Wroth's Silvesta gives voice to sovereign subjectivity of another sort:

Now love's as farr from mee as never knowne,
Then bacely tyde, now freely ame mine owne.
Slavery, and bondage with mourning care
Were then my living, sighs, and tears my fare,
Butt all thes gone, now live I joyfully,
Free, and untouch'd of thought butt chastity.   [I.157-62]

Even the presence of a faithful male suitor, the Forester, cannot compel Silvesta to exchange her independence from the "slavery, and bondage" of desire for the dependent state of a wife. For his part, the Forester laments Silvesta's enforcement of his corresponding freedom, finding "with most libertie, most griefe, most woe" (II.62). Although characters of both sexes suffer subjection to desire in *Love's Victory*, significantly it is only a woman who manages to proclaim her liberty from that subjection by finding in the independent state of chastity a basis for subjectivity.

Once again Wroth juxtaposes political and personal terms of sovereignty, as in the example of the sonnet on the sufferings of a deposed king quoted by Pamphilia, when Cupid observes that "'Tis farr more griefe from joye to bee downe throwne, / Then joy to bee advanc'd to pleasur's throuene [*sic*]" (III.377-78). Expressed in this language, the potential sovereignty of pleasure, undercut by grief, apparently pales beside the freedom from desire claimed by Silvesta. At the same time, for those characters (both male and female) who choose heterosexual bonding over chastity, Wroth intimates that not only the sovereignty of Venus, but also the cooperative authority of individual women, can produce joy after all. Thus Musella is hailed by Lissius and Simeana as "sole restorer of this joy" for resolving their difficulties in love (IV.331), and Silvesta is hailed by Philisses and Musella as "freind and priest" for her role in bringing them together despite the social obstacles blocking their union (V.252). These examples of female authority differ most notably from Sidney's fashioning of female authority in *The Lady of May* in that where Sidney's May Lady completely defers to the queen's choice between her suitors, Wroth's lovers seek the aid of female characters such as Musella and Silvesta explicitly in order to overcome the blocking power of fatherly authority and fulfill the choices they have already made.

Wroth's play further sets forth the possibility of more than one type of female sovereignty, contrasting the peremptory decisions of the goddess Venus with the supportive advice provided by Musella and Silvesta, whose discourse results in freedom rather than bondage for the lovers who submit to their authority. Both Musella and Silvesta suffer or have suffered the bondage of passion themselves, and thus their authority over other lovers is tempered by their awareness of the challenges facing any attempt to assert subjectivity in the language of desire. Even as Anne Clifford, Elizabeth Cary, and Mary Wroth achieved and maintained voices for themselves in the face of the frequently oppressive authority of their husbands or the king, so Wroth's female characters in *Love's Victory* find assertive voices only after experiencing social constraints. Moreover when Rustic unfeelingly celebrates his freedom upon learning of the apparent deaths of Musella and Philisses, Wroth underscores the double-edged nature of "libertie," whose value must be measured against the discourse of its possessor rather than through any easy equations of autonomy and subjectivity.

Unlike *The Lady of May*, where Queen Elizabeth's final judgment is narrated only briefly and without explanation, Wroth's play concludes with an explicit celebration of "love's victory," where Venus affirms her sovereignty over the lovers and explains how Silvesta was her "instrument ordain'd / To kill and save her freinds" (V.491-92).[60] As Musella and Philisses, restored to life, pay tribute in thanks first to Musella's mother, then to Silvesta, and finally to Venus herself, it becomes apparent that "love's victory" is a triumph of feminine authority as much as of lovers' desire. While Venus may be the "Princeses Crown'd with Victory" (V.580), the human female characters, from Musella to Silvesta, whose compassionate advice has aided their friends, prove to be sovereign subjects in their own right, able to shape their own and others' desire in language within the subtly feminized social parameters of Wroth's play.

The courtly subtext of the lovers' interaction in *Love's Victory* can be glimpsed from Wroth's inclusion of a similar group of characters in the manuscript continuation of *Urania*, where they are no longer shepherds and shepherdesses under the power of Venus, but instead courtiers in rustic guise. Wroth's treatment of sovereignty and subjectivity in her romance differs from her play, however, on even more significant issues than the rank of one parallel group of characters. Because the principal female characters in *Urania* can in many cases claim positions of political sovereignty as well as romantic authority, their discourse exhibits some of the tensions that marked the politics of gender in early modern England more explicitly than does the pastoral dialogue of the play. When the language of sovereignty is appropriated by figures of wise women and queens as well as by shepherdesses and goddesses, the relations between female authority and subjectivity emerge in polemical rather than primarily pastoral terms.

At the beginning of *Urania*, Wroth foregrounds the politics of gender in her representation of her title protagonist's first encounter with a male courtier. Urania's response to the self-pitying lamentations of a knight she finds in a cave is to urge him to take action to avenge the apparent death of his beloved, rather than "lie here complaining" (4). First mistaking Urania for a "divelish spirit," Perissus realizes his error and exclaims: "But now I see you are a woman; and therefore not much to be marked, and lesse resisted" (4). Perissus's reaction to Urania exposes the gendered bias of a social politics that not only defines women as the weaker sex, but construes their discourse as not worth listening to. Along those lines, he requests that Urania "leave me who am afflicted sufficiently without your companie; or if you will stay, discourse not to me" (4). Dismissing these alternatives of obedience or silence, Urania responds assertively in her turn: "Neither of these will I doe" (4). Instead, she succeeds in persuading Perissus initially to communicate with her, and subsequently to accept her counsel, which in fact leads ultimately to his reunion with his beloved Limena. This incident becomes a point of reference throughout the prose romance, as an example of the title character's authority to resolve the difficulties of other characters of both sexes. Urania is able to counsel Perissus not in spite of her gender, then, but rather because her own quest for her female identity has allowed her to "identify" with the emergent subjectivity of others.

The incident recalls as well another fictive encounter in a cave that defines, even while it subverts, a masculine politics of gender. In Sidney's *Old Arcadia*, when Basilius and Gynecia arrive at the cave that is the scene of their individual assignations with "Cleophila," Basilius believes Gynecia to be his hoped-for mistress and muses upon the "contrast" with his wife, declaring: "O who would have thought there could have been such difference betwixt women?" (*OA*, 275). In fact, of course, Basilius has actually been outwitted by another male, Pyrocles, and his comment ironically conveys masculine assumptions about the actual lack of difference between women, as if all women were only one female body, apart from the male prerogative to determine "difference." In the example of the literally short-sighted male sovereign in Sidney's romance, an imagined difference between women turns out to be nonexistent. Wroth, however, dismantles conventional masculine assumptions still further, given that the imagined sameness of all women implied in Perissus's blanket dismissal of the gender breaks down in the face of Urania's authority as an individual woman.

An even closer parallel to the Urania/Perissus encounter can be identified in Book III of *The Faerie Queene*, where Britomart comes upon Scudamore bewailing his loss of Amoret, and at first encounters a reaction of indignant scorn when she attempts to comfort him. Scudamore's reaction, however, has nothing to do with Britomart's gender, because he takes her for a male knight, whereas Wroth emphasizes the politics of gender in the exchange between Urania and Perissus. More to the point, Wroth provides her own parallel episode in the manuscript continuation of *Urania*, when Amphilanthus is interrupted by a "lady" while lamenting Pamphilia's engagement to the king of Tartaria, and responds: "What devill in woemans habitt comes thus to torture and hinder my ende" (I: fol. 51v). The "lady" who receives the appellation of "devill in woemans habitt" is none other than his sister, Urania, who once again, as with Perissus, overcomes masculine resistance to her female authority and reproves her brother for his behavior. Urania promises to help Amphilanthus as she has helped numerous other characters by this point in the narrative, adding: "Did nott I say thus much to Perissus, and did itt nott fall out soe" (I: fol. 52). No male character exerts an influence comparable to that of Urania in providing advice and guidance for friends and strangers alike.

Urania shares the role of wise female counselor, however, with several other women in the romance, the most notable of whom is the female seer, Melissea. Although Melissea's considerable powers extend to freeing other characters from enchantments and foreseeing future events, her most valuable gift to suffering lovers, including the young Urania, rests in her words of advice and encouragement. Even as Perissus was discovered by Urania in a cave, so Amphilanthus comes unaware upon the entrance to Melissea's palace on the island of Delos by first entering a great cave. Sitting down to bewail his inability to gain a clear sign of his beloved's favor—a common occupation for the otherwise heroic male knights in *Urania*—Amphilanthus is interrupted by the entrance of "a grave Ladie, apparreld in a black habit, and many more young women attending her" (115). Melissea's appearance as a female figure of authority recalls the central figure of Night who appears in "sad attire" in *Pamphilia to Amphilanthus*. Her authority is confirmed by her "skill in the Art of Astrologie," which allows her to inform Amphilanthus that "all shall love you that you wish: but yet you must bee crost in this you now affect, though contrarie to her heart" (115). While Melissea further warns Amphilanthus that "it will proove your fault if you lose her, which I thinke, you will and must" (115), she does not have the power to alter the outcome of his actions, for which he must learn to take sole responsibility.

Although not a queen, Melissea nevertheless exerts an alternative authority to that found in royal courts, commanding the various nobles who have assembled at her palace to depart for locations that she determines suitable to their fortunes (117). In an episode that parallels her advice to Amphilanthus, Melissea gives harbor to Urania and Pamphilia, and counsels them concerning their fortunes without indicating all that is to transpire (159-60). After warning Pamphilia that she must undergo many afflictions, Melissea reveals to Urania her identity as a royal princess, and encourages her to accept "change" in love, because "it is but just change" (160). As the romance unfolds, Urania comes to love and ultimately marry not her first beloved, Parselius, but rather Steriamus, who himself relinquishes an unrequited passion for Pamphilia in exchange for the love of Urania. The piece of advice on "just change" in love, bequeathed from Melissea to Urania, becomes the cornerstone for much of the subsequent discourse shared among the women throughout the narrative on the vexed relations between love and change, constancy and desire.

Despite a romance framework which includes the presence of magic enchantments, then, Wroth consistently emphasizes the power of female discourse in natural rather than supernatural terms. By contrast to the suspect and thereby monstrous femininity of the witches represented in *Macbeth* or in the notorious Lancashire trials of 1612, in which clay images or poisonous brews were associated with maleficent female powers,[61] Wroth's female mage exerts a sovereign authority over other characters, both male and female, with beneficent effects. As another wise woman tells one of the male princes, Melissea "governs as much as art can allowe onely for art, nott soe far as develish conjurations" (II: fol. 2v).

Furthermore, unlike the allegedly punitive Sycorax of *The Tempest*, who is credited with imprisoning Ariel within a cloven pine, Melissea is responsible for releasing others from the intertwined bonds of enchantment and confusion. Her wise counsel consistently strengthens the women's powers in the social world of the romance, while rebuking male characters such as Amphilanthus for their "fault" in mistreating the women they love. Where even the "natural" magic of Paulina in *The Winter's Tale* consists of keeping Hermione apart from court society and thus from her sovereignty as queen for sixteen years, Melissea's alternating use of magic and counsel uncovers and restores the sovereignty and agency of a range of female characters, including both Urania and Pamphilia.

The politics of gender comes into play throughout Wroth's narrative for both wise women and queens, female counselors and female rulers, as the women learn to confront the changeability of their male lovers with an equanimity fostered to different degrees by an emergent sense of security in their own positions as female subjects able to recognize, and thus potentially govern, their own responses to "just change" in love. Nereana is one queen whose unrequited affections initially derail both her political government as a sovereign and her personal estimation of herself as a sovereign subject. Leaving her kingdom, she comes in search of Pamphilia, whom she believes to be beloved still by Steriamus, her own object of desire. Pamphilia marvels at a woman undertaking "so Knight-like a search" (163), and praises Nereana's strength of will. Nereana herself, "despising any passion but love should dare think of ruling in her" (164), continues to be governed by desire rather than maintaining her rule over her people. Her decision to "[lay] aside State" in an attempt to "recreate her selfe after her owne liking" (164) results in her wandering in the woods, "quite lost in her selfe" (165), until a distraught male lover, Allanus, actually mistakes her first for his own beloved and then for the goddess of the woods, and strips her of her royal robes. Bereft of any appearance of authority, she attempts to assure herself that her "owne royall spirit" will never leave her (167), and yet in the next breath speaks so peremptorily to a nearby knight that he observes: "a woman and being madde, had liberty to say any thing" (167).

The disintegration of Nereana's discourse parallels the deconstruction of her subjectivity through her subjection to desire, leaving her only with the role of "madde woman." As the romance proceeds, she suffers "Winter in cold despaires, and Sommers heat in flourishing misery" (288), until she is taken under the protection of Perissus, whose own fortunes have been revived by the initial counsel of Urania. In a lucid moment of explanation to Perissus, Nereana attributes her misfortune to her having been "made in myne owne Country, and in the most perfect time of my rule, subject to a stranger" (288), acknowledging her experience of the incompatibility between subjection and subjectivity without grasping her need for self-government. Shortly thereafter, Nereana's inability to govern herself again erodes her capacity to communicate, the narrator observing that "when she had her greatnes againe in good clothes put about her, she began to grow to her wonted accustomed humours, like a garden, never so delicate when well kept under, will without keeping grow ruinous" (289). Consequently, when she finally returns to her own country she finds it "possess'd, and governd by a younger sister of hers" whom she had kept "inclosed in a strong Tower" in the past (290). As Nereana is imprisoned in the tower in her turn, the narrator comments: "Now Nereana, where is thy greatnesse, but in miserie? where the so often named title of Princesse but in bondage? where all thy glorie but in subjection?" (291). As a figure of the subjected sovereign, the unruly ruler, Nereana forfeits all her political authority, even as her own subjects interpret her personal passions, "though naturall to her," as "meere lunatick actions" (291). Finally, however, after years of imprisonment, Nereana's exclusion from political subjecthood fosters the reconstitution of her subjectivity. After her sister departs to "try the Inchantment" which has attracted many of the other characters, one of Nereana's male subjects is moved to "urge restitution," and succeeds in convincing the people to establish her "in her former government" (421). Once Nereana is restored to her place as rightful monarch of her country, she proves "an excellent Governess, and brave Lady, being able to overrule her old passions, and by them to judge how to favor, licence, and curb others" (421). Like Silvesta in Love's Victory, Nereana's experience of the bondage of passion enables her ultimately to govern her own desires as well as to judge fairly of others. Only after she learns to claim an identity for herself in isolation, then, is Nereana able to reclaim her authority over her subjects at large.[62] Once she learns to reimagine a sovereign sense of self while imprisoned, she finds that she can legitimately reclaim the political sovereignty of her position as monarch.

Female sovereignty does not always work to the advantage of female subjects, as evidenced both by Wroth's own eventual loss of her position of favor in the court of Queen Anne, and by her representation of a similar loss of favor in the story of Lindamira (whose name can be recognized to be a loose anagram for "Ladi Mari"). The narrator of Lindamira's story, significantly, is Pamphilia, who works to define her own sovereign subjectivity as a queen in relation to the many examples of feminine subjection as well as empowerment which she encounters throughout the romance. Pamphilia tells the tale of Lindamira to one of her female friends, Dorolina, instead of reading her own verses, thus substituting a tale of another's political subjection in place of the lyric representation of her own subjection to desire (424-29), even as she earlier read aloud another woman's sonnet comparing loss in love to the political subjection of a deposed king (409).

Pamphilia opens her narrative by describing Lindamira's favored position with the Queen of France, so that "by no meanes she must be absent from the Court, which indeed was the fittest place for her, being a Lady of great spirit" (424). During her time at court, Lindamira loved a male courtier in secret, and meanwhile "served the Queene faithfully, and so affectionately, as she had no love but them two of either Sexe; yet she was carefull to give no dislike to her mistris, whom she would not injure, or indeed at that time her selfe, for she was married, he not thinking that it was himselfe she loved" (424). Subsequently, the queen comes to doubt Lindamira's faithful service when

another envious female courtier initiates rumors about Lindamira's secret love
and the queen becomes jealous. As a result, the queen withdraws her favor
from Lindamira "as suddenly and directly, as if never had: Lindamira remaining like one in a gay Masque, the night pass'd, they are in their old clothes
againe, and no appearance of what was" (424).

Having participated in "gay Masques" with Queen Anne—termed
"necessary follies" of the court by another female character (456)—only to experience the Cinderella-like disenchantment of finding herself in her "old
clothes againe, and no appearance of what was," Lady Mary Wroth was certainly well positioned to represent the trials as well as the triumphs associated
with women's experiences of the competing plays for power at court. As
Pamphilia wryly remarks in recounting Lindamira's political fall from grace,
speaking from the position of a queen who has herself suffered subjection to
desire, "in Loves Court all are fellow-subjects; and thus her Majesty was deceived in her greatnesse, which could not, as she thought, be subject" (424).
Although no fairy godmother appears to rescue Lindamira from her plight,
her social disgrace brings her love to the attention of the male courtier concerned, and consequently she achieves a "strange happines" despite the loss of
the queen's favor and the continuing jealousy of her husband (425). Paradoxically, then, even as the queen's political sovereignty gives way to subjection
"in Loves Court," Lindamira's political subjection results in an emergent subjectivity associated with the eventual sovereignty of her affections.

Pamphilia concludes her narrative by sharing seven sonnets allegedly
composed by Lindamira, eliciting Dorolina's admiration for "these Sonnets,
and the story, which shee thought was some thing more exactly related then a
fixion" (429). Quilligan locates this "exactly related" connection in the parallel between the lost favor of a female superior suffered by Lindamira, and the
lack of fidelity on the part of a male lover suffered by Pamphilia, suggesting
that their situations agree "not only in the shared pain but in the insistent self-
definition created in a relationship betrayed by the powerful other."[63] A somewhat different parallel emerges in Pamphilia's tacit identification with the
queen's discovery that "in Loves Court all are fellow-subjects" and must "serve
alike" (424). Interestingly, even the unjust behavior of the queen—acting "in
a chaff," so to speak—thus serves to represent the limits of political sovereignty
across gender lines when confronted with personal desire.

Pamphilia herself, finally, serves as a figure of female rule who learns to
govern both herself and her country, if not apart from, then at least without depending upon, the authority or fidelity of male subjects or lovers. From victim
to hero, subject to sovereign, critical constructions of the figure of Pamphilia
span the gamut of her voices.[64] Indeed, at least part of the reason that Pamphilia has elicited such varied critical interpretations can be attributed to
Wroth's multiple representations of the politics of gender. No single outcome

for gendered conflicts of authority and subordination, constancy and desire, dominates the narrative of her prose romance. Unlike Nereana, for example, Pamphilia experiences at once sovereignty over her kingdom and subjection to desire, and gradually learns to define a position for herself as a speaking subject through, rather than despite, her divided condition. After being crowned queen of the country of Pamphilia at the bequest of her uncle, the former ruler of that realm, Pamphilia departs not, as Nereana, to pursue passion, but rather to conclude the enchantment on the island of Cyprus. When Amphilanthus joins her, he recognizes her authority as "soveraign of al harts," and is immediately compelled to acknowledge the justice of her estimation of his inconstancy (137-38).

Pamphilia's own definition of her sovereignty emerges in a conversation with one suitor named Leandrus, when she responds to his question: "are you not soveraigne of your selfe by judgement, yeares and authoritie, unlimited by fortunes, by government, and the love of your Parents," with the answer: "these still are but the threads that tie my dutie" (279-80). Her sovereignty of herself, then, is located not in a condition of isolation, but rather in the context of her acceptance of ties that bind. To adapt the words of Queen Elizabeth, Pamphilia knows what it is to be a sovereign *because* she has known what it is to be a subject.[65] On the other hand, in wrestling with her subjectivity as a lover, Pamphilia demands of herself: "Can thy great spirit permit thee to bee bound . . . ? Scorne such servilitie, where subjects soveraignize; never let so meane a thing ore-rule thy greatest power; either command like thy self, or fall downe vassall in despaire" (198). Her condition—"though great as any, yet in love was as much subject as the meanest borne" (198)—validates rather than undermines her subjectivity, because her capacity to "command like [her] self" stems from her ability to govern her own actions even when another is "Monarch of her heart" (481). At once sovereign and subject, Pamphilia is only eventually enabled to move beyond fluctuating experiences of political empowerment and romantic victimization by learning to share her burdens with other women who are both subject to and speaking subjects of a range of desires.

Through multiple interchanges between the struggling Pamphilia and her friends, Wroth emphasizes the importance of female ties in allowing women to come to terms with the relations between personal sovereignty and subjectivity, even as their bonds with men repeatedly tend to obscure their agency. As one female character observes regarding this dichotomy, "wee are fine creatures alone in our owne imaginations; but otherwise poore miserable captives to love" (411). Pamphilia is aided, among other female friends, by Limena, who in her turn was restored to her lover Perissus as a result of Urania's counsel. Limena urges Pamphilia to "raise up your spirit, that which is worthy to Monarchise the world, drowne it not, not make a grave by sad conceits, to bury what should live for royalty," and goes on to provide through her discourse "a perfect glasse" within which Pamphilia can view her "selfe truly free from such distresse" (189). Wroth's construction of Limena's offer can be viewed in relation to Spenser's *Faerie Queene*, where Britomart looks into the male magician's mirror owned by her father, only to find herself "subjected to loves cruell law" by the vision of the male knight she sees therein (*FQ*, III.ii.38). By contrast, Wroth represents one woman providing a mirror of the "true perfections" of another, which enables Pamphilia to glimpse her capability to be "truly free" from the "distresse" associated with subjection to love (189). Far from erasing desire, such a vision instead extends the parameters of women's subjectivity beyond the conventional terms offered by the Law of the Father for heterosexual relations, to emphasize the potentially liberating force of homosocial bonds among "this sex which is not one." Even as historians such as Amussen have documented early modern women's strategic support of one another in terms that subverted their culture's patriarchal emphasis on female obedience,[66] so Wroth's female characters succeed in supporting one another's emergent sovereignty in discursive terms, by calling attention to each other's capacity to "Monarchise the world" in the midst of their otherwise troubling subjection to desire.

The closest that a male author such as Shakespeare comes to representing the quality of female endurance explored by Wroth is in the queens of his late romances. Nevertheless, when Wroth's depiction of Pamphilia's response to the "tyranny" of male jealousy, to use Lanyer's term, is compared to Shakespeare's characterization of Hermione's suffering, it becomes clear that their representations of constant female sovereigns figure forth quite different politics of gender. Aware that her years of separation from Amphilanthus have taken their toll, Pamphilia muses: "Can he smile on these wrincles, and be loving in my decay?" (482). Her feminine perspective on their separation can be compared to Leontes's protest to Paulina upon beholding the statue of his wife in *The Winter's Tale*: "But yet, Paulina, / Hermione was not so much wrinkled, nothing / So aged as this seems" (V.iii.27-29). Having been cast off by her husband on the basis of a false accusation of inconstancy, Hermione has aged through the intervening years only to be "reborn" into a reunion with the finally repentant Leontes. However in Wroth's treatment of undeserved rejection, it is not Pamphilia but Amphilanthus who is described as figuratively frozen in stone by his act of abandonment, so that his feelings of repentance "wrought in him, like drops falling on soft stones, they weare in to them at last, though in the beginning touch and slide off" (556). Whereas in *The Winter's Tale* Leontes responds to the statue of Hermione reflexively by invoking stone-like comparisons for both himself and Perdita, in Wroth's romance the stone-like associations are exclusive to the male. Furthermore, while Hermione's statue-like passivity effectively constitutes acquiescence to her husband's authority not only to reject her but also to silence her for sixteen years, Pamphilia refuses to wait out Amphilanthus's inconstancy in silent passivity, asserting instead the continuity of her discourse both as a woman and as a ruler in her own right. Pamphilia's subjectivity, then, is tied not only to her sexuality, which can be threatened by the physicality of decay in the gaze of her male lover, but to her sovereignty as well, which is mirrored for her in the speech of her female friends.

Interestingly, in both *Urania* and *The Winter's Tale* male-female conflict is triangulated by the presence of a defender of female honor, a woman's voice to challenge masculine authority. When Amphilanthus attributes his sorrow, for example, to "inconstancie in [Pamphilia] and ingrat[it]ude in mee," Urania responds tartly: "I beeleeve the latter . . . for Pamphilia is above all worldly nations fixt, and onely fixt to you, therfor what have you dun?" (II: fol. 52). Although Urania's frank speech recalls the no-nonsense approach of Paulina, her position as Amphilanthus's sister, and a ruler in her own right, enables her to address him from a position of political equality rather than subordination, while her friendship with Pamphilia similarly is not marked by the class divisions separating Paulina and her queen.[67] Thus Wroth elevates the woman's role in the political structures of the community, while stressing the mutual sovereignty which underlies the friendships among some of her female protagonists.

Wroth indicates the extent to which her female characters rely upon each other in their struggles to claim their own powers of agency, instead of simply depending upon masculine support, when Pamphilia comes under attack by enemy forces and receives aid not only from neighboring male princes but also from her friend and neighboring sovereign, Veralinda, queen of Frigia. Wroth represents their communication as a sustaining force in a mutable world, emphasizing not only their political alliance as rulers, but also their personal bond as friends: "for never was ther greater, nor Constanter love beetweene woemen, then beetweene thes towe most excellent Ladys, continuing to ther ends, . . . soe as while the warrs might bee cruell, and curst, yett they might in sweet conversation injoye one the other" (I: fol. 39v). The physical aid provided by Veralinda's army, then, is surpassed only by the emotional support provided by her discourse. Acknowledging the cultural myth of women's inconstancy to one another in order to refute it, Wroth fashions the friendship between Pamphilia and Veralinda with an emphasis on the importance of their reciprocal "conversation," by contrast to the oppositional violence of "warrs" staged by men.

Even as Limena encouraged Pamphilia early in the narrative to raise up her spirit, "that which is worthy to Monarchise the world," so Veralinda urges Pamphilia not to let Amphilanthus's inconstancy undermine her sovereignty: "say he hath left you, lett him goe in his owne pathe, tread nott in itt, an other is more straite, follow that, and bee the Emperess of the world, comaunding the Empire of your owne minde" (I: fol. 41). Veralinda's counsel sets forth parameters of female subjectivity which anticipate Gallagher's analysis of how later seventeenth-century women writers refigure the concept of sovereignty by reimagining the absolute in feminine rather than monarchical terms, producing a "commonwealth" of the self, or in Wroth's terms, an "Empire" of the mind.[68] Rather than depending upon male fidelity, Wroth's female characters learn from each other to identify "an other" path, figuring forth within the discourse of female friendship the terms of a sovereign constancy which might allow them to be both rulers and subjects, able to "Monarchise the world."

The politics of gender in Wroth's sonnet sequence, play, and prose romance spans the discourses of subjected lover and autonomous sovereign, counselor and queen. From reconstructing personal subjection in political terms to reimagining political sovereignty in personal terms, Wroth's women voice their struggles to establish positions as speaking subjects within male-dominated structures of society. In the face of her Jacobean culture's gendering of authority in decidedly masculine terms, from domestic treatises to kingly proclamations, Wroth grants her female characters some measure of both political authority and personal sovereignty in language that recalls on the one hand the gynecocratic discourse of Queen Elizabeth, and on the other hand the less overt yet nevertheless insistent assertions of agency that marked a number of women's voices both within and beyond the alternative court of Queen Anne.

Even as women authors such as Aemilia Lanyer and Elizabeth Cary probe the limitations of feminine authority and expand the boundaries of female discourse established by their male peers, so Mary Wroth refigures both political power and sexual passion along explicitly feminized lines. The "public voices" of Pamphilia and Urania, Silvesta and Musella, Lindamira and Veralinda define multiple possibilities for expression not despite, but rather through, their experiences of abandonment and deprivation in love. Within the shared female discourse in Wroth's works, then, exists the potential for women to lay claim to sovereign subjectivity in the midst of otherwise oppressive circumstances. Although representation of potential must not be confused with celebration of mastery, nevertheless "the power of discourse," to use Irigaray's terms once again, need not necessarily produce "the subordination of the feminine" when the acknowledgment of that subordination provides the starting point for a re-production of female subjectivity in sovereign terms.

5

Engendering Discourse

In a Different Voice

Even when the social parameters of courtship and matrimony, motherhood and daughterhood, courtiership and monarchy prove repeatedly resistant to figurations of gender that challenge cultural norms, authorship offers a perpetually alternative venue for "changing the subject." A number of critical studies of early modern England, however, as discussed in my first chapter, treat authorship as the exclusive purview of privileged male writers. One apparent rationale for this focus can be found in Jonathan Crewe's new historicist study, *Trials of Authorship*, which justifies the exclusion of women from an investigation of "English Renaissance authorship" by maintaining that any attempt to "belatedly manufactur[e] female 'authors'" could only be *"pro forma,"* and thus should be abandoned in favor of acknowledging the "exclusiveness" of authorial construction in early modern England.[1] Crewe's explicit efforts to locate in sixteenth-century English culture itself the responsibility for the "invidious exclusions" [*sic*] that mark his study are based upon the premise that authorship in the Renaissance is already, by definition, a male-centered concept, if not necessarily a desirable system in the eyes of twentieth-century critics. Although his marshalling of historical data to support his reading of Renaissance concepts of authorship is persuasive to a point, it stops short of probing the implications associated with the presence of women writers who not only implicitly, through the production of written texts, but at times explicitly, through direct discussion of female authorship, asserted their authorial voices in defiance of conventional cultural constraints. Just as early modern directives urging women to be chaste, silent, and obedient coexist with abundant examples of both historical women and literary female characters who were anything but, so Crewe's examples of the ideologically gendered "exclusiveness" of authorship in "the" Renaissance must be juxtaposed with equally authentic historical examples of women authors, from Mary Sidney to Aemilia Lanyer, Elizabeth Cary to Mary Wroth, who articulated their own trials of authorship.[2]

In recognition of the need to recover not simply the voices but also the written concerns of authors in what Crewe has termed the "anti-canon," I will explore in this chapter the ways in which authorship provided some women writers in early modern England with an opportunity to "engender" discourse, or to "conceive and bear" discourse in which the gender of the subject could make a difference—even *the* difference. In the act of assailing social constraints through language, a female author could find if not a room, then more "subjectively" a voice, of her own. Nancy Miller's landmark emphasis on the need for "arachnology," or the critical practice of reading women's texts to discover the embodiment in writing of a gendered subjectivity, suggests the importance of figuring women's relation of production to the dominant culture, without reading women authors as already written by the dominant voices of that culture.[3] In this chapter, I am concerned to identify the manifestations of gendered subjectivity associated with authorship for women in early modern England, even as I focus upon the engendering of discourse in Mary Wroth's texts in particular, where not simply the number, but more significantly the variety, of speaking positions for women—both as authors and as interpretive audiences for one another's words—posed a challenge to cultural objectifications of women.

My attention to the ways in which early modern women write their relation to language by writing about the relation between women and language has been sharpened by some of the concerns articulated in Margaret Homans's *Bearing the Word*, in which she explores the significance of sexual difference to the act of writing. Homans examines how the nineteenth-century women writers who are the subject of her study endeavor to reclaim their own experiences as paradigms for writing, and probes in particular the critical contradictions between cultural myths of women's relation to and subordination within language, and individual women writers' efforts to assert agency through language.[4] While the significantly different cultural constructs and social conditions of early modern England distinguish the experiences of Mary Wroth and her female peers from those of their successors, nevertheless their texts bear related signs of their vexed and often only partially successful linguistic struggles to reclaim women's experiences as paradigms for authorship.

Feminist literary critics have proposed a range of responses to questions of whether or not men and women use language differently, and what effects gender has on the experiences of reading and writing. Homans argues, for example, that because literal language is associated with the feminine, and figurative with the masculine, nineteenth-century women writers place more value on the literal than their male counterparts. Critics such as Elizabeth Wright have analyzed the implications of traditional dichotomies between the "public language" of patriarchy and the "private language" of marginalized women's voices. On the other hand, starting from the premise that language has the potential not only to reflect but also to address existing power structures, including figurations of gender, Patricia Yaeger has explored how women write about their experience by appropriating masculine traditions in order to transform them, adapting "phallocentric" diction to fit the needs of "feminocentric" expression.[5] While no single formulation of "difference," clearly, can suffice to describe the distinctions between men's and women's speech, particularly across a range of historical periods, my reading of early modern women writers draws upon other feminist "arachnologies" in attending to the gendered dynamics of authorship in early modern England, in order to expand the terms of difference beyond what has often proved to be the primarily materialist focus of recent historicist criticism.

Speaking about women's writing, Cixous asserts that "woman must write her self: must write about women and bring women to writing . . . must put herself into the text—as into the world and into history—by her own movement." In Cixous's terms, as noted in chapter 3, that act of authorship refers particularly to women writing "through their bodies," drawing on their relation to the mother in order to write in "white ink." Although the writings of early modern women rarely display signs of this type of Cixousian connection to the female body, their authorship nevertheless works to put women into texts on the basis of gendered experience, in practical opposition to what Cixous has termed the masculine economy of male-authored discourse. Cixous's acknowledgment that all writing offers *"the very possibility of change,* the space that can serve as a springboard for subversive thought, the precursory movement of a transformation of social and cultural structures," opens space for critical attention to women authors who put themselves into the text (and into history) in other historical periods than the present, and through other linguistic relations to female experience than those defined primarily by the body.[6] Along related lines, Cixous observes that women "from the moment they venture to speak what they have to say, will of necessity bring about a shift in metalanguage."[7] Distinct traces of that shift in metalanguage, evident despite "invidious exclusions" from dominant conceptions of authorship, can be identified not solely in twentieth-century texts, but in women's constructions of authorship across the centuries.

Kristeva, in fact, emphasizes the multiplicity of female-authored expressions and concerns in her essay on "Women's Time," taking care not to overgeneralize about the nature of femininity even while she insists upon the significance of sexual difference to experience.[8] Elsewhere, however, Kristeva finds that women are "estranged from language . . . dancers who suffer as they speak."[9] In direct response to Kristeva's theories of language, Gilbert and Gubar maintain (along the lines of Homans's argument) that the female subject is not necessarily alienated from the words she writes and speaks, particularly when "the lure of the mother's lore" takes precedence over the Law of the Father.[10] The difficulty with privileging the power of maternal "lore" over paternal discourse in Gilbert's and Gubar's terms, however, resides in the apparent opposition between "lore" and discourse, which must be defined after all in language already accorded the privilege of masculine authority.

Rather than remaining on the level of linguistic argument, Irigaray probes more directly than either Kristeva or Cixous into the "subject" at hand, by foregrounding the importance of the gendering of subjectivity itself. In an essay entitled "The Power of Discourse and the Subordination of the Feminine," Irigaray develops her influential theory of female "mimesis," which explores the recuperative power of mimicry (*mimétisme*) in allowing women to uncover the operation of the feminine *in language*.[11] Irigaray emphasizes that the issue is not one of constructing a new theory of subjectivity, but rather of "jamming the theoretical machinery itself," in order to challenge the way in which the feminine often finds itself defined, within discourse, as the lack or negation of the (masculine) subject. Every "dichotomizing—and at the same time redoubling—break," according to Irigaray, must be disrupted, so that space for the feminine can be opened up not on "either a right side or a wrong side of discourse," but in the repeated (and redoubled) passage from one to the other.[12] Instead of simply identifying new (or old) gendered oppositions between linear and cyclical time, or between public and private, figurative and literal language, then, Irigaray's approach opens an alternative avenue for reading the gendering of discourse in reflectively multiple terms.

While many of the feminist literary critics cited above have applied their theories of gender and language to studies of nineteenth- and twentieth-century women writers, the texts of early modern women writers have tended to receive more critical attention, particularly in materialist terms, for their relation to social issues than for their discursive figurations of gender. The texts of Mary Wroth, for example, have been read repeatedly in terms of the social dynamics of the Jacobean court, without sufficient attention to their construction of the vexed relations between gender and language, discourse and sexual difference. My own study of Wroth attempts to situate her gendered constructions of authorship in relation to the gender ideologies of her culture, which included discursive deconstructions of the potentially productive and thus dangerous link between writing and (female) sexual difference. Furthermore, although female-authored texts like Mary Wroth's romance often did elicit responses of outrage and vilification from male readers—in Wroth's case, the male courtiers surrounding King James—the constructions of the women writers may have been directed at least as much, if not more, to their female peers than to their self-styled male superiors. Certainly the gender of an intended audience makes a "difference" to the engendering of discourse within a text. In identifying "arachnologies" for early modern women writers, then, it is particularly important to take note of what might be termed the "difference within" their texts, when gender distinctions among putative readers or listeners are brought to the fore.

As discussed in some of the preceding chapters, even as male-authored conduct books in early modern England attempted to bolster established social practices in the face of emergent discourses of social change, early female-authored polemical texts revised cultural commonplaces in order to open new avenues of debate. In the discourse of a female polemicist such as Jane Anger, the very notion of authorship itself is subject to revaluation in gendered terms. Anger opens her pamphlet with a direct attack on male authors, observing: "The desire that every man hath to show his true vein in writing is unspeakable, and their minds are so carried away with the manner as no care at all is had of the matter."[13] At once judge and executioner, Anger claims the high ground for her own authorship in the act of writing as a woman against the writings of men, de-ciphering the "unspeakable" desires embedded in men's texts.

What is more, not only the terms but also the audience for the debate are explicitly gendered, when Jane Anger addresses herself not to the men whose condemnation of women has necessitated her pamphlet, but rather to her fellow women: "I have set down unto you (which are of mine own Sex) the subtle dealings of untrue meaning men."[14] By exposing those "subtle dealings" in her pamphlet, Jane Anger challenges through her own discourse the discursive infidelities of the other sex. She goes even further in advising women to refuse to be subjected to male discourse at all, with an injunction to "stop your ears."[15] By re-gendering cultural commonplaces concerning the infidelity of women in order to lay the blame on men, now defined as "other" than her audience, Jane Anger manages to publicize the otherwise private wrongs suffered by women without resorting to a "private" female language.

A few decades later, in the first female-authored response to Joseph Swetnam's *Arraignment*, Rachel Speght attacks Swetnam's authorial construction by deconstructing publicly "the portraiture which he hath drawn of himself, his Writings being the very emblem of a Monster."[16] Similarly, Esther Sowernam's response to Swetnam relies upon the publication rather than privatization of female discourse. Where Swetnam opens his pamphlet with the admission that he has taken his "pen in hand" in a private moment, "musing with myself, being idle," Sowernam commences by recounting a "discourse concerning women" among friends, "where the number of each sex were equal." Having established a gender-balanced social context for her voice, Sowernam proceeds to recount her judgment of Swetnam's text, in which she found "the discourse as far off from performing what the Title promised as I found it scandalous and blasphemous."[17] In more measured terms than Jane Anger, but with the same preemptive force, Esther Sowernam locates not simply the desirability but more strongly the mandate for her authorship in the failings of a male-authored text.

In closing, Sowernam asserts once more the power of her authorship ("I have in my discourse touched you and all yours to the quick"), and underscores her authority as a writer by advising Swetnam himself on the most suitable construction of his discourse in the future: "write out of deliberation, not out of fury; write out of advice, not out of idleness."[18] Refusing to be defined as the lack or negation of the masculine subject, Jane Anger and Esther Sowernam in effect work to jam the ideological machinery of their culture by affirming their authority as speaking subjects on the basis of their authorship as writers. Their bold attacks not simply on men, but more specifically on the writings of men, thus serve to put male authors on the defensive, even while opening up a space for a feminine discourse engendered by female authority.

The feminine discourse of the mothers' advice books, on the other hand, claims a ground for authorship quite different from that of the female polemicists. As Crawford observes in her analysis of women's published writings in the seventeenth century, maternity offered a subject on which women could publish without implicitly attacking conventional values.[19] Instead of directly opposing the authority of men, as do the female polemicists, the mothers who author advice books, writing in "white ink," tend to present their discourse as a complement to fatherly authority within the family. At the same time, responding to the potential devaluation of female discourse even in this arena, they consistently elevate the significance of maternity from a physical condition (whose rigors are acknowledged even by Swetnam) to a discourse of wisdom, able to authorize female authorship. Although nonconfrontational, the mothers' advice books put women literally "into the text—as into the world and into history" by giving them a voice outside "the nurcery." Thus Dorothy Leigh identifies several "causes" for her decision to engage in writing—an activity she preemptively acknowledges as "a thing so unusual among us"—which extend from "motherly affection" for her children to a desire to "encourage women" directly.[20] The enormous popularity of the mothers' advice books, which had a sizable female audience, indicates that the power of maternal discourse was appreciated not simply by children, but more significantly among women themselves.[21]

Apart from the still relatively limited number of female-authored polemical pamphlets and advice books, early modern women were able to "engender" discourse, even if not published, through diaries, correspondence, and manuscripts. Ezell has demonstrated how practices of manuscript circulation and epistolary exchange allowed women to obtain a readership outside their own families without losing control over their productions. Ezell finds particularly striking the degree to which women found voices within these mediums to criticize prominent figures of male authority in their culture, asserting authorial voices in the face of social censure.[22] To borrow Cixous's terms once again, these early modern women both wrote about women and brought women to writing "by [their] own movement," however unacknowledged or unaccepted by their male peers. Using a range of textual genres which have caused many subsequent literary critics, such as Crewe, to label them "authors" only provisionally and in quotation marks, but which nevertheless found an appreciative audience among women at the time, the female authors of un-published manuscripts and letters carved out a discursive space for themselves in which gender could make as significant a "difference" as in the polemical pamphlets and mothers' advice books.

Sidonie Smith's analysis of women's experiments with "alternative lan-guages of self and storytelling," particularly in the examples of autobiographies ranging from the fifteenth to the twentieth centuries, suggests that women authors may "transform [themselves] and cultural stories generally by shift-ing generic boundaries so that there is neither margin nor center."[23] I would add that "alternative languages of self and storytelling" can be found in the diaries and correspondence of early modern women, as well as in their po-lemical and literary texts, which testify to their efforts to transform them-selves and cultural stories generally by shifting the generic boundaries that have denied their existence as writing subjects. Even if some of the texts them-selves resist the dichotomizing structure of margin/center, however, these texts admittedly remain on the margins of their culture's structures of textual pro-duction.

At the same time, as Smith observes, while margins have their limita-tions, they also have advantages of vision, being "polyvocal, more distant from the centers of power and conventions of selfhood," and fostering vital attempts to "reconcile sometimes irreconcilable readings of the self."[24] Furthermore, when we consider the gendered nature of the dynamic linking (or repelling) author and audience, the act of writing *from* the margins sometimes emerges as an art of writing *on* the margins in more than one sense. From the diaries of Lady Margaret Hoby and Lady Anne Clifford, for example, we know that these women spent a notable amount of time not only writing in their diaries, but also composing letters to others, both in friendship and (particularly in re-sponse to directives from their husbands) in occasional conflict.[25] Indeed, Ezell has documented the significant extent to which "correspondence networks" provided educated women with often quite extensive opportunities for intel-lectual engagements, both affectionate and hostile.[26]

Although female-authored correspondence is often notoriously hard to track down among historical collections of family papers, particularly given that family papers are seldom indexed under women's names, in Mary Wroth's case several striking letters survive which document her struggle to defend her authorship as a woman within the Jacobean court.[27] Immediately following the publication of *Urania* in 1621, for example, Wroth received two hostile letters from Edward, Lord Denny, charging that Wroth had slandered his family in her fictional account of Seralius and his father-in-law. Denny's attack included a poem, entitled "To Pamphilia from the father-in-law of Seralius," which comprises a compendium of many of the misogynist figurations of gender marking the Jacobean court:

Hermophradite in show, in deed a monster|
  As by thy words and works all men may conster
  Thy wrathfull spite conceived an Idell book
  Brought forth a foole which like the damme doth look
Wherein thou strikes at some mans noble blood
  Of kinne to thine if thine be counted good
Whose vaine comparison for want of witt
  Takes up the oystershell to play with it
Yet common oysters such as thine gape wide
  And take in pearles or worse at every tide
Both frind and foe to thee are even alike
  Thy witt runns madd not caring who it strike
These slanderous flying f[l]ames rise from the pott
  For potted witts inflamd are raging hott
How easy wer't to pay thee with thine owne
  Returning that which thou thy self hast throwne
And write a thousand lies of thee at least
  And by thy lines describe a drunken beast
This were no more to thee then thou hast donne
  A Thrid but of thine owne which thou hast spunn
By which thou plainly seest in thine owne glass
  How easy tis to bring a ly to pass
Thus hast thou made thy self a lying wonder
  Fooles and their Bables seldome part asunder
Work o th'Workes leave idle bookes alone
  For wise and worthyer women have writte none.[28]

The image of a "Hermophradite in show" echoes the language of the cultural debate over transvestism which had reached a climax just the previous year, with the publication in 1620 of *Hic Mulier; or, The Man-Woman* and *Haec-Vir; or, the Womanish Man*. *Hic Mulier*'s attack on the "Female-Masculine" of "these new Hermaphrodites" revealed men's simultaneous fear and loathing of women whose cross-dressing disrupted the visual boundaries of sexual difference, threatening the apparent autonomy of male subjectivity. Denny's use of the label of "Hermophradite" betrays a similar fear and loathing, elicited in his case not simply by the "show" of female appearance, but by the "deed" of female language as well. In juxtaposing Wroth's "words and works," Denny unwittingly grants her the very power of agency associated with authorship which his attack has been fashioned to undermine. Even the sexual hostility underlying his description of Wroth's "oysters," which "gape wide / And take in pearles or worse at every tide," can be read in "redoubled" terms as exposing his masculine insecurity over this woman writer's capacity actually to produce "pearles" of her own, despite his accusation that she only "takes in" what she puts out. Denny's attack finally boils down to an explicit anxiety over the cultural transgression embodied in female authorship: "Work o th'Workes leave idle bookes alone / For wise and worthyer women have writte none." In the wake of the hostile response of courtiers such as Denny to the publication of *Urania*, Wroth wrote a letter to the duke of Buckingham in which she defends her authorship: "Understanding some of the strang constructions which are made of my booke contrary to my imagination, and as farr from my meaning as is possible for truth to bee from conjecture, my purpose noe way bent to give the least cause of offence, my thoughts free from soe much as thinking of any such thing as I ame censurd for; I have with all care caused the sale of them to bee forbidden, and the books left to bee shut up."[29] In maintaining that "strang constructions" have distorted her discourse, Wroth attempts to disrupt the "dichotomizing—and at the same time redoubling—break" (to use Irigaray's words) that governed the courtly outrage over her female authorship of a secular romance. Attacked specifically on the basis of her gender as an author, condemned as a "hermophradite in show, in deed a monster," Wroth suffers the cost of the dichotomizing figurations of gender in her culture, which construct female authorship in oxymoronic terms and attempt to "shut up" her writings.

Although Wroth assured the duke of Buckingham that she had stopped the sale of her books, she meanwhile responded directly to Denny's attack with a scathing letter in which she does anything but "shut up." Even as Jane Anger and Esther Sowernam locate their mandate for authorship in the failings of male-authored texts, so Wroth professes disbelief that the "vile, rayling and scandalous thinges" which appeared under the name of Lord Denny could have proceeded "from any but some drunken poett." In observing that she "no more meant harme to my Lord Denny or his house, then to my selfe," Wroth asserts the validity of her subjecthood, which Denny has attempted to deconstruct with his labels of "Hermophradite" and "monster." Rather than "shut up," then, Wroth proceeds to construct a "redoubling break" of her own, by sending Denny his "owne lines . . . reversed" in a powerful example of what might be termed transformational mimesis. Finally, in identifying this "course" of her response to Denny as no more, nor less, than "a mornings work," Wroth maintains the agency of her authorial voice.[30]

Wroth's poem changes the subject of Denny's poem in more ways than one:

> Hirmophradite in sense in Art a monster
>   As by your railing rimes the world may conster
> Your spitefull words against a harmless booke
>   Shows that an ass much like the sire doth looke
> Men truly noble fear no touch of blood
>   Nor question make of others much more good
> Can such comparisons seme the want of witt

When oysters have enflamd your blood with it
But it appeares your guiltiness gapt wide
    And filld with Dirty doubt your brains swolne tide
Both frind and foe in deed you use alike
    And your mad witt in sherry aequall strike
These slaunderous flying flames raisd from the pott
    You know are false and raging makes you hott
How easily now do you receave your owne
    Turnd on your self from whence the squibb was throwne
When these few lines not thousands writt at least
    Mainly thus prove your self the drunken beast
This is far less to you then you have donne
A T[h]rid but of your owne all words worse spunn
By which you lively see in your owne glasse
    How hard it is for you to ly and pass
Thus you have made your self a lying wonder
    Fooles and their pastimes should not part asunder
Take this then and now lett railing rimes alone
    For wise and worthier men have written none.[31]

The opening line of Wroth's poem immediately replaces Denny's attack on the "body" of her work (and by extension on her own female body, construed as a "Hermophradite in show") with her attack on the "sense" of his language, and on the deformation of his "Art." Responding, Arachne-like, to Denny's characterization of her discourse as a spun "Thrid," Wroth spins a web of language around Denny which recasts him as a supremely incompetent author ("your owne all wordes worse spunn"), whose "railing rimes" at once expose and deflate his "brains swolne tide." In a further exchange of letters between Wroth and Denny, Wroth reminds Denny that she is, after all, not Pamphilia but rather "the author of the booke," and concludes: "be assured you shall find mee; what my blood calls mee to be, and what my words have said mee to be."[32] As both flesh and blood woman, and as "the author" of her own book, Mary Wroth claims a position of agency as a speaking subject who cannot be "shut up."

Wroth's experience of the tribulations associated with female authorship in early modern England reflects cultural figurations of gender that sought to restrict women's speech and writing to religious spheres wherever possible. Even as Denny castigated Wroth for having the effrontery to write secular fiction and poetry, in contrast to the "godly books" of her aunt, the countess of Pembroke, so Margaret Tyler opened her translation of *The Mirrour of Princely Deedes and Knyghthood* in 1578 with an "Epistle to the Reader," which expresses the hope that her "ill willers" do not attempt to force her as a woman "either not to write or to write of divinitie."[33] At the same time, women writers such as Aemilia Lanyer, Elizabeth Cary, and Mary Wroth could look back to "foremothers" with a range of authorial voices, from Christine de Pizan to Marguerite de Navarre, and from Louise Labé to the countess of Pembroke herself, whose agency as a literary figure provided Wroth in particular with an empowering example quite distinct from Denny's reductive formulation.

As Margaret Hannay has pointed out in her book-length study of Mary Sidney, although the countess remained on the margins of cultural discourse, her astute use of the permitted religious genres served in its own way as a strong political statement. For examples, Hannay points to original poems such as "To the Thrice Sacred Queen Elizabeth," and "To the Angell spirit of the most excellent Sir Philip Sidney," in which the countess of Pembroke sought to continue not only her brother's discourse, but also his involvement in Protestant politics.[34] At the same time, Mary Ellen Lamb's similarly detailed analysis of the countess's texts suggests that Mary Sidney justified the discourse of her translations by embedding her version of authorship within the art of dying.[35] The heroism of dying links the authorial voice of the countess of Pembroke, then, with the authors of the mothers' advice books, who asserted the prerogative of speech from "beyond the grave" in order to free their discourse from the apparent contamination of sexuality imposed by the gender ideologies of their culture.

Aemilia Lanyer's volume of religious poems, *Salve Deus Rex Judaeorum*, moves beyond the margins of literary discourse occupied by the countess's translations, in demonstrating that an Englishwoman could claim a lyric voice of her own. Publishing *Salve Deus* under her own name in 1611, Lanyer dared to author a celebration of good women in which gender makes not only a difference, but all the difference. With eleven dedications to women, a title poem on Christ's Passion and crucifixion which includes subsections for "Eves Apologie in defence of Women," "The Teares of the Daughters of Jerusalem," and "The Salutation and Sorrow of the Virgine Marie," and a final country-house poem, "The Description of Cooke-ham," which celebrates the countess of Cumberland's estate as a female Eden, *Salve Deus Rex Judaeorum* establishes not only the range but also the authority of feminine discourse in a religious context.

The very first dedicatory poem, "To the Queenes most Excellent Majestie," calls attention to the gendered significance of Lanyer's authorship in inviting the Queen "to view that which is seldom seene, / A womans writing of divinest things" (3-4). Even while praising the queen, the poem constantly calls attention to its own "lines" and "Text," and establishes its general audience as well, in professing to be written not simply in honor of the queen, but in honor of the queen's "sexe" (35, 74, 76). The poem concludes with the hope that Nature, the originator of "all Arts," might grace Lanyer's "barren Muse" with a voice, "and in a Woman all defects excuse" (151, 155-56). The trials of female authorship thus surface at the beginning of the volume, in the poet's apparent desire to seek "excuse" for her "defects" (discursive transgressions?) as a woman.

The poet's seemingly defensive position on the issue of gender reappears in the next dedicatory poem, "To the Lady Elizabeths Grace," where she asks the princess to accept "the first fruits of a womans wit," despite having seen "farre better Bookes" (12-13). Lanyer contextualizes her reference to "farre better Bookes," however, in her dream poem addressed to "the Countesse Dowager of Pembroke," where she compares her own written "fruits" with the "many Books" written by Mary Sidney (194-95). Even as she finds the countess's books to be "more rare" than her own, she maintains the value of her own authorship, observing that "yet there is honey in the meanest flowers: / Which is both wholesome, and delights the taste" (195-97). Far from comparing herself unfavorably with male authors, then, Lanyer situates herself in a literary community of women who compose both authors and audience, where even "the meanest flowers" can coexist harmoniously with "farre better Bookes" when produced by and for women.[36] Thus in her dedicatory poem "To all vertuous Ladies in generall," as well as in her epistle "To the Vertuous Reader," Lanyer explicitly addresses her volume to "all virtuous Ladies and Gentlewomen of this kingdome; and in commendation of some particular persons of our own sex" (48). For Lanyer, writing openly as a woman on women to women, in a society that enjoined women to silence, the engendering of discourse for female author and female audience go hand in hand.

While Renaissance authorship may be represented as a male-centered concept in the writings of men, with the Muse often configured as a mistress or female beloved answerable to the entreaties or commands of men's voices, Lanyer addresses her Muse as mother to her "Infant Verse," thus calling upon the potentially empowering force of maternity to liberate her voice even as did the contemporary authors of the mothers' advice books (SDRJ, 273, 279). Furthermore, even as she details the dangers confronting her fledgling verse, she transforms the trials of her authorship into evidence of the power of God, for whom "the Weaker thou doest seeme to be / In Sexe, or Sence, the more his Glory shines" (SDRJ, 289-90). Openly acknowledging the vulnerabilities of "Sexe, or Sence" associated with her authorship in a patriarchal culture, Lanyer identifies her words with "the Widowes Myte," whose "little All" proved "more worth than golden mynes" in the eyes of the Lord (SDRJ, 293-94). Just as the treasures of wealthy men seem as nothing by comparison to the widow's "All" in the eyes of Christ, so the abundant production of male authors in Lanyer's culture may yet, Lanyer warns, be found insignificant by comparison to her "plainest Words" (SDRJ, 311). "Invidious exclusions," in other words, may originate in the eye of the beholder.

Furthermore, in the portion of *Salve Deus* entitled "Eve's Apologie," Lanyer identifies "Eve's faire hand" with "a learned Booke," in providing the source of all men's knowledge (*SDRJ*, 807-8). This particular identification, with its implication that what comes from the hand of a woman may not only be compared to a learned book, but may even prove a source for learned books, further underscores the latent power in Lanyer's own "Hand and Quill" (*SDRJ*, 324), an image at once female and authorial. At the close of her long poem on Christ's Passion, Lanyer once again hails the countess dowager of Cumberland as her earthly inspiration for authorship, and addresses her as "the Articke Starre that guides my hand" (*SDRJ*, 1839). Illumined by female authority and guided by female affection, Lanyer's "Hand and Quill" produce a text that confronts the patriarchal exclusions of her society, and works to de-construct the social codes that authorized the marginalization of the female subject.

The proximity between the publication dates of *Salve Deus Rex Judaeorum* and Wroth's poems and prose romance (separated by only ten years) suggests Lanyer's importance, along with the countess of Pembroke, as a model of female authorship for Wroth. Indeed, a number of Wroth's representations of female authorial figures in her texts can be linked, both explicitly and implicitly, to the examples of Mary Sidney and Aemilia Lanyer, as well as to their textual engagements with issues of women's speech. At the same time, in *Pamphilia to Amphilanthus* Wroth moves in a significantly different direction from her female predecessors in the English lyric by opening up a space for feminine discourse within the male-dominated bastions of Petrarchism. Instead of grounding her constructions of female heroism in the art of dying, or in the spiritual piety of female religious devotion, Wroth finds a voice in sexual difference itself, or in a re-gendering of the tension between lover and beloved. Wroth's inscription of a female lyric subject through the voice of Pamphilia assails the conventional premises of the Petrarchan sonneteers' objectification of women by disrupting the "dichotomizing—and at the same time redoubling—break" between the vocal male lover and the silent female object of desire. Rather than defining Pamphilia, like Stella, as the lack or negation of the (masculine) subject, then, Wroth uncovers the operation of the feminine *in language*—that is, to paraphrase Irigaray, in her recuperative mimesis of the Petrarchan language of authorship and desire.

Heather Dubrow's recent reading of *Pamphilia to Amphilanthus* in terms of a dialogue between Petrarchism and anti-Petrarchism provides an illuminating model of some of the tensions marking Wroth's sequence. Specifically, Dubrow observes that even as Petrarchan discourses "define themselves diacritically, through contrast with other writers and other selves," and yet often encrypt that which they reject within themselves, so they can "mime the problematics of female subjectivity as well as male."[37] In the case of Wroth, according to these terms, the sonnet genre thus offers not only familial precedent, but also a potential model for her own subjectivity. Dubrow's incisive analysis of the influences of Petrarchism and anti-Petrarchism upon Wroth's sequence opens the possibility for reading an early modern female author in revisionary rather than reactionary terms, as providing a transformative response to the very constraints that might exclude her from authorship based upon her gender. Instead of simply reacting to "dominant" male predecessors, then, Wroth can be seen to be reworking the problematics of gendered subjectivity within the genre itself.

Throughout her lyric sequence, Wroth at once appropriates and transforms the tropes of her father and uncle, both Petrarchan poets *par excellence*. Furthermore, Wroth initially experiments with the "art of dying" approach of her aunt even as she borrows the focus for her verse from her father. In one early song, for example, Wroth apparently reverses the opening line of one of Robert Sidney's songs ("Winter is come at last" [Song #3]) with her own opening line ("The spring now come att last" [P7]), only to bring her poem into direct alignment with her father's poem after all: "Colde winter yett remaines / Noe signe of spring wee know." Whereas Robert Sidney's song is spoken by "a shepherd . . . with weights of change oppressed," Wroth's speaker is a "shepherdess . . . who was with griefe oprest." Significantly, Wroth disrupts the alignment between the two speakers almost as soon as she has established it, by extending the focus of her shepherdess's song from lament alone to the authorship of that lament: "The barck my booke shall bee / Wher dayly I will wright / This tale of haples mee." In conclusion, the shepherdess pledges to leave "thes lines" for someone to place upon her tomb, so that she may speak to other lovers from beyond the grave. The discourse of this particular song, then, can be said to be grounded in the "art of dying."

In subsequent poems, however, Wroth moves from the art of dying to the "art" of authorship itself (P8), even as she begins to identify her speaker, in distinction from the Petrarchan pose of painter, as a speaking subject rather than the "speaking object" of her own art. The conventional pose of painter can be identified in numerous male-authored sonnets, such as the first sonnet of Robert Sidney's crown, which depicts the lover's painterly skills turned impotently upon himself, as the speaker laments: "I labour shall in vain / To paint in words the deadly wounds the dart / Of your fair eyes doth give" (Sonnet #11). More famously, the first sonnet of *Astrophil and Stella* finds the speaker seeking "fit words to paint the blackest face of woe" — to paint, that is, his own face of woe, in order to win Stella's pity. Near the center of the sequence, Philip Sidney calls further attention to the failure of the speaker's art, with Astrophil's complaint that "Stella oft sees the verie face of wo / Painted in my beclowded stormie face: / But cannot skill to pitie my disgrace" (AS #45). After noting that Stella is moved by "a fable," Astrophil beseeches her to think "that you in me do reed / Of Lover's ruine some sad Tragedie," concluding: "I am not I, pitie the tale of me" (AS #45). In Philip Sidney's sequence, love makes Astrophil a painter of his own plight, a fabler of his own sad tale. His seeming self-denial — "I am not I" — actually advances an assertion of self encoded in a fiction — "pitie the tale of me." For male sonneteers such as Philip and Robert Sidney, self-objectification through art, even in failure, serves only to reify their subjective authority as writers.

Wroth, however, expands the representational purview of her art to encompass not only "this tale of haples mee," but also the image of her beloved: "Love will a painter make you, such, as you / Shall able bee to drawe your only deere / More lively, parfett, lasting, and more true / Then rarest woorkman, and to you more neere" (P83). Wroth here aligns herself as a poet with Shakespeare's position in Sonnet #24, where his speaker declares to the young man that "mine eye hath played the painter and hath stelled / Thy beauty's form in table of my heart." Yet even in appropriating Shakespeare's stance, Wroth moves away from the male Petrarchan obsession with the physical beauty of "form" to her own concern with gender relations in love. The double meaning of "true" in Wroth's sonnet, alluding not only to the accuracy of the likeness but also to the desired constancy of the male beloved, is underscored by the final phrase, "and to you more neere." In connecting the power of representation with successful passion, Wroth conveys not the impotence, but rather the potential authority, of her authorship.

While in Shakespeare's sequence the speaker's painterly obsession with the young man still works to place a masculine image at the center of the sonnet in question, elevating the complementary masculine image of the speaker himself as a result, in Wroth's sequence the speaker's representational focus upon her male beloved rather than herself might be read as a seeming example of the self-abnegation expected of a Renaissance lady.[38] From another perspective, however, to use Irigaray's definition of *mimétisme*, Pamphilia's assumption of the apparently feminine posture of serving the male beloved's image rather than foregrounding her own allows Wroth to uncover the mechanisms by which Petrarchan discourse exploits the woman. At the same time, as Masten has observed, Pamphilia's refusal to circulate as a Petrarchan sign herself signifies a repudiation (or, one might add, a "re-gendering") of public Petrarchan discourse.[39] Furthermore, Wroth's emphasis upon Pamphilia's successful agency as a poet rather than her physical "form" or appearance contrasts not only with conventional Petrarchan objectifications of the female body, but also with the failure of art bemoaned by sonneteers such as Philip and Robert Sidney. Speaking with the emerging authority engendered by her own lyric discourse, Wroth celebrates the representational power of the female lover as poet.

The crown of sonnets at the heart of Wroth's sequence both appropriates and transforms the discursive techniques of her father's and uncle's poetic "crowns." As it draws to a close, Wroth's *corona* circles back upon itself with the questioning couplet of the fourteenth sonnet: "Soe though in Love I fervently doe burne, / In this strange labourinth how shall I turne?" (P90). The question in the fourteenth line of the fourteenth sonnet echoes the question in the first line of the first sonnet, completing the circle only to continue it.[40] Even as Wroth's ongoing struggle to define her subjectivity as a female author surfaces repeatedly throughout the sequence as a whole, so the labyrinthine turns of Pamphilia's quest to define her identity as a female lover within the *corona* can have no simple end. In the *Old Arcadia*, Philip Sidney goes beyond his *corona* in order to end it, attaching a four-line tag after the tenth dizain in which Strephon calls explicitly for "an ende" (OA #72). Robert Sidney breaks his circle without ending it, cutting off the fifth sonnet of his crown after one quatrain. Wroth differentiates her crown from those of her uncle and father by maintaining a true circularity of form, which reflects the continuing rather than conclusive nature of her speaker's experience of vexed gender relations in love.

Interestingly enough, however, the circular continuity of Wroth's crown actually echoes and encompasses the essential circularity embedded in the larger sequences of her father and uncle. While the broken fifth sonnet of Robert Sidney's crown, which would have been the fifteenth sonnet of his sequence, interrupts the inner circle of the *corona*, the actual fifteenth sonnet of the sequence only reiterates the continuing nature of the speaker's plight, ending with his query "what way to fly?" (Sonnet #15). The final sonnet of Philip Sidney's sequence suggests the continuing cycle of Astrophil's experience with a circular couplet—"That in my woes for thee thou art my joy, / And in my joyes for thee my only annoy" (AS #108)—which echoes the circular plaint of Strephon and Klaius in Philip Sidney's *corona*: "I joye in griefe, and doo detest all joyes" (OA #72). The ending of Wroth's *corona* thus recalls the apparently endless trials of love expressed in the larger sequences of her male Sidney forebears. At the same time, in her own larger sequence, Wroth moves beyond the circularity of her *corona* with the final utterances of her female speaker.

The first song that follows Wroth's *corona* yields a transformed blazon which not only translates the Petrarchan obsession with fragmented body parts into Platonic rather than physical terms, but also conjoins lover and beloved in a single union. While traditional Petrarchan blazons tend to establish a dichotomizing break between the objectified female "other" and the male author of discourse, Wroth's inscription of "eyes of gladnes, lips of love, / And harts from passion nott to turne" has the effect of celebrating connection rather than distance between the lovers, suggesting the possibility of a union between two equal, even if differently gendered, subjects. In disrupting the dichotomizing effects of Petrarchan discourse, Wroth works to open up a "space for the feminine" in a different voice, which grants the potential for subjectivity to both lovers without claiming a simple resolution to trials in love.

Pamphilia to Amphilanthus closes with a sonnet conveying the speaker's conscious decision to complete her discourse: "My muse now hapy, lay thy self to rest, / Sleepe in the quiett of a faithfull love" (P103). Pamphilia directs her muse to "Leave the discource of Venus, and her sunn / To young beeginers," concluding: "And thus leave off, what's past showes you can love, / Now lett your constancy your honor prove" (P103). Just as the sequence opened with a dream vision of Venus and Cupid from which the speaker first wakes to love, the sequence closes with a call to sleep. However it is now the lady, no longer a helpless dreamer, who directs her muse to sleep.[41] As both lover and poet, Wroth's speaker has moved beyond the arbitrary power of Venus and Cupid, tracing her thread of passion from the margins through the heart of the "labourinth," until her experience enables her to articulate her own rhetoric of love. Likewise Wroth demonstrates that she has moved beyond the particular Petrarchan discourse of her father and uncle in tracing her thread of song from the margins of the Sidney family tradition to the central achievement of her own lyric sequence, whose existence re-forms the tradition.

Relinquishing the fictive "discource" of Venus and Cupid, Pamphilia turns from writing to living, from speaking her desire to acquiring agency from her speech. The silence of Pamphilia's muse in this final sonnet is a silence not of lack but of completion.[42] As she designates the point of closure for her lyric sequence, Pamphilia characteristically makes reference to the necessary continuation of that discourse in the voices of other lovers, whose presence in her sequence through her acknowledgment of the shared nature of female suffering has decentered the absence of her own beloved. Both Philip and Robert Sidney end their sequences with assertions of continuing desire as well as frustration, in which their speakers lament once again their personal plights with further versions of "the tale of me." Wroth's speaker claims no greater personal success in love than Astrophil or Rosis, yet her powers of authorship prevail not only through but also beyond her personal trials of desire. Even as Aemilia Lanyer founds her authorship of "The Description of Cooke-ham" on an experience of the loss specifically of female companionship, so Mary Wroth finds in the shared female experience of absence in love the occasion for a lyric voice of her own.

At the end of Wroth's sequence, Pamphilia takes care to contrast the "true forme of love" in her own discourse with the "ancient fictions" of her paternal forebears (P100). For male sonneteers like Philip and Robert Sidney, although the lady may be the object of affection, the speaker's "tale of me," or fiction of himself, is the true subject of the sequence. For Wroth, on the other hand, the female speaker's discursive attention to gender relations in love ultimately takes precedence over the enfabling of her experiences. When the lady speaks, in the eighth song of *Astrophil and Stella* or in the sixth song of Robert Sidney's sequence, the music of the male sonneteers is at least temporarily broken, because their "ancient fictions" are predicated upon their construction of the female beloved as listener rather than voice. Wroth's speaker maintains that the "true forme of love" is bodied forth within her language, apart from the changing whims of male response, so that no male beloved can finally fracture her authorship. The silence at the end of *Pamphilia to Amphilanthus* thus represents not the defeat of the singer, but the culmination of the song.

As a prominent early modern woman, Wroth herself was no breaker of songs, as can be gathered from the many poems written in her honor.[43] Furthermore, she is honored by other poets not just as a lady but as a maker of songs and, indeed, an author in her own right—most notably by Ben Jonson's assertion that since copying her sonnets he became "A better lover, and much better poet."[44] Even allowing for the element of hyperbole, Jonson's response to Wroth's poems does serve to accord her the status of an author, although inevitably her status functions to bolster his own ("much better") position as poet. At the same time, the attacks of a courtier such as Lord Denny bear witness to the double-edged consequences of successfully claiming a "different" lyric voice as a woman. Distinguishing herself from her aunt on the one hand, and her father and uncle on the other, Mary Wroth proves her ability to "engender" poetic discourse by putting herself "into the text" as female subject rather than object, woman author rather than "other." In inscribing "the very possibility of change" within the masculine economy of Petrarchan discourse, then, the language of *Pamphilia to Amphilanthus* can be read in Cixous's terms as providing a space for "the precursory movement of a transformation of social and cultural structures."

More explicitly within her play and prose romance than in her lyric sequence, Wroth situates women's discursive connections with one another in relation to social and cultural structures. By calling attention to the often already gendered relations between speaker and listener, author and audience, discursive production and reception, Wroth connects female authorship and authority not in isolation, but specifically among women. Wroth's treatment of feminine discourse in both *Love's Victory* and *Urania* can be examined with reference to the models of female authorship provided by Marguerite de Navarre and Elizabeth Cary, who constructed fictive worlds within secular rather than strictly religious frames, and who fashioned a significant variety of female speaking positions.

Anne Lake Prescott and Maureen Quilligan have linked Wroth to Marguerite de Navarre with the suggestion that Wroth may be imitating Marguerite's technique in the *Heptaméron* by presenting family members and court acquaintances in disguise within a narrative framework.[45] On another level, I would suggest that Wroth's awareness of the *Heptaméron* may have shaped her treatment of conflict between the sexes, not only in romantic relationships but also in interpretive discourse. As Natalie Zemon Davis has demonstrated, the *Heptaméron* conveys a remarkable range of pardonable violent sentiment for women, going beyond most sixteenth-century discussions of the implications of anger and violence between men and women. Davis finds that in the realms of test, threat, and fantasy in particular, the queen-author figure allows her ladies a wider range of feeling than women allow themselves in the letters of remission, and also pardons them for it. Because the narrative debates on how and whether men and women should act on their anger are followed by opportunities on the one hand for forgiveness and on the other hand for acceptance of desires for vengeance, Davis suggests that the *Heptaméron* succeeds in representing the liberty implicit in the act of interpretation.[46]

In her historical analysis of women of the Renaissance, Margaret King notes that Marguerite de Navarre was in fact the director of cultural matters at the court of her brother, François I, and the protector of a circle of learned men. King points out that Marguerite's standing as a woman at the center of currents of proto-reform in court circles thus positioned her effectively to raise questions, in the *Heptaméron*, about the troubled roles of women in a man's world.[47] In England less than a century later, the influential standing of Mary Sidney, the countess of Pembroke, as a patron of literary men, as well as the extensive involvement of her niece, Mary Wroth, with Jacobean court circles, can similarly be read not simply as illuminating gendered restraints upon authorship in a patriarchal society, but as enabling resistance to those very restraints at the same time. As with many other gendered representations of authority, conceptions of authorship in an early modern English society that included female readers of texts such as Marguerite's *Heptaméron* can be seen to have been more absolute in rhetoric than in practice.

In Marguerite's *Heptaméron*, the female authorship of the queen engenders a narrative form in which the sexes can share discourse on equal terms. As Marguerite's Hircan notes when the characters agree to engage in the pastime of exchanging stories: "Where games are concerned everybody is equal."[48] Interestingly, the triangle of storytellers who most consistently shape the flow of the narrative — Oisille, Parlamente, and Hircan — is formed of two women and one man, with the oldest and most authoritative of the three being a woman, so that the balance of authorial power frequently shifts toward the women, undermining the otherwise regular attempts of the male characters to dismiss the women's tales on the basis of gender.[49] Furthermore, the likelihood that Marguerite herself authored the storytelling framework in which the tales that she collected are embedded indicates the importance of the interpretive frame.[50] Within this frame of interpretive discourse, both women and men are given voices to critique the authorship of the opposite sex as well as their own, so that gendered differences of interpretation can be at once articulated and challenged.

At the conclusion of one tale concerning a wife's falsehood, for instance, the male narrator of the tale, Simontaut, immediately generalizes from his story to all women, concluding that "ever since Eve made Adam sin, women have taken it upon themselves to torture men, kill them and damn them to Hell," adding that he can testify to his own experience of "feminine cruelty" (78). But when he urges Oisille to tell the next story, asserting his confidence that she will corroborate his estimation of women, she accepts his challenge not defensively, but with a laugh, and calls into question Simontaut's strategy of "casting a slur on *all* women" by "telling a true story about *one* wretched woman" (78). Without denying the frailty of one particular woman, Oisille yet resists Simontaut's interpretive attempt to stereotype all women, from Eve to the present, in negative terms based upon their alleged difference from men. Instead, she calls attention to the differences among women themselves, which operate to undermine their potential objectification in men's eyes.

Soon thereafter, one of the other female characters, Ennasuite, follows Oisille's example of critiquing the inadequacies of gender stereotyping, again in response to a tale involving an unfaithful wife narrated by a male character, in this case Saffredent. Interestingly, Ennasuite specifically addresses her story to a female audience, asserting: "I have a story to tell, Ladies, which will show Saffredent and everyone else here that not *all* women are like the queen he has told us about, and that not all men who are rash enough to try their tricks get what they want" (89). As her subsequent narrative points out, while female infidelity requires the complicity of a man, female virtue can be maintained even in the face of male aggression. Ennasuite's tale details a violent rape attempt upon "a strong woman" who is both a widow and a princess. Once the widow realizes that her assailant "would use all his strength to dishonour her," she fights back "with all *her* strength in order to stop him," until he is forced to retreat, covered with bites and scratches (92-93). Ennasuite brings her story to a close by observing that in the aftermath of the failed rape attempt "he, who was the boldest man at court, would completely lose his self-assurance in her presence, and would frequently go to pieces" (96), suggesting that male subjectivity can be deconstructed by female presence of mind and strength of will, as manifested in active physical resistance. In her interpretive commentary, Ennasuite maintains that her story "should strike fear into the hearts of any man who thinks he can help himself to what doesn't belong to him" (96), underscoring the power of her narrative to document women's capacity for agency even in the face of attempted victimization. The interpretive emphasis upon female physical strength and will in this tale from the *Heptaméron* can be linked to the active powers of Pamphilia as a warrior queen in Wroth's *Urania*, which enable her to resist the masculine aggression of enemy kings even as she outlasts the inconstancy of her male beloved.

In a further twist upon the deconstruction of gender stereotyping in Marguerite's text, yet another female character, Nomerfide, sets out to "tell a story to show . . . that women can exercise their cleverness for bad purposes as well as for good ones," at the same time reminding her audience that just as one woman's virtue "does not redound to the honour of other women unless they actually follow in her footsteps, so the *vice* of one woman does not bring dishonour on all other women" (101). While Nomerfide's story represents an example of successful female infidelity, her interpretive commentary challenges the earlier conclusions of Simontaut and Saffredent. Nomerfide remarks that if women are "clever enough to cover up something bad," she thinks that "they'd be even more ingenious in avoiding bad deeds or in doing good ones," and concludes that "a shrewd wit is always stronger in the end" (103). Significantly, Hircan is so offended by Nomerfide's praise of "feminine cunning" that he resorts to the offensive, asserting that Nomerfide herself would never have the capability to exercise such cunning (103). Rather than being put out by his accusation, however, Nomerfide replies simply by offering Hircan the opportunity to demonstrate his belief that "male cunning . . . is superior to female cunning" with a story of his own (104). Once again, the interpretive frame allows for the voicing rather than the silencing of difference.

Nomerfide's tale and attendant commentary, along with those of many of the other female characters in the *Heptaméron*, too numerous to detail adequately here, work not simply to provide a list of "good women," along the lines of the approach adopted by Aemilia Lanyer, but rather to challenge the tendency of the male characters to dichotomize all women into virgins or whores (with an emphasis on the latter) while refusing to recognize at once the strengths and the differences among women. An example of unbridled female sexuality, then, can be used to resist gender stereotyping as vigorously as an example of female virtue in Nomerfide's story. Nomerfide's emphasis upon "feminine cunning" as a potential force for virtuous agency as well as deception distinguishes between women's bodies and their minds, and opens the playing field for "wit" to both sexes. Moreover, the fierce debates that mark the (female-authored) interpretive frame connecting the stories in the *Heptaméron* serve as occasions for demonstrating the power of women's voices and minds yet again, as "a shrewd wit is always stronger in the end."

With little precedent in the religious writings of such earlier Renaissance Englishwomen as the countess of Pembroke or Aemilia Lanyer, both the examples of freely shared discourse between the sexes and the voicing of "shrewd wit" as well as passionate desire among the female characters in Mary Wroth's play and prose romance may be related to the vocal positions of Marguerite's female characters. By contrast to the clearly "masculine economy" which shapes the romances of Montemayor and d'Urfé, Sidney and even Shakespeare, Marguerite de Navarre's *Heptaméron* may have provided Wroth with a model of alternative figurations of gender which resist conventional stereotyping of women's roles in dichotomized terms, and which allow for the discursive potential of female narrators as speaking subjects rather than simply objects of male desire.

Taking a different tack from Marguerite, Elizabeth Cary's *The Tragedy of Mariam* foregrounds the more problematic aspects of women's speech from the beginning. The women in Cary's play must face male censure for both public and private speech. Whether chaste, like Mariam, or licentious, like Salome, Cary's female characters receive only opprobrium from the governing males for their attempts to forge voices of their own. Catherine Belsey observes that "in a society where the circulation of discourses is controlled by men the definition of women is inevitably patriarchal and reductive," leaving "no space outside discourse from which women may silently intuit an alternative definition." Nevertheless, in the example of *Mariam*, Belsey finds an interrogation of the dominant definitions that problematizes both patriarchal absolutism and women's speech[51] Far more than Wroth's or even Marguerite's characters, Cary's characters fit Kristeva's description of women who are estranged from language, "dancers who suffer as they speak." In a play openly dominated by the Law of the Father in the figure of Herod, the gendered tensions between "public" and "private" language are inscribed from Mariam's opening lament over the consequences of her "public voice" (I.i.1) to Herod's closing acknowledgment that "my word though not my sword made Mariam bleed" (V.i.189). At the same time, in the space between the female characters' spoken words and the disciplinary silencing action of the patriarchal society can be glimpsed the potential power of women's voices to refashion, if not social structures, then individual social practices.

By contrast to the interpretive commentary on tales of salacious as well as virtuous women which marks the *Heptaméron*, Cary inscribes differences among women by juxtaposing such unlikely mothers as Alexandra and Doris, or by opposing the publicly outspoken but sexually chaste Mariam to the privately outspoken and sexually licentious Salome. Although, as Belsey points out, all Salome's talk of initiation of divorce by women and equality of the sexes is formulated only to be sharply repudiated,[52] nevertheless the cleverness of Salome's arguments enthralls her listeners despite the apparent duplicity of her self-fashioning. Her arguments encode the potential, articulated by Marguerite's Nomerfide, for feminine cunning and "shrewd wit" to triumph over instances of masculine domination, thus undermining, however temporarily, the patriarchal social fabric.

For all Mariam's concern over her "public voice," it is Salome who exhibits the power to shape Herod's social practices through language that plays on the insecurities implicit in Herod's simultaneous awe and distrust of Mariam's speech. Thus when a wavering Herod seeks to determine Mariam's fate in conversation with Salome, the issue of Mariam's speech itself provides a vehicle for Salome's attack:

> *Herod.* But have you heard her speak?
> *Salome.* You know I have.
> *Herod.* And were you not amaz'd?
> *Salome.* No, not a whit. . .
> She speaks a beauteous language, but within
> Her heart is false as powder: and her tongue
> Doth but allure the auditors to sin,
> And is the instrument to do you wrong. (IV.vii.425-26, 429-32)

Speaking with the authority of a woman qualified by gender to pass judgment upon another woman's voice, Salome penetrates to the heart of Herod's fears by maintaining that Mariam's "beauteous language" is only a show to cover up the "false as powder" heart within. Salome's claim that Mariam's tongue is a dangerous "instrument" thus draws directly upon cultural anxieties over female speech to discredit the already suspect powers of Mariam's "public voice."

While Belsey maintains that "to speak is to become a subject," so that "for women to speak is to threaten the system of differences which gives meaning to patriarchy," Karen Newman takes issue with Belsey's position, suggesting that "to see subjectivity as constituted through speech is problematic" because "it gives priority to presence and privileges identity; it rehabilitates immediacy, intentionality, and performance." Instead, Newman argues that female subjectivity is constituted through and by representation rather than immediacy of voice. Thus in the case of early modern witchcraft trials, Newman finds that "witches threatened hegemonic patriarchal structures precisely not through their bodies but through their representational powers: as cultural producers, as spectacle, as *representatives* . . . of an oppositional femininity."[53] Viewed in these terms, the power of Cary's Salome can be seen to reside perhaps not in her voice *per se*, let alone in her licentious body, so much as in her representation of Mariam's femininity in oppositional terms which reflect Salome's own relation to Herod. By depicting Mariam as discursively fluid, Salome succeeds in deflecting Herod's interpretive focus from her own voice to the voice of Mariam. Salome's narrative works less as a rational argument for Mariam's infidelity than as an exaggerated spectacle of female duplicity, projected upon a screen of feminine discourse.

In immediate, reflexive response to Salome's accusation of Mariam's false speech, Herod declares Mariam "unchaste" in discursive terms — and ultimately sentences her to death — because "her mouth will ope to ev'ry stranger's ear" (IV.vii.433-34), choosing a tangentially phallic image of the penetrative powers of Mariam's voice which reverses the more conventional construct of an unfaithful woman's ear opening to any man's speech. Herod's fears, like those of Constabarus discussed in chapter 2, indicate the phallic potential of female authorship in men's eyes, underscoring masculine anxieties about verbal castration. In the end, although Mariam is put to death at Herod's command, it is Herod who is defined in relation to Mariam, rather than the other way around, in the epitaph that he chooses for his tomb: "*Here Herod lies, that hath his Mariam slain*" (V.i.258). Even as Mariam's refusal to employ persuasive discourse in her defense allows her to resist Herod's efforts to define her as a Petrarchan mistress, so her silence in death elicits Herod's own words of self-condemnation. Her subjectivity thus emerges most powerfully not in speech and presence, but rather, as Newman's argument might seem to indicate, in the representation of her silence and absence, and in the spectacle of her oppositional femininity. Furthermore, the fact that Herod's epitaph is inscribed within the confines of a female-authored play, whose very title identifies the play as an epitaph not for Herod but for the central female character, provides an interesting twist on the apparent limitations of female speech. In a woman author's hands, the tragedy of Mariam and her public voice opens a space, however briefly, for a feminine economy of discourse after all, when the male tyrant is defined according to his own epitaph as the negation of the female subject rather than vice versa, and the memory of Mariam's voice outlasts the voice of her silencer.

Wroth's play and prose romance complement Cary's representation of masculine anxieties by probing similar fears in a variety of male characters. Yet where Cary's vocal women are finally either silenced (Mariam) or disgraced (Salome), Wroth's female characters speak in a wider range of settings with a greater variety of perspectives. The complex and often competing discourses in Wroth's texts attest to the fact that even as no agency can be said to be entirely accessible, whether for men or women, so no strategies of subordination can be regarded as entirely effective. And just as any efforts to achieve agency may be confronted by counter-attempts to enforce subordination, so any act of representation or authorship is subject to interpretation, and thus re-presentation.

Not limited to the same measured dichotomies between public and private language that obtain in Cary's play, Wroth's female protagonists in particular engender discourse that articulates women's potential for agency precisely in the face of forces impelling social subordination. When Wroth's *Love's Victory* is read primarily as a record of Sidney family relations, or of the obsessions and intrigues of the Jacobean court, the attention, however otherwise illuminating, to *roman a cléf* allusions tends to obscure the significance of gendered differences of representation and interpretation.[54] In Marguerite's *Heptaméron* to an even greater extent than in Cary's *Mariam*, both female and male characters adopt discursive positions located in a heterogeneous middle ground between agency and subordination, which also becomes a middle ground between representation and interpretation. The storytelling framework of the *Heptaméron*, for example, encourages acts of representation and interpretation, authorship and evaluation from both sexes, giving voice to a series of productions of gendered subjectivity. Similarly, in *Love's Victory* Wroth's characters agree to engage in a storytelling game that recalls, in abridged form, the narrative pastimes of the *Heptaméron*. As in Marguerite de Navarre's narrative, the male and female characters in Wroth's play "discourse the secretts of the mind" as equals, agreeing to let "each one heere theyr fortunes past relate, / Theyr loves, theyr froward chance, or theyr good fate" (I.303-5). When one character worries that she must "lose [her] song" because shepherding duties interrupt their pastime, Musella reassures her that her chance to speak will come (I.381). Both authorship and evaluation thus mark the explicitly narrative setting that opens Wroth's play.

Early in the play, Rustic volunteers to sing of Musella, who responds with the sentiment: "Sorry I ame I should your subject bee" (I.334). Musella would rather author her own discourse than be subjected to the domineering discourse of an unwelcome suitor. Although the consequences of choosing not to be Rustic's "subject" initially seem to result in Musella's death, recalling the death of the "outspoken" title character in Cary's play, Musella's death proves to be self-chosen rather than imposed on the one hand, and only temporary on the other. Feminine discourse in *Love's Victory* at once engages and competes with masculine discourse due to the rules of the storytelling game, in which, as in Marguerite's *Heptaméron*, both sexes are allowed to participate. At the same time, female authorship affects the dynamics of discursive exchange among the characters, so that Musella's decision to claim a subject of her own to counter Rustic's tale-telling empowers the other female characters to begin to find their own voices as well.

Outside the parameters of the narrative game, the play bears witness to the existence of alternative modes of feminine discourse than simply subjection to desire. When Silvesta maintains, for example, that she knows "what 'tis to sweare, and break itt both, / What to desire, and what itt is to love" (II.43-

44), her speech not only explains her choice of chastity over romantic passion, but also locates her confidence as a speaker in feminine experience rather than innocence. Having sworn off any desire for a man, Silvesta is enabled to assert the power of her discourse as a woman. Although Silvesta is an exceptional character in a play in which most of the characters endeavor to pair up with members of the opposite sex as a matter of course, it is significant that her assured choice of a life of chastity is associated specifically with her femininity, while the Forester's unfulfilled longing for a union with Silvesta restricts his masculine agency to his offer to die in her place. In the gap between masculine and feminine experience, then, resides the potential for at least one of the female characters in *Love's Victory* to assert ongoing agency through language, in the process engendering discourse in a different voice.

At the same time, Wroth represents the difficulty of claiming speech as a woman when connection rather than separation from the opposite sex is at issue. Thus while Silvesta can speak freely, having resolved no longer to engage in romantic relations with a man, Musella feels constrained from expressing her love to Philisses, telling Silvesta: "Somtimes I faine would speak, then strait forbear / Knowing itt most unfitt; thus woe I beare" (III.77-78). Even Silvesta agrees that for "a woman to make love is ill" (III.79), apparently reinforcing the very strictures against female speech that she herself has escaped by choosing to speak without "making love." Given these strictures, Pamphilia's discourse of love in the sonnet sequence emerges as far more daring within its Petrarchan context than the speeches of isolated female lovers within the play, because Pamphilia finds words, however embattled, to speak specifically as a woman within a relationship with a man, rather than, as in the case of Silvesta, through a choice of chastity over heterosexual love.

Yet although Wroth's play does not disrupt the dichotomizing of discourse along gendered lines to the same extent as does her lyric sequence, Silvesta's language of chastity does offer a notable example of empowered female speech. In tracing Silvesta's vocal movement from dependence to independence, Wroth charts the potential for an emergent female discourse to survive in the face of the accepted social subordination (and associated silencing) of many women within heterosexual love relationships. Furthermore, unlike Cary's Salome, whose voice is seemingly empowered by a sexual licentiousness which breaks the bonds of social decorum and yet which results only in her opprobrium at the end, Wroth's Silvesta finds in chastity a space not only for speech but also for successful agency, which allows her to influence the resolution of all the conflicts in the play.

Only amongst themselves are many of the female characters in *Love's Victory* able to voice their desires without constraint. As will be discussed more fully in the next chapter, the engendering of discourse in Wroth's play finally becomes visible most clearly not between men, nor between women and men, but between women. The issue of audience, then, must prove crucial to the question of authorship, when the nature of the gender gap between speaker and listener, author and audience, can determine the difference between the assertion or repression of female speech. As the play progresses, the voices of the female characters increasingly claim precedence over masculine discourse. During one exchange of riddling lyrics among Musella, Dalina, Simeana, and Climeana, for example, the men know better than to interrupt the course of female authorship, Philisses remarking: "Lett them alone, the woemen still will speake" (IV.379). When "the woemen" not only can but will speak amongst themselves, their discourse has the potential to challenge some of the patriarchal social codes that mandate their silence in settings that include men as well.

Furthermore, when Musella and Philisses agree in the climax of the play to exchange vows even at the cost of their lives, they entrust the telling of their tale to Simeana (V.101) and their fates to Silvesta (V.250ff). After the apparent demise of the lovers, Simeana and Silvesta appear together before the remaining characters in order to narrate, in tandem, the tragic story. In a testament to the powers of female authorship, their tale brings about the resolution of the vexed social relations that have produced the lovers' plight, as Rustic disavows his previous betrothal to Musella, and Musella's mother puts aside the "Law of the Father" to accept responsibility for her daughter's demise and openly profess her maternal love and grief. Once the lovers are restored to life by the priests of Venus, Venus herself calls for a celebratory song, bringing the play's narrative pastimes full circle to a fitting conclusion of compositely gendered authorship. Although *Love's Victory* does not finally challenge the gendered norms of its genre as extensively as do Wroth's other texts, nevertheless it represents an empowering connection between female speech and chastity, and indicates the potential for women's voices to emerge in other social contexts as well.

In her prose romance, Wroth extends the social parameters of female speech that obtain in her play in order to explore the possibilities for discursive agency among a range of female characters, while opening the contained Petrarchan world of her lyric sequence to alternative figurations of authorship and desire. As discussed earlier, it was Wroth's composition of the prose romance in particular which elicited attacks from male courtiers such as Lord Denny, whose label of "Hermophradite" serves as one example of cultural anxiety levels regarding the potential disruption of conventional boundaries of sexual difference through female authorship. Writing out of a tenuous "subculture" of women's voices in early modern England, Wroth nevertheless expands the authority of feminine discourse in her own narrative by endeavoring to adapt "phallocentric" diction—to borrow Yaeger's terms—to fit the needs of "feminocentric" expression. The simultaneous costs and benefits of such an expansion are represented within the framework of her narrative by the coexistence of examples of failed female authorship or silenced speech alongside other examples of insistent textual production and articulate female voices.

In many instances, Wroth's self-conscious revisions of male-authored conceits and conventions establish her "difference" of voice not simply through plot and characterization, but through language itself. Near the beginning of the prose romance, for example, Wroth not only represents Urania as an active presence, by contrast to her notable absence in Sidney's *New Arcadia*, but also situates her title character in a descriptive context which distinguishes her narrative discourse from the conventionally idealized conceits of her male predecessors. As she is mourning the absence of her mother, Urania hears a noise and looks up to see a "fierce she-wolfe" rushing toward her: ". . . the beast running towards her of the sudden stood still; one might imagine, seeing such a heavenly creature, did amase her, and threaten for medling with her: but such conceits were vaine, since beasts will keepe their owne natures, the true reason being, as soone appear'd, the hasty running of two youths, who with sharpe speares, soone gave conclusion to the supposed danger, killing the wolfe as shee stood hearkning to the noise they made" (16). Here Wroth displays the "different" voice of her authorship by managing to have it both ways. On the one hand, she celebrates the "heavenly" appearance of her female protagonist in terms that could rival her uncle's descriptive praise of the absent Urania at the beginning of his romance, where Urania's "very horse . . . bewailed to be so disburdened" when she alighted (NA, 62). On the other hand, she immediately undercuts Sidney's idealized objectification of female beauty by locating the emerging subjectivity of her protagonist, however beautiful, in a perishable human body whose appearance alone is not sufficient to alter the "nature" of a beast. By differentiating her descriptive language from the "vaine conceits" of other authors of romance, then, Wroth begins to establish grounds for her own discursive authority.

Throughout *Urania*, Wroth weaves distinctively feminine metaphors into her narrative which further serve to distinguish her discourse from that of her male predecessors. As Susan Frye has observed, women's texts in the Renaissance are sometimes linked metaphorically with textiles, across a range of genres.[55] Wroth's prose narrative is marked by a number of domestic metaphors which draw upon early modern women's experiences with the composition and treatment of textiles. In one description of the marriage of two lovers, for example, Wroth represents the dissolution of desire over time with reference to the storage of fine cloth: "but now three yeares being pass'd, the heate resonably cooled, other passions have crept in like Mothes into good stuffe: and discontents have risen" (440). Another textile metaphor serves for a female character's description of her appearance as "a rag of the rich piece of

beauty indeed, cutt off att the fag end of perfections truthe in beauties Court,
as threds bee of whole pieces" (II: fol. 60). Even as Wroth trims the "vaine
conceits" associated with some of the romances of her male predecessors from
the "whole piece" of her own narrative, so she weaves the "threds" of her discourse from alternative conceits as well.

Wroth engages head-on with the limitations of the cultural obsession
with women's appearances in her use of yet another "household" metaphor to
describe a group of older women, "who having young minds rumbled up their
old carcases, and rubd over their wrinckling faces like old wainscot now var-
nished" (476). Instead of reproducing typically masculine suspicions concerning the correspondence between female beauty and falsehood, Wroth gives
voice to women's anxieties over the discrepancy between the outward appearances by which, according to cultural norms, they are judged, and their capacity to become speaking subjects. Just as the chasm between (young) minds
and (old) bodies poses a threat to the masculine view of women primarily as
bodily objects of desire, so Wroth's authorship elicits the attack from Denny
which explicitly sexualizes the threat of that chasm in the label of "Hermophradite." The "rich piece" of Wroth's text is subject, by virtue of the gender of
its author, to Denny's vicious label of "Bable"—("Fooles and their Bables seldome part asunder")—which at once attempts to devalue the text's worth as a
female "bauble" or toy, and exposes his own fear of being overcome by the
"babel" of female voices which refuse to be silenced. In fact, one can argue
that it is in the very multiplicity of women's voices in *Urania* that the most
powerful challenge to masculine objectifications of women resides.

Where *Pamphilia to Amphilanthus* resuscitates Petrarchan discourse in
newly gendered terms, and *Love's Victory* includes a limited number of exceptions to the discursive gender gap of more conventional pastoral forms, Wroth
hybridizes genres in *Urania*, combining elements of lyric and drama within
her prose narrative in order to engender the discourse of her characters through
a range of speaking voices as well as strategies of textual production. Wroth's
appropriation of theatrical conventions, in particular, allows her to play upon
the discursive differences between genres in representing both the struggles
and the empowerment that attend many of the female-authored narratives in
her text.[56] In place of the stylized language and narrated summaries of conversations which Sidney, for example, relies upon to convey the communication
between Pamela and Philoclea, Wroth includes extensive passages of spoken
dialogue which give dramatic immediacy and discursive substance to the
voices of her female characters, recalling, although in frequently less oppositional form, the spoken exchanges between the female characters in Cary's
Mariam. Furthermore, she represents some of her female characters themselves as authors, whose textual production at times supports and at times subverts the struggles of their spoken voices. Significantly, several pivotal scenes

occur in "theaters," which are depicted as dramatic sites of contestation and enchantment (321ff), while portions of the narrative are described as "acts" in the ongoing drama of the protagonists' fortunes (II: fol. 42v). The extent to which *Urania* is informed by a sense of theatrical moment and dramatic speech enables Wroth to develop both her female characters' voices and their own textual production in at once more expansive and more ambivalent terms than appear in many prose romances. Wroth's hybridization of genres thus allows her some space to adopt previously phallocentric diction for feminocentric ends, initiating in the framework of her narrative what Cixous has termed "a shift in metalanguage."[57]

Describing the plight of women in love with reference to theatrical conventions, Wroth observes that "an Actor knowes when to speake, when to sigh, when to end: a true feeler is wrapped in distempers, and only can know how to beare" (314). As the female protagonists in *Urania* set out to articulate their passions, the unfeigned passion of their voices is juxtaposed with the inadequacy of speech itself, at moments, to convey desire. Wroth's female characters must learn both "when to speake" and "how to beare," how to speak without feigning and when to bear without speaking, how to claim the agency of acting without relinquishing the authority of feeling. In the self-consciously "counterfeit" discourse of playacting, where a male actor playing Rosalind can remind the audience that "it is not the fashion to see the lady the epilogue," speech alone does not necessarily engender power. Indeed Newman's argument, cited above, suggests that to see subjectivity as constituted primarily through speech has precisely the effect of privileging "performance."[58] By distinguishing between play-actors, or performers, and women subject to (and silenced by) the "distempers" of desire, Wroth begins to address the tensions associated with conflicting discursive representations of subjectivity.

The role of women authors within Wroth's prose romance has drawn attention from a number of critics. To adapt language characteristic of the otherwise quite different conflicts between new historicists and cultural materialists, Wroth critics can be divided on this issue of authorship into two groups—those who emphasize containment, and those who focus upon subversion. Although both camps acknowledge to a certain extent the finally unresolved nature of some of the discursive tensions in Wroth's narrative, they tend to stress either disempowering or enabling forces. Quilligan, for example, designates Urania's speaking position as "radically unstable," suggesting that she must in consequence "define her subject position by all its lacks," and concluding that "Wroth necessarily ends with representing the traffic in women as an inexorable shaper of their lives, the only virtuous escape from which appears to have been into the cul-de-sac of private poesis."[59] Female authorship, in such a reading, appears to function ultimately less as an enabling force than as a dead end (or "cul-de-sac"), bringing temporary relief from the traffic in women, but no new directions for discourse. Along related lines, Waller locates two "recurring patterns" in Wroth's writing: one of "male dominance and female masochism," and the other in "repeated stories of women daring to make sexual choices," and finds only a few "(literally) small spaces in which we can detect a striving for some way out of the destructive and pessimistic impasse that is Pamphilia's usual position in the *Urania*."[60] One such space, according to Waller, emerges in Pamphilia's pursuit of privacy, which allows her to "claim withdrawal as a tactic of self-affirmation for a woman's subjectivity." While Waller is particularly effective in illuminating both the inhibiting power of the male gaze and the "active and defiant exhibitionism" of Pamphilia's (and, on another level, Wroth's) response to that gaze, his identification of female storytelling as a "private space" underestimates the potentially public power of women's voices in the narrative, and tends to privilege, as does Quilligan's argument, the male traffic in women over female homosocial bonds and discourse.[61]

Although adopting a position related to that of Waller in linking Wroth's sexual defiance of her society with her authorship, Mary Ellen Lamb's analysis of *Urania* has a distinctly different tone. Lamb points out that even though the denial of subjectivity in many of the works read by women raised obstacles for women attempting to construct themselves as authors, nevertheless some women did still write, and thus "the discourse of gender difference must not be read as a description of actual practice."[62] At the same time, Lamb observes that the most successful female authors often turned out to be women who had escaped or transgressed conventional social boundaries. In the case of Wroth, Lamb argues that Wroth's own authorship, and consequently that of her female characters as well, is impelled by the dual forces of sexuality and denied anger. Lamb's primary difference from Waller emerges in her attention to the underlying heroism rather than victimization of Wroth's female storytellers. The angry "heroics of constancy" in Wroth's narrative, according to Lamb, enable her female characters to "speak rather than endure psychic destruction."[63] Also attending to Wroth's representations of female authorship, Barbara Lewalski proposes that "a major means of self-definition and agency for Wroth's heroines is literary composition." Lewalski finds that stories "allow the narrators to shape their lives artfully, giving them meaning and rhetorical power," and thus enabling the female storytellers, who far outnumber their male counterparts in *Urania*, to lay claim to agency.[64] Although she places less emphasis upon anger than Lamb, Lewalski's attention to the empowering effects of successful narrative aligns her approach with Lamb's analysis of the enabling force of Wroth's "heroics of constancy."

While the notion of women's "escape" through authorship from the social constraints of their culture can emphasize either (temporary) success or (ultimate) failure—subversion or containment—I find that the defensively reactionary and the proactively empowering examples of female speech and textual production within *Urania* must be examined in tandem, rather than in isolation, in order to identify Wroth's strategies of authorship. Wroth's treatment of female authorship in *Urania* offers, then, not merely a vision of "escape" from psychic or social destruction, but also an active engagement with the frequently misogynist figurations of gender in her culture. Wroth's own strategic responses to the court scandal associated with the publication of *Urania*, manifest both in her "defensive" letter to Buckingham and in her conspicuously "offensive" poem and letters to Denny, make clear that authorship to her was not simply an avenue of retreat or withdrawal from social victimization, but rather a space for assertion, disruption, and even active debate. Wroth's assumption of the challenge of female authorship in her lyric sequence, play, and prose romance enabled her, to borrow Cixous's terms once again, to "put herself into the text—as into the world and into history—by her own movement." The enormous canvas of *Urania* in particular, totaling over 590,000 words, encompasses narratives of desire and despair, endurance and exploration, which appropriate only to re-view and revise many of her culture's figurations of gender. Wroth's multiple representations of female authorship, then, serve to define a space for feminine discourse based upon gendered differences of voice and view.

Before attending to Wroth's focal treatment of female authorship in the figure of Pamphilia, it is necessary to consider the implications encoded in the alternative figure of Antissia. Antissia's struggles and even failures as a woman writer offer a counterpoint to the measured and hard-earned achievements of Pamphilia, and illustrate the costly gap between reactive and proactive approaches to the gendering of speech and subjectivity for women authors. Just as the subjected sovereign, Queen Nereana, provides a contrast to the sovereign subjectivity of Queen Pamphilia, so the vexed authorship of Antissia serves as a foil for Pamphilia's own discourse. The immediacy of the contrast between Pamphilia and Antissia is heightened all the more by their shared passion for Amphilanthus, whose early attention to Antissia is displaced by the appearance of Pamphilia.[65] Because at first neither Pamphilia nor Amphilanthus will admit their feelings for each other to Antissia, let alone to each other, Antissia finds herself inhabiting a vacuum of desire, where the increasing self-referentiality of her authorship reflects her inability to fashion a speaking position for herself apart from her role as an object of masculine attention.

From the beginning, Wroth indicates that Antissia's passion, which reflects many of the patriarchal figurations of gender in early modern England, has been defined at least as much by Amphilanthus's "fine discourse" as by her own (50). Subsequently, when Antissia assures Pamphilia that any man whom Pamphilia might choose would "venture his life, to gaine so pretious a prize," Pamphilia rejects Antissia's gendered construction of victor and prize, to maintain instead that "love is onely to be gaind by love equally bestowed, the giver, and the receiver reciprocally liberall, else it is no love" (77). Where Antissia assumes women's necessary subjection as objects of male conquest, then, Pamphilia asserts the need for a reciprocity of power relations between the sexes. Drawing upon her understanding of the construct of authorship, Antissia also attempts without success to force Pamphilia to confess her position as a lover by pointing to the evidence of Pamphilia's poems. Pamphilia replies in turn that poetry may exist as a purely aesthetic construct, apart from "sence of passion," so that her poems are "no proofe" against her (77). Pamphilia's response indicates her refusal on the one hand to admit publicly to passion—particularly, given the example of Antissia, in a society that tends to objectify the female lover—without first commanding the private language of her desire, and her conviction on the other hand that authorship enables a discourse that can encompass but is not necessarily restricted to "sence of passion."

As Antissia's estimation of her abandonment by Amphilanthus intensifies, her poetry begins to unravel in response, so that the final couplet in one of her sonnets serves to record her experience of being "undone": "Restlesse I live, consulting what to doe, / And more I study, more I still Undoe" (84). Indeed, when Antissia mistakes Pamphilia's brother Rosindy for Amphilanthus, and berates him accordingly for betraying her, Wroth describes her as "a meere Chaos, where unfram'd, and unorder'd troubles had tumbled themselves together without light of Judgement, to come out of them" (95). The early modern casebooks of the astrological physician, Richard Napier, covering patients seen between 1597 and 1634, indicate that romantic passion and the thwarting of love matches were perceived to be common causes of mental instability, particularly among women.[66] In Wroth's narrative it is worthy of note, then, not only that her representation of Antissia's mental "Chaos" draws upon common conceptions of the distempers of desire in early modern England, but also that her account of Pamphilia's parallel struggle with the disempowering effects of passion results in a woman claiming a position, albeit hard-won, of agency rather than insanity.

Wroth uses the concept of "unfram'd" discourse once again when representing a portion of one of Antissia's songs, with the comment: "Assuredly more there was of this Song, or else she had with her unframed and unfashioned thoughts, as unfashionably framd these lines" (122). Antissia's mental chaos thus is mirrored not only in her erratic speech, but in her tormented textual production as well, which leads her at one point to commit her written verses to the fire for destruction (272). Her inability to frame a harmonious lyric bears witness to her failure to establish a stable position as a subject, so that her texts give voice to the disintegration rather than the emergence of female subjectivity. Significantly, Antissia's torment is the direct result of her subjection rather than resistance to the dominating power of masculine discourse. Unframed, unfashioned, unordered, and undone, Antissia serves as a figure of reactive female authorship, written by masculine desire and incapable of voicing a position for herself apart from the masculine subject.

Pamphilia, by contrast, first finds her voice as a writer not in reflexive reaction to Amphilanthus's discourse, but rather in response to her own desire to write her passion in order to define a position for herself as a lover. The very first act of written authorship in the narrative is in fact Pamphilia's inscription of verses within "a little Cabinet" in her bedroom (50). As Patricia Fumerton has indicated, English Renaissance love poetry was often kept in private rooms within ornamental cabinets or boxes, and subsequently "published" between intimates in those same private rooms.[67] Wroth's decision to represent Pamphilia in the very moment of authoring a text at once "publishes" the particular privacy of female authorship—extending to her own as well—and asserts its viability apart from any response of the court. At the same time, Wroth's representation of the trials as well as the triumphs of Pamphilia's authorship attests to the difficulty of engendering discourse in a woman's voice. Thus Pamphilia criticizes her own poems more severely than any other audience could, and, like Antissia, destroys the words written in her hand more than once (52).

Yet even as Pamphilia's passions prove increasingly troubling, her confidence in her own voice grows, until she begins to extend her authorship from the privacy of her "cabinet" to the public arena of engraving sonnets upon trees, vowing to "make others in part taste my paine, and make them dumbe partakers of my griefe" (75). By taking up a knife for a pen, and writing a sonnet upon a tree, Pamphilia at once adopts a phallic tool and adapts phallocentric diction to fit the needs of feminocentric expression. Along these lines, her sonnet identifies her "ingraven" suffering with the experience of the tree she is addressing, characteristically establishing reciprocity rather than opposition with her subject. Wroth differentiates Pamphilia's bond with Amphilanthus from the discursive couplings of male-authored romantic pairs such as Rosalind and Orlando by re-gendering the dynamic of authorship in her romance. Thus while Orlando carves Rosalind's name upon trees in the forest (AYLI, III.ii), Pamphilia is the one who carves Amphilanthus's name in cipher upon an oak tree (270), along with her sonnets. Likewise, while Rosalind, as Ganymede, serves as the interpreter of Orlando's stilted poems rather than as the author of any poems of her own, Wroth emphasizes the discursive power of female authorship. By reversing the gender of the carver, Wroth underscores the potentially enabling effects of love upon the woman as writer rather than simply reader, inscriber rather than inscribed.

At the same time, Wroth's representation of Pamphilia as a sylvan sonneteer rewrites a superficially similar moment in Sidney's Old Arcadia, when Pamela carves a sonnet upon a pine tree (OA #47). Quilligan points

out that where Pamela's sonnet focuses upon the difference between speaker
and tree, Pamphilia's sonnet insists upon the shared experience of pain.[68]
Indeed, while Pamela asserts that her wound is "farr deeper" than that of the
tree, Pamphilia's identification rather than competition with the tree as subject indicates her capacity for fashioning a "testament" (75) to suffering in
other than purely egocentric terms—a capacity that is borne out, as discussed
earlier, by her lyric sequence as well. Moreover, Pamela's act of composition
is represented as part of a joint activity undertaken with her male lover, Musidorus, while Pamphilia's textual production occurs apart from masculine discourse.

  Pamphilia's act of carving can be compared, finally, with a parallel gesture on the part of Antissia in the very same text. In this case, Antissia initially
creates of a tree a domesticized text, "imbroider[ing] it all over with characters
of her sorrow" as if it were an ornamental piece of cloth, and then retreating
into that domesticized location itself for comfort by finding a seat for herself in
the "crowne" of the tree with "the armes, and branches incompassing her"
(273). In this position, she appears as "the forsaken compasse, out of which so
large and flourishing a crowne of despised love proceeded, so as take it either
way, shee was either crownd, or did crowne that wretched estate of losse, a piti-
full honor, and griefefull government" (273). Just as the "characters of her
sorrow" serve an ornamental rather than communicative function, Antissia's
"crowne of despised love" here contrasts implicitly with Pamphilia's "crowne
of Sonetts dedicated to Love" (P77-90). Whereas Antissia's carving is an act of
defensive retreat and withdrawal, and her "crowne" is devalued by the power
of the male gaze to objectify her position, Pamphilia's carving is an act of out-
reach or "testament," and her "crowne of Sonetts" is empowered by her discursive maintenance of the constancy of her passion apart from the presence
or absence of her male lover's gaze or voice.

  Where the male lover himself is concerned, it is interesting to note that
even the "failed" textual production of Antissia is included in Wroth's own
text, while Amphilanthus's poems never appear. This absence, in conjunction
with the appendage of Pamphilia's entire lyric sequence to the end of *Urania*,
indicates the vested nature of Wroth's response to the "gender gap" of authorship and the potential dominance of masculine discourse within her culture.[69]
By consistently measuring Amphilanthus's "skill in Poetry, a quallitie among
the best much prized and esteemed, Princes brought up in that, next to the
use of Armes," in terms of his "valour" (112), Wroth exposes the cultural rationale according to which Amphilanthus's relation to language is gendered
differently from that of Pamphilia. Like any conventional male Petrarchan
sonneteer, then, Amphilanthus's "excellent verse" is based upon opposition
and conquest, in contradistinction to Pamphilia's poetic concerns with connection and reciprocity.

For his part, when Amphilanthus is privileged to accompany Pamphilia to "her Cabinet" in order to fetch "some Verses of hers," he comments that they are "the best he had seene made by a woman" (266).[70] Wroth expands upon this obliquely dismissive, if representative, masculine response to a female-authored text, with Amphilanthus's conventionally masculine charge that Pamphilia "counterfeit[s] loving . . . well" (266). As discussed earlier, the issue of the "counterfeit" nature of feminine discourse is a culturally loaded one, in venues ranging from polemical pamphlets to Shakespeare's plays. But where Rosalind presumes to instruct Orlando in the art of love by denying her own passion, proclaiming in her disguise as a boy that her playing of the woman's part is mere "counterfeit" (AYLI, IV.iii.166-82), Pamphilia responds to Amphilanthus's charge with a boldly direct affirmation of her love (266). In representing Pamphilia as direct and not feigning, Wroth disrupts early modern figurations of gender which consistently associate women with inconstancy and pretense.[71] And in resisting the gendered dichotomizing of "counterfeit" discourse which governs the interaction between lovers in male-authored texts, Wroth opens new possibilities for a reciprocal communication of desire within the language of romance.

In hybridizing other textual forms, moreover, Wroth draws again upon the example of Sidney's poems as well as Shakespeare's plays in order to refashion the relation of masculine to feminine discourse within her prose narrative. Thus when Amphilanthus complains: "howe doth this sadd paceing full Moone, and her watrye shadow in thes streames, resemble my sorrowes, . . . naturally hating change, especiall the sad farewell for ever" (II.i.fol. 28), the language of his lament echoes that of Sidney's Astrophil: "With how sad steps, o Moone, thou climb'st the skies, / . . . To me that feele the like, thy state descries. / . . . Is constant love deem'd there but want of wit?" (AS #31). But while Astrophil's lament reflects his assumption of his own faithfulness by contrast to his beloved's ingratitude, Amphilanthus's complaint only underscores the contrast between his own inconstancy and Pamphilia's constant strength, particularly as embodied in her poems. Amphilanthus's inability to maintain a constant voice or stance as a lover thus places him, rather than his female beloved, in an unstable position as a subject.

Ultimately, it is not the composition of voices in isolation but rather the interrelation of author and audience which differentiates the sexes most sharply in Wroth's narrative. Just as the female authors of the polemical pamphlets address themselves to an audience of their own sex, configuring their rhetoric according to the gendered concerns of their listeners, or as the female characters in Marguerite de Navarre's Heptaméron often direct their speeches to each other, so Wroth represents the connections between author and audience in explicitly gendered terms. From the patronizing response of Amphilanthus to Pamphilia's poems — "the best he had seene made by a woman"

(266)—to the well-meaning but dim reaction of Pamphilia's father to one of her narratives—"the king good man thought noe thing of her speech, and tooke all verbally, nott feelingly, nor understandingly" (II.ii.fol. 18v)—Wroth exposes another gender gap, this time in the interpretive (dis)orientation of male audiences when confronted with a female author. Even as the interpretive framework of the *Heptaméron* reveals repeated chasms between gendered points of view, so Wroth's own experience of the gendered conflict between Edward Denny and herself confirms the cultural relevance of the interpretive fissures already documented within her text.

By contrast to these fissures, female authorship in *Urania* is consistently empowered by the reception of a female audience, in the face of otherwise uncomprehending, dismissive, or even hostile social settings. From Urania to Dorolina, Lindamira to Pamphilia, Wroth represents women not only sharing their writings with one another, but also sharpening their discursive control over their often potentially overwhelming respective plights through collaborative acts of interpretation. Although men sometimes appear in these interpretive sessions, the women's voices consistently predominate. Thus Urania and Selarina pass from discoursing with Selarinus to reading the "bookes and papers" in Pamphilia's cabinet (217), Meriana successfully entreats Pamphilia to read her verses aloud (392), and the queens of Naples and Sicily pass the time by "telling stories of themselves, and others, mixed many times with pretty fine fictions" (415). In one extended exchange, Dorolina shares at Limena's request a long poem of her own composition, which compares her plight in love with the struggles of female artists who have been abandoned by men, from Ariadne to Penelope, and with the enchantment of female "witches" who have been vilified for their powers over men, such as Medea and Circe (418). As a production that is at once performance and text, Dorolina's poem is concerned less to represent female "difference" from men than to explore differences among women themselves.

Soon thereafter, in response to Dorolina's request that she read aloud some verses of her own composition, Pamphilia recounts Lindamira's story and poems, embracing another woman's plight in metaphoric relation to her own (423ff). In urging Pamphilia to share her poetry, Dorolina intends "to take her this way something from her continuall passions, which not utter'd did weare her spirits and waste them, as rich imbroyderies will spoyle one another, if laid without papers betweene them, fretting each other, as her thoughts and imaginations did her rich and incomparable minde" (423). Interjecting yet another domestic simile conjoining texts and textiles, this one reflecting household knowledge concerning the storage of "rich imbroyderies," Wroth underscores the discursive individuality of her authorship at the same time as she conveys the complexity of the bond between women, for whom reciprocal communication is manifested through interpretive connection with one another's texts. Even as Dorolina admires Pamphilia's narrative, then, "shee thought [it] was some thing more exactly related then a fixion" (429), grasping the point of the story both "feelingly" and "understandingly," and supporting Pamphilia in the process.

While the importance of bonds between women will be explored more fully in my final chapter, the significance of female authorship in *Urania* in particular can be grasped through Wroth's representation of women's voices speaking, composing poems, telling tales, and singing songs, particularly to one another, in times of both trial and triumph. Feminine discourse forms a counterpoint in a range of instances to the sometimes antagonistic, sometimes patronizing, and sometimes merely unfeeling voices of men. Commenting upon the position of women in a patriarchal society, one female character observes that "womens honours . . . are so nice to be touched, as they are like little Sluses, that but opened, let in Rivers, and Oceans of discourses, and so blots never to be salved any more then a Floud can be withstood, or turned backe" (508). Even as a male character such as Shakespeare's Leontes can accuse wives of allowing themselves to be "sluic'd" in their husbands' absences (*Winter's Tale*, I.ii.194), so Wroth's female character calls attention to the vulnerability of women's reputations in the eyes of men, significantly representing sexual violation in discursive terms. On the other hand, within the larger framework of Wroth's narrative, women readers and listeners play an important role in fostering connections between authorship and authority, enabling women writers to speak not simply in abandonment or isolation but to receptive audiences as well. Several significant examples of female discursive production and reception in *Urania* thus bear witness over the course of the narrative to an emerging conception of female subjectivity in multiple rather than singular terms, along reciprocal rather than oppositional lines of communication.

As Lamb has pointed out, at stake in the attempted containment of women's reading and sexuality (and, one might add, occasional authorship) in early modern England was the status of women as subjects, able to think, to desire, and to produce meanings sometimes at variance with patriarchal objectives.[72] Denny's attempted dismissal of Wroth, then, is jeopardized on one level by his conflation of her sexuality and her authorship, which ironically empowers what it would seek to reduce, when his juxtaposition of her "words and works" unwittingly grants her, as discussed earlier, the very power of agency associated with authorship which his attack was apparently fashioned to undermine. At another level, Denny's attempted containment of Wroth's public and published voice is subverted even more effectively by Wroth's own refusal to construct either feminine discourse or female audiences in her text solely in accordance with dominant figurations of gender in her culture. Certainly Wroth's experience—attacked by male courtiers such as Denny for her pioneering literary venture—necessarily heightened her awareness of the dangers as well as the difficulties of writing literally out of a masculine tradition of authorship, and consequently facing the prospect of being written out of that tradition for all time.[73]

Carol Thomas Neely's call for a "reengendering" of the Renaissance[74] requires not only critical juxtapositions of male and female writers in early modern England, but also attention to the role of "gender" in "engendering" discourse. The *Oxford English Dictionary* distinguishes between two gender-specific definitions of the term "engender": "of the male: to beget," and "of the female: to conceive, bear." For the male, in biological terms, engendering is a single act, precipitating consequences but not necessarily responsibility. For the woman, the act of engendering is an ongoing and manifold process, from conception, through "bearing" the gestation, to birth. In scrutinizing the significance of sexual difference to the act of writing, Homans concludes that women writers' attempts to appropriate their own experiences as paradigms for writing may collide with their acknowledgment of a dominant cultural myth of language which presumes their silence.[75] The tension between "when to speake" and "how to beare" in silence, identified early in *Urania*, modulates later on, particularly for Pamphilia, into the challenge of how to bear speech, how to give birth to feminine discourse in the face of patriarchal constraints.

The engendering of discourse for women authors depends upon gender distinctions "begot" by male writers, but reconceived by women "bearing the word" in different voices. Mary Wroth foregrounds the gender-specific nature of speech in her narrative, writing outside the accepted boundaries of the "fashion" which Shakespeare's Rosalind appears to transgress but in fact enforces. When women's voices are constructed (and spoken) by men, female speaking positions are frequently marginalized or even erased, subsumed into a discourse where men have the last word. By contrast, women's voices in all three of Wroth's works encode some measure of female resistance to assumptions of masculine authority, even as the cost of that resistance is marked by failures such as the "Chaos" of Antissia's authorship. Although Wroth's insistent and diverse inscriptions of feminine discourse should no more be adjudged to provide a completely effective voicing of agency than should the canonical works of her male peers, nevertheless her texts can be seen to offer a particularly intense representation of ongoing metamorphoses in her culture's figurations of gender. The "reengendering" of early modern England must begin with our awareness not only of the oppositional strategies but also of the "engendering" potential of female-authored discourse. Wroth's texts give early and gendered voice to the concerns of such discourse.

6

Between Women

Becoming Visible

Mary Wroth represents bonds between women as both troubled and enduring, at once potentially restrictive and liberating, within social settings that pose multiple challenges to women's agency and subjectivity. Of the various concerns that mark Wroth's texts, from her re-vision of Petrarchan forms to her exploration of the often vexed relationship between authorship and desire, her attention to the relations among women has received a surprisingly scant amount of critical discussion thus far. My analysis in this chapter focuses upon the emergence of bonds between women in Wroth's texts, viewed in relation both to coexisting structures of heterosexual desire, and to the overlapping spheres of affection and antagonism, cooperation and competition which mark female homosocial relations in a range of early modern English texts. In foregrounding female bonds across a spectrum of social positions for women, from virginity and marriage to motherhood and widowhood, Wroth succeeds in representing complex networks of female homosocial relations with the power to foster female agency and subjectivity.

In *Between Men*, Eve Sedgwick locates her study of male homosocial desire within the structural context of triangular, heterosexual desire, alluding in explanation to the basic paradigm of male traffic in women which underlies the entire book. Within the frame of male homosocial relations, Sedgwick argues that "*any* erotic involvement with an actual woman threatens to be unmanning."[1] While Sedgwick's model illuminates the male-authored texts that she examines, her paradigmatic focus upon the isolation and subordination of women produced by male homosocial bonds proves less applicable to some of the female-authored texts in the early modern period, which accord female homosocial bonds a significant shaping force in both sexual and social relations.[2] Within Wroth's texts, while romantic and erotic involvement between the sexes often threatens to challenge or, more menacingly, to deconstruct the agency and subjectivity of individual female characters within such relationships, the simultaneous development of female homosocial relations is often sharpened rather than subverted by tangential connections to such heterosexual relations. Furthermore, the power of romantic and erotic involvement with men to undermine female subjectivity diminishes specifically when evaluated within the context of female homosocial relations. Indeed, by contrast to the male homosocial bonds scrutinized by Sedgwick, in Wroth's *Urania* same-sex bonds consistently allow female characters to re-view and sometimes revise the conventionally hierarchical dynamics of heterosexual desire.

Whereas much recent Wroth criticism has focused upon conflicting representations of heterosexual desire while frequently, if sometimes inadvertently, subordinating the significance of female homosocial bonds, my focus in the present chapter on relations "between women" runs the opposite risk of seeming to discount unnecessarily the importance of the relations between key pairs of female and male protagonists, such as Pamphilia and Amphilanthus. My intention, however, is not to underestimate the importance of such heterosexual bonds, whose dynamics unquestionably provide central structuring devices for the plot, as discussed in chapter 2, but rather to scrutinize the less commonly analyzed but often equally complex bonds between the female characters, which offer striking alternatives to conventional early modern figurations of the relations between women. Rather than discounting the presence of heterosexual relations, then, I am more concerned to "recount" the presence of alternative ties. At the same time, by examining Wroth's treatment of both tensions and triumphs in female bonding in relation to the treatment of similar issues by a range of early modern authors, I hope to demonstrate the extent to which complex constructions of agency and subjectivity for women are directly tied to representations of female homosocial bonds.

From Sidney and Shakespeare to Montemayor and d'Urfé, early modern male authors repeatedly center their fictions upon extremes of romantic conflict, emphasizing struggle and tension between the sexes that is resolved by the union or reunion of male and female characters in pairs—the traditional heterosexual unit of lyric, drama, and romance. While some male writers present friendships between women in seemingly idealized terms, such female ties remain consistently subordinate to relationships with or between men. Female authors such as Aemilia Lanyer, Elizabeth Cary, and Marguerite de Navarre, on the other hand, juxtapose their representations of the often destructive effects of heterosexual bonds upon women with central examples of potentially enabling as well as constraining relations among women themselves. Mary Wroth herself attends at once to vexed extremes of romantic conflict, and to simultaneous connections among women which both underlie and challenge hierarchical relations between the sexes. Moreover, whereas male authors of romance in particular often depict male protagonists who strive for autonomy, and who attempt to define their roles primarily by staking out their independence from one another, Wroth represents key female figures who depend to varying degrees upon affiliation with each other in realizing their subjectivity—that is to say, who grow through their interrelation with female friends as well as male lovers. Wroth's female characters, then, more consistently locate speaking positions for themselves through affirmations of connections across difference than through simple assertions of independence.[3] Assuming that autonomy equals strength, and that its opposite must imply weakness, some critics have tended to interpret the roles of early modern women, and thus of female characters as well, in terms of passivity and helplessness at best, and victimization and loss of self at worst. Wroth's poems, play, and prose romance, however, represent not only the victimization but also the resilience of women in a world where fluctuations in romantic fortune may be determined by male lovers, but constancy in love may be redefined by female friends.

This is not to say that Wroth problematizes only heterosexual bonds, while idealizing female homosocial relations. Even as the bonds between Wroth's female characters are often jeopardized by the intrusion or intervention of other characters, both female and male, some of the primary heterosexual pairings in the narrative, including the relations between Pamphilia and Amphilanthus and between Urania and Steriamus, actually grow stronger as the women forge increasingly confident voices of their own. Female homosocial bonds thus have the potential not just to disable but actually to enable heterosexual relations, by strengthening the women's positions within those relations. Indeed, in Wroth's texts heterosexual and homosocial bonds are so inextricably intertwined that any exclusive critical focus upon one dynamic can work to the neglect of the other. At stake is the consideration not only of differences between male and female same-sex ties, but of distinctions between women's positions as well.

Instead of identifying in Wroth's works a simple inversion of Sedgwick's paradigm for male-authored texts, whereby female homosocial relations are threatened by erotic involvement with men, I find that Wroth emphasizes the potentially empowering influence of women's bonds upon emergent female subjectivity and agency, without sacrificing the relevance of heterosexual ties. Given that she was writing within a society that tended to promote male social bonds while treating strong female ties as potentially suspect or subversive of the social order, Wroth succeeds to a remarkable extent in representing female bonding as neither a preferable nor a subsidiary alternative to heterosexual relations, but rather as an enabling space within which women might learn, against formidable odds, to claim different positions as speaking subjects. My examination of the relation between heterosexual desire and homosocial friendship in Wroth's texts attempts to scrutinize both troubling and empowering bonds between the female characters that allow them to articulate not simply their differences from the "opposite sex," but also their own differences of voice and view.

Irigaray explains her emphasis on attempting to secure "a place for the feminine within sexual difference" by pointing out that "the feminine has

never been defined except as the inverse, indeed the underside, of the masculine," so that "for woman it is not a matter of installing herself within this lack,
this negative," nor of "reversing the economy of sameness by turning the feminine into *the standard for 'sexual difference,'*" but rather a matter of "trying to
practice that difference."[4] While it might be argued that early modern England
offered hardly any opportunities for a woman to "practice that difference"
except as the inverse or negative of the masculine subject—as in the examples
of the cross-dressing females in James's reign—nevertheless some early modern
women did try to practice "difference" in their writings. Indeed, writing that
difference in practice could be said to offer more plausible subversive potential
than attempting to reverse "the economy of sameness" by establishing the feminine as a standard for sexual difference in the culture at large. Even granting
the vast "difference" of another sort, spanning chronology and culture, between contemporary French feminist philosophies and early modern figurations of gender, Irigaray's observations offer a useful frame of reference for an
examination of the gendering of subjectivity in earlier texts, as long as the historical specificity of those texts is attended to at the same time.

Instead of positing woman as "the difference from man," or even as "difference" itself, to use Teresa de Lauretis's formulation, women writers who
focus upon differences among and within women work to create feminine parameters for agency and subjectivity that reflect both connections and tensions
between women as well.[5] Only by "practicing difference," then, can women
attempt to move beyond the conventionally dominant parameters of masculine subjectivity to configure bonds of their own. As Rosi Braidotti points out,
the redefinition of the female subject can start with the recognition of "both
the sameness and the otherness of the other woman, her symbolic function as
agent of change."[6] When "the other" is no longer primarily a feminine inverse
of the masculine subject, but rather an/other woman among women, then the
horizontal relations between women allow for the practice of differences that
collectively can enable women to function both as individual speaking subjects and as agents of change for each other. The multiplicity of bonds between women has the potential to disrupt dichotomous divisions between
subjects based on binary sex-gender systems, according to which men can be
"unmanned" by contact with femininity, even as women can be objectified by
the male gaze alone.

The significance of bonds between women in female-authored texts by
no means precludes the importance of heterosexual relations on the one hand,
nor necessitates a fusion of individual women in the service of some overarch-
ing vision of unified female identity on the other hand. Rather, female homosocial relations can serve to foster dialogue across and through differences,
both between women and men, and between women themselves. At the same
time, just as all discourses are not created equal, so the existence of such dialogue alone does not always imply parity between the speaking subjects in

question. Even within female-authored texts, the discursive relations between women may reproduce patriarchally defined hierarchies, or may even body forth the Law of the Father despite their putative subject of feminine concerns. Nevertheless, the polyvocality of women's discourses has the potential to enable interrogation of the dominant culture from several angles at once, without compromising the different positions of the women speaking. The "practice of difference" engendered by discursive bonds among women, then, can render visible the possibilities for changing the subject of patriarchal figurations of gender.

Female homosocial bonds in early modern England receive widely varying treatments depending upon the genre and authorship of the texts in which they appear. As Crawford has pointed out, while ideology certainly shaped the context within which women interacted in early modern England, "female records" encompassing printed writings by women, unpublished diaries, autobiographies, and correspondence survive to indicate that women often communicated outside the boundaries of their prescribed roles. Thus Crawford observes that the letters and diaries of literate women reveal networks of support and advice that were not represented in the conduct books.[7] Female authors of both polemical tracts and literary texts, furthermore, often call attention to relations among women as providing the occasion (as well as the audience) for their authorship, while the role of "the other woman" emerges in the writings of some early modern women as a symbolic agent of "difference" as well as change. In this chapter, I am concerned to locate the parameters of Mary Wroth's treatment of bonds between women in relation to the varied representations of female homosocial bonds that informed her culture.

Many of the courtesy books and treatises published by the English popular press during the late sixteenth and early seventeenth centuries that scrutinized deviant female behavior, particularly viewed in relation to men, stressed the positive values of female appearance over speech, behavior to the exclusion of discourse.[8] Treatises that proffered the model of the chaste, silent, and obedient woman took care to emphasize female silence as a condition of chastity and obedience. The prospect of women meeting together to engage in shared discourse clearly undermined cultural notions of appropriate behavior for silent and obedient women, to the extent that the early Jacobean years saw the publication of numerous satirical representations of female homosocial bonds, manifest in a genre which Linda Woodbridge has termed "the gossips' meeting."[9]

In texts with titles such as *Tis Merrie when Gossips meete* (1602), and *A whole crew of kind Gossips, all met to be merry* (1609), male authors such as Samuel Rowlands satirized the domineering and deviant discourse that they associated with meetings of women. Particularly troublesome to these male authors was the potential for women to instruct each other in subversive behavior directed against men. In her survey of multiple examples of the "gossips' meeting" genre, Woodbridge emphasizes the fear of marital insubordination which underlies such texts, represented in the older gossips' supposed instruction of younger gossips concerning how to get the marital bridle into their own hands. Purported female advice, in these male-authored texts, focuses upon marital strategies ranging from relentless scolding to histrionic scenes of feigned illness and artificially induced weeping.[10] In each case, the false nature of women's speech and actions is emphasized, while female homosocial bonds are represented as directly destructive of heterosexual relations.

Another widespread conviction inscribed by the male authors of these texts was the assumption that the primary subject of any conversation among women was men. The "gossips' meeting" texts thus attempted to define female homosocial bonds in purely reactive terms, as motivated primarily by women's opposition to proper patriarchal authority rather than by connections among women themselves. In an interesting twist upon this strategy, however, the writings can also be seen implicitly to convey widespread male curiosity about what women discuss when they are alone together, suggesting once again a fear of uncontained female speech. Woodbridge concludes that the "gossips' meeting" genre ultimately expresses male anxiety and chagrin that bonds among women could absorb such an apparently formidable male intrusion as marriage "with scarcely a ripple," while male bonding was typically represented, along the lines suggested by Sedgwick, as endangered by close contact with women.[11]

In fact, the defensiveness of the male authors was a reaction to the very real presence of networks of so-called "gossip" which bound together the women of each locality in a web of relationships. As Adrian Wilson indicates in an essay on the ceremony of childbirth and its interpretation in early modern England, the "gossip" network supported a collective culture of women centering not around discussion of the dominant men in their lives, as the male authors of the "gossips' meeting" genre perhaps wishfully assumed, but rather around such shared experiences as the ceremony of childbirth, from which men were of necessity excluded.[12] In these gatherings, women of different stations of life were enabled if not to write through the mother's body, in Cixousian terms, then at least to speak to each other through the mother's body by sharing the birthing of one another's children. Regardless of whose child was being born at any given time, the "gossip" network thus opened for many women a space for discourse apart from the hypothetical or actual dominance of masculine subjects in their lives.

By contrast to the implicit criticism and suspicion of bonds between women in the male-authored "gossips' meeting" texts, female-authored polemical treatises both presume upon and celebrate the strength of female homosocial relations. Jane Anger's tract addresses her fellow women with a discursive attack on men which not only exposes their flaws and failures, but is empowered by the female bonds that provide the occasion for her polemic. As discussed in chapter 5, Anger's explicit naming of her "own Sex" as her audience at once works to exclude men from that audience, and supports her disavowal of men's capacity to practice legitimate authorship in any form ("the desire that every man hath to show his true vein in writing is unspeakable").[13] Whereas Esther Sowernam includes two dedicatory epistles in her pamphlet, one addressed to each sex, she concludes her response to Swetnam by narrating an account of his "arraignment" by a group of women whom she has assembled to discuss "what course we should take with him."[14] The result of this female caucus is Swetnam's "indictment," which is followed by a speech by Sowernam refuting all Swetnam's objections against women. Thus Sowernam, like Anger, ultimately draws upon discursive relations among women in order to repudiate the ill-conceived masculine aggression embodied in Swetnam's misogynist pamphlet.

Writing proactively rather than reactively, the female authors of the mothers' advice books often address not only their children, but other women as well. In the case of Dorothy Leigh, as Joan Klein has so perceptively pointed out, the mother's advice book becomes an occasion for establishing the position of women in a dominantly male world in positive terms.[15] Furthermore, in the context of advising her sons to treat their wives well, Leigh specifically addresses some of the social tensions distinguishing bonds between women from bonds within marriage, and warns her sons not to do "a woman that wrong as to take her from her friends that love her, and after a while begin to hate her."[16] Leigh's comment points to the same suspicion of female homosocial bonding as subversive of the marriage bond which underlies the "gossips' meeting" texts, but suggests by contrast that female friendship and marriage need not necessarily be incompatible. At the same time, Leigh calls attention to the possibility for friendship within marriage as well, by reminding her sons that their wives are "worthy to be thy fellow[s]."[17] Given that a large proportion of the public audience for mothers' advice books was female, Dorothy Leigh's articulation of women's agency and subjectivity both without and within marriage thus serves as an address not only to her sons but also to her fellow women.

Seemingly at the other end of the public spectrum from the published discourse of the polemicists and the authors of the mothers' advice books, but linked in representing the centrality of a female audience for women's voices, can be found the technically private but in practice often quite public inscription of female homosocial relations in women's diaries and correspondence. In her extensive survey of early modern women's diaries, Sara Heller Mendelson notes the frequency with which the framework of everyday life evoked in such writings included women entertaining and being entertained in each other's houses.[18] Lady Margaret Hoby records, for example, her conversation with a friend "tell diner time," during a day otherwise occupied by activities pursued in relative isolation.[19] Female friendships occupy an even more central role in Lady Anne Clifford's diary, which documents numerous occasions spent in the company of other women. Clifford makes mention several times of conversations with "Lady Worth," or Mary Wroth, as well as with Wroth's mother, Lady Lisle, Wroth's sister, Barbara Sidney, and Wroth's sister-in-law, Dorothy Sidney, countess of Leicester (August, October 1617).[20] Clifford also records "much talk" between herself and "my old Lady Pembroke," or Wroth's aunt, and "divers others of my acquaintance" (September 1619).[21] The content of Clifford's discourse with her female friends can be gathered from one entry, during the midst of her prolonged conflict with her husband and the king over the ownership of her lands, where she notes that she spent "all this week with my Sister Compton; and my Sister Sackville, being sad about an unkind letter from my Lord" (September 1619).[22] The support that Clifford garnered from her relationships with other women enabled her to endure the hostility and intimidation of her husband without relinquishing either her right to claim her own lands, or her ability to speak out frankly in defense of that right.

As Margaret Ezell has discussed with reference to bonds among women in England in the 1630s and 1640s, female friendship could possess an intensity equal to that of a marriage relationship, and could certainly provide an alternative venue for affection and stability in a culture otherwise not configured to provide women with much support.[23] While Ezell focuses upon the correspondence between Constance Aston Fowler and her future sister-in-law, Katherine, evidence for such bonds can be glimpsed a decade or so earlier in the correspondence of other pairs of Englishwomen as well. The correspondence between Lucy, countess of Bedford and Lady Jane Cornwallis Bacon, particularly between 1614 and 1627, for example, conveys the centrality of bonds of friendship between women of the courtly class in early modern England, and contains frank expressions both of affection and of the exercise of judgment independent of the attempted control of men.[24]

In Mary Wroth's own immediate family circle, surviving letters documenting the relation between Wroth's sister-in-law, Dorothy Sidney, the countess of Leicester, and Dorothy Sidney's own sister, Lucy, the countess of Carlisle, suggest that the Sidney family women relied upon each other for political news and advice where the affairs of the court were concerned as well as for emotional support.[25] While female homosocial relations in aristocratic families such as the Sidneys were by no means unvexed or indiscriminately affectionate, as attested to by descriptions of sororal conflicts as well as confidences, still the bonds between women were often expressed in passionate terms among themselves. In order to evaluate representations of female homosocial bonding in the Sidney family correspondence, it is necessary on the one hand to take account of constructions of male bonding in the family letters as well, and on the other hand to probe the distinctions between letters regarding female friendship addressed by women to men and to each other.

Wroth's brother Robert, second earl of Leicester, for example, wrote to his brother-in-law, Algernon Percy, tenth earl of Northumberland, expressing his happiness that their relations were no longer strained by some temporary misunderstandings, and concluding: "for I love you so much that I thinke I shall not prophane the word of God, the fountaine of truth, if I take this saying out of it, and apply it to myself, that my love is beyond the love of women."[26] This use of the "second sex" as a frame of reference apparently validating the greater value of male homosocial bonding is not uncommon in correspondence between upper-class men in early modern England, suggesting a need on the part of some men to dismiss the "unmanning" capacity of "actual women"—to borrow Sedgwick's terms—head-on. Another letter, this time from Algernon Percy to his own sister, Lady Leicester, reveals the relative importance accorded the sexes in a masculine estimation, in Percy's explanation of his delayed account of the birth of his most recent child: "the haveing of an other girle, I thought so little considerable, that I made no haste in acquainting you with it."[27] Labeled by fathers, husbands, and brothers as "little considerable," early modern women quite likely measured their words differently for male and female ears.

The correspondence between Lady Leicester and her husband regarding her sister, the countess of Carlisle, for example, differs quite strikingly from the correspondence between the two women themselves. Writing to her husband, Lady Leicester complains that her visiting sister "is greater in her owne consaite then ever shee was, for her to galants are more her slaves then I thinke ever men wear to any woman."[28] On this and several other occasions, Lady Leicester apparently criticizes her sister in particular for her conduct during her visits to Penshurst, observing at one point that her sister "sertainlie staies hear for other considerations then my companie."[29] Interestingly, Lady Leicester also admits casting about, in these same letters, for "any thing that I can intertaine you with," opening the possibility that her narrative of sororal tensions at Penshurst may have served as more acceptable subject matter for her husband than an account of female homosocial bonding in his absence.[30]

On the other hand, the correspondence between the sisters themselves suggests the presence of a bond shared without need for reference to the opposite sex. Thus Lady Carlisle writes to her sister, Lady Leicester, of her earnest desire for her company: "You cannot posibly imagen how mutch impations I have for your returne, there are few things cane make me happy, and your com-

pany is the prinsipale, and though I hade not ingagments and othere obliega-
tions, for my one interest I would indevor all ways posible, to have your returne
soone and satisfactory, if this be not the greatest truthe that ever wase told you,
conclude me the falsest creatur living."[31] On other occasions, their letters address topics particular to their sex, such as the dangers associated with the multiple pregnancies so often experienced by non-nursing aristocratic mothers.
Lady Carlisle observes to Lady Leicester, along these lines, that "I should be
glead to hear that you wayr not with child, that you might the better pase the
year which I hope you will doe," and in another letter remarks that she has
heard that one of their friends' "health is so good, as she is not sartine of her
being with child."[32] It is just such "female" discourse—confronting the practical realities of women's sexual experience, in which the health of individual
women is repeatedly sacrificed for the "health" of the patriarchal line—that
the male-authored "gossips' meeting" texts attempt unsuccessfully to satirize
and discourage. The gender-specific commentary embedded in the Sidney
family correspondence suggests that the "haveing of an other girle," dismissed
as "so little considerable" by husbands, in fact exerted a "considerable" toll on
the bodies of their wives, which could be acknowledged frankly in the shared
communication afforded by female homosocial bonds.

Other examples of such connections between women abound, even in
a body of correspondence in which women's letters were rarely saved by comparison to the letters of their fathers and brothers and husbands. Thus in one
surviving letter, Lady Leicester writes boldly to a male correspondent in the
service of her friendship with his wife, noting: "you have maid an unplesant
seperation betweene your wife, and me, but I hope you will recompence it to
us bothe in giveing her all the contentment you can."[33] In identifying her
interests with those of her friend, so that kindness to her friend will "recompence . . . us bothe" for the husband's evidently unsuccessful attempt to divide
them, Lady Leicester at once asserts the legitimacy of female homosocial
bonds and represents the enduring power of such bonds in the face of attempted masculine interference. The Sidney family correspondence contains
further evidence of the central place of shared discourse in bonds such as that
between Mary Wroth and several other aristocratic women, including Susan
Herbert, countess of Montgomery, who was one of Wroth's closest friends,
and for whom The Countesse of Mountgomeries Urania was named.[34]

The passionate language, both of affection and competition, with which
women give voice to their relations can be identified not only in the private
diaries and correspondence just mentioned, but within female-authored literary texts as well. Although lyric forms in early modern England often seem
configured primarily to lament or celebrate the progression of heterosexual

love relations, Sedgwick's discussion of how male homosocial desire can be located within the context of triangular, heterosexual desire opens the way for a
consideration of alternate triangulations of desire which encompass female
homosocial relations as well. The lyric is a particularly good place to begin,
given that the trope of the singular "dark lady" has so dominated both male-
authored lyric figurations of gender, as discussed in chapter 2, and critical analyses of those figurations as well.

While the religious translations of the countess of Pembroke necessarily
sublimate heterosexual relations to spiritual concerns, the original poetry of
Aemilia Lanyer's *Salve Deus Rex Judaeorum* represents religious devotion not
so much in "asexual" terms as specifically in relation to female homosocial
bonds. As noted earlier, gender makes not only a difference but all the difference to Lanyer's lyric voice. In the revised triangulation of desire in Lanyer's
sequence of poems, Christ provides a divine focal point around whom women
can join *with* one another in a worship that excludes all earthly men, from
Adam to Pilate. Rather than remaining fixed in the male gaze as objects of
desire, then, the community of women in Lanyer's poem functions as worship-
ping subjects.[35] Furthermore, their passion for Christ exhibits the potential not
only to liberate them from the sexualized foreclosure of female subjectivity
implicit in earthly heterosexual relations, but also to connect them with one
another in spiritual homosocial bonding.

Thus in her dedicatory poem, "To all vertuous Ladies in generall,"
Lanyer specifically enjoins her fellow women to embrace each other in the service of Christ, in language which celebrates the female subject. Her exhorta-
tion to her listeners to adorn their temples "with faire Daphnes crowne, / The
never changing Laurel, alwaies greene" (22-23), manages to appropriate in the
service of religious worship a myth of female escape from the prospect of male
sexual abuse. The transformed body of Daphne, liberated from rape and represented by the laurel wreath, is reconceived not as a symbol of masculine
accomplishment, but rather as a crown for the spiritual heroism of women. In
her "reincorporation" of the myth of Daphne, Lanyer succeeds in implicitly
contrasting the "never changing" fidelity of women (23) with the contrasting
behavior of the other sex—and all without yielding any space in her verse to
the male perpetrator implicated by the myth.

In a further extension of the community of women to whom her poem is
addressed, Lanyer urges her audience to "let the Muses your companions be, /
Those sacred sisters that on Pallas wait" ("To all vertuous Ladies," 29-30). Once
again, Lanyer revises the conventional male-authored literary subordination of
feminine figures, representing the Muses here not as objects of inspiration for
male poets, but rather as a sisterly community attendant upon the specifically
female authority of Pallas Athena. From Athena, the mythic embodiment of all
human wisdom, to Eve, the mother of all humankind, to Mary, the mother of

"our Lord," Lanyer identifies women throughout *Salve Deus Rex Judaeorum* as the shaping forces within society at large, and calls upon her female listeners to recognize that power within each other as well. In observing that Mary is "from all men free," being "farre from desire of any man" (*SDRJ*, 1077-78), Lanyer deconstructs the conventional dynamic of heterosexual desire in the service of liberating women to bond with one another in religious devotion instead. The effect of her repeated invocations of a community of female be-lievers who can understand and identify with Christ's sufferings far more effec-tively than can the men who were responsible for Christ's death is to dignify female homosocial bonds in a religious context that excludes deleterious bonds with men.

At the same time, several critics have commented upon the extent to which the homosocial bonds between women within Lanyer's poem involve a dynamic of competition as well as cooperation. Lanyer's own relation to the historical women whom she addresses as patrons can be viewed as occasionally ambivalent as well as celebratory. Kari McBride suggests, for example, that Lanyer ultimately displaces the aristocratic female contemporaries whom she addresses in her poems, by shifting her praise to biblical models of heroism, so that her own voice finally is seen to govern all the constructions within her poetic world.[36] Along related lines, Ann Baynes Coiro argues that Lanyer's ser-vice to the women whom she hopes to win as patrons is complicated by an underlying anger against both gender and class roles which reveals the strain of that service upon her writing.[37] On the other hand, it is necessary to remember that Lanyer's decision to claim the authority of her writing voice specifically in relation to a community of women, however ambivalently constructed, is in itself a daring move which insists upon the enabling potential of female homo-social bonds, not only in "gossips' meeting" conversations focused upon mar-riage or childbirth, but also in feminine praise of divine authority.

In her concluding country-house poem, "The Description of Cooke-ham," Lanyer's erasure of the masculine presence from her revised triangula-tion of desire enables her to position herself as the "other woman" in a potentially cooperative, rather than conventionally competitive, triangular bond which includes the countess of Cumberland and her daughter, Anne Clifford. No longer situating her language in a primarily religious context, Lanyer crafts an explicitly female version of the heterosexual family state and estate subsequently idealized by such male poets as Jonson in "'To Penshurst." Where Jonson's poem extols the virtues of a procreative fertility which encom-passes fish and fruits, "better cheeses," and "ripe daughters," all cultivated apparently for the purposes of consumption, and culminating in the lord's "fruitful" lady and his children (53-54, 90), Lanyer's poem celebrates the bond among three women, made visible in the beauty of the landscape. Cookham emerges as at once an estate and a family state informed by female subjectivity, where the effects of both presence and absence are defined solely in relation to female subjects.

In the context of the biblical subject matter of *Salve Deus Rex Judaeorum*, Lewalski has observed that Cookham takes on the appearance of a ravaged Eden after the expulsion of the first human couple, with the difference that in Lanyer's poem it is not a heterosexual couple but rather a female trio who depart.[38] The female poet's sojourn in this Edenic community, governed by a "Mistris" rather than a master, enables her participation in that sisterhood of "the Muses" to which she first refers in her dedicatory poem to "all vertuous Ladies," so that here, at the end of *Salve Deus*, she is able to claim "powre" for her verse from those very same Muses ("Cooke-ham," 3-4, 11). Although the dispersal of the countess of Cumberland, her daughter, and Aemilia Lanyer from Cookham results, according to the poet, in the disintegration of the beauty of the estate, it also produces the music of the poem itself, whose lament offers a visible and lasting memorial to bonds between women which otherwise can prove neither visible nor lasting within a society dominated by masculine subjects.

Near the end of "Cooke-ham," Lanyer describes a kiss bestowed by the countess of Cumberland upon "that stately Tree" which figures so importantly in the poem as a haven for feminine communion with "Christ and his Apostles" (53, 82). Immediately thereafter, Lanyer claims that she herself takes back the kiss from the tree, "scorning a sencelesse creature should possesse / So rare a favour, so great happinesse" (167-68). This kiss-once-removed epitomizes the displaced homosocial bonding that informs "Cooke-ham" even more clearly than the patronage poems. Through her verbal recounting of the mute kiss of the "Mistris," at once deflected and redirected through the body of the tree, the female poet constructs a position for herself as author outside the realm of potential threat or competition.[39] Within the elegiac frame of "Cooke-ham," connection occurs most clearly across social and physical distance.

Lanyer offers her poem not as a static monument to the estate, which itself is "deface[d]" by dust and isolation once the women depart (202), but rather as a living testimony to the bonds among women that have informed a single location with such communicative vitality. In closing, Lanyer declares that the virtues of the countess, lodged within her, tie "my heart to her by those rich chaines" (210). The "rich chaines" here at the end of "Cooke-ham" thus represent ties that bind, even in separation. Lanyer's "last farewell" (205) to the departed female inhabitants of the estate, as well as to the (female) readers of *Salve Deus Rex Judaeorum*, can be viewed, finally, as a proactive strategy predicated on "both the sameness and the otherness of the other woman, her symbolic function as agent of change," which allows her to appropriate the absence of those "other" women as the authorization for the emergent subjectivity of her own valedictory voice.

Mary Wroth chooses a lyric voice for ends far different from those of Aemilia
Lanyer, and yet the poetry of both women figures forth the importance of
female bonds to women's discourse. By contrast to Lanyer, who clearly identifies the countess of Cumberland and Anne Clifford by name in representing
the effects of bonds among women, Wroth builds her lyric sequence around
the voice of her speaking subject, with little reference to contemporary events
or individuals. In noting the poems' sustained lack of reference, Masten observes that "they seem to speak an almost inscrutable private language," and
concludes that the poems "encode a withdrawal from circulation."[40] On the
other hand, given that Petrarchism itself constituted a public language for
poets in the early modern period, I would argue that the apparently nonrefe-
rential discourse of the poems "publishes" a subtext of communication
between women which openly revises male-authored Petrarchan strategies.
Without naming any contemporary women in her sequence, Wroth nevertheless manages to evoke strong female ties to personified figures ranging from
"Night" and "Fortune" to the mythic "Philomeale," specifically to counteract
the perennial absence of the male Petrarchan lover. Furthermore, the lack of
reference to contemporary female figures in Wroth's sequence preemptively
reduces the potential threat to self-fashioning of possibly competitive women's
voices, such as appear in Lanyer's patronage poems. Thus while Wroth's
poems may encode a withdrawal from "the traffic in women" associated with
circulation between the sexes, as well as from the traffic between historical
women placed in competitive relation by a patriarchal social system, they
point at the same time to an alternative framework of female bonds that underlie and may even outlast the changing dynamics of heterosexual romance.

   In accord with the Petrarchan frame of the sequence, Wroth's speaker
seems at moments to probe the conventional options available to her as a
"dark lady," observing: "Yett though I darke do live I triumph may" (P9).
Drawing upon traditional Petrarchan alternations of day and night in the expression of grief, she opens one sonnet with the question: "Which should I
better like of, day, or night," and concludes with the lament: "Darke to joy by
day, light in night oprest / Leave both, and end, thes butt each other spill"
(P20). Male sonneteers often experimented with these traditional alternations
as well, so that Philip Sidney, for example, intensifies the dichotomy, alternating his images until the two states are superimposed in one experience of
heightened suffering: "no night is more darke then is my day, / Nor no day
hath lesse quiet than my night" (AS #89). Robert Sidney, in a fashion characteristic of the tone of his sequence, emphasizes the suffering of his speaker
with metaphors of physical pain.[41] Thus one sonnet portrays the lover as a
galley slave "who on the oar doth stretch / His limbs all day, all night his
wounds doth bind," and ends with the speaker's complaint that no day is so
long that new wounds are not received, "Nor longest night is long enough for

me / To tell my wounds, which restless bleeding be" (Sonnet #19).

When Wroth's sonnets upon the relative merits of day and night are viewed as a larger group, however, it becomes apparent that instead of maintaining the dichotomy insisted upon by her male predecessors, she more often moves beyond that dichotomy to a choice, which suggests her emerging definition of female subjectivity in multiple rather than singular terms. Thus one sonnet which begins with the day/night alternation becomes a comparison of the speaker and "Night" as female companions in grief. Pamphilia's litany of parallels between herself and Night leads to her concluding embrace of the sustaining company of Night:

> My thoughts are sad; her face as sad doth seeme:
> My paines are long; Her houers taedious are:
> My griefe is great, and endles is my care:
> Her face, her force, and all of woes esteeme:
> Then wellcome Night, and farwell flattring day.   [P13]

While the male lover's absence governs the dynamic of heterosexual desire (and pain) which informs the Petrarchan frame of much of the sequence, nevertheless the sustained lack of reference either to the male lover himself—named only in the title—or to his absence in so many words, shifts the focus of the speaker's discourse from the masculine subject to her own construction of homosocial bonds with the female figures of Night, Time, Fortune, and even Philomela. Unlike the male lover, these alternate figures of female authority and companionship offer a complex (and occasionally ambivalent) context of support for the female speaker's attempts to claim a position of her own. Significantly, that position as a speaking subject is most effectively attainable, in each of Wroth's texts, in conjunction with the publication of bonds between women to balance the challenges to female subjectivity encoded in heterosexual ties.

A subsequent sonnet opens with that same welcome—"Truly poore Night thou well-come art to mee"—and proceeds to delineate Pamphilia's reasons for loving this companion who gives quiet "to uss, and mee among the rest oprest" (P17). Rather than focusing upon the exclusivity of her pain in love, as do many of the male poets, Wroth's speaker declares herself part of a larger community of "oprest" lovers and embraces the character of Night as a female friend in a shared time of trouble. Three times, in fact (lines 2, 5, 9), Pamphilia declares her love for Night in language that conveys not her subjection to the forces of Cupid, but rather her assertion of her own agency in choosing to love: "Truly poore Night . . . I love thee." Furthermore, in defining Night's response of "loving grace" to the speaker as well as "the rest oprest," Wroth manages to underscore, even in suffering, the strength of mutual love between women. Although it is true, as Gary Waller has pointed out, that the female roles that Wroth invokes in her sequence often share qualities of helplessness or anger,[42] nevertheless I would argue that Wroth's revision of the solipsistic Petrarchan model of self-centered suffering proves ultimately more empowering than constraining for her female speaker, who finds her voice not in a vacuum but in an explicitly feminized community.

In yet another sonnet which welcomes "darkest night," Wroth expands upon the "absence" which oppresses the female speaker with a description of the distress manifest in the natural landscape at "sweet sommers parting," in which summer is represented not as a male figure but rather as a feminine presence now departed: "The very trees with hanging heads condole / Sweet sommers parting, and of leaves distrest / In dying coulers make a griefe-full role; . . . / Thus of dead leaves her farewell carpett's made: / Theyr fall, theyr branches, all theyr mournings prove" (P22). The language of mourning here unexpectedly recalls Lanyer's description of nature's lament in "Cooke-ham": "The trees that were so glorious in our view, / Forsooke both floures and fruit, when once they knew / Of your depart, their very leaves did wither, / Changing their colours as they grewe together" (133-36). In both cases, nature's lament testifies to a feminine experience of loss.

While Philip Sidney compares "night" and "thought" in terms of their aesthetic similarities (AS #96), Wroth embraces the triple companionship of "silence," "grief," and "Night" in personal terms which not only stress her awareness of a shared female bond of suffering, but even more significantly decenter the role of the male beloved, relegating him in effect to the margins of this "freindship" (P43). Elsewhere Pamphilia finds comfort in the "blesse'd armes" of Fortune, another feminine figure who instructs Pamphilia to "depend" upon her (P36). In response, Pamphilia observes: "I, her obay'd, and rising felt that love / Indeed was best, when I did least itt move" (P36). As Nona Fienberg points out, in this sonnet Wroth revises the traditionally misogynist representation of "Lady Fortune," so that the once indifferent or hostile figure of Fortune becomes instead a friend.[43] Supported by the love of female companions, Wroth's speaker finds herself able to escape the torments to which she has been subject, "possessing mee as if I ought t'obay," and instead begins to reclaim possession of her own agency as a speaking subject (P36). To similar ends did Aemilia Lanyer inscribe in her poem her bonds with the countess of Cumberland and Anne Clifford, and Anne Clifford herself inscribe in her diary the support she garnered from female friends such as Wroth when suffering the disapproval and opposition of her husband.

Even as Lanyer invokes the "mournefull Ditty" of "faire Philomela" in representing the sorrowful songs of the birds in the bereaved landscape of Cookham (189), so Wroth includes the music of "Philomeale" in her sequence as well (P93). Examining a variety of Renaissance depictions of Philomela,

Mary Ellen Lamb makes a convincing argument that "with her anger as present/absent as her tongue, the nightingale Philomela presents a powerful analogy for women writers in the Renaissance," suggesting along these lines that with "her tongue mutilated so that she cannot speak, Philomela becomes a figure for silenced anger."[44] The classical myth itself initially seems to subvert any possibility of female agency or subjectivity, given its tale of the brutal rape of a woman's body followed by the apparent silencing of her voice. Yet despite the excision of her tongue by her rapist brother-in-law, Tereus, Ovid's Philomela weaves her story into a tapestry, creating a text for her sister Procne's eyes, after which they murder the son of Tereus (and Procne) and serve him in a dish for his father's consumption, perpetuating a cycle of violent revenge that is broken only when all three are transformed into birds.

Given that the use of the nightingale as a figure for the poet was already a commonplace by the end of the sixteenth century, Lamb notes that Philomela paradoxically embodies an authorial role already endorsed by the Renaissance patriarchy which yet accommodates the gender of a woman poet. At the same time, Lamb argues that the revision of the vengeful Philomela of Ovid into the grieving Philomela of most Renaissance adaptations of the story indicates the anxiety elicited by women's anger within Renaissance culture. Lamb concludes that the "cultural dislocutions" which deny Philomela's anger to emphasize her pathos create a "formidable barrier" to female authorship in the Renaissance.[45] Although Lamb usefully stresses Philomela's significance as a figure of "silenced anger," it is also revealing to consider the potential for alternative readings of Ovid's tale which focus not only upon the emotions of anger or grief associated with the characters, but also upon the practices of textual refashioning embedded in the narrative. Deprived of her tongue, Philomela nevertheless overcomes her attempted silencing by authoring her own text for a specifically female audience. While the consequent fate of Tereus's son admittedly shadows Philomela's authorship with horrific undertones after the fact, it is useful to recall that Edward Denny's construction of Wroth in explicitly monstrous terms was precipitated by her authorship alone.

Wroth's own use of the figure of Philomela reveals an appropriation of the mythic tale which can be seen to emphasize not so much silenced anger as insistent communication in a feminized context. Whereas Lanyer's Philomela ceases to sing upon the departure of the countess and her daughter, her music "drownd in dead sleepe" (190) and thus effectively silenced, Wroth's Philomela sings anew in the "arbour" of female companionship provided by Silvia and her nymphs:

> Philomeale in this arbour
> Makes now her loving harbour
> Yett of her state complaining

Her notes in mildnes straining
  Which though sweet
  Yett doe meete
Her former luckles payning.   [P93]

The "meeting" between Philomela's mild yet strained notes and "her former luckles payning" points directly to her physical violation and the attempted silencing of her voice, even as the presence of her song, literally embodied in Wroth's text, serves as a reminder that the silencing was unsuccessful.[46] Furthermore, Philomela's song is represented here in an unexpected "harbour" of female homosocial bonding rather than solely in relation to the conventional heterosexual passion associated with the nightingale's song in male-authored Renaissance love poetry, recalling the original female audience of her sister for whom the tongueless Philomela refashioned her story.

In the larger context of Wroth's *Urania*, the nightingale motif reappears when Pamphilia's aunt, the queen of Naples—associated, as noted earlier, with Wroth's own aunt the countess of Pembroke—composes a poem for an audience of her ladies after she hears the song of a nightingale, "upon which she grounded her subject" (I: fol. 416). Comparing her "sighs and teares" to the "notes" of the nightingale, the queen of Naples concludes that the bird has the advantage because "Thy griefe thou utterest, mine I utter not" (U34). And yet, as Lamb points out, in the very writing of a poem on the impossibility of authorship the queen of Naples demonstrates its possibility.[47] Furthermore, given that the queen of Naples' unuttered grief becomes the "subject" of her poem, even as Philomela's unuttered suffering becomes the subject of her tapestry, the text/textile conjunction becomes particularly apposite, suggesting that authorship can take more than one form.

The song of the nightingale thus serves, in Wroth's textual configurations, to convey both a conventional Renaissance lament of frustrated heterosexual desire and a revisionary insistence upon a shared context of female homosocial bonding, which recalls the painful yet enduring bond of sisterly loyalty in the face of masculine violation and oppression which informs the original myth. Interestingly, both Wroth and Lanyer, for all the differences in their poetic occasions, associate the voice of Philomela with the presence of a community of women. In Wroth's sequence in particular, with its explicit framework of heterosexual desire, the restored voice of Philomela signifies the reemergent agency of the female subject despite masculine abuse. For all the grief inscribed in the sequence, then, what endures after all is the song.

Near the end of the sequence, Wroth calls upon "clowdy night to governe this sad place," commemorating "thes haples rooms"—playing on the Italian *stanza*, as Jeff Masten has pointed out[48]—to the female authority of Night, whose presence has supported the speaker's voice throughout the sequence (P100). Wroth closes the sequence with an affirmation of Pamphilia's discursive bond with her muse, the last figure of female authority in the poem apart from the speaker herself (P103). The collaboration between Wroth's female speaker and her female muse, recalling Lanyer's representation of the bond between herself and her "sacred sisters," has resulted in a discourse of love which encompasses not only heterosexual passion, but homosocial bonding as well. Pamphilia's commemoration of her poems to Night, and her injunction of her muse to silence, reveal at once the centrality of bonds between women to female discourse, and the potential for a female-authored lyric protagonist finally to choose, unlike Ovid's Philomela, the terms of her own silence. Instead of finding her voice stifled or suppressed by a man, then, Wroth's speaker is enabled to choose the point of closure for her song.

While female homosocial bonds play apparently little part in male-authored lyric poetry in early modern England, a significant number of male-authored plays and prose romances feature friendships among women in the background of plots driven by heterosexual desire. As Woodbridge's survey of a range of male-authored Renaissance literary examples suggests, female friendships conventionally are characterized by a note of social dependency and domesticity absent from parallel depictions of male friendships.[49] Most such literary depictions of bonds between women, furthermore, present those friendships in reactionary, subordinate, or at best parallel relation to male homosocial bonds. In fact, many of the examples of female friendship in both continental and English male-authored plays and romances serve to emphasize not female homosocial bonding but rather heterosexual desire, by representing pairs of women who serve primarily to fulfill the romantic quests of pairs of male friends.

    In her recent analysis of what she terms "transvestite ventriloquism" in the early modern period, Elizabeth Harvey argues that a number of the texts written by male authors include representations of women's speech that actually serve to marginalize women's voices or to reinforce women's silence. In Harvey's view, these examples of apparently feminine voices function "either to erase the gender of the authorial voice or to thematize the transvestism of this process," according to which women's voices are seemingly linked with a whole set of "feminine" characteristics, including popular accounts of women's emotional makeup and sexualized bodies. Harvey concludes that such ventriloquism is an appropriation of the feminine voice which at once reflects and contributes to a larger cultural silencing of women.[50] Harvey's observations can be applied to women's voices not simply in heterosexual bonds but in homosocial relations as well, where male-authored representations of female friendship function to marginalize female agency or silence feminine voices, through metaphorical or even literal transvestite ventriloquism.

While women play a prominent role in the romances of Montemayor and d'Urfé, for example, the friendships between the female characters in *Diana* and *Astrée* commonly serve only to underscore the primacy of love between the sexes, effectively subordinating women's to men's voices. Significantly, the central example of "female friendship" in *Astrée* actually features the heterosexual relation between Astrée and Celadon in transvestite disguise as the druidess "Alexis." Far from developing the implications of homosocial bonds between women, then, d'Urfé locates in this "female friendship" the occasion for representing an extensive objectification of the female body by the male lover. Astrée's naked female body is exposed to Celadon's gaze in several sensual dressing scenes, while d'Urfé's nominal use of the female pronoun associated with "Alexis" quickly gives way to the operative masculine subject: "Celadon had a good will to continue his caresses longer, but some considerations moved him to give over sooner than he had a mind, and helping her to dress her selfe, her Breasts, and almost every part of her fair Body was open to his eye, which being ravished at the sight of so many transcendent perfections, she [*sic*] desired that Celadon were another Argus, full of eyes, that he might the better contemplate all those excellencies."[51] An epitome of the masculine gazer or "peeping Tom," the one-hundred-eyed figure of Argus is set by one jealous female (Hera) to spy upon another (Io), and is ultimately killed by Hermes upon the orders of a yet more powerful male (Zeus) who had his eye on Io all along. On the one hand, d'Urfé's descriptive appropriation of the mythical figure of Argus focuses upon the masculine capability to possess the female body through "the gaze." On the other hand, the associated Ovidian tale of feminine conflict and triumphant masculine sexual power underlies his narrative transformation of "female friendship" into a safely heterosexual bond. Furthermore, by apparently ventriloquizing the feminine voice of "Alexis" while actually emphasizing the masculine gaze of Celadon in relation to Astrée, d'Urfé succeeds in replacing the voice of Astrée with her sexualized body, thus erasing in one "homosocial" stroke any suggestion of female agency or subjectivity. By contrast to d'Urfé, in an unambiguously gendered reversal of the terms of the Argus myth, Mary Wroth actually attributes to the female figure of "Night" even greater power than that of "the God, whose pleasant reede did smite / All Argus eyes into a deathlike night," when Night liberates Pamphilia by closing "from priing sight" the spiteful eyes of those who wish her ill (P65). In Wroth's text, then, the objectifying male gaze is at least temporarily extinguished due to superior forces of female friendship.

In Sidney's *Arcadia*, as discussed in chapter 2, the relation between Philoclea and "Zelmane" provides another example, as in *Astrée*, of the collapse of an apparently female homosocial bond before the demands of heterosexual desire. In both cases, the "female friendships" are actually controlled by men, whose feminine cross-dressing or transvestism, so far from signaling the dissolution of "difference" between the sexes, serves only to highlight the resolutely masculine subjectivity which governs the terms of the relationships. Constance Jordan observes that in Sidney's construction of the relation between Philoclea and "Zelmane," the inexperienced woman must learn to separate "the signs of femininity" from "the female sex" in order to be a wife.[52] On the other hand, it might be argued that the completion of heterosexual desire in this case necessitates the deconstruction of an only temporarily idealized "female friendship," where hitherto problematic signs of (ventriloquized) femininity can be replaced by unambiguously dominant signs of masculinity, in a reification of the patriarchal institution of marriage.

The more traditional female friendship between Pamela and Philoclea, moreover, merely echoes the primary male homosocial bond between Musidorus and Pyrocles, while completing a tetrad of heterosexual desire. Although it can be argued that the conversations between Pamela and Philoclea, particularly in the *New Arcadia*, provide an antecedent in prose romance for the intimate exchanges between Wroth's female characters, in fact the interaction of the Arcadian sisters consists less of a mutual interchange (such as can be found between Musidorus and Pyrocles) than a frequently one-sided discourse, where Pamela confides in Philoclea, who draws parallels between their situations to herself rather than in direct response to her sister. Sidney's authorial ventriloquization, to use Harvey's term once more, thus stops short of according this female homosocial bond the same potential for independent subjectivity which distinguishes the speaking voices of Pyrocles and Musidorus. As will shortly be discussed in more detail, the conversations shared by Wroth's female characters, on the other hand, rely upon the mutual voicing rather than the isolated sublimation of thoughts and emotions. Speaking among themselves, Wroth's female characters forge at once distinct and interdependent voices.

Along the lines of the male-authored prose romances discussed above, the double friendship/marriage of Cambell and Triamond with Cambina and Canacee in Book IV of Spenser's *Faerie Queene* brings homosocial bonds into parallel relation with heterosexual desire, while consistently subordinating the women to the men. The title of Book IV announces "The Legend of Cambel and Telamond [subsequently spelled Triamond], or of Friendship," explicitly calling attention to a narrative of male homosocial bonding. Significantly, the first of the two women to be paired off with these male heroes is introduced not as a subject, but rather as an object of male desire. Thus Canacee must wait while the three brothers, Priamond, Diamond, and Triamond, battle with Cambell for her possession, each attempting "as his most worthie wage" to "purchase [her] with his lives adventur'd gage" (IV.iii.4). A lengthy description of this triple battle culminates in an apparent stalemate between Cambell and

Triamond, broken finally by the appearance of Cambina, whose role is to serve the warriors a liquid whose consumption transforms their enmity into friendship. Having brought about the "legend" of friendship between the two men, Cambina and Canacee are then free to greet each other as friends, even as they are taken "to wife" by the heroes (IV.iii.52). Given the presence of thirty-eight stanzas detailing the physical engagement which sets the context for the legendary bonding between the men, the single stanza depicting the exchange of "curt'sies meet" (IV.iii.50) between the women only underscores their ancillary position within the social structure of homosocial bonding as well as within the "bands" of marriage (IV.iii.52).

Although the relationship between Britomart and Amoret might seem initially to diverge from this pattern of female ties subordinated to masculine dominance, in fact their pairing reproduces the dynamics of the patriarchal social system. The emergent friendship between Britomart and Amoret is cast initially in terms of heterosexual relations, so that Amoret believes her rescuer to be a man and fears "his will" (IV.i.8). Indeed, Britomart is so successful in her attempts "to hide her fained sex" by alternately offering Amoret propositions "of love, and otherwhiles of lustfulnesse," that the latter "feard *his* mind would grow to some excesse" (IV.i.7; emphasis mine). The rather convoluted reference to the attempted masking of Britomart's "fained sex"—when logic would dictate that it is precisely her "fained" masculinity that should be published while her true gender as a woman be hidden—relies upon conventional cultural associations of femininity and feigning, so that the connotations of "excesse" can be seen to apply not simply to masculine behavior but to the feminine capacity for deception as well.

It is only after Britomart is challenged and fights successfully with a(nother) male knight for the possession of Amoret that she unlaces her helmet and reveals her golden hair. The response of some observers that her femininity must be "a maske of strange disguise" (IV.i.14) further underscores the latent associations of femininity and feigning that mark Spenser's text even in the figure of a female hero. Thus although this representation of a relation between two women, one in male apparel, might seem at first glance to offer a reversal of the romance convention of false "female friendships" between a woman and a male knight in feminine disguise, the emerging bond between Amoret and Britomart does not actually overturn the dominance of heterosexual expectations over homosocial bonding. Even when Amoret discovers Britomart's sex and willingly agrees to share her bed with the female knight, Spenser takes only four lines to refer in passing to their shared conversation, and soon separates them, apparently finding their conjunction more useful for indicating complementary types of female relation to men than for exploring in any depth the configuration of a bond between women.

One of the most prominent female homosocial relationships in *The Faerie Queene* is of course the competition between Britomart and Radigund represented in Book Five. As Susanne Woods has so effectively pointed out, Britomart's conquest of Radigund functions as a conquest of all other women as well, enacting on the one hand a "typical male fantasy of female competition for men," and on the other hand "a tragedy of female powerlessness" in the figure of Radigund.[53] By contrast to the lengthy description of the battle between Cambell and Triamond, Spenser allots only eight stanzas to the battle between Britomart and Radigund. Interestingly, although some parallel metaphors appear, particularly in the use of beast imagery, the comparison of the male warriors with "two Tygers" attempting to "gaine a feastfull guerdon of their toyle" in order to "asswage" their "famine" (IV.iii.16) conveys overtones of a righteous competition for survival, which are less evident in the comparison of the female warriors with "a Tygre and a Lionesse" who "challenge" their prey "with equall greedinesse" (V.vii.30). Even more strikingly, Britomart's victory over Radigund results, unlike the competition between Cambell and Triamond, not in legendary homosocial bonding, but rather in death for the vanquished Radigund and in Britomart's erasure of the Amazonian system of female rule, so that Britomart "the liberty of women did repeale," restoring them "to mens subjection" and the authority of Arthegall. As Harvey points out, it is only by setting two powerful female figures against each other that Spenser can effectively represent the defeat of "female supremacy" and the restoration of appropriate masculine authority.[54] This destruction rather than celebration of potential female homosocial bonding, then, provides the ultimate assurance of the "true Justice" of the patriarchal order (V.vii.42).

Similarly, in Shakespeare's plays, bonds between women consistently yield primacy to the simultaneously heterosexual and patriarchal claims of marriage. Louis Montrose has suggested, in his exploration of gender in Elizabethan culture, that "men make women, and make themselves through the medium of women," using *A Midsummer Night's Dream* as one of his examples. According to Montrose, the examples of male and female doubling in that work result in "the maidens remain[ing] constant to their men at the cost of inconstancy to each other," while the marriages at the end "dissolve the bonds of sisterhood at the same time that they forge the bonds of brotherhood."[55] In fact, the marriages at the end of many Shakespearean comedies place women primarily in relation to men rather than to each other, as the "counter-universe" of female friends, to use Carole McKewin's term, is subsumed under the patriarchy.[56]

The female conversations in Shakespeare's comedies in particular have prompted feminist critics such as McKewin to praise Shakespeare's mimetic skill in "creating the sound of women's voices placing themselves in a man's world."[57] Some critics have pointed to the interaction between Shakespeare's female friends as suggestive of a female "subculture" in contrast to the dominant male order.[58] As Peter Erickson has convincingly argued, however, the possibilities for female bonds throughout Shakespeare's plays are severely restricted by comparison to masculine bonds, with relations between women commonly represented either as lost opportunities or as subsidiary events, and never allowed to appear equal in strength or scope to male bonds.[59] Furthermore, the cross-dressed females in Shakespeare's comedies, from Rosalind to Viola, serve to advance heterosexual relations as surely as do the cross-dressed males in the romances of Sidney and d'Urfé, with actual female friendships consistently taking second place to the governing forces of heterosexual desire. Thus at the conclusions of the plays, the cross-dressed females compliantly relinquish their temporarily assertive roles for subordinate positions as wives, even as male homosocial bonds are reinstated.

The relative absence of female homosocial bonds in Shakespeare's tragedies in particular only underscores the significant fate of one exception, in *Othello*, where Desdemona and Emilia converse at length in the "willow scene" (IV.iii) on relations between the sexes. In that case, the vividly discursive bond between Desdemona and Emilia is silenced when both women suffer death at the hands of their husbands. Furthermore, although Emilia's longest conversation with Desdemona is marked by bold challenges to a gendered hierarchy of emotions, in such questions as: "have not we affections, / Desires for sport, and frailty, as men have?" (IV.iii.100-101), still she is constrained to define women in relation to men's faults: "The ills we do, their ills instruct us so" (IV.iii.103). And while Paulina's vehement defense of Hermione provides a similar exception to the relative absence of female homosocial bonds in Shakespeare's romances, the bonds between women in *The Winter's Tale* are marginalized, in the male-dominated social world of the play, through their suspect association with "magic" (V.iii.39, 110). In insisting that she is unaided by "wicked powers," Paulina must defensively anticipate charges of witchcraft for her act of preserving Hermione's life in the face of masculine abuse (V.iii.91). Leontes, as discussed in chapter 3, literally has the final word, accepting his wife back under his patriarchal authority and silencing Paulina by assigning her to a husband. The notable absence of any dialogue between Paulina and her queen in the final scene further reinforces the sublimation of female homosocial bonds throughout the play, where women are given voices to speak primarily to men rather than to one another.

By contrast to the range of male-authored literary texts just surveyed, female-authored literary antecedents of Wroth as varied as Marguerite de Navarre's *Heptaméron* and Elizabeth Cary's *Mariam* can be seen both to celebrate and problematize female homosocial bonding, while in any case according it greater depth as well as prominence than the "ventriloquized" versions of male writers from Montemayor to Shakespeare. Some of the most empowering female bonds in the *Heptaméron* are depicted in relation to the threat of masculine aggression, as in the tale of the failed rape attempt upon the widowed princess discussed in chapter 5. In that example, the princess revises her initial desire to "have the man's head" (93) after a long conversation with her lady-in-waiting, who advises her to protect her reputation from suspicion by refraining from publicizing the attempt, thus in effect erasing the agency of the male aggressor. Upon following the advice of her female friend, the princess finds that she is able to maintain both her pride and her peace of mind, while the putative rapist completely loses his "self-assurance" in her presence thereafter (96). Unlike the ultimate impotence of Emilia's advice to Desdemona, given their deaths despite (or because of) their speech, these female characters in the *Heptaméron* successfully reverse the threat of masculine aggression through the alternative force of female homosocial bonding.

While representations of strong female bonds abound in the *Heptaméron*, they are by no means uniformly idealized. In the commentary that connects the tales, the women frequently argue with one another, even as they identify with each other's struggles. Thus near the conclusion of Marguerite de Navarre's text, Longarine, Ennasuite, and Parlamente all adopt conflicting perspectives on the significance of the tale just narrated, differing most particularly on guidelines for appropriate relations between a woman and her husband (505). Parlamente points out elsewhere, however, that "the burdens borne by men and by women are often very different" (253), and even goes so far as to assert to the men, on behalf of the assembled women, an argument that runs counter to the "shared frailty" position adopted by Emilia, in maintaining that "our temptations are not the same as yours" (305). Interestingly, her opening statement—that "we are all in need of God's grace, since we all incline to sin"—does not differentiate between the sexes, and yet in her very next sentence that "we" has split into an "us" versus a "you," with "all your pleasure" derived from "dishonouring women" and "killing other men" (305). Unlike Saffredent's sexualized insistence that "underneath all those skirts . . . you *are* all women" (202), Parlamente's articulation of gender differences extends beyond anatomical distinctions to embrace the subjectivity and agency of women who face different challenges and enact different choices, both from men and from one another. In Marguerite de Navarre's *Heptaméron*, then, female homosocial bonds support a gender group identification that is flexible enough to allow for differences among women themselves.

Like the *Heptaméron*, and by contrast to male-authored treatments of women's relationships in early modern England, Elizabeth Cary's *Mariam* grants female homosocial relations a central rather than peripheral position. Yet the multiple examples of discourse among women in Cary's play, while not construed as witchcraft by the male characters as in *The Winter's Tale,* prove vexed at best, and in many instances downright hostile. Far more frequently than in Marguerite de Navarre's text, female homosocial relations in *Mariam* enact conflict rather than connection, competition rather than support. Indeed, the finally limited power of female speech in Cary's play can be attributed at least in part to the consistently oppositional patterns of discourse that govern not only the relations between the sexes, but the interaction among the female characters as well. Particularly because most of the female characters, from Mariam herself through Alexandra and Doris to Salome, are frequently compelled to construct both their speech and their actions in reaction to the powerful masculine figure of Herod, their multiple relations to this singular male subject undermine the potential for homosocial bonding among themselves.

In the scene that follows Mariam's opening soliloquy, for example, Mariam and her mother, Alexandra, engage in a combative discussion over the appropriateness of Mariam's mourning for "the tyrant's end" (I.ii.80), revealing the extent to which, even in "death," the figure of Herod still effectively obscures their bond. In the very next scene, Mariam and Salome debate their respective positions of social stature in terms that once again center upon the women's relation to Herod, as Salome postulates that "Mariam hopes to have another king," while Mariam stands upon her elevated position as "Judea's queen" in dismissing Salome as no better than "Mariam's servants" (I.iii.209, 225-26). Directly thereafter, Salome has a soliloquy (I.iv) to match Mariam's earlier soliloquy (I.i), in which she contemplates her limited social options in the aftermath of Herod's death and plots to exchange one husband for another.[60] Although not one single man appears in the first four scenes of the play, the figure of Herod serves as a dominating "absent presence," informing the often oppositional speech of the female characters even as they compete to preserve their social standing in a patriarchal society.

Despite the seeming centrality of the absent Herod, however, Cary consistently foregrounds the shaping force of women's voices in domestic politics. Moreover, by contrast to the blurring of distinctions between the female characters in Josephus's *Antiquities,* Cary emphasizes distinctions in her configuration of female homosocial relations. On the one hand, the discursive combat amongst the women throughout the play works to isolate their voices, so that they seem to be speaking constantly against each other rather than with each other, leaving no space for any collective discourse of female concerns. On the other hand, their spirited engagements with one another often function to sharpen their respective positions as subjects able to claim voices for themselves within the otherwise overdetermined social roles afforded them by male-authored codes of feminine conduct. The shared conversations and/or arguments among the major female characters seem at times to serve as release valves for their pent-up frustration at containing their speech in the presence of the men who wield social authority over them. Oddly enough, then, the very conflicts conceived in relation to male authority which define female homosocial bonds in Cary's play work not simply to distinguish, but occasionally even to empower, the voices of female protagonists as otherwise apparently opposed as Mariam and Salome.

Significantly, the one female character who does not speak in conflict with the others is also the epitome of feminine silence and subjection to male authority: namely, Graphina, who does not appear in Cary's source. Graphina actually can be seen to function as a striking foil for the other female characters, pointing up their emergent assertions of agency and subjectivity, not only despite but through their conflict with one another, as well as their varying degrees of resistance to patriarchal authority, by contrast with her own passivity and self-doubt. Only Graphina takes pains to efface her voice even in the act of speech, replying reluctantly to Pheroras's command that she "move [her] tongue" with the explanation that "if I be silent, 'tis no more but fear / That I should say too little when I speak" (II.i.41, 49-50). Even Mariam's concerns over the effects of her too "public" voice reflect not a fear of saying "too little" when she speaks, but rather her awareness that any public speech at all from a woman can be construed as too much, while Salome is rarely silent.

When Cary's Salome rails against male "privilege," her language seems to assert female agency where Shakespeare's Emilia only begins to question the terms of male domination. On the other hand, like Emilia after all, Salome defines women only in comparative relation to men:

> Why should such privilege to man be given?
> Or given to them, why barr'd from women then?
> Are men than we in greater grace with Heaven?
> Or cannot women hate as well as men?
> I'll be the custom-breaker: and begin
> To show my sex the way to freedom's door.   [I.iv.305-10]

Whereas Emilia claims for women the same "affections" as men, Salome claims equal power to "hate," and goes on to fashion for herself the role of "custom-breaker," most particularly insofar as customs interfere with her own desires. For all her aggressive language, Salome proves ultimately far more bound by the patriarchal system which she professes to despise than is Emilia, desiring after all to remain a wife, while Emilia warns her husband: "Perchance, Iago, I will ne'er go home" (Othello, V.ii.194). The "freedom's door" for Salome, then, seems to consist of skill at manipulating men rather than a resolve to escape their authority. Furthermore, for all her seeming dedication to her "sex," it is female homosocial bonds which Salome sacrifices in the service of her own advancement, when she finally succeeds in convincing Herod to execute Mariam, not through her wide-ranging enumeration of means (including decapitation, drowning, and burning), but rather through her ironic proposal that Herod "let her live for me," which results in his immediate resolve that "she shall die" (IV.vii.381).

After manipulating Herod to achieve Mariam's execution, Salome receives for her reward only Herod's curses upon her head, as he terms her an "ape" and a "sun-burnt blackamoor" by comparison to the Mariam whom he has sentenced to death (IV.vii.460, 462). And far from deriving any comfort from bonds with other women, Salome "the custom-breaker" ultimately stands condemned, in Herod's words, of "envy . . . / To see thyself out-matchèd in thy sex" (V.i.161-62). Given Herod's own view of the competitive relation between women, it is not surprising that the female characters' focus upon Herod leads them into oppositional relations with each other. And yet even those seeming oppositions collapse upon closer scrutiny, given the women's shared experience of male tyranny. As Weller and Ferguson point out, Salome herself is not simply Mariam's antitype, but rather "the active double of Mariam's passive resistance to patriarchal power and to definition by the male."[61] Herod himself conflates the two women when he accidentally names Mariam in place of Salome and corrects himself in mid-breath, observing that the death of Constabarus will "requite / Thee gentle Mariam—Salom I mean," and adding that "the thought of Mariam doth so steal my spirit, / My mouth from speech of her I cannot wean" (IV.ii.84-86). Ironically, for all the power of his position, it is ultimately Herod who finds his speech increasingly dependent upon the women whose voices he is constantly attempting to contain and control.

Even as Mariam's first discursive engagement with another woman is a combative discussion with her mother, so her final scene in the play consists of yet another argumentative dialogue with a woman, in this case Herod's first wife, Doris, who closes their exchange, as discussed in chapter 3, by delivering a curse upon Mariam and her offspring (IV.viii.601-3, 609ff). Instead of representing relations between women in a patriarchal society as supportive or empowering, then, Cary demonstrates the mutually destructive potential of female homosocial bonds in the face of masculine oppression. Although Cary's female characters exhibit the ability to speak out strongly against male tyranny when heard in isolation from each other, their collective jostling for position in a society governed by male subjects leaves them little room to stand together, so that finally their alternatives seem limited to drowning out each other's voices or subsiding into silence. And yet the swelling dissonance of the women's voices, speaking "in concert," provides a fitting counterpoint to the diminishing authority of Herod's singular voice, which finally can achieve definition only in relation to the "absent presence" of the dead Mariam. Not simply despite, but rather through conflict, then, the female characters in Cary's play find positions as speaking subjects after all.

The numerous female characters in Wroth's play and prose romance prove instrumental in opening a space for discourse which is potentially both mutual and enduring in homosocial terms, even as they simultaneously negotiate complex heterosexual relations. Through her representations of female bonds, Wroth "changes the subject" not only of such male authors as Sidney and Shakespeare, but also of such female authors as Lanyer and Cary. Instead of simply shifting the emphasis away from the practice of male traffic in women, as does Lanyer, or working to displace the dominance of masculine subjects by focusing upon oppositional relations between women, as does Cary, Wroth structures her texts, both implicitly and explicitly, around interdependent configurations of heterosexual and homosocial bonding. Just as *Pamphilia to Amphilanthus* uncovers new speaking positions for the female lover in conjunction with female homosocial bonds, so *Love's Victory* and *Urania* explore a range of female relations that exert a shaping influence upon the dynamics of heterosexual romance. Far from positioning female homosocial bonds in direct opposition to heterosexual ties, Wroth exposes their interdependence. It is precisely in the acknowledgment of that interdependence that Wroth's female protagonists learn to locate consistent positions as speaking subjects within both heterosexual and homosocial relations.

Indeed, Wroth figures forth a multiplicity of bonds between women which allow her female protagonists initially to function as potential agents of change for each other, and ultimately to begin to fashion, collectively, feminine parameters for agency and subjectivity. Wroth's female characters are enabled to claim multiple positions as speaking subjects, then, not only in relation to men, but also by "practicing difference" among themselves. If the redefinition of the female subject can be said to start with the recognition of both "the sameness and the otherness of the other woman," then the horizontal relation between women in Wroth's texts can be scrutinized for the emergence into visibility of "this subject which is not one." Moreover, in representing both connections and tensions between heterosexual desire and homosocial friendship, Wroth at once challenges and redefines some of the figurations of gender governing constructions of sexual difference in her culture.

From the beginning of *Love's Victory*, Wroth features the importance of homosocial bonds within the world of the play. When Venus, for example, commands Cupid to make her power felt among the humans, he pledges to disrupt friendships even before love relationships: "Freinds shall mistrust theyr freinds, lovers mistake, / And all shall for theyr folly woes partake" (I.27-28). In representing ties of friendship, Wroth begins with homosocial bonds between men, develops cross-gender friendships and sexual bonds as the plot proceeds, but focuses the climactic energies of the play upon the agency of women. As Barbara Lewalski has pointed out, Wroth transforms the genre of pastoral from a traditional articulation of masculine desire and political commentary into a

vehicle for "women's voices, values, and vision."[62] Furthermore, Wroth's attention to female agency and subjectivity serves not only to revise the generic
boundaries of pastoral drama, but also gradually to change the subject of the
play itself from an opening concern with masculine friendship to a closing celebration of bonds between women. By contrast to the ventriloquized "female
friendships" in such male-authored texts as the *Arcadia* and *Astrée*, which
prove actually to be sites of heterosexual desire dominated by masculine subjects, Wroth explores the bonding of gendered subjects in homosocial as well
as heterosexual terms, which encompass nonhierarchical relations between
characters of both sexes, and extend the possibilities for female agency beyond
the conventional parameters of social passivity and sexual subordination encoded in cultural figurations of gender in early modern England.

The play opens with a representation of the tension between heterosexual and homosocial bonds, when apparently strong ties between men are
disrupted by the presence of a woman. In the first act of the play, Philisses attempts to suppress his passion for Musella because he mistakenly believes her
to be loved by his friend Lissius, observing that he would rather neglect himself
than wrong his friend (I.69-70). Unlike superficially similar moments in romances by male authors such as Montemayor and d'Urfé, however, in Wroth's
play the woman refuses to become a passive object of masculine desire, or a
mere counter to be exchanged between two male friends in a game of romance, asserting her presence instead as one of the leading figures in the rec-
reational gatherings among the shepherds and shepherdesses. Musella's first
conversation with Philisses, significantly, concerns the power of friends to
comfort one another when suffering the pangs of desire:

> *Phil.* Yett when the paine is greatest, 'tis some ease
>   To lett a freind partake his freind's disease.
> *Mus.* That were noe freindly part in this you miss,
>   Impart unto your freind noe harme butt bliss.
> *Phil.* Some freind will reddy bee to ease one's smart.
> *Mus.* Soe to befreind your self they showld bear part   [I.295-300]

Where Philisses argues at once for the dominance of heterosexual desire and
its power to infect homosocial bonds, with one (male) friend partaking "his
freind's disease," Musella maintains that friendship should provide an alternate source of affection rather than infection, so that one friend can impart
unto another "noe harme butt bliss." This latter view of friendship proves to
inform the bonds particularly among the women in the play, so that instead of
simply suffering together, they are supported by their love for one another.

The relations between male friends in the play seem the most vulnerable
to fluctuations of heterosexual desire, with Philisses avoiding Lissius in the
midst of his uncertainty over Lissius's affections rather than seeking to confide

in him. When Lissius confronts Philisses with his concern that his friend's recent coldness threatens "that band of freindship of our long held love," Philisses replies with an affirmation of his "first affection" for his friend, counterpoised with his conviction that he finds his "self undun" by that affection at the same time (II.255-58), particularly given his assumption of the mutually exclusive nature of homosocial versus heterosexual bonds. In the midst of such conflict, the language of love nevertheless continues to inform the homosocial bonds between men in Wroth's play even as it shapes their expressions of heterosexual desire. And when Philisses is convinced that Lissius desires only Musella's "freindship," he finds himself able to reaffirm the strength of his bond with Lissius even as he discovers himself finally free to voice his passion for Musella. Thus as the play proceeds, cross-gender friendship comes to be recognized by male characters as well as by female characters as one acceptable configuration of relations between the sexes, which provides a possible resolution to otherwise apparently competing heterosexual and homosocial ties.

The bonds among the women in Wroth's play, on the other hand, prove not only more resistant to fluctuations of heterosexual passion than those of the men, but capable of shaping female subjectivity through the "practice of difference" among women as well. The friendship between Silvesta and Musella in particular, although predated by their shared passion for a single man, evolves over the course of the play into a bond of love as strong as any of the romantic bonds between members of the opposite sex. Achieving a resolve that Philisses himself only contemplates in frustration with regard to Musella and Lissius (and ultimately is freed of the necessity of addressing), Silvesta determinedly forsakes her original desire for Philisses in order to embrace chastity when she observes his love for Musella. Far from resenting or avoiding Musella, however, Silvesta empathizes with her feminine subjection to love, having only recently claimed liberty for herself. In declaring that "Musella is my love" (III.37), Silvesta thus asserts her own freedom from the bondage of heterosexual desire even as she pledges fidelity to another woman. When Musella confides in Silvesta as one "who I know will not mee beetray," Silvesta responds in kind, fulfilling Musella's own earlier representation of friendship: "Betray Musella? Sooner will I dye . . . I'le wish butt the meanes to work your blis" (III.47-48, 68). In couching Silvesta's love for Philisses in the past tense, and her love for Musella in the present tense—"Butt th'one I lov'd, and love the other tooe" (III.60)—Wroth refigures cultural stereotypes of the abandoned woman which stress the destructive dominance of the past heterosexual bond upon the female victim's subsequent self-fashioning, instead emphasizing the potential autonomy of the willingly chaste woman, who can choose female friendship over heterosexual desire.

In scenes where the female characters speak among themselves, Wroth expands her representation of the relationship between homosocial bonds and gendered self-fashioning. In the middle of the play, the women gather at Dalina's suggestion to discourse together upon their shared experiences:

Now w'are alone lett every one confess
Truly to other what our lucks have bin,
How often lik'd, and lov'd and soe express
Owr passions past: shall wee this sport begin?
Non can accuse us, non can us betray
Unles owr selves, owr owne selves will bewray.   [III.125-30]

Significantly, the female characters perceive themselves to be "alone" together when not in the company of men, with "non" to accuse or betray them, "unles our selves." Their "selves," then, represent a collective subjectivity gendered in explicitly feminine terms. Freed from the social constraints of cross-gender discourse, the women are enabled to "truly tell" (III.131) not only their past love affairs, but also their present bonds with one another, however fraught with conflict as well as affection.

As in the contrasting female-authored narratives of Marguerite de Navarre's *Heptaméron*, or in the arguments between a number of the female characters in Cary's *Mariam*, the feminine discourse in *Love's Victory* encompasses far more perspectives than appear in male-authored ventriloquizations of women's voices, particularly given the limited amount of space actually allocated to conversations among women in male-authored texts. The figure of Dalina, for example, can be compared to the outspoken Salome, given not only their shared qualities of sexual inconstancy and verbal aggression, but also their simultaneous frustration and contempt for the social dominance of the opposite sex. Thus Dalina advises the other women to "lett [men] alone, and they will seeke, and sue, / Butt yeeld to them and they'll with scorne pursue" (III.252-53). The contrasts between Dalina and Silvesta, both of whom resist masculine domination and yet adopt diametrically opposed sexual stances, resist simple dichotomization into polarized stereotypes of femininity, suggesting instead women's potential for making connections with one another across their differences.

When the connections among the female characters emerge in the context not only of social familiarity but more particularly of friendship, the bonds themselves allow for the differences. Speaking from a shared position of gendered subjectivity, Musella advises her friend, Simeana, to trust her own judgment, or her "self," in determining the extent of her desire: "For this beleeve while you your self are just, / You cannott any way your love mistrust" (IV.265-66). Both the chaste Silvesta and the loving Musella demonstrate the possibility for women to claim agency as speaking subjects, while "practicing difference" from one another in their courtship relations with male lovers, past and present. While Wroth includes several examples of cross-gender

friendship in her play, as when Musella aids both Lissius and Simeana to realize their passion for one another, she emphasizes the potential for discourse
between women to serve as both a motivating and a sustaining force in enabling her female characters to learn to be true to their "selves."

Silvesta, in fact, not only supports Musella through counsel, but is willing to die in the attempt to preserve her friend's happiness.[63] In particular,
Silvesta refuses to watch her friend's agency destroyed: "Musella to bee
forc'de, and made to ty / Her faith to one she hates, and still did fly. / Itt showld
nott bee, nor shall bee; noe, noe, I / Will rescue her, or for her sake will dy"
(V.174-77). When Silvesta finds Musella and Philisses about to take their lives
in the Temple of Love and intervenes before they can shed their own blood,
they embrace her as both "freind and priest" for providing them with a "sweet
potion" that will allow them to die "imbracing" (V.248-52). The "priest" in
this Temple of Love, significantly, is a friend first. In the event, although
Silvesta's potion proves to mimic the effects of the Friar's potion in *Romeo and
Juliet*, the tragic outcome of the somewhat bumbling Friar's plans in Shakespeare's play is avoided by the forethought of the wise female friend in Wroth's
play, whose simultaneous administration of the potion to both lovers guarantees their mutual reawakening. Far from opposing heterosexual relations,
then, the female homosocial bonds between Musella and Silvesta in this case
enable the realization of heterosexual desire.

Musella's other friend, Simeana, who comes upon the scene just after
Silvesta has administered the potion, joins with Silvesta in appearing before
the remaining characters in order to share the telling of the tale. Speaking
across their own differences as two women devoted, respectively, to chastity
and to heterosexual passion, but united through their friendship with the dead
lovers as well as with one another, Silvesta and Simeana manage to bring
about a resolution to the altercations which have marked the play. When
Simeana comments on Musella's conflict with her mother—who submits to
the "Law of the Father" until her daughter's apparent death—that "her mother
growne her foe, and death her freind, / Her freind she chose" (V.335-36), her
speech indicates how Musella's choice of her friend Silvesta's means of death
allowed her to escape the patriarchal constraints of her social world. As in
Mariam, masculine tyranny functions, at least initially, to divide mother and
daughter in Wroth's play. Unlike Cary, however, Wroth reenvisions the evolu-
tion of maternal authority in relation to the development rather than the destruction of female bonds. Not only is Musella released from the bondage of
her mother's acquiescence to her father's will by Silvesta's solution, then, but
after Silvesta narrates the circumstances of the lovers' deaths, Musella's
mother herself wishes to be released from the effects of those same constraints
by "death alone, my freind" (V.400). Just as Night signifies a powerful female
presence in Wroth's lyric sequence, so the conflation of Silvesta and death en-

codes an alternative authority gendered feminine in Wroth's play, and associated with homosocial rather than heterosexual bonds.

If *Love's Victory* were a tragedy along the lines of Cary's *Mariam*, these deaths would end the play, with the remaining female characters able to voice only their loss of agency in the face of the governing power of masculine subjects. Instead, the tyrannical masculine subjects in Wroth's play are reduced to temporary impediments unable to withstand the agency of the female characters, as Musella's appointed suitor Rustic disappears, the malicious Arcas is unmasked, and even the retroactive force of Musella's father's will is dismissed by her mother, who finds herself newly empowered by the company of women. Once the lovers have been revived by the priests of Venus, Musella recalls Silvesta's position of honor as "freind and priest." Musella's observation that only in Silvesta "was true freindship found" (V.506) fulfills her initial articulation of friendship as a source of strength which need not be subordinated to heterosexual desire, but might even, as in this case, prove both comforting and empowering. Silvesta's own praise for the friendly love manifest in Venus's ultimate care for them all, meanwhile, suggests that maternal authority, in the example of Musella's mother as well as Venus, has the potential to complement rather than undermine bonds of love in friendship and sexual passion alike.

Cupid's final speech is marked by the same emphasis on friendship which distinguished the opening of the play: "Now my warrs in love hath end, / Each one heere injoys theyr freind" (V.555-56). The nongendered reference to "freind," moreover, encompasses cross-gender as well as same-sex friendship, even while pointing to the possible coexistence of friendship and desire in the same bond. Venus herself, termed a "Princeses [*sic*] Crown'd with Victory" (V.580), thus becomes not simply an overseer of the perpetually vexed relations between the sexes, but rather a celebratory voice for the intersection of homosocial and heterosexual ties. Rather than attempting to define a single "female identity" along the lines of Montemayor or d'Urfé, or even Sidney in *The Lady of May*, Wroth represents in *Love's Victory* the "otherness" among women themselves, and highlights their individuality through the breakdown of fixed Petrarchan stereotypes of heterosexual desire. At the same time, instead of playing opposing female "types" against each other, as does Cary with Mariam and Salome or Doris, Wroth brings differing female characters into relation with each other, and thus can expand the range of speaking positions for women within her play. The "Triumph of love's victory" at the end of the play (V.486), then, is a triumph not merely of conventional heterosexual desire, but also of homosocial bonding, most specifically as manifest in the enduring relations between women, whose "practice of difference" among themselves serves increasingly to heighten the power of their collective subjectivity.

Wroth's prose romance encompasses more voices than her lyric sequence, and represents more bonds among women both in connection with and apart from men than her play. While the lyric sequence, the play, and the prose romance all are framed by the dynamics of heterosexual desire, Wroth develops the relationships among the characters in *Urania* not only before but also after marriage, so that her narrative patterns are not cut off by the traditional terminus of heterosexual couplings so common to the many of the male-authored literary texts of the period. Furthermore, because Wroth does not always match up her male and female characters in pairs, avoiding the "Noah's ark" convention which defines many romances in particular, she is able to expand her characterizations of female homosocial bonds without necessarily subordinating them to parallel examples of male friendship. To an even greater extent in *Urania* than in her other two works, Wroth explores the nature not of a female "subculture," but of a female culture, to create the sound not simply of women's voices in a man's world, but of a world of women's voices which sometimes intersect, sometimes subvert, and sometimes even override or outlast the voices of men. At the same time, at the heart of Wroth's narrative of "the woman's part" in all three of her texts can be located not only the potentially disabling effects of romantic desire upon women, but the potentially enabling force of female friendship as well.

Carolyn Ruth Swift, one of the earliest critics to pay any sustained attention to *Urania*, is also one of the few to emphasize the importance of relations between women to the narrative, observing that Wroth "transforms the earlier romance pattern of heroine and confidante into genuine friendship among women."[64] Most of her discussion of the text, however, focuses less upon friendship between women than upon women's victimization by men. Along related lines, Waller's psychoanalytic reading of "family romance" attends in great detail to the frequently victimized or subordinated positions of women within heterosexual relationships, while suggesting only in passing that "friendship between women provides the opportunity for private spaces in which the more brutal aspects of hegemonic male power might be escaped."[65] Although such references to female bonds indicate a critical awareness of their existence, the absence of any extended discussion of those bonds has the effect of marginalizing their significance.

Perpetuating this pattern, Quilligan's analysis of female authority in the family romance attends primarily to heterosexual relations in Wroth's narrative. Given this focus, Quilligan concludes that "no one ends up with the 'right' person in the second part of the *Urania*," and that "women are the bonds between men, the cultural glue, as it were, that holds society together as they are exchanged between groups of men."[66] Although the designation of "no one" is perhaps a bit extreme, given the longstanding marriage of Urania and Steriamus, as well as the enduring, although troubled, relation between

Pamphilia and Amphilanthus which outlasts both their marriages to others, it is certainly true that many of the heterosexual pairings remain changeable, while, from the male characters' points of view, women sometimes function more as "glue" than as subjects. Many of the female characters "end up" with exactly the "right" female friends, however, and their shared discourse suggests, as was frequently the case in the culture at large, that their perspectives on their own roles often differed radically from those of their fathers and brothers, husbands and lovers.[67]

Lamb acknowledges that "to foreground the relationship between Pamphilia and Amphilanthus is of course to neglect others," citing the long-lasting friendship between Pamphilia and Urania as one example. Furthermore, contextualizing Wroth's authorship in relation to her own circle of friends, Lamb notes that the family of Susan Vere Herbert, who was the countess of Montgomery and wife to Mary Wroth's cousin, Philip Herbert, as well as the dedicatee of *Urania*, quite likely provided one "safe house" (in addition to the other Sidney/Herbert family households) in which women could write. All the same, the larger patterns which Lamb identifies in *Urania* center upon heterosexual desire, resulting in an overview in which she suggests that "various narratives about women married against their will gradually yield to narratives about the happiness of second loves, which gradually yield to narratives about sad constant heroines whose beloveds leave them for yet a second time."[68] The body of Lamb's analysis of *Urania*, then, like that of other Wroth critics from Swift to Waller and Quilligan, tends to focus upon romantic relations between the sexes rather than upon the intricacies of female homosocial bonds.[69]

In this final chapter of my own study, I endeavor to extend the parameters of some of the previous discussion of romantic passion and victimization in *Urania* by attending more particularly to Wroth's representations of homosocial bonds, which shape heterosexual relations even as they body forth "differences among" women. Moreover, by contextualizing those differences with reference to other cultural as well as literary texts by both female and male authors, I seek to expand the textual boundaries of previous critical work on Wroth, so that her representations of gender relations can be located in relation not just to her family circle or her generic sources, but also to the complex and sometimes conflicting figurations of gender in early modern culture at large.

Just as Wroth "changes the subject" of her play from her initial focus upon men's discursive relation to heterosexual desire to a deepening exploration of bonds between women, so she expands the scope of her prose romance from a seemingly conventional focus upon love affairs between the sexes to an increasingly multifaceted representation of the simultaneous difference and connection among her female characters as well. While heterosexual relations occupy a prominent place throughout the narrative, then, Wroth allocates an increasing amount of space to the triangulation of heterosexual desire with homosocial bonds. Two of the major group enchantment episodes which dominate the published *Urania* provide some indication of this progression, even as the unpublished manuscript continuation of the romance refashions the relations between the sexes yet further.

The first enchantment episode occurs upon the island of Cyprus, where Urania, Parselius, and a group of other characters discover an "admirable Pallace" on a hill, which they are told is called "the throne of Love" (39-40). After drinking from the river on the hill, the male knights immediately are overcome by "severall Passions" and rush off in search of warlike adventures, while the women investigate the Throne of Love, only to find themselves imprisoned in the towers of "Desire" and "Love" until "the valiantest Knight, with the loyallest Lady come together" to rescue them (40). Significantly, it is the women rather than the men who are literally captivated by heterosexual love at this early point in the narrative, and their captivity can only be terminated by the initial union of a man and a woman, apparently "come together" in a romantic bond. Wroth immediately problematizes the nature of this union, however, as well as its promise for bringing about any enduring resolution to the trials of heterosexual desire, which indeed become only more challenging as the male and female characters begin to pair off.

As this first enchantment progresses, more lovers join the initial prisoners after making unsuccessful attempts to end the enchantment. Once Pamphilia and Amphilanthus arrive, they are distinguished by their separate relations to the towers of Desire, Love, and Constancy. Amphilanthus is responsible for opening the gate to the first tower, based upon his knowledge that "he had as much strength in desire as any" (141), while together they open the gate to the tower of Love. The third tower, however, is accessible only to Pamphilia. At its gate, "*Constancy* stood holding the keyes, which Pamphilia tooke; at which instant Constancy vanished, as metamorphosing her self into her breast" (141). Only when Pamphilia hands the keys to Amphilanthus is he enabled to open the gate, after which the imprisoned lovers are released on the basis of their gender, Pamphilia liberating the women while Amphilanthus "give[s] freedome to the Knights" (141). Even at this stage of the narrative, then, the gender-based scene of liberation suggests the extent to which homosocial bonds can serve a necessary function in disentangling problematic heterosexual ties.

Without discounting the importance of the early bond between Pamphilia and Amphilanthus, it is nevertheless interesting to note that at this point in the plot they are not yet lovers themselves. After this point, in fact, it is quite a while before they are able to act together as mutually and effectively as they do in bringing the first enchantment to a close. Furthermore, it is Urania rather than Amphilanthus whom Pamphilia actually embraces once the enchantment is concluded, telling her "the worth which shee knew to bee in her, had long since bound her love to her, and had caus'd that journey of purpose to doe her service" (141). Thus although the "throne enchantment" requires a heterosexual couple to bring it to an end, a profession of love between women marks the release of those captive to heterosexual desire.

By contrast to the first enchantment, the mass imprisonment resulting from the subsequent "theater enchantment" finds resolution specifically through female homosocial bonds. This enchantment commences when Pamphilia and Urania are shipwrecked with two other ladies, and come upon "a round building like a Theater, carved curiously, and in mighty pillars" (321). When Pamphilia dismisses Urania's fears of another enchantment by asserting: "Let it be what it will . . . I will see the end of it," Urania reminds her friend to "take heed, all adventures were not framed for you to finish" (321). Indeed, even as the initial connection between Pamphilia and Amphilanthus which brought about the end of the first enchantment produces more trials of desire than it concludes over the course of the narrative, so Pamphilia herself must learn to draw upon her bonds with "other" women as well as the "other" sex in claiming a position of agency for herself. Urania's tart reminder that "all adventures were not framed for you to finish" thus serves as a useful caution, from one woman to another, regarding "differences among" occasions for agency as well as subjectivity.

Sure enough, as soon as Pamphilia manages to unlock the gate and the ladies enter the theater, sitting in four marble chairs, "the gate was instantly lock'd againe, and so was all thought in them shut up for their comming forth thence, till the man most loving, and most beloved, used his force, who should release them, but himselfe be inclosed till by the freeing of the sweetest and loveliest creature, that poore habits had disguised greatnesse in, he should be redeem'd, and then all should bee finished" (322). Neither Pamphilia, then, nor Amphilanthus—"the man most loving, and most beloved"— can end this enchantment by their own powers, either jointly or alone. On this occasion, neither "strength in desire" nor constancy are sufficient, in and of themselves, to overturn the bondage of romantic enchantment. Furthermore, unlike the first enchantment, heterosexual bonds function here as part of the problem rather than the solution. Thus not only is Amphilanthus enclosed upon his arrival with the ladies even as they are restored to "their best senses," but he sits with an/other woman, Musalina, leaving Pamphilia to return to her seat, "not only as she did alone, but viewed by all to be so" (377). Not yet having learned, at this point in the narrative, to draw strength from bonds with women, Pamphilia experiences the isolation of romantic dependency upon a changeable male lover. Even the restored "senses" of the women in the "theater" serve only to heighten their awareness of the enchantment, bringing "misery to them that were subjects to it" (377), rather than release.

Meanwhile, in an unusual twist upon the prose romance convention of "female friendship" between a woman and a man in female disguise, discussed earlier, Wroth represents a friendship between the shepherdess Veralinda and the "nimph Leonia," without disclosing for quite a while that "Leonia" is actually the knight Leonius, younger brother to Urania herself. The effect of this lack of information is to place the reader in the position of Veralinda, who learns to trust "Leonia" first as a female friend. Wroth's depiction of the transformation of this relationship from an apparently homosocial to an actually heterosexual bond depends upon a striking difference of view from seemingly parallel examples in the male-authored romances. In Sidney's *Arcadia* or d'Urfé's *Astrée*, the reader is "in the know" about the operative strategy of "transvestite ventriloquism," in effect sharing the male gaze which consumes the unknowing female character in each text, and thus identified with the position of voyeur adopted by the cross-dressed male character. In Wroth's *Urania*, however, the reader is placed in an implicitly feminized position, identified with the "unknowing female" rather than the potentially voyeuristic male, in accepting the seeming femininity of a character only subsequently revealed to be a man. Like the central female character, then, the reader must first learn "difference" in homosocial terms, before reevaluating the emergent subjectivity thus revealed in relation to heterosexual desire.

Moreover, in another notable difference from the male-authored prose romance tradition, where Sidney's and d'Urfé's cross-dressed male characters go to great lengths to assert their masculinity despite their surface appearances, "Leonia" is not afraid to adopt the position of a woman in order to offer love to a woman. Thus Leonius explains to Veralinda when he discloses his true identity: "I am the Knight you loved as a Knight, I am the man, who for feare you lov'd me not, to move your love *made my self a woman*" (389; emphasis mine). Instead of reinscribing the pattern of transvestite ventriloquism, where male authors give male characters a feminine appearance clearly designated as superficial in order to underscore their masculine desire—so that Pyrocles, as noted earlier, makes haste to assure Musidorus that "there is nothing I desire more than fully to prove myself a man in this enterprise" (*OA*, 22-23)—Wroth creates a male character whose passion leads him actually to identify with a woman, conjoining "self" and other in a discursive union whose purpose is to appreciate rather than deconstruct female subjectivity.

Veralinda embraces Leonius's proffered identification as a testament of honesty rather than deceit, responding: "I am . . . the woman that loves you as much, or more, if possible, then I did, having so many more bonds to tye me unto it" (389). Veralinda's acknowledgment of the doubly gendered bonds of their love allows her to embrace Leonius not as a dominant masculine subject along the lines of Pyrocles or Celadon, then, but rather as a friend as well as a lover. Furthermore, unlike Sidney, who represents the relationship between Pyrocles and Philoclea as taking precedence over the latter's friendship with Pamela, or d'Urfé, who restricts his representation of "female friendship" to the heterosexual coupling of "Alexis" and Astrée, Wroth situates the bond between Veralinda and Leonius in relation to her already extensive representations of bonds between women. Far from serving as a false front for heterosexual desire, female homosocial bonds in *Urania* set a standard against which the depth of heterosexual ties can be measured, and through which the emergence of female subjectivity, necessary for any mutual heterosexual relations, can be fostered even in a patriarchal society.

Furthermore, although Veralinda arrives at the island of the "theater enchantment" in the company of Leonius (whose true identity she does not yet know), she ends the enchantment through her own agency as a woman, without any aid from a man. Her appearance causes the enchanted chairs to vanish, leaving a "Pillar of Gold" on which hangs a book, which most of the other characters try in vain to take down. After Urania, with the encouragement of Pamphilia, removes the book, Amphilanthus tries unsuccessfully to open it, once again exposing his position in this enchantment as part of the problem rather than the solution. Ultimately Amphilanthus must yield place to Urania once more, who "must have Veralindas help to open it" (388). The book turns out to contain "the whole story of Urania," followed by the story of Veralinda, who, like Urania, is revealed to be a princess rather than a shepherdess after all. This revelation of the identities of the two women responsible for ending the enchantment enacts, in a "theater," their mutual identification on several levels, given their identical pastoral appearances as well as their jointly empowered homosocial agency.

Unlike the "throne enchantment," then, the "theater enchantment" requires the conjoined agency of two women to achieve a conclusion which even the most valiant of the male knights has been unable to bring about. The enchantment only concludes, moreover, when Urania and Veralinda together open the book that contains their "stories," finding in its written text the verification of their positions as women rulers as well as friends. By representing Amphilanthus's inability to open, let alone read, this narrative of female agency and subjectivity, Wroth underscores her ability to "change the subject" of cultural figurations of gender which attempted to prohibit women from reading, let alone writing, romance.[70] Transgressing those prohibitions, Wroth's female characters begin to learn, in the company of other women, to read and write their own stories.

Even as Urania and Veralinda find each other to be kindred spirits when they bring the "theater enchantment" to a conclusion together, so Pamphilia and Veralinda discover each other to be "neighbours" (389), and develop an equally strong bond of their own. As the narrative progresses, Wroth highlights the growing bonds among her female characters, often locating those bonds in triangulated contrast to fluctuations of romantic fortune between the sexes, as when Urania and Pamphilia discuss their differing relations to Amphilanthus as sister and lover, by contrast to their ties with one another as cousins and friends. The friendship between Urania, Pamphilia, and Veralinda in particular endures many changes in their respective situations, from adolescent virginity to marriage, from motherhood to widowhood, while their discourse casts light upon their maturing perspectives as sovereign subjects, authors, and friends. When Wroth's female protagonists confront the transforming power of desire, bonding in friendship often relieves bondage to passion. At the same time, Wroth's attention to the gradual passage of her protagonists through generational stages of maturation over time distinguishes her representation of gender relations not only from male-authored prose romances, but also from Marguerite de Navarre's *Heptaméron*, and from the plays of Cary as well as Shakespeare, in which both heterosexual desire and homosocial bonding are foreshortened and in many senses foreclosed by the relative textual focus upon the present moment.

To use Braidotti's terms once again, both Urania and Veralinda in effect serve as "agents of change" for Pamphilia, demonstrating both "the sameness and the otherness of the other woman" through their supportive but also frequently argumentative relations with her, which at once encompass and outlast multiple alterations in their heterosexual ties over the same extended period of time.[71] In neglecting these relations, many Wroth critics have tended accordingly to focus upon Pamphilia's constancy, to Amphilanthus in particular, as the defining characteristic not simply of her role, but of female subjectivity in the romance as a whole. I find, by contrast, that whereas Wroth's lyric sequence inscribes Pamphilia's simultaneous voicing of constancy and desire, the prose romance contextualizes Pamphilia's discourse, exposing—by comparison to "other women" such as Urania and Veralinda— some of the limitations that Pamphilia's initial idealization of heterosexual constancy as the defining quality of her subjectivity entails. In representing the potentially destructive effects of such an idealization, Wroth can be seen to be responding to early modern handbooks for women which advocate chastity and obedience, constancy and silence, and represent (implicitly heterosexual) constancy in particular as necessarily more appropriate for the feminine than the masculine temperament.[72]

At the same time, Wroth's narrative addresses head-on a variety of literary and cultural stereotypes which depict women as the obverse of their prescribed roles. Both polemical pamphlets and male-authored romances and sonnet sequences repeatedly construct women as potentially fickle at best, and duplicitous at worst. Each of these cultural configurations of female sexuality functions to objectify women, whether dwelling upon their "seeming" virtues or their "actual" failings. Wroth's decision to individualize both the strengths and the weaknesses of the otherwise apparently abstract and singular virtue of constancy, within the complex character of Pamphilia rather than merely through the allegorized figure of "Constancy" that appears in the "throne enchantment," has the effect of "changing the subject" from the gendering of virtue to the engendering of female subjectivity.

In identifying constancy in heterosexual love as a governing characteristic of Wroth's representation of female subjectivity, critics of *Urania* also have tended to treat Pamphilia as the embodiment of the ideal of constancy to which she apparently aspires, imperfect only insofar as the cultural stereotype itself leaves something to be desired, rather than ambivalent in her self-fashioning.[73] Yet Wroth provides a far more complex response to her culture's gendering of constancy than the objectification of another female stereotype. In the first place, Pamphilia's willed constancy to Amphilanthus, as discussed in chapter 2, enables her to bolster her subjectivity against the destructive effects of inconstant masculine passion, by allowing her to construct a context for her agency which cannot be diminished by an inconstant male lover. Furthermore, with the aid of female friends such as Urania and Veralinda, Pamphilia learns to expand her conception of constancy to encompass homosocial bonding as well as heterosexual desire.

When Pamphilia and Urania are read not merely in oppositional relation to their putative male lovers, but rather in triangulated relation to each other as well as to a male figure such as Amphilanthus (at once lover and brother), the "difference" of Wroth's construction of female subjectivity can be recognized. In Braidotti's terms, only when women, as speaking subjects, "fasten on to the presence of the other woman, of *the other as woman*," are they enabled to begin to define their identities in relation to "the otherness of the other woman."[74] Wroth stresses the importance of "the other as woman" even in the dynamics of heterosexual courtship, where female homosocial bonding expands women's abilities to find voices within what might otherwise prove to be male-dominated relationships. Far from subordinating heterosexual to female homosocial bonds in a simple reversal of male-authored configurations, then, Wroth brings them into immediate conjunction, representing connections between strong female homosocial bonds and enduring rather than temporary heterosexual ties.

The variety of Wroth's female characters further illuminates the multiple speaking positions accorded women within her narrative. While Urania's emergent subjectivity finds expression in her capacity to identify with the positions of others, for example, Pamphilia's subjectivity initially remains confined to the private discourse of her poems. Unable to speak her passion aloud, Pamphilia experiences the bondage of desire far more severely than Urania, her speaking voice constrained even as she most publicly attempts to proclaim her autonomy. Only once she begins to participate in shared discourse with other women, most particularly through her bonds with Urania and Veralinda, does Pamphilia begin to identify a speaking position for herself that can include both her private and public roles, a constancy that can embrace homosocial bonding as well as heterosexual desire, and a "self which is not one" not because it is split in two, but because it encompasses the multiple "otherness" of female subjectivity.

The conclusion of the "theater enchantment," which brings Urania, Veralinda, and Pamphilia into close conjunction, marks a turning point in Pamphilia's appreciation of bonds between women. From that point on, Pamphilia's discourse with "other" women begins to expand her ability to assert a speaking voice on subjects other than the exclusive virtue of constancy in heterosexual desire. After the initial revelation of Amphilanthus's inconstancy, however, Pamphilia descends into such melancholy that even with Urania "she still put it off, and would not (unto her) confes, but dissembled" (390). Retreating into a self-imposed silence, Pamphilia "with her owne thoughts discoursed," and "could bee in greatest assemblies as private with her owne thoughts, as if in her Cabinet" (390-91). In voluntarily embracing a "private," because self-referential, communion with her own thoughts, Pamphilia responds initially to the inconstancy of masculine desire by adopting the self-effacing (and thus socially acceptable) behavior prescribed for women in heterosexual relations. Using language reminiscent of the sonnets, Pamphilia addresses Night as the only friend to whom she has yet learned to speak frankly: "my waylings fitter were to bide in you, afflictions founded best in you . . . my fortune like your face, my hopes blacker than your saddest Mantle . . . you truely shewed my selfe unto my selfe, you were mine eyes to make mee see my selfe" (396). The limitations of this "bond," however, are apparent in Pamphilia's language, which constructs Night as the same rather than "other" to her suffering self.

Only when Urania challenges Pamphilia's solipsistic isolation with a difference in view does Pamphilia start to find a new voice, and stance, of her own, as she learns to "fasten on to the presence of the other woman, of *the other as woman.*" Refusing to leave Pamphilia in solitary silence, Urania confronts her friend on the assumption that she has been mourning the inconstancy of her still publicly unidentified beloved, "a thing familiar with men," and advises her to "hate that humour by your owne worthy constancy, . . . and let not so uncertaine a qualitie hurt you," concluding: "This I advise as my selfe would be advised if in such extremity, and this I say to you my dearest

Cosin, and would say, though I knew it were my owne brother caused this mischiefe" (398-99). Urania's advice reveals at once her capacity for identification
with her friend even as she advises her from an "other" point of view—"this I
advise as my selfe would be advised"—and her unerring perspicuity about the
nature of the relationship involved—"though I knew it were my owne brother
caused this mischiefe." Although Pamphilia maintains the constancy of her
desire, her revealing choice of superlatives in naming Urania her "onely friend
and dearest Cosin" (399) suggests for the first time that her "other" cousin,
Amphilanthus, no longer so exclusively dominates her affections. Indeed,
Urania's characteristic frankness initiates a probing exchange between the
cousins on the respective merits of constancy and love which includes
Urania's discourse on the "limits" of constancy (400), and which leads not to
any simple resolution of the challenges to be faced, but rather to an opening of
the lines of communication between the women.[75]

    At moments, some of the lively and dramatic interchanges between
Wroth's female protagonists recall the verbal wit of Shakespeare's comic
heroines, but often with a subversive re-gendering of conventional cultural
metaphors. When one of Wroth's female characters, known as the "Merry Marquess," warns another that "husbands are strange things if nott discreetly han-
dled," and proceeds to compare husbands to horses which must be kept on a
tight rein (II: fol. 24v), her sally suggests the independence and humor of a
Beatrice or a Rosalind. At the same time, the comment by the Merry Marquess
ironically reverses the common Renaissance comparison between horses and
wives.[76] When the Merry Marquess warns women to guard against the potential tyranny of husbands lest they "like horses gett the bitt beetweene their
teeth, and run the full race, or course of their owne humour, and the wives
slaverye" (II: fol. 24v), Wroth's character refashions the metaphor from a
woman's perspective. In this instance, Wroth's narrative exhibits affinities with
the sixteenth-century feminist admonitions of Jane Anger, who compares male
lovers to horses and warns women not to trust them, "for although a jade may
be still in a stable when his gall backe is healed, yet hee will showe himselfe in
his kind when he is traveling."[77] Summoning up a misogynist metaphor only to
subvert its terms, Wroth uses the very language of patriarchy to undermine
masculine assumptions of dominance within a context of homosocial bonding,
along precisely the lines that the "gossips' meeting" satirists so evidently feared.

    The sisterly sharing of fortunes and misfortunes in love in Wroth's nar-
rative often takes the form of extended dramatic dialogues not commonly
found in other prose romances, but comparable to the conversations of Beatrice and Hero, Rosalind and Celia, and even of such later Shakespearean
female characters as Desdemona and Emilia, Hermione and Paulina. Nevertheless, Wroth re-forms the "heroine/confidante" pattern governing many of
the close female friendships in Shakespeare's plays, to establish more equality

of role and voice in the homosocial bonds joining Urania, Veralinda, and Pamphilia. The hierarchical separation between heroine and confidante in Shakespeare's plays encodes, and in the process enforces, the hierarchical dynamic governing the relation between man and woman, husband and wife, in which love consists of accepting service on the one hand, and offering it on the other. Even when the women share a comparable social rank, in most scenes one of them serves primarily as voice, the other as interpreter or echo, just as in the Sidnean example of Pamela and Philoclea. Beatrice's voice, for instance, often overrides that of her friend Hero, while when Hero does give voice to her thoughts on Beatrice, it is in her hearing rather than to her face. Urania and Pamphilia speak *with* each other rather than simply to or for each other, not only offering their own thoughts aloud but also responding directly to each other's narratives. And when Wroth's female friends are rulers, as in the cases of Urania, Pamphilia, and Veralinda, their discourse becomes an occasion for sharing, rather than delegating, authority.

On Shakespeare's stage, women's voices often acquire their greatest resonance when addressed to men—Beatrice demanding that Benedick "Kill Claudio," for example, or Rosalind instructing Orlando that men have died, but not for love—or achieve their greatest pathos when silenced by men, as in the cases of Desdemona and Hermione. In Wroth's romance, the most witty or impassioned speeches by women are often addressed to other women. In fashioning these speeches along dramatic lines, Wroth subverts the narrative conventions limiting female discourse in the prose romance, while remaining unconstrained by the cultural expectations restricting the range of dialogue between female characters on the stage. And in emphasizing the enabling effects of a female audience upon women's voices, she draws upon an ideological base for feminine discourse already represented in female-authored texts as various as the mother's advice books and polemical tracts, the letters and diaries of literate women, and the dedicatory poems of Aemilia Lanyer.

Yet just as McBride has pointed out how the dedicatory poems of Lanyer can be viewed as functioning at once to empower and to displace the figures of her female patrons, whose social standing encodes a potential threat to her own authority as author,[78] so the discourse between women in Wroth's narrative yields evidence of competition and conflict as well as cooperation. At such times, heterosexual ties prove dominant over or even destructive of female homosocial bonding, although notably more frequently in the subplots than in the interactions among the major protagonists. In one such example, a lady threatens to betray the secret romance between her female friend and her friend's lover, in order to force the assistance of her friend in reclaiming the affections of her own lover, which have been diverted to her friend's maid (358). Long after repudiating this attempted blackmail attempt, the second lady finds herself abandoned by her original lover, and forced to greet his new mistress "as a friend" because they both share the same object of desire (359-60). This convoluted tale of failed female homosocial bonding is rendered further abstruse in the retelling due to the dearth of proper names which marks many of the subplots, thus distinguishing them from the adventures of the clearly named major protagonists, who more successfully mediate between the competing forces of heterosexual and homosocial ties.

On another occasion, Wroth provides an example of a triangulation of desire involving, as in Sidney's *Lady of May* and Shakespeare's *Sonnets*, a pair of male friends competing for the affections of a single lady. But whereas in those male-authored texts the lady is represented primarily as a silent object of desire rather than a speaking subject, in Wroth's narrative the (male) character who agrees to adjudicate their dilemma calls upon the lady to speak for herself and "likewise tell her opinion" (383), even as the men. Despite this beginning, the tale seems increasingly to objectify the lady, as the two male lovers and the male judge strive to determine her "place" without sacrificing the primacy, in their eyes, of the male homosocial bond. Furthermore, as the male lovers narrate the origins of this dilemma, it becomes apparent that their problematic competition has arisen because the first lover initially wished his friend to "enjoy" his mistress also, so that they "had both what [they] desired, and she was free to both," until the male lovers become more possessive, "desiring to have our loves each onely to himselfe" (384-85), at which point their concern with the lady's "freedom" apparently drops out of the picture.

The lady's refusal to choose between the two men, upon their request, gives rise to their suspicions that "she is still willing to hold both," indicating a potentially threatening capacity for desire even greater than their own (385). Meanwhile, her own account of the affair emphasizes her delight in their "difference" from each other rather than simply their otherness from her, so that she is "contented" with both (385-86). At this point, the lovers begin to vie with each other to yield rather than claim possession of the lady, citing the primacy of their mutual bond. When the adjudicator prescribes a course of blindfolding the lady and letting her sightless "choice" of a recipient for her garland of flowers determine the outcome of the conflict, the men decide instead to "equally leave her" (386). While she is still blindfolded and before she can speak, then, they leave her "like all-changing women to glory in her owne folly, or to cover her selfe with her owne shame" (386), effectively attempting to blame the woman for their own construction of her as a shared object of desire.

It is at this very moment, however, that Wroth reverses the conventionally patriarchal impetus of this tale by depicting the female character's bold reclamation of her voice in abandonment to proclaim her own agency and autonomy after all. Wroth thus concludes the sentence describing the male lovers' departure with the narrator's observation that the lady now "took a changers boldnesse on her" (386). Speaking directly to the male judge, the lady observes: "I am no more troubled with their leaving, then I should have enjoyed in having them," and asserts that "the fault lyes on your sexe." She concludes, confidently: "I liv'd before I loved them, and shall (I trust) live, and love againe without them" (386). Refusing to accept the implicit blame associated with the male characters' rationale for their departure, the lady successfully reasserts her voice as a speaking subject apart from their construction of her as an object of desire, proclaiming agency literally in the face of gendered social subordination. Furthermore, she rejects all three male characters' identification of her as the third point of a triangle of affection whose primary import is homosocial bonding between men, maintaining instead her right to pursue her own desires, so that she can "live, and love againe without them."

Interestingly, in a parallel example of female homosocial bonding interrupted by heterosexual desire, Wroth does not simply reverse the dynamic described above. Thus neither do the two women in this case objectify the man they love, nor does Wroth focus upon the male beloved's singularity, attending instead to the complex nature of the bond between the women. In one of the few examples in Wroth's narrative which seemingly can be linked with Sedgwick's hypothesis of a potential continuum between homosocial bonding and homoerotic desire,[79] these "lover-like" women are described as kissing and embracing until "their owne passions were a little satisfied" (541). Rosilea, who already loves a man, adopts her own experience of heterosexual desire as a scale to measure the intensity of her bond with her "chosen friend," assuring Celina that "my love to you shall be no lesse, but rather more, since the better I know how to love, the better, I shall love you" (543). Within the frame of female homosocial relations for this particular character, erotic involvement with a man apparently fosters, rather than diminishes, the intensity of her bond with another woman.

Celina, however, observes to Rosilea that if she ever "fall[s] into" the "servitude" of love, "it will be to keepe you company, yet dearely should I buy such friendship" (543). Already the contrast between these two different female characters—one who asserts her agency in her "chosen" bond with her friend, while the other is unable to maintain her "difference" from the "other woman," and thus anticipates helplessly "falling into" love's servitude to keep her friend company—indicates the only limited applicability of Sedgwick's continuum to this female-authored text, where female bonding resists distillation into a singular paradigm.

As Wroth's narrative proceeds, Celina discovers Rosilea's male beloved upon the riverbank, nearly drowned, and in sharing Rosilea's concern to revive him, Celina "falls into" the very state that she feared, that of loving her friend's beloved (543-44). As Rosilea embraces her beloved, Celina "embraced both, loving both as their kinds were," while the Venetian prince who loves Celina "held all three, so as the foure made in their crosse embracements a true lovers knot, and so it was on some parts" (544). While the previous homosocial bond between the women was labeled a "twined" union which "could not be unwoven by any workeman but death" (543), the intersection of a competing heterosexual desire produces a "knot." Although a "true lovers knot" has positive connotations of fidelity as well as desire, Wroth characteristically emphasizes the multiplicity of the relation, whereby a continuum "on some parts" may represent a crossroads for others. "Loving both as their kinds were," Celina can neither dismiss nor reconcile her competing affections, and thus finds herself tormented by a continuing tension between heterosexual and homosocial bonds.

In several additional examples of intersections between heterosexual desire and female homosocial bonding which involve more prominent protagonists, however, Wroth represents the potentially empowering effects of female ties in enabling balanced interpretive judgments of problematic heterosexual relations. Indeed, over the course of the narrative a significant number of Wroth's female protagonists experience the regenerative effects of communication among themselves, throughout the course of and by contrast to their fluctuating relationships with their male lovers. Unlike instances of male inconstancy in *Diana* or *Astrée*, such inconstancy in *Urania* is understood, rather than simply scorned or feared, by the major female characters. Through their shared discourse, the women confront not only "sexual difference," but also their collective differences as members of the same sex. Homosocial bonding thus allows some of the women in Wroth's romance to come to terms with their subjectivity through interrelation, freed from the dependence upon a dominant context of masculine subjectivity which characterizes feminine experience in the romances of Montemayor and d'Urfé. Similarly, where the relationships not only of Shakespeare's women but also of Cary's female characters often take shape in reaction to male tyranny, whether of fathers (*As You Like It*), lovers (*Much Ado About Nothing*), or husbands (*Othello, The Winter's Tale, Mariam*), the homosocial bonds between many of Wroth's female protagonists consistently predate, coexist with, and outlast their fluctuating relationships with the men in their lives.

Particularly in the manuscript continuation of *Urania*, conversations between the women serve to interrogate gender-specific assumptions concerning the dynamics of heterosexual bonding. Pamphilia and Veralinda, for example, engage in a heated exchange over the implications of Amphilanthus's inconstancy:

Those days are past, my deere Veralinda, cride Pamphilia, and hee is changed, and proved a man; hee was ever thought soe, sayd Veralinda,

but when hee shall see you againe, bee assured hee will bee, nay hee can
bee noe other then as truly, ore att least as passionately loving you as ever;
what care I for passion, lett mee have truthe, cride she; I, that is best, sayd
the delicate Veralinda, butt you were, and are the discreetest of your sex,
yett you would have impossibilities; you say Amphilanthus is a man, why
did you ever know any man, especially any brave man, continue constant
to the end? . . . all men are faulty, I would nott my self have my Lord
Constant, for feare of a miracle . . . say he hath left you, lett him goe in
his owne pathe, tread nott in itt, an other is more straite, follow that, and
bee the Emperess of the world, comaunding the Empire of your owne
minde. [I: fol. 40-40v]

Veralinda's wry distinction between "passion" and "truth" exposes the limitations of the masculine subject even as her emphasis on the faultiness of all men
encodes her refusal to idealize the object of her own or any other woman's
desire. Practicing difference, Veralinda points Pamphilia to an "other" path, instead, leading away from feminine subjection and passivity in the face of male
inconstancy, toward the potential empowerment of female agency: "bee the
Emperess of the world, comaunding the Empire of your owne minde." While
both Shakespeare's Emilia and Cary's Salome, as discussed earlier, construct
women's roles in relation to men's faults, Wroth's Veralinda asserts the possibility that women may choose a path of their own.

Moreover, while Mariam, Emilia, and Desdemona are ultimately silenced, for all their courage, at the hands of their husbands, Wroth's female
protagonists demonstrate the potential not only to endure, but to prevail. Male
inconstancy thus ironized by Veralinda becomes less of a force to victimize
women than when subject to control or release only through magic, as in the
examples of Montemayor's Don Felix or d'Urfé's Hylas. Instead, specifically
female precedents for Wroth's representation of male inconstancy can be
found in the feminist pronouncements of "Jane Anger" and "Joane Sharp" on
the nature of men.[80] Supported by constancy of love between women, Wroth's
female protagonists exhibit the ability to evaluate their male lovers with ironic
humor, and even ultimately to respond with forgiveness. Instead of allowing
their subjectivity to be threatened by heterosexual relations, the female protagonists prove able in notable instances to "fasten on to the presence of the other
woman, of *the other as woman*," and thus to maintain their equilibrium as subjects without sacrificing otherwise problematic heterosexual ties. Their response deprives male inconstancy of its potentially pervasive force to dominate
or victimize, as the women affirm through their shared discourse their capacity to command different positions as speaking subjects.

In the latter part of the manuscript continuation of *Urania*, Wroth conjoins the mutuality of homosocial friendship and heterosexual desire, and
transforms some of the boundaries distinguishing masculine and feminine be-

havior and discourse. Florizel and Lindavera, the younger generation of lovers, come together more as equals than as wooer and wooed, while Pamphilia and Amphilanthus now prove able to move beyond some of the gender-specific expectations that previously bound them. Josephine Roberts points out that Pamphilia ultimately arrives at a revolutionary model of heterosexual relations between "youke fellows, noe superior, nor commanding power butt in love betweene united harts" (II: fol. 51).[81] As my analysis in this chapter indicates, the origins of this heterosexual model can be located in Pamphilia's widening experience of the mutual rather than hierarchical affection offered by female homosocial bonds, which expands not only her formerly "limited" conception of constancy in purely heterosexual terms, but also her active engagement with other "youke fellows" of both sexes.

In *As You Like It*, Shakespeare's Rosalind maintains gendered expectations of behavior by remarking: "I could find in my heart to disgrace my man's apparel and to cry like a woman; but I must comfort the weaker vessel" (*AYLI*, II.iv.4-6). Amphilanthus, on the other hand, weeps much more copiously than Pamphilia in the second portion of Wroth's narrative, and even faints upon the occasion of one reunion between them, so that it is Pamphilia who must revive him. The "feminine" comparisons which Wroth uses to describe him — hands more delicate than those of a lady, and behavior "as if hee had bin bred in a ladys chamber" (II: fol. 2) — parallel his increased capacity for friendship and mutual bonding. Like Pamphilia, it is in the manuscript continuation that Amphilanthus arrives at a revised conception of his role as "a new man as new borne, new fram'd and noe thing as I was before" (II: fol. 52).[82] Instead of cloaking her women in masculine disguises which provide them artificial entry into a world of patriarchal discourse, as do Spenser and Shakespeare, Wroth represents a male character coming to terms with feminine qualities not as weaknesses but as strengths within himself, and learning to appreciate social bonds not only with male comrades but also with women.[83] No longer approaching Pamphilia solely as a lover, Amphilanthus thus becomes her loving friend as well.

At the same time, Wroth subverts cultural and literary norms to emphasize the increasingly articulate voices of the women in her fictive society. In one late scene, reminiscent of the mutual tale-telling in Marguerite de Navarre's *Heptaméron*, Wroth depicts a circle of friends, including both Pamphilia and Amphilanthus, staying up into the night and sharing tales of their youth, "the flowering time of their first lovings, every one, nott nice, butt truly telling their infinitely suffering passions" (II: fol. 57v). By this point in the narrative, "truth" and "passion" can coexist in both heterosexual and homosocial discourse. Whereas Pamphilia initially suffered love not as "an Actor [who] knowes when to speake," but rather as a "true feeler" who "only can know how to beare" (314), by the end of *Urania* she has learned to "truly tell"

her passions, to speak with her own voice. And unlike Rosalind at the conclusion of *As You Like It,* Pamphilia need not excuse any lack of "fashion" in
speaking as she likes.[84] With the encouragement of female friends such
as Urania and Veralinda, Pamphilia moves beyond the dependency of her
"first loving" to realize her capability, as a woman, to command her mind's
"Empire" and to claim the authority of her own discourse.

It is worth remarking that, although often touted as the most vocal
women in early modern English literature, Shakespeare's female characters
often lose their voices, effectually if not literally, by the endings of the plays.
Desdemona and Hermione can be silenced by their husbands because both
women function primarily not as speakers, but as listeners, as the recipients
and interpreters of masculine discourse. Even Beatrice and Rosalind move
from speeches of their own to the relative suppression of women's discourse
predicated by Shakespeare's dramatic denouements: Beatrice's mouth is literally "stopped" by Benedick's kiss (rather than the other way around), and
Rosalind finally disavows her woman's voice in the epilogue by calling attention to the male actor who speaks it. Wroth's women, however, not only are
not reduced to silence as the romance progresses, but instead are increasingly
empowered to construct their subjectivity through the authority of their own
language. Instead of looking primarily to Amphilanthus, Pamphilia learns to
look to herself, as well as to "other" women, to articulate women's capacity for
constancy within both heterosexual and homosocial relations. And once
Urania matures through her initial search for self-definition, she becomes a
touchstone for other characters seeking to represent—that is, to give voice
to—their identities, through "difference" as well as similarity.

By depicting female homosocial bonds that do not depend upon a "primary" context of heterosexual desire or a "parallel" context of male friendship,
Wroth rewrites the figurations of gender that govern the romances of her predecessors. Once Pamphilia learns from friends like Urania and Veralinda to recognize the regenerative potential of change over stasis, she can begin to accept
the dynamic potential of constancy to inform bonds not only between lovers,
but between women as well. When two female characters near the end of the
published *Urania* declare themselves to be "called the true loving friends, a
rare matter (as men say) to bee found amongst us" (450), that declaration acknowledges the patriarchal bias of early modern English society, while affirming Wroth's own determination to locate female homosocial bonding at the
heart, rather than the margins, of her narrative.

By contrast to many male-authored lyric sequences, plays, and prose romances, then, where examples of female friendship are either nonexistent or
repeatedly subordinated to representations of male homosocial bonding or the
gendered hierarchies of heterosexual desire, each of Wroth's texts works to
render bonds between women not only viable, but also eminently visible.

Most particularly in the complex and capacious frame of her prose romance, Wroth's female characters voice differences in the company of "other" women which can expand our appreciation of the otherwise partial glimpses of female homosocial bonding to be found in such cultural texts as the diary of Wroth's friend, Anne Clifford, and the correspondence of her sisters-in-law, the countesses of Leicester and Carlisle, as well as in female-authored polemical texts and mothers' advice books. While not attempting to disguise or idealize the suffering often attendant upon heterosexual desire for women in early modern England, Wroth dares to represent the simultaneous existence of an alternative network of affection, connection, and communication between women, which offers an empowering source for constructions of female agency and subjectivity in both heterosexual and homosocial relations. Although the basic paradigm of male traffic in women which previous critics have identified in Wroth's texts certainly shapes one facet of her treatment of sexuality, nevertheless I find in Wroth's insistent inscription of female homosocial bonds an equally important, and considerably less conventional, re-vision of her culture's figurations of gendered subjectivity. The community of women in Wroth's works may not eliminate the problematic dynamics of power in either heterosexual or homosocial relations, but it does open possibilities for female agency in the figures of women enabled finally, in concert, to command positions as speaking subjects.

Epilogue

Changing the Subject

Dale Spender's *The Writing or the Sex?* includes a revealing appendix containing comments by male critics who dismiss writings by women (poets, playwrights, novelists, and critics) as insignificant without having read them. One of the most blatant comments, as quoted by Elaine Showalter, comes from a male academic who, after castigating a feminist critic, responds to the question of whether he has in fact read her book by saying: "Of course not, it would take a miracle to make me change my mind."[1] Extreme? Indeed. Exceptional? Not as much as we might sometimes like to think. I myself found that changing the subject of my own research from an early interest in the canonical Sir Philip Sidney to a subsequent focus on the less than canonical Lady Mary Wroth exposed me to some intriguing attitudes which betrayed an underlying measure of gender bias.

One of my early grant applications to support the initial research for the present book, for example, met with the dismissive response that Wroth "is now widely read, taught, and written about," followed by the claim that studies of Wroth are "already an overworked field." Interestingly, at the time of that grant application in 1990, there was not one single book-length study of Wroth's complete works in existence. The first collection of critical essays on Wroth, co-edited by myself and Gary Waller, was still in process. While several essays on Wroth, some by me, had appeared in recent journals and critical anthologies, not one of the five major collections of essays concerned with early modern women that appeared in the second half of the 1980s included an essay on Mary Wroth.[2] It is worthy of note, moreover, that *The Norton Anthology of Literature by Women: The Tradition in English*, edited by Sandra Gilbert and Susan Gubar, did not even mention Wroth, let alone include any excerpts from her works.[3] With only one available (hardcover) edition of her poems at the time, one ($300) limited edition of her play, and no modern edition of her prose romance, it was hard to see how Wroth could be considered so "widely read," let alone "taught, and written about." Apparently for this particular reviewer, the preliminary attention already paid to this uncanonical woman writer could be judged to have overloaded an already "overworked field."

At the moment of writing this epilogue, in 1995, I can testify with pleasure to the extent to which the critical climate for studying women and gender in early modern England has changed notably even in the half-decade since that early grant proposal. Certainly works by Mary Wroth are far more widely read, taught, and written about than when I began my study, and the recent founding of the Society for the Study of Early Modern Women is only one of many signs of a significant blossoming of scholarship and teaching in the field. Nevertheless, Margaret Ezell's articulation of the tension between the recent burgeoning of scholarly attention to early modern women and the continuing influence of theoretical models of women's literary history and studies which assume the ultimate containment or co-option of those women's voices within patriarchal structures provides a useful reminder that canon revision is an ongoing process.[4]

Even as Carol Thomas Neely has called for a "reengendering" of the Renaissance by finding new ways to surround, contextualize, and "overread" men's canonical texts with women's "uncanonical" ones, so Nancy Miller advocates a practice of "overreading" women's writing in order to focus on those moments in which the representation of writing itself might be said to figure the production of the female artist.[5] In order to "overread" men's texts, it is necessary first to read and reread women's hitherto uncanonical ones. And I have learned, as well, that it is important to be wary lest such uncanonical texts are too hastily "overread" themselves, which is to say read primarily in relation to men's texts, and soon deemed "overworked" as a result. Furthermore, I find that bringing the intimate interconnections between what we now term canonical and uncanonical texts, as well as "literary" and "cultural" texts, to bear upon figurations of gender in early modern England allows new questions to be raised regarding the seeming dominance of widely publicized gender ideologies both in the early modern period and in our own.

In discussing the relation between the emergent articulations of female agency and subjectivity in Wroth's texts and the varied figurations of gender in her culture, I have attempted to identify not a single, oppositional dynamic, but rather a range of constantly changing constructions of femininity in early modern England. From lover to mother, sovereign to "subject," author to friend, the women in Wroth's texts speak with voices to some extent already shaped by discourses ranging from handbooks for women to mothers' advice books, from polemical tracts to courtly correspondence, from monarchs' speeches to gossips' conversations, and from Petrarchan sonnet sequences to continental romances. On the other hand, those same voices serve to engage, and sometimes even to transform, the gendered parameters of such discourses. Writing both within and against the strictures of her culture, Wroth represents a striking measure of women's capability for agency and subjectivity.

By defining the roles of individual women in her lyric sequence, play, and prose romance not solely, or even necessarily, in relation to husbands and lovers, but also in relation to a larger community of parents and children, siblings and cousins, neighbors and friends, Wroth refashions the emphasis of her culture's governing constructions of femininity. The female subjects in her works emerge not simply as mimetic mirror images or parodic shadows of masculine subjects, then, but instead as multiple agents of change: this sex/self/subject which is not one. By illuminating female bonding and representing mutuality rather than hierarchy as a viable basis for communication in friendship and love, Wroth feminizes the discourses of "romance" across generic boundaries. She translates the "subculture" of gossips' networks and male-authored representations of female homosocial bonds into a governing force in her texts, re-forming the focus on patriarchal tensions to be found in the texts of her male literary predecessors in particular with her own emphasis on matrilineal bonds and shared women's speech.

At the same time, extending the boundaries of the treatments of sexual difference by such female predecessors as Aemilia Lanyer and Elizabeth Cary, Wroth begins to change "the subject" by representing the practice of differences among women, which collectively enable them to function both as speaking subjects and as agents of change for one another. The multiplicity and variety of women's voices in Wroth's works resist an essentialist interpretation of the nature of femininity in early modern England, inviting rather our renewed awareness of the constructed nature of every voice. Mary Wroth's narrative of "the woman's part" conveys the potential for women—as writers and mothers, friends and lovers—to find not one but many voices of their own. To paraphrase Cixous's words, it is not the sum but the differences that matter.[6] And it is the differences, finally, that change the subject, and open fields not just to work over (and "overwork"), but to work anew.

Notes

1. Figurations of Gender

1. For superb examples of the recent critical attention to gender and culture in early modern England, particularly with reference to the drama, see Karen Newman, *Fashioning Femininity and English Renaissance Drama* (Chicago: Univ. of Chicago Press, 1991); Valerie Wayne, ed., *The Matter of Difference: Materialist Feminist Criticism of Shakespeare* (Ithaca: Cornell Univ. Press, 1991); and Theodora A. Jankowski, *Women and Power in the Early Modern Drama* (Urbana: Univ. of Illinois Press, 1992). Other excellent studies similarly concerned with constructions of gender in relation to male Renaissance dramatists, particularly Shakespeare, include Carol Thomas Neely, "'Documents in Madness': Reading Madness and Gender in Shakespeare's Tragedies and Early Modern Culture," *Shakespeare Quarterly* 42 (Fall 1991): 315-38, and "Constructing Sexuality in the Renaissance: Stratford, London, Windsor, Vienna," in *Feminism and Psychoanalysis*, ed. Richard Feldstein and Judith Roof (Ithaca: Cornell Univ. Press, 1989), 209-29; Mary Beth Rose, "Where Are the Mothers in Shakespeare? Options for Gender Representation in the English Renaissance," *Shakespeare Quarterly* 42 (Fall 1991): 291-314, and *The Expense of Spirit: Love and Sexuality in English Renaissance Drama* (Ithaca: Cornell Univ. Press, 1988); Jean E. Howard, "Renaissance Antitheatricality and the Politics of Gender and Rank in *Much Ado About Nothing*," in *Shakespeare Reproduced: The Text in History and Ideology*, ed. Howard and Marion F. O'Connor (New York: Methuen, 1987), 163-87; and Catherine Belsey's influential study, *The Subject of Tragedy: Identity and Difference in Renaissance Drama* (New York: Methuen, 1985). Recent studies concerned with nondramatic male-authored representations of women and gender in the Renaissance include Pamela Benson, *The Invention of the Renaissance Woman* (University Park, Penn.: Pennsylvania State Univ. Press, 1992) and Elizabeth D. Harvey, *Ventriloquized Voices: Feminist Theory and English Renaissance Texts* (London: Routledge, 1992). One of the most influential essay collections on the topic remains that edited by Margaret W. Ferguson, Maureen Quilligan, and Nancy J. Vickers, entitled *Rewriting the Renaissance: The Discourses of Sexual Difference in Early Modern Europe* (Chicago: Univ. of Chicago Press, 1986).

2. Modern published editions include *The Poems of Lady Mary Wroth*, ed. Josephine A. Roberts (Baton Rouge: Louisiana State Univ. Press, 1983); *Lady Mary Wroth's "Love's Victory": The Penshurst Manuscript*, ed. Michael G. Brennan (London: The Roxburghe Club, 1988); and Roberts's recent edition of the first part of *Urania* (Binghamton, N.Y.: Renaissance English Text Society, 1995), which unfortunately appeared too late for me to use. Only twenty-eight copies of the 1621 edition of *The Countesse of Mountgomeries Urania* and only one copy of the manuscript continuation of the romance (Case Msfy 1565.W95, Newberry Library) survive today.

Subsequent citations of Wroth's poems and play will refer to the modern published editions, using Roberts's numbering scheme for the poems, and act and line numbers for the play. Quotations from Wroth's *Urania* will refer by page number to the 1621 edition. The unpublished second part of *Urania* will be cited by book and folio number from the Newberry manuscript. Whenever possible, I have reproduced the orthography of the original manuscript, with the exceptions that *u* is silently normalized to *v*, and *i* to *j*, and abbreviations (such as "La:" for "Lady") are expanded in full.

3. Wayne, "Historical Differences: Misogyny and *Othello*," in *Matter of Difference*, ed. Wayne, 174.

4. The phrase "fashion femininity" is borrowed from the title of Newman's study, cited above in note 1. While Newman focuses upon male-authored texts, her emphasis on analyzing gender in terms of its local and specific formations, and on the need for "a different kind of textual intercourse, a promiscuous conversation of many texts, early modern elite and non-elite, historical records and ideological discourses, contemporary theory and popular culture," has helped shape the parameters of my own approach (*Fashioning Femininity*, xix, 146).

5. For a thoughtful analysis of the implications of "selectivity" for a feminist literary critic concerned with the writing of women's literary history, see Margaret J.M. Ezell, *Writing Women's Literary History* (Baltimore: Johns Hopkins Univ. Press, 1993), 2.

6. See, for example, Katherine Usher Henderson and Barbara F. McManus, *Half Humankind: Contexts and Texts of the Controversy about Women in England, 1540-1640* (Urbana: Univ. of Illinois Press, 1985), 48.

7. Belsey, *Subject of Tragedy*, 221. Belsey herself suggests, in conclusion, that "women disrupt the discourses designed to contain them," and that "the subject, however defined, addressed, enticed, enlisted, does not finally stay in place" (223-24).

8. See Irigaray, "This Sex Which Is Not One," in *This Sex Which Is Not One*, trans. Catherine Porter (Ithaca: Cornell Univ. Press, 1985), 26, 28-29; "Questions," in *This Sex*, 159; and "The Power of Discourse and the Subordination of the Feminine," in *This Sex*, 84-85.

9. David Simpson, *Subject to History: Ideology, Class, Gender* (Ithaca: Cornell Univ. Press, 1991), 3-4, 32.

10. Carol Thomas Neely, "Constructing Sexuality in the Renaissance," in *Feminism and Psychoanalysis*, ed. Feldstein and Roof, 211-12, 229.

11. Barbara K. Lewalski, *Writing Women in Jacobean England* (Cambridge: Harvard Univ. Press, 1992), 10-11.

12. Heather Dubrow, *Echoes of Desire: English Petrarchism and Its Counterdiscourses* (Ithaca: Cornell Univ. Press, 1995), 274.

13. See Lawrence Stone, *The Family, Sex, and Marriage in England, 1500-1800* (New York: Harper & Row, 1977) and David Cressy, "Foucault, Stone, Shakespeare and Social History," *English Literary Renaissance*, 21 (Spring 1991): 128-31.

14. Keith Wrightson, *English Society, 1580-1680* (London: Hutchinson, 1982); Linda A. Pollock, *Forgotten Children: Parent-Child Relations from 1500-1900* (Cambridge: Cambridge Univ. Press, 1983); Ralph A. Houlbrooke, *The English Family, 1450-1700* (London: Longman, 1984); Alan Macfarlane, *Marriage and Love in England: Modes of Reproduction, 1300-1840* (Oxford: Basil Blackwell, 1986); and J.A. Sharpe, *Early Modern England: A Social History, 1550-1760* (London: Edward Arnold, 1987). Also of note are anthologies of Renaissance writings on the subject of the family, including Linda Pollock, *A Lasting Relationship: Parents and Children over Three Centuries* (London: Fourth Estate, 1987); Ralph Houlbrooke, ed., *English Family Life,*

1576-1716: An Anthology from Diaries (Oxford: Basil Blackwell, 1988); and Joan Larsen Klein, ed., *Daughters, Wives and Widows: Writings by Men about Women and Marriage in England, 1500-1640* (Urbana: Univ. of Illinois Press, 1992). In their anthologies as well as their historical studies, both Pollock and Houlbrooke are concerned to refute not only Stone but also Philippe Aries, whose *L'Enfant et la Vie Familiale sous l'Ancien régime* (Paris: Librairie Plon, 1960) [reprinted as *Centuries of Childhood*, trans. R. Baldick (London: Jonathan Cape, 1962)] influenced much subsequent evaluation of parent-child relations within the family. For more politically oriented studies, see David Underdown, *Revel, Riot, and Rebellion: Popular Politics and Culture in England, 1603-1660* (Oxford: Clarendon Press, 1985) and J.P. Sommerville, *Politics and Ideology in England, 1603-1640* (New York: Longman, 1986), as well as Anthony Fletcher and John Stevenson, eds., *Order and Disorder in Early Modern England* (Cambridge: Cambridge Univ. Press, 1985) and Linda Levy Peck, ed., *The Mental World of the Jacobean Court* (Cambridge: Cambridge Univ. Press, 1991).

15. See Susan Dwyer Amussen, *An Ordered Society: Gender and Class in Early Modern England* (Oxford: Basil Blackwell, 1988) and Margaret L. King, *Women of the Renaissance* (Chicago: Univ. of Chicago Press, 1991). Collections of essays on women's history by editors from Berenice Carroll and Renate Bridenthal and Claudia Koonz (containing the much-quoted essay by Joan Kelly-Gadol entitled "Did Women Have a Renaissance?") to Mary Prior, Barbara Hanawalt, and most recently Valerie Fildes, have covered an immense amount of ground in discussing topics ranging from women in the labor force to women as mothers. See Carroll, ed., *Liberating Women's History* (Urbana: Univ. of Illinois Press, 1976); Bridenthal and Koonz, eds., *Becoming Visible: Women in European History* (Boston: Houghton Mifflin, 1977); Prior, ed., *Women in English Society, 1500-1800* (London: Methuen, 1985); Hanawalt, ed., *Women and Work in Preindustrial Europe* (Bloomington: Indiana Univ. Press, 1986); and Fildes, ed., *Women as Mothers in Pre-Industrial England* (New York: Routledge, 1990).

16. Specialized studies by single authors such as Hilda Smith, Retha Warnicke, Linda Woodbridge, and Katherine Henderson and Barbara McManus have provided a bridge between historical and literary topics (see Smith, *Reason's Disciples: Seventeenth-Century English Feminists* [Urbana: Univ. of Illinois Press, 1982]; Warnicke, *Women of the English Renaissance and Reformation* [Westport, Conn.: Greenwood Press, 1983]; Woodbridge, *Women and the English Renaissance: Literature and the Nature of Womankind, 1540-1620* [Urbana: Univ. of Illinois Press, 1984]; Henderson and McManus, *Half Humankind*. On the heels of many of the literary-historical studies followed a quite remarkable series of anthologies of literary criticism in the second half of the 1980s, including those of Margaret Hannay, Mary Beth Rose, Carole Levin and Jeanie Watson, Sheila Fisher and Janet Halley, Anne Haselkorn and Betty Travitsky [see Hannay, ed., *Silent But for the Word: Tudor Women as Patrons, Translators, and Writers of Religious Works* (Kent, Ohio: Kent State Univ. Press, 1985); Rose, ed., *Women in the Middle Ages and the Renaissance: Literary and Historical Perspectives* (Syracuse: Syracuse Univ. Press, 1986); Levin and Watson, eds., *Ambiguous Realities: Women in the Middle Ages and the Renaissance* (Detroit: Wayne State Univ. Press, 1987); Fisher and Halley, eds., *Seeking the Woman in Late Medieval and Renaissance Writings* (Knoxville: Univ. of Tennessee Press, 1989); Haselkorn and Travitsky, eds., *The Renaissance Englishwoman in Print: Counterbalancing the Canon* (Amherst: Univ. of Massachussetts Press, 1990)].

17. See Elaine Beilin, *Redeeming Eve: Women Writers of the English Renaissance* (Princeton: Princeton Univ. Press, 1987); Elaine Hobby, *Virtue of Necessity: English*

Women's Writing, 1646-1688 (London: Virago Press, 1988); Ann Rosalind Jones, *The Currency of Eros: Women's Love Lyric in Europe, 1540-1620* (Bloomington: Indiana Univ. Press, 1990); Marilyn Williamson, *Raising Their Voices: British Women Writers, 1650-1750* (Detroit: Wayne State Univ. Press, 1990); Tina Krontiris, *Oppositional Voices: Women as Writers and Translators of Literature in the English Renaissance* (London: Routledge, 1992); and Lewalski, *Writing Women in Jacobean England.*

18. Ezell, *Writing Women's Literary History,* 3-4.

19. Having assumed the necessary usefulness of such an approach myself in my earlier work on Wroth, from my doctoral dissertation on Sidney's *Arcadia* and Wroth's *Urania,* through an early article analyzing Wroth's poetry in relation to that of her father and uncle, to a subsequent article on Wroth and Shakespeare, I was not surprised when my successful proposal for an MLA special session entitled "Sexual/Textual Poetics: Mary Wroth and the Sidney Family Men" followed on the heels of my unsuccessful proposal, the previous year, which focused on Wroth alone (see Naomi J. Miller, "Strange Labyrinth: Pattern as Process in Sidney's *Arcadia* and Wroth's *Urania*" [Ph.D. diss., Harvard Univ., 1987]; "Rewriting Lyric Fictions: The Role of the Lady in Lady Mary Wroth's *Pamphilia to Amphilanthus*," in *Renaissance Englishwomen in Print,* ed. Haselkorn and Travitsky, 295-310; "Engendering Discourse: Women's Voices in Wroth's *Urania* and Shakespeare's Plays," in *Reading Mary Wroth,* ed. Miller and Waller, 154-72; "Sexual/Textual Poetics: Mary Wroth and the Sidney Family Men," MLA special session, December 1990). Another of my articles, "'Not much to be marked': Narrative of the Woman's Part in Lady Mary Wroth's *Urania,*" *Studies in English Literature, 1500-1900* 29 (1989): 121-37, addresses a wider range of texts, but still focuses primarily on Wroth's textual relation to her male literary predecessors.

20. For a meticulously researched summary of the details of Wroth's biography, see Josephine Roberts's introduction to *The Poems of Lady Mary Wroth,* especially pp. 6-27. For a longer account, see Gary Waller, *The Sidney Family Romance: Mary Wroth, William Herbert and the Early Modern Construction of Gender* (Detroit: Wayne State Univ. Press, 1993).

21. See Brennan, ed., introduction to *Wroth's "Love's Victory",* 8-9; Margaret Hannay, *Philip's Phoenix: Mary Sidney, Countess of Pembroke* (Oxford: Oxford Univ. Press, 1990); Mary Ellen Lamb, *Gender and Authorship in the Sidney Circle* (Madison: Univ. of Wisconsin Press, 1990), 21; Maureen Quilligan, "The Constant Subject: Instability and Female Authority in Wroth's *Urania* Poems," in *Soliciting Interpretation: Literary Theory and Seventeenth-Century Poetry,* ed. Elizabeth D. Harvey and Katherine Eisaman Maus (Chicago: Univ. of Chicago Press, 1990), 307-8; Barbara K. Lewalski, "Writing Women and Reading the Renaissance," *Renaissance Quarterly* 44 (Winter 1991): 809, and her chapter on Wroth in *Writing Women in Jacobean England;* and Waller, *Sidney Family Romance.* For a range of critical approaches to Wroth, see *Reading Mary Wroth: Representing Alternatives in Early Modern England,* ed. Naomi J. Miller and Gary Waller (Knoxville: Univ. of Tennessee Press, 1991).

22. Gayatri Chakravorty Spivak, "The New Historicism: Political Commitment and the Postmodern Critic," in *The New Historicism,* ed. H. Aram Veeser (New York: Routledge, 1989), 281.

23. Teresa de Lauretis, *Technologies of Gender: Essays on Theory, Film, and Fiction* (Bloomington: Indiana Univ. Press, 1987), 26.

24. Ezell, *Writing Women's Literary History,* 33, 38, 65.

25. Roberts, *Poems*, 30-31, has argued convincingly for the likelihood that Wroth did much of her writing when her involvement in court activities had diminished. See Stephen Mullaney's argument, in the context of a discussion of the Elizabethan stage, for the importance of exploring the ways in which apparently marginalized works can not only "reflect" their marginality but also "put it to use," deriving from their removed, exterior vantage point a critical perspective as well as a certain license of expression concerning the cultural conditions that made their existence possible (*The Place of the Stage* [Chicago: Univ. of Chicago Press, 1988], 9, 30-31, 131).

26. For more extensive analysis of Wroth's exchange with Denny, see chapter 5, "Engendering Discourse: In a Different Voice." For further discussion of the historical context, see John J. O'Connor, "James Hay and *The Countess of Montgomeries Urania*," *Notes & Queries*, n.s. 2 (1955): 150-52; Josephine A. Roberts, "An Unpublished Literary Quarrel Concerning the Suppression of Mary Wroth's *Urania* (1621)," *Notes & Queries*, n.s. 24 (1977): 532-55; Paul Salzman, "Contemporary References in Mary Wroth's *Urania*," *Review of English Studies* 29 (1978): 178-81; and Roberts, *Poems*, 31-36.

27. For reproductions of Denny's verses, Wroth's rebuttal, and the accompanying correspondence, see Roberts, *Poems*, 32-35, 233-45.

28. Peck, *Jacobean Court*, 3-4; see especially the essays in that collection by Malcolm Smuts ("Cultural Diversity and Cultural Change at the Court of James I," 99-112) and Leeds Barroll ("The Court of the First Stuart Queen," 191-208).

29. J.J. Jusserand, *The English Novel in the Time of Shakespeare* (1908; reprint, New York: AMS Press, 1965); Ernest A. Baker, *The History of the English Novel*, Vol. II (London: H.F. & G. Witherby, 1929); Frederic Rowton, ed., *The Female Poets of Great Britain* (1848; reprint, Phildelphia: Carey & Hart, 1849); Bridget MacCarthy, *Women Writers: Their Contribution to the English Novel, 1621-1744*, 2 vols. (Cork: Cork University Press, 1944). For an early treatment of Wroth in primarily historical terms, see Charlotte Kohler, "The Elizabethan Woman of Letters: The Extent of Her Literary Activities," (Ph.D diss., Univ. of Virginia, 1936).

30. Individual articles include: Carolyn Ruth Swift, "Feminine Identity in Lady Mary Wroth's Romance *Urania*," *English Literary Renaissance* 14 (1984): 328-46; Miller, "'Not much to be marked', 121-37; Maureen Quilligan, "Lady Mary Wroth: Female Authority and the Family Romance," in *Unfolded Tales: Essays on Renaissance Romance*, ed. George M. Logan and Gordon Teskey (Ithaca: Cornell Univ. Press, 1989), 257-80; Swift, "Feminine Self-Definition in Lady Mary Wroth's *Love's Victorie*," *English Literary Renaissance* 19 (1989): 171-88; Margaret McLaren, "An Unknown Continent: Lady Mary Wroth's Forgotten Pastoral Drama, 'Loves Victorie,'" in Haselkorn and Travitsky, eds., *Renaissance Englishwoman in Print*, 276-94; Miller, "Rewriting Lyric Fictions: The Role of the Lady in Lady Mary Wroth's *Pamphilia to Amphilanthus*," in *Renaissance Englishwoman in Print*, 295-310; Josephine Roberts, "Radigund Revisited: Perspectives on Women Rulers in Lady Mary Wroth's *Urania*," in *Renaissance Englishwoman in Print*, 187-207; Quilligan, "The Constant Subject: Instability and Female Authority in Wroth's *Urania* Poems," in Harvey and Maus, eds., *Soliciting Interpretation*, 307-35; Barbara Lewalski, "Revising Genres and Claiming the Woman's Part: Mary Wroth's *Oeuvre*," in *Writing Women in Jacobean England*. See also the full-length collection of essays on Wroth, *Reading Mary Wroth*, ed. Miller and Waller; the two book-length studies that address Wroth in relation to her Sidney and Herbert/Pembroke family connections: Lamb, *Sidney Circle*, and Waller, *Sidney Family Romance*; and Josephine Roberts's modern edition of *Urania*. For more

extensive discussion of earlier Wroth scholarship, see introduction and annotated bibliography in *Reading Mary Wroth*, 6-8, 229-34.

31. Jankowski, *Women and Power*, 12; Ezell, *Writing Women's Literary History*, 43, 55.

32. Swift, "Feminine Identity," 329.

33. Waller, "Struggling into Discourse: The Emergence of Renaissance Women's Writing," in *Silent But for the Word*, ed. Hannay, 239, 247.

34. Jane Marcus, "Still Practice, A/Wrested Alphabet: Toward a Feminist Aesthetic," in *Feminist Issues in Literary Scholarship*, ed. Shari Benstock (Bloomington: Indiana Univ. Press, 1987), 81-82.

35. Patricia Yaeger, *Honey-Mad Women: Emancipatory Strategies in Women's Writing* (New York: Columbia Univ. Press, 1988), 29-30.

36. Karen Newman, "Directing Traffic: Subjects, Objects, and the Politics of Exchange," *differences* 2.2 (Summer 1990): 47.

37. Having determined upon the rubric of "changing the subject" for my study of Wroth and early modern figurations of gender before reading Nancy K. Miller's illuminating collection of feminist essays in comparative literature, *Subject to Change: Reading Feminist Writing* (New York: Columbia Univ. Press, 1988), I decided not to change my title after all (despite the even further coincidental similarity between our names), because our "subjects" are so different. Nevertheless, having now read Miller, I find her explanation of the rationale behind her own original title of "Changing the Subject" both deeply persuasive and enduringly influential (18), and am indebted in more instances than I can detail to the incisive lucidity of her feminist approach to the construction of gendered subjectivity. On this subject, see also B. Radhakrishnan, "The Changing Subject and the Politics of Theory," *differences* 2.2 (Summer 1990): 126-52.

38. I have borrowed Catherine Stimpson's term, "multilogue," from her preface to Newman's *Fashioning Femininity*, xiv, with the aim of further extending the implications of Ezell's timely analysis of the "dialogue" between women's writings and more canonical texts (*Writing Women's Literary History*, 65).

39. The approaches of Wayne, Stallybrass, Howard, and Belsey are represented in Wayne's collection, entitled *The Matter of Difference: Materialist Feminist Criticism of Shakespeare* (see note 1). While the interests of Carol Thomas Neely, Karen Newman, and Mary Beth Rose (also cited in note 1) tend to focus upon male Renaissance dramatists, Margaret Ferguson and Ann Rosalind Jones have turned their attention to early modern women writers as well (see Ferguson, "A Room Not Their Own: Renaissance Women as Readers and Writers," in *The Comparative Perspective on Literature*, ed. Clayton Koelb and Susan Noakes [Ithaca: Cornell Univ. Press, 1988], 93-116, and her edition, with Barry Weller, of Elizabeth Cary's *The Tragedy of Mariam*, in conjunction with *The Lady Falkland: Her Life* [Berkeley: Univ. of California Press, 1994]; Jones, "Nets and Bridles: Early Modern Conduct Books and Sixteenth-Century Women's Lyrics," in *The Ideology of Conduct: Essays on Literature and the History of Sexuality*, ed. Nancy Armstrong and Leonard Tennenhouse (New York: Methuen, 1987), 39-72, and *Currency of Eros*.

40. Carol Thomas Neely, "Constructing the Subject: Feminist Practice and the New Renaissance Discourses," *English Literary Renaissance* 18 (Winter 1988): 7. It is instructive to recognize, along the lines of Neely's critique, the extent to which the bias toward "the dominant culture" and the male-authored canon still prevails even among many otherwise critically astute studies of "the Renaissance." Two of many examples are Stephen Greenblatt's collection, *Representing the English Renaissance* (Berkeley:

Univ. of California Press, 1988), which reinscribes "the" Renaissance in wholly masculine terms through its failure to consider any female-authored texts, and Jonathan
Dollimore's influential study, *Radical Tragedy: Religion, Ideology and Power in the
Drama of Shakespeare and His Contemporaries* (Chicago: Univ. of Chicago Press,
1984), the subtitle of which indirectly bespeaks his allegiance to canonical male-
authored texts.

41. Margaret Homans, *Bearing the Word: Language and Female Experience in
Nineteenth-Century Women's Writing* (Chicago: Univ. of Chicago Press, 1986), 28.

42. See Nancy Chodorow, *The Reproduction of Mothering: Psychoanalysis and the
Sociology of Gender* (Berkeley: Univ. of California Press, 1978), 169, 176, 207; also
Chodorow, *Feminism and Psychoanalytic Theory* (New Haven: Yale Univ. Press, 1989),
3-7, 14-18. For a related perspective, see Carol Gilligan, *In a Different Voice: Psychological Theory and Women's Development* (Cambridge: Harvard Univ. Press, 1982).
See note 8 for Irigaray citations. For a collection of representative essays by Kristeva,
see *The Kristeva Reader*, ed. Toril Moi (New York: Columbia Univ. Press, 1986).
Elizabeth Grosz, *Sexual Subversions: Three French Feminists* (Sydney: Allen & Unwin,
1989), provides a useful analysis of Kristeva's relation to feminism (especially pp. 63-
68), as well as an extended discussion of the differences between Kristeva and Irigaray
(104-9). *New French Feminisms*, ed. Elaine Marks and Isabelle de Courtivron (New
York: Schocken Books, 1981), includes several significant essays by Cixous.

43. Ezell, *Writing Women's Literary History*, 7-8, 17; Eve Kosofsky Sedgwick,
Between Men: English Literature and Male Homosocial Desire (New York: Columbia
Univ. Press, 1985), 11-12.

44. See Jankowski, *Women and Power*, 5-6, 9, 12, 16; Ezell, *Writing Women's
Literary History*, 8-10, 12-13. Dubrow, *Echoes of Desire*, 280, 283, usefully warns
against the "intemperance and intolerance" which often characterize the academy's
common constructions of binary distinctions between "our own work and that of opposing camps."

45. Maggie Berg, "Luce Irigaray's 'Contradictions': Poststructuralism and Feminism," *Signs* 17 (Autumn 1991): 51.

46. Diana Fuss, "'Essentially Speaking': Luce Irigaray's Language of Essence," in
Revaluing French Feminism: Critical Essays on Difference, Agency, and Culture, ed.
Nancy Fraser and Sandra Lee Bartky (Bloomington: Indiana Univ. Press, 1992), 94,
109.

47. Not simply nonfeminists, but even materialist feminists, attempt to distance
themselves from these other, more psychoanalytic feminists by asserting that materialist feminism "offers a potentially radical alternative . . . to the idealised or essentialised
effects of some feminist criticism" (Wayne, intro. to *Matter of Difference*, 11).

48. Marilyn Williamson deconstructs the artificial extremity of the choice
between the essentialist and the genderless subject in *Raising Their Voices: British
Women Writers, 1650-1750* (Detroit: Wayne State Univ. Press, 1990), 10, while Rosi
Braidotti, "The Politics of Ontological Difference," in *Between Feminism and
Psychoanalysis*, ed. Teresa Brennan (London: Routledge, 1989), 92-93, elucidates the
need for feminism to refuse the separation of polarized terms such as sex and gender,
and elaborates on the metaphysical question of essence. See also *differences: A Journal
of Feminist Cultural Studies* 1 (Summer 1989), which includes articles on the topic of
essentialism by Teresa de Lauretis, Naomi Schor, Luce Irigaray, Diana Fuss, Robert
Scholes, Leslie Wahl Rabine, and Gayatri Spivak (interview with Ellen Rooney).

49. De Lauretis, "The Essence of the Triangle or, Taking the Risk of Essentialism
Seriously: Feminist Theory in Italy, the U.S., and Britain," *differences* 1 (Summer

1989): 3. In the same volume, see also Naomi Schor's critique of "the excesses perpetrated in the name of anti-essentialism," in "This Essentialism Which Is Not One: Coming to Grips with Irigaray," 38-58. See also de Lauretis's discussion of "difference" in "The Technology of Gender," in *Feminist Studies/Critical Studies*, ed. de Lauretis (Bloomington: Indiana Univ. Press, 1986), 1-14.

50. See Judith Newton and Deborah Rosenfelt, "Introduction: Toward a Materialist-Feminist Criticism," in their *Feminist Criticism and Social Change: Sex, Class and Race in Literature and Culture* (New York: Methuen, 1985), xv-xxxix, esp. xvi-xviii; cited in Belsey, "Afterword," *Matter of Difference*, 257.

51. Fraser, intro. to *Revaluing French Feminism*, 4, 16-17.

52. Brennan, *Between Feminism and Psychoanalysis*, 91.

2. Dark Lady: *This Self Which Is Not One*

1. Irigaray, "This Sex Which Is Not One," in *This Sex*, 26, 28-29.

2. In line with the emphasis of many new historicist studies, Jankowski observes that it is "virtually impossible to think of women except in terms of how they relate to the marriage bond or to their use by men: as virgins (unmarried women); wives; or widows" (*Women and Power*, 24).

3. Irigaray, "The Power of Discourse and the Subordination of the Feminine," in *This Sex*, 84-85.

4. Ezell, *Writing Women's Literary History*, 16.

5. Kristeva, "Women's Time," in *The Kristeva Reader*, ed. Moi, 209-10.

6. Marcus, "A/Wrested Alphabet," 81-82.

7. Sedgwick, "Gender Asymmetry and Erotic Triangles," in *Between Men*, 21, 27.

8. Valerie Traub, "Prince Hal's Falstaff: Positioning Psychoanalysis and the Female Reproductive Body," *Shakespeare Quarterly*, 40 (Winter 1989): 459. See also Elizabeth Meese, *Crossing the Double-Cross: The Practice of Feminist Criticism* (Chapel Hill: Univ. of North Carolina Press, 1986), 75, on how "woman, defined by negation, opposition, limitation, and lack, is appropriated in the service of the male prerogative to define itself."

9. Marjorie Garber, "Spare Parts: The Surgical Construction of Gender," *differences* 1 (Fall 1989): 137.

10. Braidotti, "Ontological Difference," 98.

11. Nancy Fraser, "The Uses and Abuses of French Discourse Theories for Feminist Politics," in *Revaluing French Feminism*, ed. Fraser and Bartky, 191.

12. See Wrightson, *English Society*, 71, 73-74.

13. Ibid., 84.

14. Houlbrooke, *English Family*, 51, and Macfarlane, *Marriage and Love*, 246-47.

15. See Wrightson, *English Society*, 86, on the potential severity of the social response to women who became not simply pregnant brides, but mothers of bastards.

16. Rose, *Expense of Spirit*, 3-5. For additional discussion of ballads, pamphlets, letters, domestic handbooks, and sermons as well as plays, see Linda T. Fitz, "'What Says the Married Woman?': Marriage Theory and Feminism in the English Renaissance," *Mosaic* 13 (Winter 1980): 1-22.

17. See Henderson and McManus, *Half-Humankind*, 74-75, and Nancy Armstrong and Leonard Tennenhouse, "The Literature of Conduct, the Conduct of Literature, and the Politics of Desire," in *Ideology of Conduct*, ed. Armstrong and Tennenhouse, 1-24.

18. See Houlbrooke, *English Family Life*, 13, on the tensions and frustrations recorded in women's diaries over the conflict between their duty of spousal obedience and their own wishes, despite the "ideal" of married friendship articulated by Macfarlane, *Marriage and Love*, 321-22. Constance Jordan, *Renaissance Feminism: Literary Texts and Political Models* (Ithaca: Cornell Univ. Press, 1990), 286-87, discusses the relation of the treatises to the hierarchy of sex and gender in the early seventeenth century. See also Ann Rosalind Jones's analysis of class images in Gervase Markham's *The English Huswife* (1615), in "Nets and Bridles," 63.

19. Heather Dubrow, *A Happier Eden: The Politics of Marriage in the Stuart Epithalamium* (Ithaca: Cornell Univ. Press, 1990), 4, 7, 12-16.

20. Amussen, *An Ordered Society*, 104; see also Amussen, "Gender, Family and the Social Order, 1560-1725," in *Order and Disorder in Early Modern England*, ed. Fletcher and Stevenson, 207.

21. The William Herbert/Mary Wroth affair is only one of many examples; for more extensive discussion of their relationship, see Waller, *Sidney Family Romance*. See also Lawrence Stone, *The Family, Sex, and Marriage in England, 1500-1800* (New York: Harper & Row, 1977), 527.

22. See discussion of widows especially in Houlbrooke, *The English Family*, 209; Macfarlane, *Marriage and Love*, 237; and Underdown, *Revel, Riot and Rebellion*, 11. Jankowski, *Women and Power*, 36, points out that since widows were often executors of their husbands' estates and trustees of their children's inheritance, they had a legal identity and legal rights where married women had neither.

23. Jane Anger, *Her Protection for Women* (1589), in *Half-Humankind*, ed. Henderson and McManus, 185, 178. Henderson and McManus present several arguments to support their contention that "Jane Anger" and other pseudonyms were used by actual woman authors (14, 20-24). While I cite excerpts from the ongoing pamphlet controversy about women from the edition of Henderson and McManus, the complete texts of Anger, Rachel Speght, Esther Sowernam, and Constantia Munda can be found in Simon Shepherd, ed., *The Women's Sharp Revenge: Five Women's Pamphlets from the Renaissance* (London: Fourth Estate, 1985).

24. Joseph Swetnam, *The Arraignment of Lewd, idle, froward, and unconstant women* (1615), and Esther Sowernam, *Esther hath hanged Haman* (1617), in *Half-Humankind*, 204, 200, 243.

25. Swetnam, *Arraignment*, 190.

26. Ibid., 194.

27. *Hic Mulier; or, The Man-Woman* (1620), in *Half-Humankind*, 275-76.

28. Linda Woodbridge, *Women and the English Renaissance*, 141-45, discusses the significance of the hermaphrodite as "the great symbol of the age."

29. For more extensive discussion of Edward Denny's condemnation of Mary Wroth, see chapter 5.

30. *Haec Vir; or, The Womanish-Man* (1620), in *Half-Humankind*, 288.

31. See Amussen, "Gender, Family, and the Social Order," 200-201, and *Ordered Society*, 41.

32. See Wrightson, *English Society*, 94, and Houlbrooke, *English Family*, 23.

33. Dubrow, *Happier Eden*, 22-23, notes that the marriage manuals in particular "move back and forth between emphasizing the husband's dominion and bestowing some measure of both power and authority on the wife as well," concluding that the manuals attempt "at once to grant and to delimit power."

34. Rowland Whyte to Robert Sidney, 2 Dec. 1595, De L'Isle MS U1475, C12/35,

Kent County Archives Office, Maidstone, England. As with the text of Wroth's unpublished continuation of *Urania*, whenever possible I have reproduced the orthography of the original manuscripts, with the exceptions that *u* is silently normalized to *v* and *i* to *j*, and abbreviations (such as "La:" for "Lady") are expanded in full. I am grateful to the Viscount De L'Isle for permission to quote from the De L'Isle manuscript collection.

35. Rowland Whyte to Robert Sidney, 2 Dec. 1595, De L'Isle MS U1475, C12/54, 64, 73.

36. Rowland Whyte to Robert Sidney, 19 April 1600, De L'Isle MS U1475, C12/25.

37. For example, Robert Sidney to Barbara Sidney, 18 Sept. 1591, U1500, C1/19, and 2 Aug. 1595, U1475, C81/61 (De L'Isle MSS).

38. Lady Leicester to Robert, second earl of Leicester, 10 Jan. 1636, U1500, C2/40; 19 Dec. 1636, U1475, C82/9; and 7 Feb. 1636/37, U1475, C82/15 (De L'Isle MSS).

39. Lady Leicester to Robert, second earl of Leicester, 15 Feb. 1636/37, De L'Isle MS U1475, C82/16.

40. See *Oxford English Dictionary*, s.v. "passion," especially definitions for 1588 and 1641.

41. Lady Leicester to Robert, second earl of Leicester, 20 Feb. 1636/37, U1475, C82/17 and 20 Sept. 1637, U1475, C82/29 (De L'Isle MSS). See also De L'Isle MSS U1475, C82/19, and 20.

42. Lady Leicester to Robert, second earl of Leicester, 11 Dec. 1638, U1475 C82/35, and 9 Dec. 1638, U1475, C82/33 (De L'Isle MSS.)

43. Amussen, "Gender, Family and the Social Order," 208-9, and *Ordered Society*, 117.

44. Amussen, "Gender, Family and Social Order," 209; in related terms, Amussen notes that "women's independence and autonomy were critical to their success as wives and mothers" (*Ordered Society*, 121-22).

45. See Lady Margaret Hoby, *Diary of Lady Margaret Hoby, 1599-1605*, ed. Dorothy M. Meads (Boston: Houghton Mifflin, 1930), especially the introductory discussion of kinship and marriage ties, 11-13; and Lady Anne Clifford, *The Diary of Lady Anne Clifford*, ed. Vita Sackville-West (New York: George H. Doran, 1924). While my citations of Clifford are drawn from Sackville-West's edition, a more recent edition of the diary, which also contains Anne Clifford's later memoirs, can be found in D.J.H. Clifford, ed., *The Diaries of Lady Anne Clifford* (Wolfeboro Falls, N.H.: Alan Sutton, 1991).

46. Amussen, *Ordered Society*, 132-33 and Lewalski, *Writing Women in Jacobean England*, 125. Lewalski discusses how Clifford's emphasis on the web of her paternal family connections is dictated largely by her desire to substantiate her claims as her father's rightful heir, allowing her to both accept and challenge the patriarchal family structure as she sought to "rewrite her place within it" (130-31).

47. Clifford, *Diary*, 28.

48. Ibid., 65, 112.

49. Robert Sidney to Barbara Sidney, 10 Oct. 1604, De L'Isle MS U1475, C81/117.

50. Ben Jonson, *Discoveries*, ed. G.B. Harrison (Edinburgh: Edinburgh Univ. Press, 1966), 15.

51. Mary Wroth to Robert Sidney, 17 Oct. 1614, De L'Isle MS U1475, C52; this letter has been inaccurately listed in the De L'Isle MSS. catalogue as written by

"H. Lansbrocke," due to a misreading of Mary Wroth's characteristic signature.
52. Houlbrooke, *English Family*, 209.
53. See for example David Underdown's discussion of court records from Tisbury in 1637, in *Revel, Riot, and Rebellion*, 33.
54. Nancy J. Vickers, "Diana Described: Scattered Woman and Scattered Rhyme," *Critical Inquiry* 8 (1981): 266-67.
55. Louis Montrose, "The Elizabethan Subject and the Spenserian Text," in *Literary Theory/Renaissance Texts*, ed. Patricia Parker and David Quint (Baltimore: Johns Hopkins Univ. Press, 1986), 325.
56. Vickers, "Diana Described," 273.
57. Newman, *Fashioning Femininity*, 10-11.
58. Henry Smith, *A Preparative to Marriage* (London, 1591), D1v, D2v, cited in Newman, *Fashioning Femininity*, 149, n. 12.
59. Astrophil resumes his first-person voice to lament: "With what she had done and spoken / . . . therewith my song is broken" (Eighth Song of *Astrophil and Stella*, from *The Poems of Sir Philip Sidney*, ed. William A. Ringler, Jr. [Oxford: Clarendon Press, 1962]). In Robert Sidney's poem, the lady's expression of love is an epitaph (Sixth Song of Robert Sidney's sequence, from *The Poems of Robert Sidney*, ed. P.J. Croft [Oxford: Clarendon Press, 1984]). The poems of Robert and Philip Sidney (including the *Old Arcadia* poems) will hereafter be cited from these Oxford editions, by poem number in the text. Subsequent references to Philip Sidney's prose romance will be drawn from *The Countess of Pembroke's Arcadia* (*The Old Arcadia*), ed. Jean Robertson (Oxford: Oxford Univ. Press, 1973), and from Vol. 1 (1590 text of the "New Arcadia") of *The Prose Works of Sir Philip Sidney*, ed. Albert Feuillerat (1912; rpt. Cambridge: Cambridge Univ. Press, 1969), hereafter cited as OA and NA by page number in the text.
60. Although Clark Hulse, "Stella's Wit: Penelope Rich as Reader of Sidney's Sonnets," in *Rewriting the Renaissance*, ed. Ferguson et al., 272-86, stresses Penelope Rich's authority as glimpsed in the voice of Stella, Nona Fienberg, "The Emergence of Stella in *Astrophil and Stella*," *Studies in English Literature* 25 (Winter 1985): 5-19, perceptively points out that the prevailing themes of Stella's absence and illness in the latter part of the sequence effectively manipulate Stella into a "silence of negation" (19).
61. Dubrow, *Echoes of Desire*, 274-75.
62. Edmund Spenser, *Amoretti* #23, from *Spenser: Poetical Works*, ed. J.C. Smith and E. De Selincourt (Oxford Univ. Press, 1989). Spenser's poems will be cited hereafter from this edition by number in the text.
63. Samuel Daniel, *Delia* #3, and Michael Drayton, *Idea* #6, from *The Anchor Anthology of Sixteenth Century Verse*, ed. Richard S. Sylvester (New York: Anchor Books, 1974). Drayton's sonnet juxtaposes in the figure of a single woman the dichotomized "good angel" and "bad angel" of Shakespeare's Sonnet 144, which even more insistently demonizes the female beloved, as will shortly be discussed.
64. Bartholomew Griffin, *Fidessa* #4, and Richard Lynche, *Diella* #2, from Sylvester, ed., *Anchor Anthology*.
65. William Shakespeare, Sonnets #20 and #127, from *The Riverside Shakespeare*, ed. G. Blakemore Evans (Boston: Houghton Mifflin, 1974). Shakespeare's sonnets will be cited hereafter from this edition by number in the text. An odd twist on the intermittent critical obsession with "identifying" the characters in the sequence is provided by the speculation that the young man may have been William Herbert, third earl of Pembroke, which opens the intriguing but factually unlikely possibility that the "Dark

Lady" might have been Herbert's lover, Mary Wroth, a title that was also applied to another contemporary woman poet, Aemilia Lanyer (see Douglas Bush and Alfred Harbarge, intro. to *The Sonnets* [New York: Penguin Books, 1970], 9; and A.L. Rowse, *Shakespeare's Sonnets* [New York: Harper and Row, 1973], xxxiv-xliii). Finally, however, the at best dubious value of such "identifications" is succinctly articulated by Susanne Woods, who observes in the case of Lanyer that "Rowse's fantasy has tended to obscure Lanyer as a poet" (see Woods's introduction to *The Poems of Aemilia Lanyer* [Oxford: Oxford Univ. Press, 1993], xix).

66. Joel Fineman, "Shakespeare's 'Perjur'd Eye'," in *Representing the English Renaissance*, ed. Greenblatt, 146-47.

67. Sedgwick, "Swan in Love: The Example of Shakespeare's Sonnets," in *Between Men*, 29, 32, 47.

68. Robert Herrick, "The Night-Piece, To Julia," in *Hesperides*, from *The Poetical Works of Robert Herrick*, ed. L.C. Martin (Oxford: Oxford Univ. Press, 1956).

69. May Nelson Paulissen, *The Love Sonnets of Lady Mary Wroth: A Critical Introduction* (Salzburg: Univ. Salzburg Press, 1982), 157, 173, argues for the direct influence of both Jonson and Donne upon Wroth through her membership in their group of "coterie poets."

70. Ezell, *Writing Women's Literary History*, 55.

71. Ben Jonson, "A Sonnet to the Noble Lady, the Lady Mary Wroth," in *The Underwood* (1640), from *Ben Jonson: Poems*, ed. Ian Donaldson (Oxford: Oxford Univ. Press, 1975). Jonson's poems will be cited hereafter from this edition by title and number in the text.

72. Kathleen McLuskie, *Renaissance Dramatists* (New York: Harvester Wheatsheaf, 1989), 161.

73. Maureen Quilligan, "Doctor John Donne and Lady Mary Wroth: New World Erotics," unpublished paper delivered at 1992 MLA convention, in special session entitled "Writing Women, Rewriting Culture: Gendered Discourses in Early Modern England."

74. John Donne, "The Good-Morrow," in *Poems* (1633), from *Donne: Poetical Works*, ed. Sir Herbert Grierson (Oxford: Oxford Univ. Press, 1977). Donne's poems will be cited hereafter from this edition by title in the text.

75. See particularly Joan M. Ferrante, "Notes Toward the Study of a Female Rhetoric in the Trobairitz," 63-72, and H. Jay Siskin and Julie A. Storme, "Suffering Love: The Reversed Order in the Poetry of Na Castelloza," 113-28, in *The Voice of the Trobairitz: Perspectives on Women Troubadours*, ed. William D. Paden (Philadelphia: Univ. of Pennsylvania Press, 1989). For an earlier study which provides useful historical background, see Meg Bogin, *The Women Troubadours* (New York: W.W. Norton, 1980).

76. Ann Rosalind Jones, "Assimilation with a Difference: Renaissance Women Poets and Literary Influence," *Yale French Studies* 62 (1981): 136,148. See also "City Women and Their Audiences: Louise Labé and Veronica Franco," in *Rewriting the Renaissance*, ed. Ferguson et al., 299-316; and, most recently, *Currency of Eros*. François Rigolot, "Gender versus Sex Difference in Louise Labé's Grammar of Love," in *Rewriting the Renaissance*, 287-98, provides a linguistic analysis of Labé's use of gender forms.

77. Gary Waller, "Struggling into Discourse: The Emergence of Renaissance Women's Writing," in *Silent But for the Word*, ed. Hannay, 245-46.

78. Elizabeth I, "On Monsieur's Departure," in *The Poems of Queen Elizabeth I*, ed. Leicester Bradner (Providence: Brown Univ. Press, 1964).

79. For more discussion of the significance of gender to Elizabeth I's rhetoric of

authority, see Susan Frye, *Elizabeth I: The Competition for Representation* (Oxford: Oxford Univ. Press, 1993); Mary Thomas Crane, "'Video et Taceo': Elizabeth I and the Rhetoric of Counsel," *Studies in English Literature* 28 (1988): 1-15; and Allison Heisch, "Queen Elizabeth I and the persistence of patriarchy," *Feminist Review* 4 (1980): 45-56, and "Queen Elizabeth I: Parliamentary Rhetoric and the Exercise of Power," *Signs* 1 (1975): 31-55. See chapter 4, "Sovereign Subject: The Politics of Gender," for further analysis of Queen Elizabeth's discursive positions.

80. Aemilia Lanyer, "To the Queenes most Excellent Majestie," 37-38, and "To all vertuous Ladies in generall," 6-7, *Salve Deus Rex Judaeorum* (London, 1611), in *The Poems of Aemilia Lanyer*, ed. Susanne Woods (Oxford: Oxford Univ. Press, 1993). All subsequent citations of the dedicatory poems and title poem of Lanyer's work will refer to titles and line numbers from this edition.

81. See also Wendy Wall, *The Imprint of Gender: Authorship and Publication in the English Renaissance* (Ithaca: Cornell Univ. Press, 1993), 319-30, who examines Lanyer's reversal of the dynamics of the blazon and her simultaneous deconstruction of its relationship between subject and object.

82. Kari McBride, "Engendering Authority in Aemilia Lanyer's *Salve Deus Rex Judaeorum*," (Ph.D. diss., Univ. of Arizona, 1994), 56-57.

83. For a perceptive analysis of Lanyer's vision of female community, see Barbara K. Lewalski, "Imagining Female Community: Aemilia Lanyer's Poems," chapter 8 in *Writing Women in Jacobean England*, 213-42.

84. *Pamphilia to Amphilanthus*, #100, in *The Poems of Lady Mary Wroth*, ed. Josephine Roberts. Hereafter cited in the text as P, according to Roberts's numbering scheme.

85. Swift, "Feminine Identity," 335-36, 342-43, for example, has suggested that the heroic constancy of Wroth's female characters is only "painful and self-destructive," because directed toward unfaithful lovers, while Waller, "Struggling into Discourse," 247-48, and "Watch, gaze, and marke: The Poetry of Mary Wroth," in *The Sidney Family Romance*, 238-39, 242-45, finds that "like the romance, the poems are dominated by betrayal, deception, broken promises, and erotic frustration," and are focused upon "love's location within discourse as an activity for men, a passivity for women."

86. Beilin, *Redeeming Eve*, 208, 212-13.

87. Lamb, "The Countess of Pembroke and the Art of Dying," in *Women in the Middle Ages*, ed. Rose, 222; *Sidney Circle*, 142-43. Lamb's emphasis on the sublimation or denial of anger as characteristic of Wroth's authorial voice may be read in relation to Ezell's analysis of that model of women's literary history in which anger provides a "linking mechanism in the chain of female literary awareness" (*Writing Women's Literary History*, 25-26). Ezell cautions, however, that the image of "the angry and alienated female artist" arises from a nineteenth-century male image of authorship. She questions the value for early modern women's literary history of focusing upon anger as "the characteristic mode of feminist writing" against which the co-option or assimilation of women writers into the dominant culture can be measured, because the result can be an emphasis on reading women writers yet again as victims of a patriarchal literary system (55, 64). Although Lamb nowhere explicitly defines anger as "the characteristic mode of feminist writing," her argument that Wroth's heroines "demonstrat[e] their worth through their psychological victories over their own rage," resulting in a "heroics of constancy predicated upon the intensity of their anger, without which such victories would scarcely be impressive," does serve to privilege anger as the most powerful mode of response to the dominant figurations of gender in Wroth's culture (*Gender and Authorship*, 142-43).

88. Dubrow, *Echoes of Desire*, 137.

89. Recent critics who have started to argue for Wroth's resistance to the subordinate position assigned to women in masculine lyric conventions include Ann Rosalind Jones, "Feminine Pastoral as Heroic Martyrdom: Gaspara Stampa and Mary Wroth," in *Currency of Eros*, 118-54 and "Designing Women: The Self as Spectacle in Mary Wroth and Veronica Franco," in *Reading Mary Wroth*, ed. Miller and Waller, 135-53; Jeff Masten, "'Shall I turne blabb?': Circulation, Gender, and Subjectivity in Mary Wroth's Sonnets," in *Reading Mary Wroth*, 67-87; and Nona Fienberg, "Mary Wroth and the Invention of Female Poetic Subjectivity," in *Reading Mary Wroth*, 175-90 and "Mary Wroth's Poetics of the Self in the Petrarchan Tradition" (unpublished manuscript).

90. See note 43.

91. Elaine Beilin, "'The Onely Perfect Vertue': Constancy in Mary Wroth's *Pamphilia to Amphilanthus*," *Spenser Studies* 2 (1981): 240, explains Amphilanthus's exclusion by suggesting that "he has no place within the scheme of constancy, because he represents change."

92. See Roberts, introduction to *Poems*, 325, and Beilin, "'Onely Perfect Vertue'," 233-34, for two separate considerations of the "dual" image of Cupid in Wroth's sequence.

93. See also Dubrow, *Echoes of Desire*, 159, who suggests that while the passivity of the Petrarchan lover is commonly a sign of weakness and failure, Wroth "turns that passivity into a positive value" by adducing the concept of constancy, and further "wrest[s] agency from objectification" by investigating her own emotions, although Dubrow takes care to remark that "the transformations are not wholly successful or consistent."

94. Masten, "'Shall I turne blabb?', 81.

95. Nancy Miller, "Arachnologies: The Woman, the Text, and the Critic," in *Subject to Change*, 77.

96. Anger, *Her Protection*, 185. Dubrow, *Echoes of Desire*, 152, notes that the spelling of "labourinth" may also contain a punning reminder of how much work is involved in the types of love Wroth evokes.

97. Penelope Reed Doob, *The Idea of the Labyrinth from Classical Antiquity through the Middle Ages* (Ithaca: Cornell Univ. Press, 1990), 1-2.

98. *The Countesse of Mountgomeries Urania* (London, 1621), STC 26051, p. 138, hereafter cited by page number in the text. The unpublished manuscript of the second part of *Urania*, Newberry Library, Case Msfy 1565.W95, will hereafter be cited by book and folio number in the text.

99. For substantiation of Wroth's likely knowledge of French, see Margaret Anne Witten-Hannah, "Lady Mary Wroth's *Urania*: The Work and the Tradition,"(Ph.D. diss., Univ. of Auckland, 1978), 59, and Roberts, intro. to *The Poems*, 9.

100. As with d'Urfé's *Astrée*, Wroth could have read the *Heptaméron* either in the abridged English translation of Elizabeth's reign, or directly in French, as the 1559 French edition was available in England in the early seventeenth century.

101. P.A. Chilton, intro. to *The Heptaméron* (London: Penguin Books, 1984), 18. Passages from *The Heptaméron* will be identified hereafter by page number from this edition in the text.

102. Ibid., 10. Chilton maintains that although the stories themselves may have been contributed by a number of different people in Marguerite's entourage, Marguerite was most likely responsible not only for composing some of the individual stories, but also for editing the tales and providing the story-telling framework.

103. See, for example, Judith M. Kennedy's introduction to *A Critical Edition of Yong's Translation of George of Montemayor's "Diana" and Gil Polo's "Enamoured Diana"* (Oxford: Oxford Univ. Press, 1968), and Miriam Yvonne Jehenson, *The Golden World of Pastoral: A Comparative Study of Sidney's "New Arcadia" and d'Urfé's "L'Astrée"* (Ravenna: Longo Editore, 1981).

104. Honoré d'Urfé, *Astrea, a Romance, written in French*, trans. John Davies (London, 1657), I:335. Subsequent quotations from d'Urfé's romance will be drawn from this edition.

105. Ibid., I:25.

106. See Harvey, *Ventriloquized Voices*, 1, 4-5. I discuss the implications of Harvey's theories more extensively in chapter 6.

107. Jordan, *Renaissance Feminism*, 223. Where Jordan interprets Pyrocles's female disguise as "a renunciation of the *primacy* of man over woman and male over female interests" (224), I argue that Sidney's representation of the failure to survive of comparable women in male disguise (see my discussion in the text) indicates rather a reinscription of "the primacy of man over woman." Furthermore, I find it curious that Jordan's argument for Sidney's "defense of women" (227) takes no account of Wroth's quite different (and notably more feminist) treatment of the gendering of subjectivity in the same genre.

108. See Margaret M. Sullivan, "Amazons and Aristocrats: The Function of Pyrocles' Amazon Role in Sidney's Revised *Arcadia*," in *Playing with Gender: A Renaissance Pursuit*, ed. Jean R. Brink, Maryanne C. Horowitz, and Allison P. Coudert (Chicago: Univ. of Illinois Press, 1991), 62, and Lamb, *Sidney Circle*, 84.

109. Edmund Spenser, *The Faerie Queene*, book III, cantos i & ii, in *Spenser: Poetical Works*, ed. J.C. Smith and E. De Selincourt (Oxford: Oxford Univ. Press, 1989). All subsequent quotations from *The Faerie Queene* will refer to book, canto, and, where relevant, stanza number from this edition in the text.

110. For more extensive discussion of the implications of Spenser's doubled and sometimes contradictory representations of women's rule through female characters in male disguise such as Britomart and Radigund, see particularly Jonathan Goldberg, *Endlesse Worke: Spenser and the Structures of Discourse* (Baltimore: Johns Hopkins Univ. Press, 1981) and Susanne Woods, "Spenser and the Problem of Women's Rule," *Huntington Library Quarterly* 48 (Spring 1985): 141-58.

111. For further discussion, see Marianne Novy, "Shakespeare's Imagery of Gender and Gender Crossing," in *Love's Argument: Gender Relations in Shakespeare* (Chapel Hill: Univ. of North Carolina Press, 1984), 188-202 and Phyllis Rackin, "Androgyny, Mimesis and the Marriage of the Boy Heroine on the English Renaissance Stage," in *Speaking of Gender*, ed. Elaine Showalter (New York: Routledge, 1989), 113-33.

112. Jonathan Goldberg, "Shakespearean inscriptions: the voicing of power," in *Shakespeare and the Question of Theory*, ed. Patricia Parker and Geoffrey Hartman (New York: Methuen, 1985), 130.

113. For further discussion of Wroth's involvement with court masques, see Roberts, *Poems*, 12-15. Andrew Gurr, *Playgoing in Shakespeare's London* (Cambridge: Cambridge Univ. Press, 1987), 57-63, 167, documents the large number of "ladies" in attendance at Shakespeare's plays during the early seventeenth century, as does Richard Levin, "Women in the Renaissance Theatre Audience," *Shakespeare Quarterly* 40 (1989): 165-74 and Kathleen McLuskie, "What Should Chaste Ears Do at a Play?," in *Renaissance Dramatists* (New York: Harvester Wheatsheaf, 1989), 87-99. For analysis of the implications of women's theater-going, see Jean Howard, "Women

as Spectators, Spectacles, and Paying Customers," in *Staging the Renaissance: Reinterpretations of Elizabethan and Jacobean Drama*, ed. David Scott Kastan and Peter Stallybrass (New York: Routledge, 1991), 68-74.

114. Stephen Greenblatt, *Shakespearean Negotiations: The Circulation of Social Energy in Renaissance England* (Oxford: Clarendon Press, 1988), 92.

115. See, for example, Catherine Belsey, *Subject of Tragedy*, 171-75; Sandra K. Fischer, "Elizabeth Cary and Tyranny, Domestic and Religious," in *Silent But for the Word*, ed. Hannay, 225-37; Betty S. Travitsky, "The *Femme Covert* in Elizabeth Cary's *Mariam*," in *Ambiguous Realities*, ed. Levin and Watson, 184-96; Elaine Beilin, "the Making of a Female Hero: Joanna Lumley and Elizabeth Cary," chapter 6 in *Redeeming Eve*, 151-76; Margaret W. Ferguson, "Running On with Almost Public Voice: The Case of 'E.C.,'" in *Tradition and the Talents of Women*, ed. Florence Howe (Urbana: Univ. of Illinois Press, 1991), 37-67; Barbara K. Lewalski, "Resisting Tyrants: Elizabeth Cary's Tragedy and History," chapter 7 in *Writing Women in Jacobean England*, 179-212; Maureen Quilligan, "Staging Gender: William Shakespeare and Elizabeth Cary," in *Sexuality and Gender in Early Modern Europe*, ed. James Grantham Turner (Cambridge: Cambridge Univ. Press, 1993), 208-32; Dympna Callaghan, "Re-reading Elizabeth Cary's *The Tragedy of Mariam*," in *Women, "Race," and Writing in Early Modern England*, ed. Margo Hendricks and Patricia Parker (London: Routledge, 1994), 163-77; and Karen L. Rabin, "Gender and the Political Subject in *The Tragedy of Mariam*," *Studies in English Literature* 35 (1995): 321-43.

116. De Lauretis, *Technologies of Gender*, 26.

117. Elizabeth Cary, *The Tragedie of Mariam, The Faire Queene of Jewry*, ed. Barry Weller and Margaret W. Ferguson, in joint edition with *The Lady Falkland: Her Life* (Berkeley: Univ. of California Press, 1994). Subsequent citations in the text will refer to this edition.

118. See Underdown, "The Taming of the Scold: The Enforcement of Patriarchal Authority in Early Modern England," in *Order and Disorder*, ed. Fletcher and Stevenson, 120-21, 126-27; also *Revel, Riot, and Rebellion*, 38-39.

119. For further textual history, see Brennan, ed., intro. to *Wroth's "Love's Victory"*, 16-20. Critical articles to date include Josephine A. Roberts, "The Huntington Manuscript of Lady Mary Wroth's Play, *Loves Victorie*," *Huntington Library Quarterly* 46 (1983): 156-74; Swift, "Feminine Self-Definition"; Margaret Anne McLaren, "An Unknown Continent: Lady Mary Wroth's Forgotten Drama, 'Love's Victory'," in *Renaissance Englishwomen in Print*, ed. Haselkorn and Travitsky, 276-94; and Barbara K. Lewalski, "Mary Wroth's *Love's Victory* and Pastoral Tragicomedy," in *Reading Mary Wroth*, ed. Miller and Waller, 88-108.

120. Jankowski, *Women and Power*, 26, 30.

121. See Houlbrooke, *English Family Life*, 219.

122. See Swift, "Feminine Identity," 329, 344, and Waller, *Sidney Family Romance*, 329.

123. I differ here from Maureen Quilligan, "The Constant Subject," in *Soliciting Interpretation*, ed. Harvey and Maus, 311-12, who maintains that the poem is actually spoken in the voice of Echo, thus positioning the female speaker as able, in absence, only to imitate the discourse of others.

124. Maureen Quilligan, "Feminine Endings: The Sexual Politics of Sidney's and Spenser's Rhyming," in *Renaissance Englishwoman in Print*, ed. Haselkorn and Travitsky, 321-23, draws comparisons primarily between Pamphilia's role and those of Britomart and Scudamour in these scenes, concluding that Wroth reverses the moral positions of the differently gendered principals.

125. See in this case Waller, *Sidney Family Romance*, 243.

126. Katharine Eisaman Maus, "Horns of Dilemma: Jealousy, Gender, and Spectatorship in English Renaissance Drama," *ELH* 54 (1987): 578.

127. Miller, *Subject to Change*, 164. See, for example, *The Mothers Counsell or Live Within Compass* (Ent 1623, publ. 1630), as well as the admonitions of *The Ladies Dictionary* (London, 1694), which epitomizes many earlier warnings as well: "Your eyes too must be kept within compass, their wanderings, restrained . . . Eyes are the casements of the body, and many times by standing too much open, let in things hurtful to the mind" (reproduced in *The Whole Duty of a Woman: Female Writers in Seventeenth Century England*, ed. Angeline Goreau [Garden City, N.Y.: Doubleday, 1984], 56-57).

128. Roberts, "'The Knott Never to Bee Untide': The Controversy Regarding Marriage in Mary Wroth's *Urania*," in *Reading Mary Wroth*, ed. Miller and Waller, 109-32.

129. Lady Leicester to Robert, second earl of Leicester, 13 April 1637, De L'Isle MS U1475, C82/24.

130. Irigaray, "When Our Lips Speak Together," in *This Sex*, 205, 212, 214.

3. Matriarch's Daughter: *Ties That Bind*

1. See Shirley Nelson Garner, Claire Kahane, and Madelon Sprengnether, eds., intro. to *The (M)other Tongue: Essays in Feminist Psychoanalytic Interpretation* (Ithaca: Cornell Univ. Press, 1985), 24-25; Traub, "Prince Hal's Falstaff," 456-58, 470.

2. See, for example, Brenda O. Daly and Maureen P. Reddy, "Narrating Mothers: Theorizing Maternal Subjectivities," introductory essay to their collection of essays by that title (Knoxville: Univ. of Tennessee Press, 1991), 1-18.

3. See Berg, "Luce Irigaray's 'Contradictions'," 62, for more analysis of the discursive implications of Lacan's theory.

4. Julia Kristeva, "Women's Time," in *Kristeva Reader*, ed. Moi, 191-93, maintains that maternity is a corporeal process outside the willed control of a subject, and thus "maternal subjectivity" can only exist insofar as the female subject undergoing the experience of maternity manages to resist the splitting and fusing process of objectification to which the mother's body is inevitably subjected. Irigaray, "Psychoanalytic Theory: Another Look," in *This Sex*, 63-64, questions more specifically why the maternal function must traditionally take precedence over the erotic function in women, and argues that when women allow themselves to be subjected to a hierarchical choice between the two, they accede not only to a masculine economy and ideology of reproduction, but also to the objectification imposed by a desiring male subject. Cixous, "Sorties" and "The Laugh of the Medusa," in *New French Feminisms*, ed. Elaine Marks and Isabelle de Courtivron (Amherst: Univ. of Massachusetts Press, 1980), 90-98, 245-64, locates the symbolic essence as well as the discursive potential of femininity in the womb, and maintains that "a woman is never far from 'mother'," suggesting that "there is always within her at least a little of that good mother's milk," so that "she writes in white ink" ("Medusa," 251).

5. Chodorow, *Feminism and Psychoanalytic Theory*, 185.

6. Stone, *Family, Sex, and Marriage*, 7, 101-2, 105.

7. Houlbrooke, *English Family*, 135, 146, 178-79, 182-83, 187.

8. Sharpe, *Early Modern England*, 70, 75; see also Alan Macfarlane's review article in *History and Theory* 18 (1979): 103-26, cited by Sharpe.

9. Leah Marcus, *Childhood and Cultural Despair* (Pittsburgh: Univ. of Pittsburgh Press, 1978), 4-5; Pollock, *Forgotten Children*, 2, 68, 199, 203-4.

10. See Wrightson, *English Society*, 117.

11. Amussen, *Ordered Society*, 34, 38, 91-94.

12. See Dorothy McLaren, "Marital Fertility and Lactation, 1570-1720," in *Women in English Society*, ed. Prior, 22-53.

13. King, *Women of the Renaissance*, 20, 23.

14. See Patricia Crawford, "The Construction and Experience of Maternity in Seventeenth-Century England," in *Women as Mothers in Pre-Industrial England*, ed. Fildes, 3-38.

15. See Jonathan Goldberg, "Fatherly Authority: The Politics of Stuart Family Images," in *Rewriting the Renaissance*, ed. Ferguson et al., 3-32. Significantly, Goldberg bases his analyses of the "pervasive politics of the family in the 17th century" (8) on the studies of Stone and Aries, whose conclusions have been refuted by subsequent social historians, as discussed above. For an extension of the implications of Goldberg's conclusions, see Debora Shuger, "Nursing Fathers: Patriarchy as a Cultural Ideal," in *Habits of Thought in the English Renaissance: Religion, Politics, and the Dominant Culture* (Berkeley: Univ. of California Press, 1990), 218-50.

16. Amussen, "Gender, Family, and the Social Order," 200, 203.

17. Margaret Ezell, *The Patriarch's Wife: Literary Evidence and the History of the Family* (Chapel Hill: Univ. of North Carolina Press, 1987), 34-35, 163. Hilda Smith, "Gynecology and Ideology in Seventeenth-Century England," in *Liberating Women's History*, ed. Berenice Carroll, 97-114, examines the subjection of women by virtue of their female anatomy in the gynecological and obstetrical writings of the period. Gordon J. Schochet, *The Authoritarian Family and Political Attitudes in 17th-Century England: Patriarchalism in Political Thought* (New Brunswick, N.J.: Transaction Books, 1988), 54-55, attends more explicitly to the political and social implications of the family as symbol and institution than to the gendered dynamics of familial authority.

18. Dubrow, *Happier Eden*, 23.

19. Wall, *Imprint of Gender*, examines the effect of the marketplace upon representations of women, concluding with a chapter on women writers, feminine tropes, and problems of publication (279-340).

20. Anger, *Her Protection*, 183.

21. Swetnam, *Arraignment*, 213-14.

22. Constantia Munda, *The Worming of a mad Dog* (1617), in *Half Humankind*, ed. Henderson and McManus, 254.

23. *Hic Mulier*, 265.

24. Pamela Benson points out, for example, that despite Anger's profeminist rhetoric, "female power remains sexual power" (*Invention of Renaissance Woman*, 229).

25. McLaren, "Marital Fertility," 45. See also Stone, *Family, Sex, and Marriage*, 4-7, 90-95, 114, and Warnicke, *Women of the English Renaissance*, 10.

26. Elizabeth Clinton, Countess of Lincoln, *The Countess of Lincolns Nurserie* (Oxford, 1622); cited in McLaren, "Marital Fertility," 28.

27. Elizabeth Crashaw, *The Honor of Virtue* (1620), in *Half Humankind*, ed. Henderson and McManus, 346.

28. *A pitiless Mother. That most unnaturally at one time, murt two of her owne Children* (1616), in *Half Humankind*, ed. Henderson and McManus, 363-65.

29. Ibid., 362-63.

30. Ibid., 366-67.

31. Elizabeth Joceline, *The Mothers Legacie to her Unborne Childe* (London, 1622), reprinted in Pollock, *Lasting Relationship*, 174.

32. Dorothy Leigh, *The Mother's Blessing* (London, 1618), prefatory material reprinted in Pollock, *Lasting Relationship*, 174.

33. Leigh, *The Mother's Blessing*, reprinted in *Daughters, Wives and Widows*, ed. Klein, 292. See Klein's introduction, especially p. 288. All subsequent citations from *The Mother's Blessing* will be taken from Klein's edition.

34. Ibid., 293-94.

35. Ibid., 292, 295.

36. See Klein, ed., *Daughters, Wives and Widows*, 289.

37. Leigh, *Mother's Blessing*, 301-2.

38. See Rose, "Where Are the Mothers?," 311; also Warnicke, *Women of the English Renaissance*, 193 and Klein, ed., *Daughters, Wives and Widows*, 290.

39. Rose, "Where Are the Mothers?," 295-96, 307-8.

40. Ibid., 310-13.

41. Crawford, "Construction and experience of maternity," 16.

42. Felicity Heal, *Hospitality in Early Modern England* (Oxford: Clarendon Press, 1990), 179, 182-83. Newman, *Fashioning Femininity*, 18.

43. Dod and Cleaver, *A Godlie Forme of Householde Government* (London, 1598), cited in Belsey, *Subject of Tragedy*, 159-60.

44. Belsey, *Subject of Tragedy*, 154-56.

45. Sara Heller Mendelson, "Stuart Women's Diaries and Occasional Memoirs," in *Women in English Society*, ed. Prior, 199, discusses the social rationale behind this dichotomy.

46. Clifford, *Diary*, 10, 14.

47. Ibid., 23.

48. Lewalski, *Writing Women in Jacobean England*, 133-34.

49. Clifford, *Diary*, 25, 27-28, 32.

50. Ibid., 72.

51. Robert Sidney to Barbara Sidney, 26 April and 2 Sept. 1588, De L'Isle MSS U1475, C81/2 and C81/10.

52. Robert Sidney to Barbara Sidney, 20 April 1596, De L'Isle MS U1475, Z53/49.

53. Rowland Whyte to Robert Sidney, 5 April 1597, De L'Isle MS U1475, C12/81.

54. Robert Sidney to Barbara Sidney, 20 April 1597, De L'Isle MS U1475, C81/97.

55. Robert Sidney to Barbara Sidney, 20 and 22 April 1597, De L'Isle MS U1475, C81/97 and 98.

56. Robert Sidney to Barbara Sidney, 20 Feb. and 30 March 1596/7, De L'Isle MS U1475, C81/92 and 93.

57. See, for example, Robert Sidney to Barbara Sidney, 2 Sept. 1604, U1475, C81/110; 10 Oct. 1604, U1475, C81/117; 25 Aug. 1605, U1475, C81/145; 10 Nov. 1607, U1475, C81/158 (De L'Isle MSS).

58. Belsey, *Subject of Tragedy*, 156.

59. Mary Wroth to Robert Sidney, 17 Oct. 1614, De L'Isle MS U1475, C52.

60. Waller, "Wroth and Family Romance," 38; also *Sidney Family Romance*, 44, 115-16, 159.

61. Rowland Whyte to Robert Sidney, 12 Nov. 1595, U1475, C12/23; Robert Sidney to Barbara Sidney, 8 and 28 Nov. 1608, U1475, C81/159, and 160 (De L'Isle MSS).

62. Hannay, *Philip's Phoenix*, 143, and "The Countess of Pembroke as Mentor," in *Reading Mary Wroth*, ed. Miller and Waller, 20-23. See also Houlbrooke, ed., *English Family Life*, 103, on the range of godparent relationships depicted in diaries of the period.

63. Mary Sidney, the countess of Pembroke, to Barbara Sidney, 9 Sept. 1590, British Library Addit. MS 15,232.

64. For more extensive treatment of Lanyer's constructions of maternity, see Naomi J. Miller, "(M)other Tongues in Aemilia Lanyer's *Salve Deus Rex Judaeorum* (1611)," [under submission].

65. Leigh, *Mother's Blessing*, 297-98.

66. Barbara K. Lewalski, "Of God and Good Women: The Poems of Aemilia Lanyer," in *Silent But for the Word*, ed. Hannay, 203-24, analyzes Lanyer's "Edenic myth" in careful detail; see also Lewalski, "Imagining Female Community: Aemilia Lanyer's Poems," chapter 8 in *Writing Women in Jacobean England*, 213-42.

67. For additional sonnets on Venus as mother figure, see especially P85 and P95; sonnets that represent Night as a comforting maternal presence include P13, P17, and P43.

68. Susan Stanford Friedman, "Creativity and the Childbirth Metaphor: Gender Difference in Literary Discourse," in *Speaking of Gender*, 74.

69. Countess of Pembroke, Psalm 58, ll. 23-24, cited in Beth Wynne Fisken, "Mary Sidney's *Psalmes*: Education and Wisdom," in *Silent But for the Word*, ed. Hannay, 177.

70. See Crawford, "Experience of Maternity," 3-38.

71. Rose, "Where Are the Mothers?" 298-301; Robert Sidney to Barbara Sidney, 20 April 1596, De L'Isle MS U1475, Z53/49. Cixous observes that "in the extreme the world of 'being' can function to the exclusion of the mother" ("Sorties," in *New French Feminisms*, ed. Marks and Courtivron, 92).

72. Irigaray, "Psychoanalytic Theory: Another Look," in *This Sex*, 63-64.

73. See *A pitiless Mother*, 364.

74. See Louis A. Montrose's extended discussion of these issues in "'Shaping Fantasies': Figurations of Gender and Power in Elizabethan Culture," *Representations* 1 (1983): 70-75.

75. For a psychoanalytic discussion of masculine appropriation of maternal power in one of Shakespeare's tragedies, see Janet Adelman's analysis of the figure of Duncan, in "'Born of Woman': Fantasies of Maternal Power in *Macbeth*," in *Cannibals, Witches, and Divorce: Estranging the Renaissance*, ed. Marjorie Garber (Baltimore: Johns Hopkins Univ. Press, 1987), esp. 94. Newman, "Discovering Witches: Sorciographics," in *Fashioning Femininity*, 62, points out in her critique of Adelman's article that "psychoanalysis need not inevitably make ahistorical claims about human development that preclude historical analysis."

76. Goldberg, "Fatherly Authority," 32.

77. For more extended analysis of constructions of maternity in the play, see Naomi J. Miller, "Domestic Politics in Elizabeth Cary's *The Tragedy of Mariam* (1613)," *Studies in English Literature* 37 (forthcoming, Spring 1997).

78. Susan Suleiman, "Writing and Motherhood," in *The (M)other Tongue*, ed. Garner et al., 372. Laurie Langbauer, "Motherhood and Women's Writing in Mary Wollstonecraft's Novels," in *Romanticism and Feminism*, ed. Anne K. Mellor (Bloomington: Indiana Univ. Press, 1988), 209-10, has suggested that the romance genre in particular may be aligned by women writers with maternal rather than paternal forces. Although Langbauer is concerned with the romantic rather than the early modern period, her analysis of the female-authored dynamic of mothers and daughters replacing fathers and sons sheds suggestive light upon the mother-daughter bonds in Wroth's romance in particular.

79. See Weller and Ferguson's double edition of *The Tragedy of Mariam* and *The Lady Falkland Her Life*, *"by one of her daughters"* (1994).

80. For more discussion of Cary's revisions of Josephus, see Betty S. Travitsky, "The *Feme Covert* in Elizabeth Cary's *Mariam*," in *Ambiguous Realities*, ed. Levin and Watson, 184-96, and Beilin, *Redeeming Eve*, 151-76.

81. Belsey, *Subject to Tragedy*, 172, 174; 149.

82. Rose, "Where Are the Mothers?," 314, closes her discussion with a brief reference to the figure of Cary's Alexandra, but concludes that her "troubling presence exceeds the bounds of meaning: she does not make sense."

83. Belsey, *Subject to Tragedy*, 192-93.

84. Hallett Smith, intro. to *Venus and Adonis*, in *The Riverside Shakespeare*, ed. Evans, 1704, notes that of all Shakespeare's works, *Venus and Adonis* was the most popular during his lifetime, being printed in at least nine editions. Although the figure of Venus as mother does appear in some male-authored texts, such as Spenser's *Amoretti*, Venus often is represented in such examples as a nurturing comforter for Cupid, who reifies her son's status as a central subject, rather than being cast as a figure of female authority in her own right.

85. For extensive analysis of the connections between Wroth's play and the pastoral tragicomedies of Tasso, Guarini, Daniel, and Fletcher, see Barbara K. Lewalski, "Mary Wroth's *Love's Victory* and Pastoral Tragicomedy," in *Reading Mary Wroth*, ed. Miller and Waller, 88-108.

86. Cixous adds: "*In* her, matrix, cradler; herself giver as her mother and child; she is her own sister-daughter. . . . Everything will be changed once woman gives woman to the other woman" ("Medusa," 252).

87. While Quilligan, "Constant Subject," 310, finds that Urania's opening speech betrays "a complete lack of self-presence," I would suggest that her speech indicates an initiatory movement toward self-definition, particularly when viewed in relation to Wrightson's analysis of the "ego-centred" system of ancestry in early modern England, "pivoting on the individual who traced kin outwards from himself [*sic*]" (*English Society*, 46-47).

88. Swift, "Feminine Identity," 333, 346, interprets this comment as a direct expression of Wroth's own perspective, without considering that it is spoken by a fictional character, and a male character at that.

89. Basing her historical analysis upon male-authored texts, Rich adds: "We acknowledge Lear (father-daughter split), Hamlet (son and mother), and Oedipus (son and mother) as great embodiments of the human tragedy; but there is presently no enduring recognition of mother-daughter passion and rapture" ("Motherhood and Daughterhood," in *Of Woman Born: Motherhood as Experience and Institution* [New York: W.W. Norton, 1986], 237).

90. Jeff Masten, "'All Arcadia on Fire': Mary Wroth reads Philip Sidney," paper delivered at 1990 MLA convention, in special session entitled "Sexual/Textual Poetics: Mary Wroth and the Sidney Family Men."

91. See chapter 6, "Between Women: Becoming Visible," for more discussion of this issue.

92. Irigaray, "Psychoanalytic Theory," in *This Sex*, 63-64.

93. My argument about the multiple "varieties" of family bonds in *Urania* runs counter to that of Swift, "Feminine Identity," 339, who bases her conclusion that Wroth "presents families in *Urania* as more tyrannical than they are in Shakespeare or in Sidney" solely upon the subplots. See Lewalski, *Writing Women in Jacobean*

England, 289, and Lamb, *Gender and Authorship*, 147, for additional discussion of illegitimate children in Wroth's narrative.

94. Hannay, "'Your Vertuous and Learned Aunt'," in *Reading Mary Wroth*, ed. Miller and Waller, 24.

95. Lewalski, *Writing Women in Jacobean England*, 292.

96. Pollock, *Lasting Relationship*, 13; Houlbrooke, *English Family*, 25, 44, 52, 192.

97. Crawford, "Experience of Maternity," 26.

98. See Lamb, *Gender and Authorship*, 146-47, for a discussion of possible connections between "Wroth's experience of motherhood" and "the combination of physical distance and continued concern which characterizes parental relationships in the manuscript portion."

99. Lewalski, *Writing Women in Jacobean England*, 289.

100. Homans, *Bearing the Word*, 287.

101. Rose, "Where Are the Mothers?," 308.

4. Sovereign Subject: *The Politics of Gender*

1. Luce Irigaray, "The Power of Discourse and the Subordination of the Feminine," in *This Sex*, 69, 81.

2. John Knox, *The First Blast of the Trumpet Against the Monstrous Regiment of Woman* (1558), in *The Works of John Knox*, ed. David Laing (Edinburgh: Thomas George Stevenson, 1855), 4:373.

3. Cited in Linda Levy Peck, "The Mentality of a Jacobean Grandee," in *Jacobean Court*, 154-55.

4. Greenblatt, *Renaissance Self-Fashioning*, 164-66, argues that Elizabeth's use of power was closely bound up with her use of fictions, so that courtiers such as Sir Walter Raleigh or Sir Robert Carey found their roles as civil servants refigured through Petrarchan politics. Montrose, "Shaping Fantasies," 64-65, focuses upon the relation between gender and power in considering the tensions generated by the "rule of a woman" within a patriarchal society, but tends to characterize that society as if its relevant actors were all men, with one exceptional woman.

5. See Allison Heisch, "Queen Elizabeth I: Parliamentary Rhetoric and the Exercise of Power," *Signs* 1 (1975): 31-55 and "Queen Elizabeth I and the Persistence of Patriarchy," *Feminist Review* 4 (1980): 45-56.

6. Leah S. Marcus, "Erasing the Stigma of Daughterhood: Mary I, Elizabeth I, and the Henry VIII," in *Discontented Discourses*, ed. Barr and Feldstein, 400-417, and "Elizabeth," in *Puzzling Shakespeare: Local Reading and Its Discontents* (Berkeley: Univ. of California Press, 1988), 51-109, argues that the queen gained authority as a woman by assimilating aspects of Henry VIII's royal identity, so that she could be perceived as a "composite" of male and female attributes, although Marcus maintains that the queen envisioned her primary public identity as ruler in "male terms." Following Marcus, Jankowski, "The Body Natural and the Body Politic: Early Modern Political Theory and the Anomaly of the Woman Ruler," chapter 3 in *Women and Power*, 54-76, concludes that Elizabeth relied upon "sexually ambiguous formulae" in order to present herself as "an androgynous ruler" (65). Mary Thomas Crane, "'Video et Taceo': Elizabeth I and the Rhetoric of Counsel," *Studies in English Literature* 28 (1988): 1-15, explores Elizabeth's use of the symbolic system of political counsel, and demonstrates how the queen's assumption of the stance of educated advisor in her own speeches and writings served to assert and protect her authorial involvement in the

making of public policy. Treating Elizabeth I as a "discursive subject," Susan Frye, *Elizabeth I: The Competition for Representation* (Oxford: Oxford Univ. Press, 1993), maps the queen's authority within her contemporaries' views of gender and power by examining particular historic records of the competition for public representation, and emphasizes the female terms of power residing in her self-representation of virginal chastity. See also Philippa Berry, *Of Chastity and Power: Elizabethan Literature and the Unmarried Queen* (New York: Routledge, 1989).

7. Lisa Gim, "'Authorizing Women': The Representation of Queen Elizabeth I by Three Seventeenth Century Women Writers," 2-3, paper delivered at 1993 MLA convention, in special session entitled "Author-izing Queens." Gim's paper is excerpted from her book-length study entitled *Representing Regina: Literary Representations of Queen Elizabeth I by Women Writers of the Sixteenth and Seventeenth Centuries* (unpublished).

8. Elizabeth I, "Second Version of the Speech Concerning the Queen's Marriage" (1558), in *The Public Speaking of Queen Elizabeth: Selections from Her Official Addresses*, ed. George P. Rice, Jr. (New York: Columbia Univ. Press, 1951), 117.

9. Elizabeth I, "On Marriage and Succession" (1566), in *Public Speaking*, ed. Rice, 81.

10. Elizabeth I, "To the Troops at Tillbury" (1588), and "Reply to the Petition Urging Execution of Mary Queen of Scots" (1586), in *Public Speaking*, ed. Rice, 96, 89.

11. Within that masculine order, Newman has pointed out that "a woman, then, is doubly a subject: subjected to her husband in obedience, according to God's ordinance in Genesis and thus modeling the relation of a subject to sovereign, but also, and more importantly, constructed as a subject by a system of relations—textual, social, institutional—that fashioned her very subjectivity and the shape and kind of available perceptions of her" (*Fashioning Femininity*, 18).

12. James I, *Basilikon Doron* (1599), in *The Political Works of James I*, reprinted from the edition of 1616, ed. Charles Howard McIlwain (Cambridge: Harvard Univ. Press, 1918), 34.

13. James I, *Basilikon Doron*, 36.

14. James I, *The Trew Law of Free Monarchies* (1598), in *Political Works*, ed. McIlwain, 53.

15. Ibid., 66.

16. James I, "Speech of 1603," in *Political Works*, ed. McIlwain, 272. Leonard Tennenhouse, *Power on Display: The Politics of Shakespeare's Genres* (New York: Methuen, 1986), 149, downplays the significance of James's "adjusting the sex" of Elizabeth's construction of power in this statement, emphasizing instead that "this figure invokes natural law as the basis for [James's] claim to patriarchal power."

17. Stephen Orgel, "Jonson and the Amazons," in *Soliciting Interpretation*, ed. Harvey and Maus, 126.

18. See Marcus, *Puzzling Shakespeare*, 184.

19. See Jonathan Goldberg, *James I and the Politics of Literature: Jonson, Shakespeare, Donne, and Their Contemporaries* (Baltimore: Johns Hopkins Univ. Press, 1983), xi, 25; "Fatherly Authority," 18, 30, 32.

20. Amussen, *An Ordered Society*, 34, 38-39, emphasizes the "reciprocal" dynamic of relationships within the household, which held implications for the state as well. See also Amussen, "Gender, Family, and the Social Order," 204-5, on the "challenges to order and the extent of disorder in the century leading up to 1640."

21. See Leeds Barroll, "The Court of the First Stuart Queen," in *Jacobean Court,* ed. Peck, 191-208.

22. Lewalski, "Enacting Opposition: Queen Anne and the Subversions of Masquing," chapter 1 in *Writing Women in Jacobean England,* 15, 26, 28-29, 43.

23. Clifford, *Diary,* 4-5.

24. Sommerville, *Politics and Ideology,* 145, 147, 151.

25. Clifford, *Diary,* 48-49.

26. Ibid., 49.

27. Ibid., 50.

28. See Roberts, intro. to *Poems,* 9-12, for a more detailed account of the Wroths' position at the court of James.

29. See for example Mary Wroth's letter to Queen Anne (c. 1612), *HMC, Salisbury,* XXII, 3, cited in Roberts, *Poems,* 233-34, requesting the queen's support in matters concerning the renovation of Loughton Hall.

30. Lady Leicester to Robert, second earl of Leicester, 14 March 1636, De L'Isle MS U1475, C82/21.

31. See Roberts, intro. to *The Poems,* 24-26.

32. Esther Sowernam, "Esther hath hanged Haman," 220, 230-31.

33. Constantia Munda, "The Worming of a mad Dog," 250-51.

34. Reported in a letter of John Chamberlain (25 Jan. 1620), and cited in Henderson and McManus, *Half-Humankind,* 17.

35. *Hic Mulier,* 269-70.

36. *Haec-Vir,* 282.

37. See for example Montrose, "'Eliza, Queene of Shepheardes'," *English Literary Renaissance* 10 (1980): 153-82 and Clark Hulse, "Stella's Wit: Penelope Rich as Reader of Sidney's Sonnets," in *Rewriting the Renaissance,* ed. Ferguson et al., 272-86.

38. Goldberg, *Politics of Literature,* 222-23, 226, 230.

39. Waller, *Sidney Family Romance,* 238.

40. Jones, "Designing Women," 137.

41. See Catherine Gallagher, "Embracing the Absolute: The Politics of the Female Subject in Seventeenth-Century England," *Genders* 1 (Spring 1988): 24-39.

42. Jones, "Designing Women," 147.

43. Masten, "'Shall I turne blabb?'," 72; Jones, "Designing Women," 147-48.

44. See Katherine Duncan-Jones and Jan van Dorsten, eds., *The Miscellaneous Prose of Sir Philip Sidney* (Oxford: Oxford Univ. Press, 1973), 17.

45. Sidney, *The Lady of May,* in *Miscellaneous Prose ,* ed. Duncan-Jones and van Dorsten, 21.

46. Jordan, *Renaissance Feminism,* 220-22.

47. See particularly Maureen Quilligan, *Milton's Spenser: The Politics of Reading* (Ithaca: Cornell Univ. Press, 1983) and Josephine Roberts, "Radigund Revisited: Perspectives on Women Rulers in Lady Mary Wroth's *Urania,*" in *The Renaissance Englishwoman in Print,* ed. Haselkorn and Travitsky, 187-207, who provides a detailed consideration of Spenser's treatment of female sovereignty in relation to *Urania.* Landmark work on these issues in Shakespearean texts includes Montrose, "'Shaping Fantasies'," and Goldberg, *Politics of Literature,* cited above, as well as Jean E. Howard, "Renaissance Antitheatricality and the Politics of Gender and Rank in *Much Ado About Nothing,*" in *Shakespeare Reproduced,* ed. Howard and O'Connor, 163-87, and Carol Thomas Neely, "Constructing Sexuality in the Renaissance: Stratford, London, Windsor, Vienna," in *Feminism and Psychoanalysis,* ed. Feldstein and Roof, 209-29.

48. Susanne Woods, "Spenser and the Problem of Women's Rule," *Huntington Library Quarterly*, 48 (Spring 1985): 146, 149, argues that Spenser's presentation of figures for Queen Elizabeth, from Belphoebe and Gloriana to the more oblique example of Britomart, suggests that he finds the potential for rule "inherent in women, not exceptional to them." Pamela Benson, "Praise and Defense of Woman in *The Faerie Queene*," and "Praise and Defense of the Queen in *The Faerie Queene*," chapters 10 and 11 in *Invention of Renaissance Woman*, 251-306, maintains that Spenser's female rulers represent "the superiority of feminine virtue," but finds that "the independent woman is an enemy in this text because she is masculine," and concludes that Spenser removes political action from the sphere of most women by writing political ambition out of their characters (253, 281).

49. See Roberts, "Radigund Revisited," 187-207, for more extended comparison of Spenser's Radigund and several of Wroth's female ruler figures, viewed primarily in terms of their relation to men.

50. Goldberg, "Speculations: *Macbeth* and Source," in *Shakespeare Reproduced*, ed. Howard and O'Connor, esp. 253ff, positions the masques entirely in relation to the fatherly authority of King James, and finds that in Jonson's masques "the representation of the king's claims to totality offers the possibility of endless replications within the system of reflecting power in which the king was placed" (253). Lewalski, *Writing Women in Jacobean London*, 15-44, focuses instead upon Queen Anne's relation to the masques, arguing that the queen was able to use the court masque "as a vehicle for self-affirmation and for subversive intervention in Jacobean politics" (15).

51. Ben Jonson, *The Masque of Queens*, in *Ben Jonson's Plays and Masques*, ed. Robert M. Adams (New York: W.W. Norton, 1979), line 45, p. 323. Subsequent quotations from the masques will be cited from this edition by line and/or page number in the text.

52. For more historical discussion of witches, see Underdown, "The Taming of the Scold," in *Order and Disorder*, ed. Fletcher and Stevenson, 116-36; also *Revel, Riot, and Rebellion*, 40.

53. Suzanne Gossett, "'Man-maid, begone!': Women in the Masques," *English Literary Renaissance* 18 (Winter 1988): 99-101. For a contrasting view of *The Masque of Queens*, which argues that the "frivolity" of the actual courtly ladies played into Jonson's representation of women as "caricatures of male virtue," see Margaret Maurer, "Reading Ben Jonson's *Queens*," in *Seeking the Woman*, ed. Fisher and Halley, 233-64.

54. Stephen Orgel, "Jonson and the Amazons," in *Soliciting Interpretation*, ed. Harvey and Maus, 130-33.

55. Lewalski, *Writing Women in Jacobean England*, 28, 32-33, 37-39.

56. Belsey, *The Subject of Tragedy*, 172.

57. Lewalski, *Writing Women in Jacobean England*, 179, 200-201.

58. Margaret W. Ferguson, "The Spectre of Resistance: *The Tragedy of Mariam* (1613)," in *Staging the Renaissance*, ed. Kastan and Stallybrass, 235-36, 238-39.

59. McLaren, "An Unknown Continent," 284-85.

60. Wroth's play may also be contrasted with the recently rediscovered *Cupid's Banishment* (1617), a masque put on by Ladies Hall, an academy for daughters of the elite, for the patron Lucy, countess of Bedford, in homage to Queen Anne, where men played all the major roles (for more detailed discussion of the production of *Cupid's Banishment*, see Susan Wiseman, "Gender and Status in Dramatic Discourse," in *Women, Writing, History, 1640-1740*, ed. Isobel Grundy and Susan Wiseman [London: B T. Batsford, 1992], 163).

61. See Newman, "Discovering Witches: Sorciographics," in *Fashioning Femininity*, 53-70, for extensive analysis of the relation between historical persecutions of witches and literary representations in early modern England.

62. For a different perspective see Beilin, *Redeeming Eve*, 225, who finds that Nereana's restoration to monarchy "reflects Wroth's view of a woman's potential, which is not to become manly, but actively and publicly to exercise her best womanly qualities."

63. Quilligan, "Constant Subject," 327.

64. Whereas some critics, like Beilin (*Redeeming Eve*, Ch.8) and Lewalski (*Writing Women*, Ch.9), read *Urania* as a narrative of female heroism centering upon the figure of Pamphilia, others, like Waller ("The Sidney Family Romance," in *Reading Mary Wroth*, ed. Miller and Waller, 58), find Pamphilia to be "predominantly a victim, unhappy, unrewarded, 'molested'." Roberts suggests that Pamphilia's commitment to the body politic as a strong female monarch is threatened by her attachment to Amphilanthus ("Radigund Revisited," 200), while Quilligan focuses upon the relation between absolutist politics and erotic desire in Wroth's characterization of Pamphilia ("Constant Subject," 327). More directly addressing connections between sovereignty and subjectivity, Masten argues that Wroth figures Pamphilia's self-control in the discourse of political sovereignty ("Circulation, Gender, and Subjectivity," 78), while Heather Weidemann maintains that within the split between Pamphilia's appearance and her innermost thoughts Wroth locates the queen's individual subjectivity ("Theatricality and Female Identity," in *Reading Mary Wroth*, 202).

65. Elizabeth I, "Reply to the Petition Urging Execution of Mary Queen of Scots" (1586), in *Public Speaking*, 89: "I have known what it is to be a subject, and I now know what it is to be a sovereign."

66. Amussen, "Gender, Family and Social Order," 208-9, and *An Ordered Society*, 117.

67. For a contrasting view of Urania's relation to her brother, see Maureen Quilligan, "Lady Mary Wroth: Female Authority and the Family Romance," in *Unfolded Tales*, ed. Logan and Teskey, 278, who argues that "Urania has no story of her own: it is tied directly to her brother's story."

68. See Gallagher, "Embracing the Absolute," 24-39.

5. Engendering Discourse: *In a Different Voice*

1. Jonathan Crewe, *Trials of Authorship: Anterior Forms of Poetic Reconstruction from Wyatt to Shakespeare* (Berkeley: Univ. of California Press, 1990), 13-15. Crewe's study is part of a series entitled *The New Historicism: Studies in Cultural Poetics*, edited by Stephen Greenblatt.

2. Rather than using the year 1600 as a rigid dividing point, as does Crewe, I find it more useful to address ongoing patterns of authorial construction in the late sixteenth and early seventeenth centuries. Along these lines, it is important to remember that the authorial voices of Lanyer, Cary, and Wroth were certainly shaped by sixteenth-century notions of "authorial construction," even if their texts technically appeared in the first two decades of the seventeenth century.

3. See Miller, *Subject to Change*, 80-81.

4. Homans, *Bearing the Word*, xi-xiii.

5. Homans, *Bearing the Word*, 5; Elizabeth Wright, "Thoroughly Postmodern Feminist Criticism," in *Between Feminism and Psychoanalysis*, ed. Brennan, 141;

Patricia S. Yaeger, "'Because a Fire Was in My Head': Eudora Welty and the Dialogic Imagination," *PMLA* 99 (1984): 955.

6. Cixous, "Medusa," 245, 249, 251, 256.

7. Cixous, "Castration or Decapitation?", trans. Annette Kuhn, *Signs* 7 (1981): 51; cited in Ezell, *Writing Women's Literary History*, 161.

8. Julia Kristeva, "Women's Time," in *Kristeva Reader*, ed. Moi, 193.

9. Julia Kristeva, "Oscillation between Power and Denial," an interview by Xaviere Gauthier in *Tel Quel* (Summer 1974), in *New French Feminisms*, ed. Marks and Courtivron, 166.

10. Sandra M. Gilbert and Susan Gubar, *No Man's Land: The Place of the Woman Writer in the Twentieth Century*, Vol. I: *The War of the Words* (New Haven: Yale Univ. Press, 1988), 262.

11. Irigaray, "Power of Discourse," 74, 76.

12. Ibid., 78-80.

13. Anger, *Her Protection*, 174.

14. Ibid., 184.

15. Ibid., 185.

16. Rachel Speght, *A Muzzle for Melastomus* (1617), Sig. A4, cited in *Half Humankind*, ed. Henderson and McManus, 16.

17. Swetnam, *Arraignment*, 190, and Esther Sowernam, *Esther hath hanged Haman*, 218-19.

18. Sowernam, *Esther hath hanged Haman*, 243.

19. Crawford, "Women's Published Writings, 1600-1700," in *Women in English Society*, ed. Prior, 222.

20. Leigh, *Mother's Blessing*, 292, 295.

21. Joan Larsen Klein, "Women and Marriage in Renaissance England: Male Perspectives," *Topic: The Elizabethan Woman* 36 (1982): 29, discusses the extent of this popularity in more detail.

22. Ezell, *The Patriarch's Wife*, 83.

23. Sidonie Smith, *A Poetics of Women's Autobiography: Marginality and the Fictions of Self-Representation* (Bloomington: Indiana Univ. Press, 1987), 59.

24. Ibid., 176.

25. Hoby, *Diary*, 133; Clifford, *Diary*, 69.

26. Ezell, *Patriarch's Wife*, 73, 99. For analysis of the differences between men's and women's voices in early modern letters of remission in France, see Natalie Zemon Davis, *Fiction in the Archives: Pardon Tales and Their Tellers in Sixteenth-Century France* (Stanford: Stanford Univ. Press, 1987), especially chapter 3, "Bloodshed and Woman's Voice," 77-110.

27. For more extensive discussion of historical access or lack thereof to women's papers, see Hilda Smith, "Feminism and the Methodology of Women's History," in *Liberating Women's History*, ed. Carroll, 369-84.

28. Lord Denny, "To Pamphilia from the father-in-law of Seralius," University of Nottingham MS Cl LM 85/1-5; *HMC*, Series 55, pt. 7; reprinted in Roberts, *Poems*, 32.

29. Lady Mary Wroth to the duke of Buckingham, 15 Dec. 1621, Bodleian Library MS Add.D. III, ff. 173r-v; *HMC*, 2nd report, item 392, p. 60; reprinted in Roberts, *Poems*, 236.

30. Lady Mary Wroth to Sir Edward Denny, 15 Feb. 1621/2, *HMC*, Salisbury, XXII, 160; reprinted in Roberts, *Poems*, 237.

31. "Railing Rimes Returned upon the Author by Mistress Mary Wrothe," University of Nottingham MS Cl LM 85/1-5; *HMC*, Series 55, pt. 7; reprinted in Roberts, *Poems*, 34-35.

32. Lady Mary Wroth to Sir Edward Denny, 27 Feb. 1621/2, University of Nottingham MS Cl LM 85/4; *HMC*, Denbigh, V, 3; reprinted in Roberts, *Poems*, 240.

33. Sir Edward Denny to Lady Mary Wroth, 26 Feb. 1621/2, University of Nottingham MS Cl LM 85/1; *HMC*, Denbigh, V, 3; reprinted in Roberts, *Poems*, 239; Margaret Tyler, "Epistle to the Reader," reproduced in *The Paradise of Women: Writings by Englishwomen of the Renaissance*, ed. Betty Travitsky (Westport, Conn.: Greenwood Press, 1981), 146.

34. Hannay, *Philip's Phoenix*, x; see also Hannay, "'Doo What Men May Sing': Mary Sidney and the Tradition of Admonitory Dedication," in *Silent But for the Word*, 149.

35. Lamb, *Gender and Authorship*, 24.

36. In her illuminating analysis of Lanyer's dedicatory poem to the countess of Pembroke, Kari McBride observes that "Mary Sidney is silenced as poet at the same time that she seems to be praised excessively," showing "Lanyer to be in control of poetic construction" ("Engendering Authority," 127, 129).

37. Dubrow, *Echoes of Desire*, 157, 161.

38. Gary Waller, for example, finds that Wroth gives "the conventional Petrarchan emphasis on love as an invasion . . . a distinctively masochistic edge" ("Mary Wroth and the Sidney Family Romance," in *Reading Mary Wroth*, ed. Miller and Waller, 54), while Ann Rosalind Jones discusses Pamphilia's "rhetoric of submission" (*Currency of Eros*, 148-49).

39. Masten, "'Shall I turne blabb?'," 75.

40. Beilin, "'The Onely Perfect Vertue'," 239, 241, interprets the repetition of the question in spiritual terms.

41. Dubrow, *Echoes of Desire*, 139, concludes that the speaker "chooses passivity" in the final sonnet on sleep, while I would argue, by contrast, that the speaker's command to her Muse to sleep leaves her own agency intact.

42. On this point I differ from Waller, who maintains that "Pamphilia projects Amphilanthus as presence, herself only as absence — as lack, incompleteness, and finally, as silence waiting to be completed" ("Struggling into Discourse," 249).

43. For examples, see Roberts, intro. to *Poems*, 15-22.

44. Ben Jonson, "A Sonnet to the Noble Lady, the Lady Mary Worth" [sic], *Underwood* #28, in *Poems*, ed. Donaldson, 175.

45. Conversation between Margaret Hannay and Anne Prescott, 9 May 1990, Kalamazoo, Mich., cited in Hannay, "'Your vertuous and learned Aunt,'" 24, 33; Maureen Quilligan, "The Resistance to Fiction: Mary Wroth and Marguerite de Navarre," unpublished paper delivered at 1991 MLA convention. See also Prescott's analysis of Marguerite's power and influence in England, in "The Pearl of Valois and Elizabeth I: Marguerite de Navarre's *Miroir* and Tudor England," in *Silent But for the Word*, ed. Hannay, 61-76.

46. Davis, *Fiction in the Archives*, 107-8, 110. For additional discussion of issues of interpretation in the *Heptaméron*, see Karen F. Wiley, "Communication Short-Circuited: Ambiguity and Motivation in the *Heptaméron*," in *Ambiguous Realities*, ed. Levin and Watson, 133-44.

47. King, *Women of the Renaissance*, 161.

48. De Navarre, *Heptaméron*, 70.

49. See Chilton, intro. to *Heptaméron*, 12-13, for further analysis of the effect of this triangular or "three-cornered" dynamic upon the narrative.

50. Ibid., 10.

51. Belsey, *Subject of Tragedy*, 164-65.

52. Ibid., 175.

53. Ibid., 191; Newman, *Fashioning Femininity*, 68-69.

54. See, for example, Josephine Roberts's discussion of Philisses and his sister Simena in terms of the anagramatic relation of their names to Sir Philip Sidney and Mary Sidney (*Poems*, 38), and Margaret McLaren's suggestion that the play offers a "view of the court" ("An Unknown Continent," 279).

55. Susan Frye, "Seventeenth-Century Women's Texts and Textiles," unpublished paper delivered at American Historical Association of the Pacific conference, August 1995.

56. Only a few critics have taken account of Wroth's incorporation of dramatic elements into her prose romance. McLaren (Witten-Hannah), "Wroth's *Urania*," 170-95, makes a case for the influence of "late Elizabethan and Jacobean spectacular theatre" upon Wroth's motifs and settings, without attending to her dialogue and action. Swift, "Feminine Identity," 336-7, 344-6, draws only brief comparisons between some of Wroth's and Shakespeare's female characters, concluding that Wroth's women appear trapped and victimized by contrast to the strong heroines of Shakespeare. More developed discussions can be found in Michael Shapiro, "Lady Mary Wroth Describes a 'Boy Actress'," *Medieval and Renaissance Drama in England* 4 (1989): 187-94, who focuses upon specific dramatic metaphors in exploring the "dual consciousness" elicited by cross-gender impersonation (see also Quilligan's very brief discussion of one of the same metaphors in "Female Authority," 264-65), and in Weidemann, "Theatricality and Female Identity," 191-209, who analyzes Wroth's vision of "femininity as theater."

57. Cixous, "Castration or Decapitation?", 51 (see note 7).

58. Newman, *Fashioning Femininity*, 68.

59. Quilligan, "Constant Subject," 310, 312, 324.

60. Waller, "Wroth and Family Romance," 40-41, 59.

61. Waller, *Sidney Family Romance*, 123-24, 250, 255.

62. Lamb, *Gender and Authorship*, 7, 9.

63. Ibid., 16, 25, 143, 185.

64. Lewalski, *Writing Women in Jacobean England*, 314, 439-40.

65. In commenting upon the parallels between Pamphilia and Antissia, Lamb finds that "Antissia serves as a container, a disposal site, into which rage over inconstant lovers and anxiety over authorship can be placed to prevent contamination from spreading further into the romance," and by implication from infecting Pamphilia as well (*Gender and Authorship*, 168). Similarly, Lewalski observes that Antissia serves as an "obvious foil for Pamphilia (and Wroth), a scapegoat created to deflect from those good poets society's cautionary tale of the psychic dangers that threaten female authors" (*Writing Women in Jacobean England*, 294).

66. Houlbrooke, *English Family*, 78.

67. Patricia Fumerton, "Secret Arts: Elizabethan Miniatures and Sonnets," in *Cultural Aesthetics: Renaissance Literature and the Practice of Social Ornament* (Chicago: Univ. of Chicago Press, 1991), 70-72.

68 Quilligan, "Constant Subject," 316.

69. By contrast to Lamb, who argues that "Wroth's romance simply denies any difference between the conditions controlling the production of poetry by men or by

women" (*Gender and Authorship*, 178), I find that the textual production associated with women characters in *Urania*, including both Pamphilia and Antissia, serves to call attention to the vastly more difficult conditions of female authorship.

70. See Fienberg, "Female Poetic Subjectivity," 179-80, for more extensive discussion of the relation between Pamphilia's physical self and her writings in this episode.

71. Henderson and McManus, eds., *Half-Humankind*, 47-53, summarize such popular Renaissance stereotypes.

72. Lamb, *Gender and Authorship*, 214.

73. The everpresent danger of being written out of the tradition is suggested by the relatively recent yet inaccurate reference to *Urania* as "a collection of poems" in Simon Shepherd's *Amazons and Warrior Women: Varieties of Feminism in Seventeenth-Century Drama* (Sussex: Harvester Press, 1981), suggesting that what Jonathan Crewe terms "invidious exclusions" (*Trials of Authorship*, 13-15) may be located not simply in the Renaissance, but in the present as well.

74. Neely, "Constructing the Subject," 17-18.

75. Homans, *Bearing the Word*, xi-xiii.

6. Between Women: *Becoming Visible*

1. Sedgwick, *Between Men*, 16, 36.

2. Sedgwick herself acknowledges that her focus "fails to do justice to women's own powers, bonds, and struggles" (ibid., 18).

3. A psychoanalytic parallel to my argument can be found in Nancy Chodorow's theory that feminine identification processes stress relationship to others, especially the continuity of identity linking one woman with another, while masculine identification processes stress differentiation from others, especially distinction from the opposite sex, which is predicated upon the presence of a female primary caretaker during a child's early years (*Reproduction of Mothering*, 169, 176, 207)—a situation that predominated in early modern upper-class families through the use of wet nurses, as well as through the direct nurture of aristocratic mothers. From a related perspective, Jonathan Goldberg, "Shakespearean Inscriptions," in *Question of Theory*, 118, observes that "in making arguments about the patriarchalism of Shakespeare's culture, critics forget that boys and girls in the Renaissance wear female clothes in their early years; femininity is there the undifferentiated sex from which maleness comes."

4. Irigaray, "Questions," in *This Sex*, 159.

5. See de Lauretis, *Technologies of Gender*, 2, 24, for a discussion of the limits of "sexual difference(s)."

6. Rosi Braidotti, "The Politics of Ontological Difference," in *Between Feminism and Psychoanalysis*, ed. Brennan, 93-95, 100-102.

7. Crawford, "Experience of Maternity," 14, 16.

8. Sara J. Eaton, "Presentation of Women in the English Popular Press," in *Ambiguous Realities*, ed. Levin and Watson, 180-1, exposes the "rhetorical fabrications" that governed such treatises.

9. Woodbridge, *Women and the English Renaissance*, 224. Waller uses the term "gossip" more loosely, as a contemporary critical term, in discussing the conversations initiated by women in Wroth's texts (*Sidney Family Romance*, 124).

10. Woodbridge, *Women and the English Renaissance*, 231-32.

11. Ibid., 236, 239.

12. Adrian Wilson, "The Ceremony of Childbirth and its Interpretation," in *Women as Mothers*, ed. Fildes, 96-97.

13. Anger, *Her Protection*, 174, 184.
14. Sowernam, *Esther hath hanged Haman*, 233.
15. Klein, ed., *Daughters, Wives and Widows*, 289.
16. Leigh, *Mother's Blessing*, 301.
17. Ibid., 302.
18. Sara Heller Mendelson, "Stuart Women's Diaries and Occasional Memoirs," in *Women in English Society*, ed. Prior, 199.
19. Hoby, *Diary*, 138.
20. Clifford, *Diary*, 74-78.
21. Ibid., 107.
22. Ibid.
23. Ezell, *Patriarch's Wife*, 120-22.
24. See *The Private Correspondence of Lady Jane Cornwallis (1613-1644)*, ed. Lord Braybrooke (London: S. & J. Bentley, Wilson, & Fley, 1842), especially letters of Lucy, countess of Bedford, 22-173. Barbara Lewalski, "Lucy, Countess of Bedford," in *Politics of Discourse: The Literature and History of Seventeenth-Century England*, ed. Kevin Sharpe and Steven N. Zwicker (Berkeley: Univ. of California Press, 1987), 52-77, provides an extensive discussion of the relationship between the two women.
25. See particularly the correspondence between Dorothy, countess of Leicester and her sister Lucy, countess of Carlisle, 1639/40, U1475, C129; also Lady Leicester to Robert, second earl of Leicester, 17 Jan. 1636/37, U1475, C82/12 (De L'Isle MSS).
26. Robert, second earl of Leicester to Algernon Percy, tenth earl of Northumberland, 8 Oct. 1632, De L'Isle MS U1475, C85/1.
27. Algernon, tenth earl of Northumberland, to his sister, Lady Leicester, 5 Dec. 1636, De L'Isle MS U1475, C127/1.
28. Lady Leicester to Robert, second earl of Leicester, 17 Nov. 1636, De L'Isle MS U1475, C82/5.
29. Lady Leicester to Robert, second earl of Leicester, 19 Dec. 1636, De L'Isle MS U1475, C82/9.
30. Lady Leicester to Robert, second earl of Leicester, 15 Feb. 1636/37, De L'Isle MS U1475, C82/16.
31. Lady Carlisle to her sister, Lady Leicester, 13 Jan. 1639/40, De L'Isle MS U1475, C129/6.
32. Lady Carlisle to Lady Leicester, 3 and 17 Dec. 1640, De L'Isle MSS U1475, C129/10 and 11.
33. Lady Leicester to unnamed male correspondent, n.d., De L'Isle MS U1475, C130/9.
34. See, for example, Robert Sidney to Barbara Sidney, 22 Nov. n.d., De L'Isle MS U1475, C81/320.
35. For further discussion of this transformation, see Wall, *Imprint of Gender*, esp. 319-30.
36. McBride, "Engendering Authority," 27-28, 41, 75.
37. Ann Baynes Coiro, "Writing in Service: Sexual Politics and Class Position in the Poetry of Aemilia Lanyer and Ben Jonson," *Criticism* 35 (1993): 365-69.
38. Barbara Lewalski, "Of God and Good Women," in *Silent But for the Word*, ed. Hannay, 224.
39. The displacement of the kiss in Lanyer's poem serves to disrupt what Sedgwick, *Between Men*, 1-2, identifies as a potential continuum between homosocial and homoerotic bonds, by underscoring instead the heightened intensity of some female homosocial bonds in physical separation rather than union.

40. Masten, "'Shall I turne blabb?'," 67, 69.
41. Croft, ed., intro. to *Poems*, 3-4, suggests that Wroth's father can be viewed as "the author of a collection of 'war poems'" which depict a continual process of suffering and dying.
42. Waller, *Sidney Family Romance*, 258.
43. Fienberg, "Female Poetic Subjectivity," 188-89.
44. Lamb, "Singing with the (Tongue) of a Nightingale," chapter 5 in *Gender and Authorship*, 195.
45. Lamb, *Gender and Authorship*, 210; 218, 220; 214.
46. For further discussion of Wroth's poem, see Lamb, *Gender and Authorship*, 223, and Fienberg, "Female Poetic Subjectivity," 188.
47. Lamb, *Gender and Authorship*, 224.
48. Masten, "'Shall I turne blabb?'," 73.
49. Woodbridge, *Women and the English Renaissance*, 240-41.
50. Harvey, *Ventriloquized Voices*, 1, 4-5, 12.
51. D'Urfé, *Astrea*, II:83.
52. Jordan, *Renaissance Feminism*, 228-30.
53. Woods, "Amazonian Tyranny: Spenser's Radigund and Diachronic Mimesis," in *Playing with Gender*, ed. Brink et al., 59.
54. Harvey, *Ventriloquized Voices*, 41-42; see also Roberts, "Radigund Revisited," esp. 189-96, for a historicized reading of the relation between Radigund and Britomart.
55. Montrose, "'Shaping Fantasies'," 69. Similarly, Peter Erickson, *Patriarchal Structure in Shakespeare's Drama* (Berkeley: Univ. of California Press, 1985), observes that "ties between men remain central" (4-8) and that "men originally divided are reunited . . . but women undergo the reverse process" (36), while Janet Adelman, "Male Bonding in Shakespeare's Comedies," in *Shakespeare's "Rough Magic": Renaissance Essays in Honor of C.L. Barber*, ed. Erickson and Coppelia Kahn (Newark: Univ. of Delaware Press, 1985), 81, suggests further that "the breach in bonding felt as potentially tragic when it occurs between men is felt as negligible or even as deeply comic when it occurs between women."
56. Carole McKewin, "Counsels of Gall and Grace: Intimate Conversations Between Women in Shakespeare's Plays," in *The Woman's Part: Feminist Criticism of Shakespeare*, ed. Carolyn Ruth Swift Lenz, Gayle Greene, and Carol Neely (Urbana: Univ. of Illinios Press, 1980), 122-23.
57. McKewin, "Gall and Grace," 117. See also Shepherd, *Amazons and Warrior Women*, 159, on the nature of the "separate female group" created by the presence of female companions in Shakespeare's later comedies.
58. Lenz et al., eds., intro. to *Woman's Part*, 5.
59. Erickson, *Patriarchal Structures*, 7-8.
60. See earlier chapters for more extensive discussion of these soliloquies of Mariam and Salome.
61. Weller and Ferguson, intro. to their edition of *The Tragedy of Mariam* and *The Lady Falkland: Her Life*, 40.
62. See Lewalski's discussion of the distinctions between *Love's Victory* and its predecessors in the genre of pastoral tragicomedy, in "Revising Genres and Claiming the Woman's Part: Mary Wroth's *Oeuvre*," chapter 9 in *Writing Women in Jacobean England*, esp. 297ff, 306-7.
63. Swift, "Feminine Self-Definition," 179, observes that Wroth "creates a situation that may be unique in early English drama: a female friend is willing to sacrifice her own life for another woman who is not her relative or mistress."

64. Swift, "Feminine Identity," 334.

65. Waller, *Sidney Family Romance*, 123.

66. Quilligan, "Female Authority ," 268-69.

67. Although Quilligan, "Female Authority," 268-69, maintains that Urania's brother, Amphilanthus, exerts his "culturally granted power to 'trade' her, that is, to help her select a suitable suitor" in throwing her from the rock of St. Maura in obedience to an "obscure prophecy," she neglects to mention the origination of the prophecy with Melissea, who functions as an influential figure of female authority throughout the narrative, and whose voice shapes the agency of a number of male as well as female characters.

68. Lamb, *Gender and Authorship*, 145, 150.

69. One exception is Lewalski's single chapter on all of Wroth's texts in *Writing Women in Jacobean England* ("Revising Genres and Claiming the Woman's Part: Mary Wroth's *Oeuvre*," 243-307), which accords Wroth credit for representing both female agency and female friendship.

70. Lamb, "Women Readers in Mary Wroth's *Urania*," in *Reading Mary Wroth*, ed. Miller and Waller, 212-14, discusses many of these strictures in more detail.

71. See Braidotti, "Ontological Difference," 93-95, 100-102.

72. See Ruth Kelso, *Doctrine for the Lady of the Renaissance* (Urbana: Univ. of Illinois Press, 1978), 25-26, 30, 108, 191-92; Catherine M. Dunn, "The Changing Image of Women in Renaissance Society and Literature," in *What Manner of Woman: Essays on English and American Life and Literature*, ed. Marlene Springer (New York: New York Univ. Press, 1977), 15-38; Hull, *Chaste, Silent and Obedient*, 133-35; and Henderson and McManus, eds., *Half-Humankind*, 62, 99-100.

73. See Lamb, *Gender and Authorship*, 163, on Wroth's construction of a "heroics of constancy," and Waller, *Sidney Family Romance*, 43, on Pamphilia's "fantasy" of adulation for Amphilanthus, which "takes the form of expecting rejection, even abuse," and receiving "some perverse comfort that her expectations are thus fulfilled."

74. Braidotti, "Ontological Difference," 98.

75. See chapter 2 for previous discussion of Urania's perspective on the "limits" of constancy. Although Quilligan, "Female Authority," argues that "Urania has no story of her own: it is tied directly to her brother's story" (278), and that "the sister's story is only tellable as the brother's tale" (280), her conclusion not only relegates homosocial bonds to the background, but also privileges Amphilanthus's conventionally heroic activity over Urania's striking powers of influence. I find, on the other hand, that Wroth's *Urania* can be read as the tale of its title character more plausibly than that of her brother, given the extent to which Urania's successful interpretation of and intervention in the experiences of most of the other major protagonists at once makes their "tales" dependent upon her agency as well as her subjectivity, and testifies to her pervasive influence with regard to both heterosexual and homosocial bonds.

76. Jeanne Addison Roberts explores that comparison at some length in "Horses and Hermaphrodites in *The Taming of the Shrew*," *Shakespeare Quarterly* 34 (1983): 159-71.

77. Anger, *Her Protection*, 186.

78. McBride, "Engendering Authority," 27.

79. Sedgwick, *Between Men*, 1-2.

80. Anger, *Her Protection*, and "Joane Sharp," "A Defence of Women" (1617) [long poem which closes Sowernam's pamphlet], reproduced in *First Feminists: British Women Writers, 1578-1799*, ed. Moira Ferguson (Bloomington: Indiana Univ. Press, 1985).

81. Roberts, "Radigund Revisited," 202.

82. Once again, I am indebted to Josephine Roberts for calling attention to this citation in "Radigund Revisited," 202.

83. Contrast with Sedgwick's analysis, *Between Men*, 36, 45-47, of feminization as a degeneration of masculine identity in Shakespeare's sonnets.

84. The Shakespearean collapsing of categories dividing women and actors, which Wroth resists, is further illuminated by Jean Howard's essay, "Renaissance Antitheatricality," 163-87, which demonstrates that the antitheatrical tracts construct women and actors "interchangeably, in the same rhetoric of contamination and adulteration."

Epilogue: *Changing the Subject*

1. Dale Spender, *The Writing or the Sex? or Why You Don't Have to Read Women's Writing To Know It's No Good* (New York: Pergamon Press, 1989), 201.

2. Hannay, ed., *Silent But for the Word*; Rose, ed., *Women in the Middle Ages and the Renaissance*; Ferguson et al., eds., *Rewriting the Renaissance*; Levin and Watson, eds., *Ambiguous Realities*; Fisher and Halley, eds., *Seeking the Woman*. The 1990 collection entitled *The Renaissance Englishwoman in Print*, edited by Haslkorn and Travitsky, was the first to contain essays on Wroth.

3. Sandra M. Gilbert and Susan Gubar, eds., *The Norton Anthology of Literature by Women: The Tradition in English* (New York: W.W. Norton, 1985). Ezell, *Writing Women's Literary History*, 41, notes more encompassingly regarding Gilbert's and Gubar's anthology that "it is of no small concern to both feminist literary historians and literary critics working in the pre-Romantic periods to discover that 'the tradition in English' of women's literature before 1800 occupies only 172 pages out of 2,390."

4. Ezell, *Writing Women's Literary History*, 3-4.

5. Neely, "Constructing the Subject," 17-18, and Miller, *Subject to Change*, 83.

6. Cixous, "Medusa," 264, observes concerning women's relations with each other that "at the end of a more or less conscious computation, she finds not her sum but her differences," concluding: "In one another we will never be lacking."

Index

Adelman, Janet, 75, 268 n 55
Alchemist, The (Jonson), 28
Amoretti (Spenser), 31, 257 n 84
Amussen, Susan, 7, 22, 24, 26-27, 39, 67-68, 114, 246 nn 43, 44, 246 n 46, 259 n 20
Anger, Jane, 63, 100, 151, 230;
Protection for Women, 23, 69, 147-48, 187-88, 225
Anne (queen of England), 11, 27, 37, 109, 114-17, 119-20, 122, 128-29, 131, 137-38
Antiquities of the Jews (Josephus), 50, 52, 92, 207
arachnologies, 144-46
Arcadia (Sidney), 47-48, 56, 89, 98, 171, 201, 211, 220-21. *See also New Arcadia; Old Arcadia*
Aries, Philippe, 66-67
Arraignment of Lewd, idle, froward, and unconstant women (Swetnam), 23, 69, 147
Astrée (d'Urfé), 45, 47, 54-55, 89, 201, 211, 220, 229
Astrophil and Stella (Sidney), 30, 38, 41-42, 79-80, 84-85, 101, 156-60, 178-79, 195, 197, 201
As You Like It (Shakespeare), 49, 176, 178, 225-26, 229, 231-32
authors, 2, 143, 152-53, 183. *See also* female authorship

Bacon, Jane Cornwallis, 189
Baker, Ernest A., 12
Barroll, Leeds, 11, 115
Basilikon Doron (James), 113
beast imagery, 31, 51, 204
Bedford, Lucy (Russell), countess of, 189

Beilin, Elaine, 7, 39, 41, 250 n 91, 262 nn 62, 64
Belsey, Catherine, 4, 14, 74, 77, 92, 93-94, 128, 164-65, 238 n 7
Benson, Pamela, 125, 254 n 24, 261 n 48
Berg, Maggie, 15
Berry, Philippa, 259 n 6
blazon imagery, 31, 37-38, 158
Boccaccio, Giovanni, 45
Book of the City of Ladies, The (Christine), 35
Bradstreet, Anne, 111
Braidotti, Rosi, 20, 185, 222-23, 243 n 48
Brennan, Michael, 8, 12
Brennan, Teresa, 17
Bridenthal, Renate, 7
burning metaphors, 101-2

Carey, Robert, 258 n 4
Carlisle, Lucy, countess of, 189-91, 233
Carroll, Berenice, 7
Cary, Elizabeth, 2, 49-50, 110, 112, 124, 132, 142-43, 153, 160, 183; *The Tragedy of Mariam*, 58, 60-61, 63, 102, 105, 107, 167, 213, 230; —, and female homosocial bonds, 205-10, 222, 229; —, and female sexuality, 51, 129-31, 164-66, 168, 213; —, and female subjectivity, 128-30, 215; —, and maternity, 91-95, 98, 214; —, and women's speech, 49-52, 128, 164-66, 171, 208-9
Cary, Henry, 50
changing the subject, 36, 143, 217
chastity, 22, 26, 39, 62, 130-31, 164, 168
childbirth metaphors, 79, 84-87
childhood, 66-67
Chilton, P.A., 45, 250 n 102

endogamy, 21
Epigrams (Jonson), 33
Erickson, Peter, 205, 268 n 55
eroticism, and spiritualism, 38
essentialism, 15-16, 236
Ezell, Margaret, 7-8, 10, 12, 14-15, 19, 33, 68, 148-49, 189, 238 n 5, 242 n 38, 249 n 87

Faerie Queene, The (Spenser), 48, 56-57, 89, 125-26, 134, 140, 202-4, 261 n 48
familial relationships, 67-69, 102
female authority: in early modern England, 71-73, 109, 114; Lanyer's treatment of, 80-82; Marguerite's treatment of, 161-62, 164; MW's treatment of, 98-99, 107-8, 142, 232
female authorship: Cary's treatment of, 164-66; critics' focus on, 143-46; in early modern England, 147-49; Lanyer's treatment of, 153-55, 159; Marguerite's treatment of, 161-63; MW's experience of, 149-52; MW's treatment of, 38, 155-60, 167-68, 170-81
female homosocial bonds: Cary's treatment of, 205-10, 222, 229; critics' focus on, 217; in early modern England, 149, 186, 188-91, 197, 200; in heroine/confidante pattern, 3-4; and heterosexual desire, 183-84, 187, 199-201, 218, 221, 223, 228-29, 232; Lanyer's treatment of, 130, 159, 192-95, 197, 199, 210, 226; liberating force of, 140; Marguerite's treatment of, 178, 205-6; MW's treatment of, 3-5, 195-200, 210-15, 216-33; Shakespeare's treatment of, 205; shaping force of, 182; Sidney's treatment of, 201-2; Spenser's treatment of, 202-4; and spirituality, 192-93
female identity, 55-56, 59, 61, 63, 99, 221-25
female sexuality: Cary's treatment of, 51, 129-31, 164-66, 168, 213; in early modern England, 18, 22-23, 25-26, 112, 150, 180; in male-authored texts, 29, 31, 42, 45, 47; Marguerite's treatment of, 46, 163; MW's treatment of, 53, 62-63, 102-3, 141, 180

female sovereignty: Cary's treatment of, 129; Clifford's treatment of, 115-16; in early modern England, 109, 110, 112; Lanyer's treatment of, 119-21; in male-authored texts, 124-28, 140; Marguerite's treatment of, 46, 163; MW's treatment of, 121-24, 130-33, 135, 136-42
female subjectivity: Cary's treatment of, 52, 95, 128-30, 215; in context of maternal authority, 82; and heterosexual love, 223; as inverse of male subjectivity, 20, 21; Lanyer's treatment of, 37-38, 80, 82, 194; Marguerite's treatment of, 45-46; in marriage context, 61; multiple terms of, 4, 18-19; MW's treatment of, 4-6, 39-44, 53-63, 87, 95, 98-99, 103, 107-8, 122, 141-42, 158, 196, 210-11, 213, 215, 223, 232-33
female voices: consideration of, 20; deconstruction of, 34; emergence of, 2, 3, 30; limitations on, 39; in opposition to silence, 12-13; subordination of, 130; women authors on, 52
feminine metaphors, 170, 177, 179
feminist criticism, 14-15
feminist historicism, 15
feminist literary criticism, 146
feminist pamphlets, 69. *See also* pamphlet wars
feminist psychoanalysts, 64-65
feminocentric expression, 144-45, 169-70, 172, 176
Ferguson, Margaret, 14, 130, 209
fidelity, 26, 43-44
Fidessa (Griffin), 31
Fienberg, Nona, 247 n 60, 250 n 89
Fildes, Valerie, 7, 67
Fineman, Joel, 32
First Blast of the Trumpet Against the Monstrous Regiment of Women, The (Knox), 111
Fletcher, John, 96
Forest (Jonson), 34
Fowler, Constance Aston, 189
Franco, Veronica, 36; *Terze rime*, 35
Fraser, Nancy, 17, 21
French feminism, 15-16, 65, 185
French feminist criticism, 14-15

Frye, Susan, 111, 170, 259 n 6
Fumerton, Patricia, 176
Fuss, Diana, 16

Gallagher, Catherine, 122, 142
Gamage, Barbara. *See* Sidney, Barbara
Garber, Marjorie, 20
garden metaphor, 86, 87
Garnier, Robert, 39
gendered subjectivity, 10-11
genre hybridization, 171-72, 178
Gilbert, Sandra, 145, 234
Gim, Lisa, 111
Godlie Forme of Householde Government, A (Dod, Cleaver), 74
Goldberg, Jonathan, 48, 68, 71, 91, 114, 118, 251 n 110, 260 n 47, 261 n 50, 266 n 3
Gossett, Suzanne, 127, 261 n 53
gossips' meeting texts, 186-88, 191, 193, 225
Greenblatt, Stephen, 14, 49, 242 n 40, 258 n 4
Greene, Robert, 45, 47, 89
Griffin, Bartholomew, 31
Guarini, Giovanni, 96
Gubar, Susan, 145, 234
Guillet, Pernette du, 36; *Les Rhymes*, 35
Gurr, Andrew, 251 n 113
gynecocracy, 110-14, 117, 119

Haec Vir; or, the Womanish Man, 24, 69, 118, 150
Hannay, Margaret, 9, 79, 104, 153
Harvey, Elizabeth, 47, 200, 202, 204
Heal, Felicity, 74
Heisch, Allison, 111
Heptaméron (Marguerite), 35; and female authority, 161-62, 164; and female authorship, 161-63; and female homosocial bonds, 178, 205-6; and female identity, 46, 59, 162-63, 213; and female sexuality, 46, 163; and gender relations, 45-46, 163, 167, 222, 231
Herbert, Philip (fourth earl of Pembroke), 27, 217
Herbert, Susan (de Vere, countess of Montgomery), 115, 117, 191, 217

Herbert, William (third earl of Pembroke), 8-9, 21-23, 27, 33, 103-4, 115, 117, 247 n 65
hermaphrodites, 24, 150-52, 245 n 28
heroine/confidante pattern, 3-4, 225-26
Herrick, Robert, 33
Hesperides (Herrick), 33
Hic Mulier; or, The Man-Woman, 23, 69, 118, 150
historicism. *See* new historicism
historicist feminist criticism, 15
Hobby, Elaine, 7
Hoby, Margaret, 27, 149, 189
Holy Sonnets (Donne), 38
Homans, Margaret, 14, 107, 144-45, 181
homosocial bonds. *See* female homosocial bonds; male homosocial bonds
Honor of Virtue, The, 70, 92
Houlbrooke, Ralph, 7, 21, 28, 66
household manuals, 67, 74
Howard, Henry, 111
Howard, Jean, 14, 251 n 113, 260 n 47, 270 n 84
Hulse, Clarke, 247 n 60

Idea (Drayton), 31, 247 n 63
illegitimacy, 21, 103-4
incest, 102-3
Irigaray, Luce, 4, 14-16, 18-19, 54, 65, 100, 110, 146, 184, 253 n 4

James I (king of England), 10-11, 27, 110-11, 114-20, 128-29, 146, 185, 259 n 16; *Basilikon Doron*, 113; *The Trew Law of Free Monarchies*, 113
Jankowski, Theodora, 12, 15, 53, 111, 243 n 44, 258 n 6
Joceline, Elizabeth, 100; *The mother's legacie to her unborn child*, 72
Jones, Ann Rosalind, 7, 14, 36, 121, 123, 248 n 76, 250 n 89, 264 n 38
Jonson, Ben, 118-19; *The Alchemist*, 28; *Epigrams*, 33; *Forest*, 34; *The Masque of Beauty*, 27, 49, 127; *The Masque of Blackness*, 49, 127-28; *The Masque of Queens*, 127-28; "Penshurst," 85-86, 118, 193; *Underwood*, 41, 160; *Works*, 33
Jordan, Constance, 47, 124-25, 202, 251 n 107

sexuality, 53, 62-63, 102-3, 141, 180; and female sovereignty, 133, 136-42; and female subjectivity, 54-63, 98-99, 103, 141-42, 223, 232-33; and maternity, 98-108
—*Love's Victory*, 1, 8, 52, 58, 62, 100, 105, 107, 124, 128, 137, 160; and female authorship, 167-69; and female homosocial bonds, 210-15; and female sovereignty, 130-33; and female subjectivity, 53-54, 95, 210-11, 213, 215; and maternity, 95-98

—*Pamphilia to Amphilanthus*, 1, 8, 12, 30, 52, 54, 58, 82, 87, 95, 98, 107, 121, 135, 171, 177, 210; and female authorship, 38, 155-60; and female homosocial bonds, 195-200; and female sovereignty, 121-24; and female subjectivity, 39-44, 87, 122, 158, 196; and pregnancy and childbirth, 84-87
Wroth, Robert, 27, 28, 50, 76, 79, 104, 117, 190

Yaeger, Patricia, 13, 144